OXFORD ILLUSTRATED DICTIONARY OF 19TH CENTURY LANGUAGE

OXFORD
UNIVERSITY PRESS

OXFORD
UNIVERSITY PRESS

Great Clarendon Street, Oxford, OX2 6DP, United Kingdom

Oxford University Press is a department of the University of Oxford.
It furthers the University's objective of excellence in research, scholarship,
and education by publishing worldwide. Oxford is a registered trade mark of
Oxford University Press in the UK and in certain other countries

Copyright © Oxford University Press 2018

Database right Oxford University Press (maker)

First published 2018

All rights reserved. No part of this publication may be reproduced, stored in a retrieval system, or transmitted, in any form or by any means, without the prior permission in writing of Oxford University Press, or as expressly permitted by law, or under terms agreed with the appropriate reprographics rights organization. Enquiries concerning reproduction outside the scope of the above should be sent to the Rights Department, Oxford University Press, at the address above

You must not circulate this book in any other binding or cover
and you must impose this same condition on any acquirer

British Library Cataloguing in Publication Data

Data available

ISBN: 978 0 19 276400 3

10 9 8 7 6 5 4 3 2 1

Printed in China

Paper used in the production of this book is a natural,
recyclable product made from wood grown in sustainable forests.
The manufacturing process conforms to the environmental
regulations of the country of origin.

Contributors include lexicographers, writers, history, and literature consultants: Jenny Watson, Rosalind Combley, Christopher Edge, Aaron Wilkes, Seamus Perry.

The publisher would also like to thank the education consultants
and teachers who have advised on this title.

PICTURE CREDITS:

Position key:
t l = top left
l = left
r = right
b l = bottom left
b r = bottom right
b = bottom
m = middle
m l = middle left
m r = middle right

Mary Evans Picture Library: iv b l; vii b r; 130 b r; 131 t l; 133 t l; 133 b l (The David Pearson Collection); 135 m l; 136 b r (GROSVENOR PRINTS); 137 t (GILL STOKER); 137 m l; 138 b l; 138 m r; 139 t (The National Army Museum); 139 m r; 139 b r; 140 m; 140 b; 140 b r (Iberfoto); 141 m; 142 b; 143 t r (The Institution of Mechanical Engineers); 144 m l (Illustrated London News Ltd); 144 m r; 145 t l (JOHN MACLELLAN); 146-147 b; 147 t l (Illustrated London News Ltd); 147 m (The National Archives, London, England); 148 b ;149 t r; 149 m (Photo Researchers); 150 m l (Everett Collection); 150 m r (Library of Congress); 151 m r; 151 b l (Illustrated London News Ltd); 153 t; 153 m l (Illustrated London News Ltd)

TopFoto: 130 b l (Ann Ronan Picture Library/Heritage Images); 131 m (World History Archive); 132 m r; 132-133 (Stapleton Historical Collection/Heritage Images); 133 t r; 134 b l (World History Archive); 134 m r (Granger, NYC); 134 b r (Fotomas); 136 b l (Granger, NYC); 137 m r (Ann Ronan Picture Library/ Heritage Images); 143 m (Oxford Science Archive/Heritage Images); 144 b r (Oxford Science Archive/Heritage Images); 146 m ; 153 m r (Granger, NYC)

Getty Images: 135 m r (Historical Picture Archive/CORBIS/Corbis via Getty Images); 147 r (Science & Society Picture Library)

Bridgeman Images: 141 b r (English School, 19th century/ Private Collection/ Photo© David Pearson); 148 m l (Skin Diseases, colour litho., English School, 19th century/ Private Collection / © Look and Learn)

Shutterstock: 131 b r (Studio DMM Photography, Designs & Art); 141 t l (Becky Stares); 143 b l (aodaodaodaod); 145 b (Birgit Reitz-Hofmann); 151 m (Everett Historical); 152 m (Gary Blakeley)

CONTENTS

iv
INTRODUCTION

1
DICTIONARY: A–O

129
ILLUSTRATED THEMES

130 CHILDHOOD

132 WORKING LIFE

134 RICH AND POOR

136 AT HOME

138 FASHION

140 SPORT AND ENTERTAINMENT

142 TRANSPORT

144 SCIENCE

146 CRIME

148 DEATH AND DISEASE

150 POLITICS

152 WAR AND EMPIRE

154
DICTIONARY: P–Z

INTRODUCTION

This dictionary will help you to understand the meanings of the words and the language used in 19th century novels and other writing of the period. With over 3000 words from **aback** to **zoophagous** and panels, notes, and illustrated thematic pages to browse through, you will quickly be able to get the most out of your reading.

In this dictionary you will find explanations for:

- unusual words such as **pottle** and **fratch**

- words that are used differently from modern English such as **recede** and **traffic** (note that we have only included the 19th century and unusual senses of these words)

- difficult words or words which are less familiar or less frequently used in modern English such as **abode**, **changeling**, **ire**, and **coeval**

- words which reflect 19th century life such as **poorhouse** and **sal-volatile**.

You will find words from these titles and many more:

- A CHRISTMAS CAROL
- THE STRANGE CASE OF DR JEKYLL AND MR HYDE
- FRANKENSTEIN
- GREAT EXPECTATIONS
- JANE EYRE
- PRIDE AND PREJUDICE
- THE SIGN OF FOUR
- SILAS MARNER
- THE WAR OF THE WORLDS

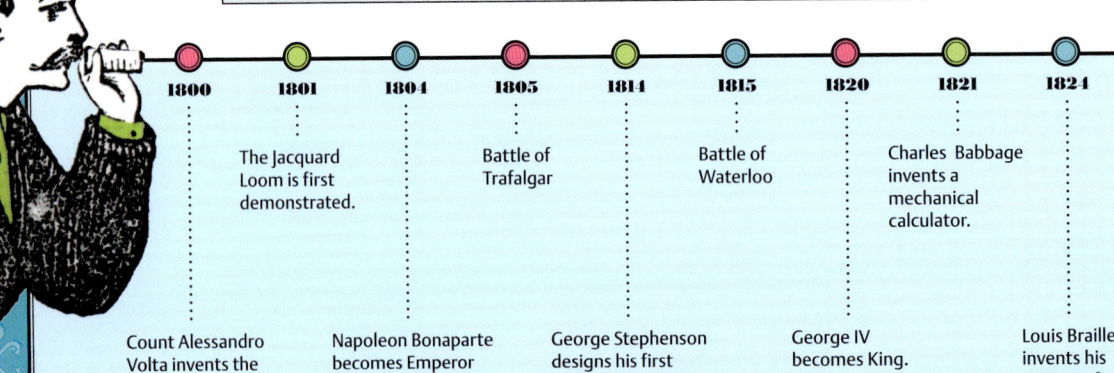

TIMELINE

1800 — Count Alessandro Volta invents the battery.

1801 — The Jacquard Loom is first demonstrated.

1804 — Napoleon Bonaparte becomes Emperor of France; Richard Trevithick builds the first steam locomotive.

1805 — Battle of Trafalgar

1814 — George Stephenson designs his first steam locomotive.

1815 — Battle of Waterloo

1820 — George IV becomes King.

1821 — Charles Babbage invents a mechanical calculator.

1824 — Louis Braille invents his system of printing for blind people.

Alphabetical letter openers

———•◆•———

These contain information on a specific person, place, object, or event. For instance, you can find out about the beginnings of **antiseptic** at **A**, **Charles Darwin** at **D**, the invention of **Morse code** at **M**, the **Penny Black** at **P**, and the ending of **slavery** at **S**.

Language and culture panels

———•◆•———

Look out for the panels at these entries to understand more about vocabulary and language:

abroad	chany	negus	thou
amour propre	defect	profession	Tophet
balk	ecod	progress	unwept
Barmecide	faugh	rive	violent
broider	gammon	sentence	wast
brooklet	girt	sovereign	worrit

You will find information about **familiar words with unfamiliar meanings**, foreign languages, local accents, exclamations, and expressing emphasis.

There is also language information on **different spellings**, **capital letters**, **past tenses**, **similes**, **sentence structure**, **nouns**, **prefixes** and **suffixes**, and the use of **thou** and **thine**, and **wast** and **wert**.

At the following entries you can discover cultural facts about **Christmas**, **daguerreotype**, **etiquette**, **fairy tales**, **penny dreadfuls** (under **library**), **money**, and **religion**.

USAGE notes help you to understand the differences between the modern and 19th century usage and meanings.

RELATED WORDS provide words linked to the word you are looking up.

📖 **Word origins** tell you where the word came from.

Illustrated themes

———•◆•———

Visit the centre section to build a picture of world events and the people and language around them. Topics include **Transport**, the kinds of jobs people did for a living at **Working life**, and the ways people spent their spare time at **Sport and entertainment**.

1829 — Sir Robert Peel forms the first police force (with officers known as 'bobbies' or 'peelers').

1830 — William IV is made King.

1831 — Michael Faraday invents an electric dynamo.

1832 — Great Reform Act

1833 — Slavery abolished in the British Empire; Factory Acts improve conditions for children.

1837 — Victoria is crowned Queen.

1838 — Samuel Morse invents the Morse Code; the first railway from London to Birmingham is officially opened.

1839 — Louis-Jacques-Mandé Daguerre invents Daguerreotype, a type of early photograph.

1840 — Penny post is implemented.

1845 — Irish potato famine begins. It lasts several years.

1848 — Pre-Raphaelite art movement is founded.

v

Why is 19th Century writing different from modern writing?

The more you read from this period, the more you get used to the ways in which writing is different. Think of these differences as part of setting the scene of the story, along with the clothes that people wore, or the ways that people travelled.

Some examples of differences include:

Sentences
Compared with modern writing, the style may seem laborious, with very long sentences and unusual grammar and punctuation.
• *Not so much in obedience, as in surprise and fear: for on the raising of the hand, he became sensible of confused noises in the air; incoherent sounds of lamentation and regret; wailings inexpressibly sorrowful and self-accusatory.*—A CHRISTMAS CAROL, CHARLES DICKENS

This sentence uses repeated semicolons, and the phrase describing the 'wailings' (not normally a plural noun) does not have typical word order. However, if you find the natural breaks, re-read some parts, and look up words which seem to carry important meaning, you can start to understand it. The word 'sensible', for example, is not used with today's ordinary everyday sense and you can look it up in this dictionary to find its meaning.

Formal or odd vocabulary
The vocabulary may seem formal and sometimes words are used in odd combinations compared to modern English.
• *Let us not **dispute** about our views.*—THE WOMAN IN WHITE, WILKIE COLLINS

Some 19th century titles contain language from an even earlier period, or references to things that were common in an earlier period.
• *The Knight undid the clasp of the **baldric**.*—IVANHOE, WALTER SCOTT
• *an old gentleman with a **powdered head***—DOMBEY AND SON, CHARLES DICKENS

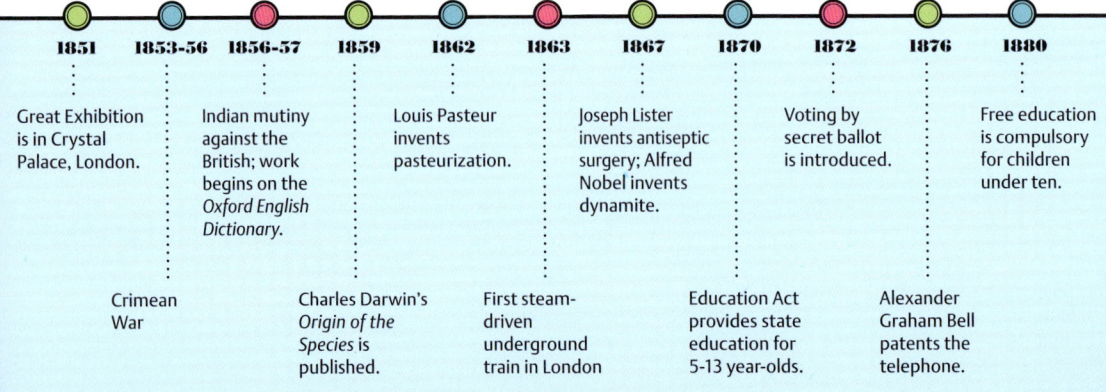

vi

Different punctuation
Punctuation may be different from the punctuation that you use in your own writing. For example, in this extract we would not expect to use a full stop with a dash.
• *For you were not brought up in that strange house from a mere baby.—I was.*
—*GREAT EXPECTATIONS,* CHARLES DICKENS

In the following extract, the commas are not used to enclose information that could be omitted; these commas would not be used in modern English.
• *It is a truth universally acknowledged, that a single man in possession of a good fortune, must be in want of a wife.—PRIDE AND PREJUDICE,* JANE AUSTEN

Different spellings
Many words may be spelled differently from modern Standard British English. For example, you may see *-or* instead of *-our* endings (such as **favor** instead of **favour**).
• *I have a **favor** to ask of you.—THE MILL ON THE FLOSS,* GEORGE ELIOT

You will also see the endings *-ise* and *-isation* as well as *-ize* and *-ization*.

More words were hyphenated, such as **ball-room** and **water-colours**.
• *These pictures were in **water-colours**. The first represented clouds . . . over a swollen sea.*
—*JANE EYRE,* CHARLOTTE BRONTË

Some characters speak with a dialect which may look strange. The easiest way to understand this is to say it aloud.
• *They aren't **worreted wi'** thinking what's the rights and wrongs **o' things**.—SILAS MARNER,* GEORGE ELIOT

Important to know
As far as possible, examples are faithful to the original texts. Some have been shortened so that they are easier to read. If you are quoting in an essay, ensure you use the version in your exam text, with the spelling and punctuation as they appear there.

Language reflects attitudes and habits of the time which may now be considered stereotypical or inappropriate. We have tried to avoid giving examples which, particularly out of the context of the story, are likely to be misconstrued.

1884 — George Eastman patents paper-strip photographic film.

1885 — Karl Benz invents the first practical automobile powered by an internal combustion engine.

1886 — Gottlieb Daimler invents the first four-wheeled motor vehicle.

1888 — John Dunlop patents the pneumatic tyre.

1892 — Rudolf Diesel patents the diesel engine.

1895 — The Lumière brothers invent the cinematograph projector.

1897 — Women's suffrage gains momentum; Guglielmo Marconi patents radio communication.

1899 — The second Boer war in South Africa begins.

1901 — Queen Victoria dies and is succeeded by Edward VII.

aback to ablutions

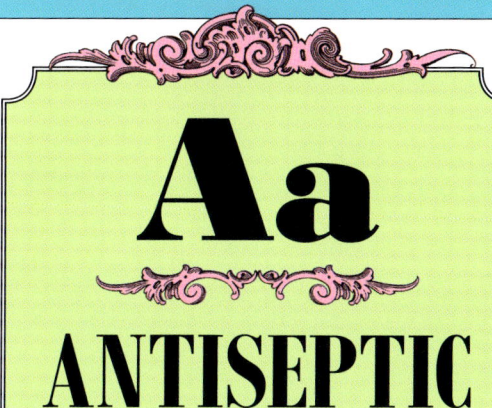

Aa

ANTISEPTIC

The Scottish surgeon **Joseph Lister** pioneered the use of carbolic acid to dress wounds and sterilize medical instruments in the **1860s**. Although his work was initially mocked, this **antiseptic** cut the number of patient deaths that followed surgery dramatically. Previously many patients survived operations only to succumb to infection afterwards. Lister also developed the first **antiseptic spray**. He is often referred to as 'the father of modern surgery'.

aback ADVERB
so that the wind is pressing the sail back against the mast
• [The ship] fell right into the wind's eye, was taken dead aback, and stood there a while helpless, with her sails shivering.—TREASURE ISLAND, ROBERT LOUIS STEVENSON

abase VERB
to lower something
• He cast his eyes full on Mr Dombey with an altered and apologetic look, abased them on the ground, and remained for a moment without speaking.—DOMBEY AND SON, CHARLES DICKENS

abashed ADJECTIVE
embarrassed, ashamed, or disconcerted
• Jem entered, looking more awkward and abashed than he had ever done before.—MARY BARTON, ELIZABETH GASKELL
➤ **abash** VERB to make someone feel embarrassed, ashamed, or disconcerted • He had never blushed in his life; no humiliation could abash him.—SHIRLEY, CHARLOTTE BRONTË

abate VERB
to become less intense, or to make something become less intense
• When the snow storm abated a moment we looked again.—DRACULA, BRAM STOKER
• I could not now abate my agitation, though I tried hard.—JANE EYRE, CHARLOTTE BRONTË

abed (say uh-bed) ADVERB
in bed
• Martha intends 'to lie abed to-morrow morning for a good long rest'.—A CHRISTMAS CAROL, CHARLES DICKENS

abhor VERB
to detest something
• Shall I not then hate them who abhor me?—FRANKENSTEIN, MARY SHELLEY

abhorrence NOUN
hatred; loathing and disgust
• I cannot think of it without abhorrence.—PRIDE AND PREJUDICE, JANE AUSTEN
• My abhorrence of this fiend cannot be conceived.—FRANKENSTEIN, MARY SHELLEY
➤ **abhorrent** ADJECTIVE hateful; disgusting
• He gloated over every abhorrent adjective.—GREAT EXPECTATIONS, CHARLES DICKENS

abide VERB
to live or stay somewhere
• She could not abide there.—THE MAYOR OF CASTERBRIDGE, THOMAS HARDY

abigail NOUN
a lady's maid
• The abigails, I suppose, were upstairs with their mistresses.—JANE EYRE, CHARLOTTE BRONTË

abject ADJECTIVE
1 wretched; without dignity
• From the foldings of its robe it brought two children; wretched, abject, frightful, hideous, miserable.—A CHRISTMAS CAROL, CHARLES DICKENS
2 dreadful; often used emphatically, to mean 'total' or 'utter'
• That abject hypocrite, Pumblechook, nodded again.—GREAT EXPECTATIONS, CHARLES DICKENS

abjure VERB
to reject or denounce someone or something
• Dot seems to have 'abjured the vanities of the world'.—THE CRICKET ON THE HEARTH, CHARLES DICKENS
🏛 Latin *ab* meaning 'away' + *jurare* meaning 'swear'

ablutions (also ablution) NOUN
an act of washing yourself or another person
• When my ablutions were completed, I was put into clean linen of the stiffest character.—GREAT EXPECTATIONS, CHARLES DICKENS

1

abode to accent

abode NOUN
a place to live; the time spent living somewhere
• *I shall take up my abode in … a nunnery.*—JANE EYRE, CHARLOTTE BRONTË

abode VERB
lived; stayed
• *I abode in London betwixt a month and five weeks' time.*—LORNA DOONE, R. D. BLACKMORE

abortive ADJECTIVE
not having formed fully
• *The pattern, or grain, in the wood is produced by 'abortive buds'.*—OUTLINES OF LESSONS IN BOTANY, JANE H. NEWELL

abridge VERB
to shorten or lessen something
• *Tess wishes to 'abridge her visit'.*—TESS OF THE D'URBERVILLES, THOMAS HARDY
• *Little by little we have seen our rights abridged.*—A LITTLE GIRL IN OLD PHILADELPHIA, AMANDA MINNIE DOUGLAS

abroad ADVERB
all around; out and about
• *There is 'an air of cheerfulness abroad'.*—A CHRISTMAS CAROL, CHARLES DICKENS
• *The monster says he 'never ventured abroad during daylight'.*—FRANKENSTEIN, MARY SHELLEY

Familiar words with unfamiliar meanings

Abroad is a familiar word, used here in an unfamiliar way.

Sometimes familiar words appear in combinations that reflect the period in which the texts were set. In modern English we would not describe a horse as 'breaking down'.
• *It had become known that she had had a fearful journey … that **the horse had broken down**, and that she had been more than two days getting there.*—FAR FROM THE MADDING CROWD, THOMAS HARDY

The example below reflects the fact that lights consisted of a naked flame, which could set fire to things.
• *He put out the expiring lights, that the barn might not be endangered.*—FAR FROM THE MADDING CROWD, THOMAS HARDY

abstract VERB
to remove something from somewhere
• *Bounderby tells how 'some fellows … got to young Tom's safe, forced it, and abstracted the contents'.*—HARD TIMES, CHARLES DICKENS

abstract NOUN
a summary
• *Mr Carker had been fluttering his papers, and muttering little abstracts of their contents to himself.*—DOMBEY AND SON, CHARLES DICKENS

abstracted ADJECTIVE
distracted or preoccupied
• *Sherlock Holmes leaned back in his chair with an abstracted expression.*—THE SIGN OF FOUR, ARTHUR CONAN DOYLE
➤ **abstractedly** ADVERB • *Maggie sat apart … , listening abstractedly to the music.*—THE MILL ON THE FLOSS, GEORGE ELIOT

abstraction NOUN
1 being distracted or preoccupied
• *Mr Nickleby … gazed with an air of abstraction through the dirty window.*—NICHOLAS NICKLEBY, CHARLES DICKENS
2 removal
• *the abstraction of the keys*—THE WOMAN IN WHITE, WILKIE COLLINS
3 an abstract idea
• *I am not a poet; I cannot live with abstractions.*—SHIRLEY, CHARLOTTE BRONTË

abundant ADJECTIVE
plentiful
• *Of this preparation a tolerably abundant plateful was apportioned to each pupil.*—JANE EYRE, CHARLOTTE BRONTË
• *She was not a woman who could shed abundant tears.*—THE MILL ON THE FLOSS, GEORGE ELIOT
➤ **abundantly** ADVERB • *[The] pantry … was far more abundantly supplied than usual.*—GREAT EXPECTATIONS, CHARLES DICKENS
• *Mr Collins … was … most abundantly supplied with coffee and muffin.*—PRIDE AND PREJUDICE, JANE AUSTEN

abuse VERB
to say critical or insulting things about someone or something
• *When Mr Bennet says all his daughters are silly, Mrs Bennet says, 'How can you abuse your own children in such a way?'*—PRIDE AND PREJUDICE, JANE AUSTEN
• *The whole conversation ran on the breakfast, which one and all abused roundly.*—JANE EYRE, CHARLOTTE BRONTË
➤ **abusive** ADJECTIVE • *[She was] uttering very abusive expressions towards my wife.*—THE ADVENTURES OF SHERLOCK HOLMES, ARTHUR CONAN DOYLE

accent NOUN
a tone of voice
• *'Come, Master Marner, have you got nothing to say to that?' said Mr Macey at last, with a slight accent of impatience.*—SILAS MARNER, GEORGE ELIOT

accident to accumulate

USAGE In modern English you would expect an *accent* to show where someone is from, rather than how they are feeling.

accident NOUN
1 chance; fortune
• *[The letter] convinced her, that accident only could discover to Mr Bingley her sister's being in town.*—PRIDE AND PREJUDICE, JANE AUSTEN
2 an unimportant part of something
• *Sunday bells were a mere accident of the day, and not part of its sacredness.*—SILAS MARNER, GEORGE ELIOT

accidental ADJECTIVE
1 happening by chance
• *this accidental meeting*—PRIDE AND PREJUDICE, JANE AUSTEN
2 unimportant; minor, occasional, or incidental
• *the removal of any accidental impurities which might be discovered on the coins*—THE WOMAN IN WHITE, WILKIE COLLINS

acclamation NOUN
loud or strong approval; a shout of approval
• *The Court received the new King with joyful acclamations.*—THE YELLOW FAIRY BOOK, ANDREW LANG

accommodate VERB
to settle or resolve an argument
• *By the landlord's intervention, however, the dispute was accommodated.*—SILAS MARNER, GEORGE ELIOT
➢ **accommodate yourself to something:** to adapt yourself to your circumstances • *It was a remarkable quality of the Ghost ... that notwithstanding his gigantic size, he could accommodate himself to any place with ease.*—A CHRISTMAS CAROL, CHARLES DICKENS

accomplished ADJECTIVE
having many accomplishments (skills)
• *Such a countenance, such manners! and so extremely accomplished for her age!*—PRIDE AND PREJUDICE, JANE AUSTEN

accomplishment NOUN
a skill, or skill generally, for example, in conversation, music, or hobbies
• *What will you do with your French, drawing, and other accomplishments, when they are acquired?*—SHIRLEY, CHARLOTTE BRONTË
• *Besides, it's not as if I was an accomplished girl who had any right to give herself airs.*—BLEAK HOUSE, CHARLES DICKENS

accord VERB
1 to grant or give someone something
• *Mrs Fairfax had begged a holiday for Adèle ... and ... I accorded it.*—JANE EYRE, CHARLOTTE BRONTË
2 to match, agree, or fit in with something
• *This seemed to accord with his desire.*—THE MAYOR OF CASTERBRIDGE, THOMAS HARDY
• *But your ideas and mine never accord.*—THE MILL ON THE FLOSS, GEORGE ELIOT

accordant ADJECTIVE
agreeable; in harmony; as it should be
• *All correct there. Everything accordant there.*—HARD TIMES, CHARLES DICKENS

accost VERB
to approach and speak to someone
• *I managed to accost him sedately, yet cheerfully.*—VILLETTE, CHARLOTTE BRONTË

accost NOUN
a greeting or way of speaking to someone
• *Her accost was quiet and friendly.*—MARY BARTON, ELIZABETH GASKELL
USAGE In modern English you might expect *accost* to suggest that someone approaches you in an annoying or unpleasant way.

accoucheur NOUN
a person trained to assist in childbirth; a midwife
• *I think my sister ... had some ... idea that I was a young offender whom an Accoucheur Policeman had ... delivered ... to her.*—GREAT EXPECTATIONS, CHARLES DICKENS

account NOUN
a piece of business, especially a bad-natured one; something to be avenged
• *Nicholas ... resolved that the outstanding account between himself and Mr Squeers should be settled.*—NICHOLAS NICKLEBY, CHARLES DICKENS
➢ **go to his / her account:** to die • *Hyde is gone to his account; and it only remains for us to find the body.*—THE STRANGE CASE OF DR JEKYLL AND MR HYDE, ROBERT LOUIS STEVENSON
➢ **turn to account:** to make use of something; to profit from something • *A chance influx of visitors ... rendered it necessary to turn to account all the accommodation.*—JANE EYRE, CHARLOTTE BRONTË

accoutrement NOUN
an item of equipment or clothing
• *His clothes, which are too big, are a 'ludicrous accoutrement'.*—THE STRANGE CASE OF DR JEKYLL AND MR HYDE, ROBERT LOUIS STEVENSON

accumulate VERB
to gather or increase; to build something up
• *There was no furniture ... and the accumulated dust of years lay thick upon the floor.*—THE SIGN OF FOUR, ARTHUR CONAN DOYLE
➢ **accumulation** NOUN a mass of something; an amount built up • *I myself was about to sink under the accumulation of distress.*—FRANKENSTEIN, MARY SHELLEY

achromatic to address

achromatic (say ak-ruh-mat-ik, ak-roh-mat-ik) ADJECTIVE
colourless; white
- The snowflakes swirl in *'achromatic chaos'*.
—TESS OF THE D'URBERVILLES, THOMAS HARDY

acquaintance NOUN
1 friendship; the fact of knowing someone
- He broke off acquaintance with all the gentry, and shut himself up like a hermit at the Hall.—JANE EYRE, CHARLOTTE BRONTË

2 friends or acquaintances
- Mr Darcy does not like speaking to anyone *'unless among his intimate acquaintance. With them he is remarkably agreeable'*.—PRIDE AND PREJUDICE, JANE AUSTEN

acquirement NOUN
something acquired, especially a quality or skill
- He was … a man of great acquirements—a Doctor.
—A TALE OF TWO CITIES, CHARLES DICKENS

acquit VERB
to remove guilt, an obligation, or punishment from someone; to absolve someone from something
- I cannot acquit him of that duty.—PRIDE AND PREJUDICE, JANE AUSTEN

➤ **acquit yourself**: to behave in a particular way
- I was not at all at my ease regarding the manner in which I should acquit myself under that lady's roof.
—GREAT EXPECTATIONS, CHARLES DICKENS

activity NOUN
busyness; activeness; speed
- Elizabeth continued her walk alone, crossing field after field at a quick pace, jumping over stiles and springing over puddles with impatient activity.
—PRIDE AND PREJUDICE, JANE AUSTEN
- They were soon gone again, rising from their seats with an activity which took their brother by surprise.
—PRIDE AND PREJUDICE, JANE AUSTEN

actual ADJECTIVE
current
- The thought of the money he would get by his actual work … was only a fresh reminder of his loss.
—SILAS MARNER, GEORGE ELIOT

actuate VERB
1 to motivate someone to do something
- When actuated by selfish and vicious motives, I asked you to undertake my unfinished work.—FRANKENSTEIN, MARY SHELLEY

2 to make something happen; to cause activity
- [The] delicate tentacles actuated [the machine's] movements.—THE WAR OF THE WORLDS, H. G. WELLS

Adam NOUN
➤ **child** (also **son**) **of Adam**: a human being

adamant NOUN
great hardness; the quality of being like a diamond, but in the sense of being hard rather than beautiful or valuable
- When the Ghost says to Scrooge, *'if man you be in heart, not adamant,'* he is suggesting that Scrooge may have a heart of stone.—A CHRISTMAS CAROL, CHARLES DICKENS

adamant ADJECTIVE
hard-hearted; unwilling to give in or change your mind
- Utterly heedless … and adamant to her pathetic sneezes, Mr Bounderby immediately crammed her into a coach.—HARD TIMES, CHARLES DICKENS

🏛 Ancient Greek: *a* meaning 'not' + *daman* meaning 'to tame'. The idea of being impossible to tame, or break, led to the idea of toughness, with the word *adamant* also being used for a diamond (a very hard stone).

adamantine (say ad-uh-man-tyn) ADJECTIVE
1 unbreakable; impossible to change or overcome
- His aunt's determination is *'adamantine in its firmness'*.—THE ADVENTURES OF TOM SAWYER, MARK TWAIN

2 shiny; diamond-like
- The angels have *'adamantine shields'*.—SHIRLEY, CHARLOTTE BRONTË

addle (also **addled**) ADJECTIVE
1 (said about eggs) rotten
2 muddled or confused; foolish
- She … slowly nodded her addle head at me.
—THE WOMAN IN WHITE, WILKIE COLLINS

➤ **addle-headed** (also **addle-brained**) ADJECTIVE foolish • You know he has nothing … but money and … addle-headed predecessors.—GREAT EXPECTATIONS, CHARLES DICKENS

addle VERB
to muddle or confuse someone
- If you shake your head in that violent way you'll addle what brains you have got.—JO'S BOYS, LOUISA M. ALCOTT

address NOUN
1 someone's manner of speaking to others
- She thanked him … and, with a sweetness of address which always attended her, invited him to be seated.
—SENSE AND SENSIBILITY, JANE AUSTEN

2 an approach or act of speaking to someone, especially in a romantic way
- Here is a young man wishing to pay his addresses to you.—MANSFIELD PARK, JANE AUSTEN

address VERB
to say something to someone
- The remark was addressed to a woman who stood behind his shoulder.—THE MAYOR OF CASTERBRIDGE, THOMAS HARDY

4

adduce to advert

• *Pumblechook was now addressing the landlord.*
—GREAT EXPECTATIONS, CHARLES DICKENS
➣ **address yourself to someone:** to speak or direct your words to someone • *I was addressing myself to you.*—HARD TIMES, CHARLES DICKENS

adduce VERB
to say that something is evidence or an example of something
• *[Justine's] confusion had ... been adduced as a proof of her guilt.*—FRANKENSTEIN, MARY SHELLEY

adjure VERB
1 to urge or command someone to do something, especially in the name of God
• *I adjured him to write by the first post.*—THE TURN OF THE SCREW, HENRY JAMES
• *Thus adjured, we set to work.*—KING SOLOMON'S MINES, H. RIDER HAGGARD
2 to call up or cast out a spirit
• *The landlord ... took on himself the task of adjuring the ghost.*—SILAS MARNER, GEORGE ELIOT
➣ **adjuration** NOUN • *I only caught the adjuration, 'For God's sake!'*—VILLETTE, CHARLOTTE BRONTË

admit VERB
to allow someone to go somewhere or do something
• *He had entertained hopes of being admitted to a sight of the young ladies.*—PRIDE AND PREJUDICE, JANE AUSTEN
➣ **admit of something:** to allow something; to make something possible • *The subject did not admit of a doubt.*—BLEAK HOUSE, CHARLES DICKENS

admixture NOUN
a mixture or addition; the state of being mixed or added to
• *Although I was glad to hear the sound, yet my gladness was not without admixture.*—TREASURE ISLAND, ROBERT LOUIS STEVENSON

admonish VERB
1 to reprimand someone; to tell someone off
• *You ... would have gently and wisely admonished her; and ... you would have very sweetly forgiven her.*—SHIRLEY, CHARLOTTE BRONTË
2 to warn or advise someone
• *Mr Crackenthorp ... admonished Silas that his money had probably been taken from him because he thought too much of it and never came to church.*—SILAS MARNER, GEORGE ELIOT

admonition NOUN
a warning, telling-off, or piece of advice
• *Silas [felt] bound to accept rebuke and admonition as a brotherly office.*—SILAS MARNER, GEORGE ELIOT
➣ **admonitory** ADJECTIVE • *She held up her small hand with an admonitory gesture.*—SHIRLEY, CHARLOTTE BRONTË

adopt VERB
to start doing, thinking, or using something
• *[Mr Godfrey] adopted a gentleness of tone in answering her.*—THE MOONSTONE, WILKIE COLLINS
• *She has been allowed to dispose of her time in the most idle and frivolous manner, and to adopt any opinions that came in her way.*—PRIDE AND PREJUDICE, JANE AUSTEN
➣ **adoption** NOUN • *I felt ... that I must ... force myself to the adoption of pursuits for which I had no natural vocation.*—JANE EYRE, CHARLOTTE BRONTË

adroit ADJECTIVE
skilful; clever
• *[Nancy] was so instinctively neat and adroit in all her actions.*—SILAS MARNER, GEORGE ELIOT
➣ **adroitly** ADVERB • *I ... adroitly dropped Mrs Dean's note on to her knee.*—WUTHERING HEIGHTS, EMILY BRONTË

advance VERB
1 to become closer friends or more intimate with someone
• *What is your own experience of him? Do you advance with him?*—GREAT EXPECTATIONS, CHARLES DICKENS
• *When the ... party met at breakfast, William and Fanny were talked of as already advanced one stage.*—MANSFIELD PARK, JANE AUSTEN
2 to improve something, such as someone's social position
• *I had begun to advance Herbert's prospects by stealth.*—GREAT EXPECTATIONS, CHARLES DICKENS
3 to lend or give someone money
• *I might secretly advance a small loan towards a little furniture.*—NICHOLAS NICKLEBY, CHARLES DICKENS

advance NOUN
a stage in the process of becoming closer friends with someone
• *I can safely say, that every advance to intimacy began on her side.*—PRIDE AND PREJUDICE, JANE AUSTEN

advantage NOUN
➣ **have the advantage of someone:** to be in a better position than someone • *Then, my dear, you may have the advantage of your friend.*—PRIDE AND PREJUDICE, JANE AUSTEN

advent NOUN
arrival
• *Silas's advent from an unknown country*—SILAS MARNER, GEORGE ELIOT

advert (say uhd-vurt) VERB
to refer to something
• *It was strange she never once adverted either to her mother's illness, or her brother's death.*—JANE EYRE, CHARLOTTE BRONTË

advertise to afford

advertise NOUN
to announce something; to inform someone of something
• That night ... I communicated with the police, and next morning we advertised in all the papers.—THE SIGN OF FOUR, ARTHUR CONAN DOYLE
• As they opened the door they were advertised of the uselessness of further search.—THE STRANGE CASE OF DR JEKYLL AND MR HYDE, ROBERT LOUIS STEVENSON
➤ **advertisement** NOUN an announcement • About six years ago ... an advertisement appeared in the Times asking for the address of Miss Mary Morstan.—THE SIGN OF FOUR, ARTHUR CONAN DOYLE

advocate NOUN
a lawyer
• The trial began, and after the advocate against her had stated the charge, several witnesses were called.—FRANKENSTEIN, MARY SHELLEY

aegis (say ee-jiss) NOUN
a shield, typically considered to be made of goatskin, belonging to a god and seen as a symbol of the god's protection
• He bore aloft the terrible aegis with its shaggy fringe.—THE PRINCESS AND CURDIE, GEORGE MACDONALD
🏛 Greek *aigis* meaning 'shield of Zeus'

aerial ADJECTIVE
1 delicate; light
• You are a beauty in my eyes ... delicate and aerial.—JANE EYRE, CHARLOTTE BRONTË
2 high up
• [the mountains'] aerial summits—FRANKENSTEIN, MARY SHELLEY

affable ADJECTIVE
friendly, good-natured, and kind
• His son will be just like him—just as affable to the poor.—PRIDE AND PREJUDICE, JANE AUSTEN
➤ **affably** ADVERB • I saw her make the effort to converse affably with Dr John on general topics.—VILLETTE, CHARLOTTE BRONTË
➤ **affability** NOUN • She is all affability, goodness, sweetness, and beauty.—NICHOLAS NICKLEBY, CHARLES DICKENS

affect VERB
to pretend to feel or do something
• I [was] affecting a coolness that I was far from truly possessing.—THE STRANGE CASE OF DR JEKYLL AND MR HYDE, ROBERT LOUIS STEVENSON
• Affecting not to see him, Mr Squeers feigned to be intent upon mending a pen.—NICHOLAS NICKLEBY, CHARLES DICKENS
➤ **affectation** NOUN pretence • What affectation of diffidence was this at first?—JANE EYRE, CHARLOTTE BRONTË

➤ **affected** ADJECTIVE put on; not genuine • He even looked at her with a smile of affected incredulity.—PRIDE AND PREJUDICE, JANE AUSTEN

affecting ADJECTIVE
moving; touching
• This is one of the most powerful and affecting stories ever conceived.—SHIRLEY, CHARLOTTE BRONTË

affianced (say uh-fy-uhnst) ADJECTIVE
engaged to be married
• She was the affianced bride of the noble Athelstane.—IVANHOE, WALTER SCOTT

affianced NOUN
someone's fiancé or fiancée
• Sally's affianced, Farmer Charles Darton—WESSEX TALES, THOMAS HARDY

affirm VERB
to state, assert, or confirm something
• My uncle would affirm it unhesitatingly.—SHIRLEY, CHARLOTTE BRONTË
➤ **affirmative** NOUN a response affirming something • She replied in the affirmative.—PRIDE AND PREJUDICE, JANE AUSTEN

afflatus (say uh-flay-tuhss) NOUN
inspiration from God
• [Jo] sat at her desk, settling papers or ... nibbling her pen while waiting for the divine afflatus to descend upon her.—JO'S BOYS, LOUISA M. ALCOTT
🏛 Latin *afflare*, from *ad* meaning 'to' + *flare* meaning 'to blow'

afflict VERB
to bother or torment someone; to make someone ill
• [Joe] was afflicted with such remarkable coughs.—GREAT EXPECTATIONS, CHARLES DICKENS
• aches, cramps, rheumatisms, and every species of ailment that can afflict the old and the feeble—SENSE AND SENSIBILITY, JANE AUSTEN

affluence NOUN
abundance; a lot of something
• that wealth of muscle, that affluence of flesh—VILLETTE, CHARLOTTE BRONTË

affluent NOUN
a stream or river that flows into a larger stream, river, or lake

affluent ADJECTIVE
plentiful; flowing freely
• affluent rain—SHIRLEY, CHARLOTTE BRONTË

afford VERB
to provide or offer something to someone
• But sleep did not afford me respite from thought and misery.—FRANKENSTEIN, MARY SHELLEY

affright to alchemist

affright NOUN
fear
- The monster knows that his ugliness will cause *'disgust and affright'.*—FRANKENSTEIN, MARY SHELLEY

affrighted ADJECTIVE
frightened
- *'Let her go!' cried the … affrighted parent, hastily.*—DOMBEY AND SON, CHARLES DICKENS
- ➤ **affrightedly** ADVERB • *'I never wrote it,' she gasped affrightedly.*—THE WOMAN IN WHITE, WILKIE COLLINS

afore PREPOSITION
1 before
- *It was the night afore the great race.*—GREAT EXPECTATIONS, CHARLES DICKENS

2 in front of
- *folks making haste all one way, afore the front window*—SILAS MARNER, GEORGE ELIOT

afore ADVERB & CONJUNCTION
before
- *And if he don't marry her afore he will after.*—TESS OF THE D'URBERVILLES, THOMAS HARDY
- *Did you ever go a-begging afore you came here?*—JANE EYRE, CHARLOTTE BRONTË

after ADJECTIVE
later
- *those events which led, by insensible steps, to my after tale of misery*—FRANKENSTEIN, MARY SHELLEY

agency NOUN
action; means
- *By some invisible agency, my guardian wound him up to a pitch little short of ferocity.*—GREAT EXPECTATIONS, CHARLES DICKENS

agent NOUN
1 a person or thing making something happen
- *We felt that they were … the agents and creators of all the many delights which we enjoyed.*—FRANKENSTEIN, MARY SHELLEY

2 a person working on behalf of someone else
- *I am the mere agent.*—GREAT EXPECTATIONS, CHARLES DICKENS

aggravate VERB
to make something worse
- *That cruel man … aggravated my sufferings.*—DAVID COPPERFIELD, CHARLES DICKENS
- ➤ **aggravation** NOUN • *an aggravation of my trials*—GREAT EXPECTATIONS, CHARLES DICKENS
- 🏛 Latin *aggravare* meaning 'to make something heavy', 'to weigh down', or 'to burden'

agin ADVERB
again
- *You're at it agin, are you?*—A TALE OF TWO CITIES, CHARLES DICKENS

agin PREPOSITION
against
- *I backed up agin the wall to have another think.*—THE ADVENTURES OF TOM SAWYER, MARK TWAIN

agitation NOUN
anxiety or excitement; emotional turmoil
- *She saw Mr Darcy rise also and follow [Mr Bennet], and her agitation on seeing it was extreme.*—PRIDE AND PREJUDICE, JANE AUSTEN

agone ADVERB
ago
- *It was but a month agone.*—WESTWARD HO!, CHARLES KINGSLEY

ague (say **ay-gyoo**) NOUN
fever; an illness causing fever and shivering
- *He seemed to be all in a quiver with fear, for his hands twitched as if he had the ague.*—THE SIGN OF FOUR, ARTHUR CONAN DOYLE

air NOUN
1 a look or impression
- *Mr Jaggers … said, 'I thought so!' and blew his nose with an air of satisfaction.*—GREAT EXPECTATIONS, CHARLES DICKENS

2 a song or tune
- *Safie sang to him the divine airs of her native country.*—FRANKENSTEIN, MARY SHELLEY

alack EXCLAMATION
used for showing strong regret or upset
- *Alack, my poor master!*—THE PRINCE AND THE PAUPER, MARK TWAIN

alacrity NOUN
speed; eagerness
- *[Mrs Bennet's] invitation was accepted with alacrity.*—PRIDE AND PREJUDICE, JANE AUSTEN

Albion NOUN
Britain or England
- *the cliffs of Albion*—JANE EYRE, CHARLOTTE BRONTË

alchemist NOUN
a person who tried or was believed to be able to change metals such as iron into gold
- *[I] mentioned … alchemists as the principal authors I had studied. The professor stared. 'Have you,' he said, 'really spent your time in studying such nonsense?'*—FRANKENSTEIN, MARY SHELLEY

alderman to alow

alderman NOUN
a senior town or county councillor
• Scrooge is as sensible as *'any man in the city of London, even including ... aldermen'.*—A CHRISTMAS CAROL, CHARLES DICKENS

alehouse NOUN
a tavern (similar to a pub or bar today)
• *[He would] be ... at the alehouses.*—GREAT EXPECTATIONS, CHARLES DICKENS

alembic NOUN
an alchemist's device for distilling chemicals

alien NOUN
a stranger or foreigner
• The workers, who have moved from the town to the country, are *'regarded as aliens'.*—SILAS MARNER, GEORGE ELIOT

alien ADJECTIVE
strange; unknown
• *And we men, the creatures who inhabit this earth, must be to them at least as alien and lowly as are the monkeys and lemurs to us.*—THE WAR OF THE WORLDS, H. G. WELLS

alight VERB
1 to get down from a horse, carriage, etc.
• *I alighted and was conducted to my solitary apartment.*—FRANKENSTEIN, MARY SHELLEY
• *I alighted at the Halfway House.*—GREAT EXPECTATIONS, CHARLES DICKENS
2 to land somewhere
• *A great moth ... alights on a plant.*—JANE EYRE, CHARLOTTE BRONTË

aliment NOUN
food; nourishment
• *an aliment divine*—VILLETTE, CHARLOTTE BRONTË

allow VERB
to admit that something is true
• *Mrs Hurst and her sister allowed it to be so.*—PRIDE AND PREJUDICE, JANE AUSTEN

allowance NOUN
an amount or portion
• *Here's her allowance of bread, and here's her slice of cheese.*—GREAT EXPECTATIONS, CHARLES DICKENS
➤ **on a short allowance:** only receiving small amounts; on rations • Rob eats greedily, *'as if he [has] been on very short allowance for a considerable period'.*—DOMBEY AND SON, CHARLES DICKENS

alloy NOUN
something mixed in with something else that weakens it or makes it less pure
• *My pleasure was without alloy.*—GREAT EXPECTATIONS, CHARLES DICKENS

alloy VERB
to weaken something or make it less pure
• *If it had been Sid, she would have had no misgivings to alloy her delight.*—THE ADVENTURES OF TOM SAWYER, MARK TWAIN

allurement NOUN
an attraction
• *He mentioned the beauties of his native country and asked us if those were not sufficient allurements to induce us to prolong our journey.*—FRANKENSTEIN, MARY SHELLEY

alms NOUN
money and food given to the poor
• *No pity had he for the poor ... so that none ... came twice to that village to ask for alms.*—THE STAR-CHILD, OSCAR WILDE

almshouse NOUN
a charitable home for the poor
• The Spirit takes Scrooge to miserable places: *'almshouse, hospital, and gaol'.*—A CHRISTMAS CAROL, CHARLES DICKENS

along ADVERB
➤ **along of**
1 on account; because of
• *But they said it was along of his wife's dying.*—GEORGE ELIOT, SILAS MARNER
2 with; alongside
• *Only Annie seemed to go softly in and out, ... with nobody along of her.*—LORNA DOONE, R. D. BLACKMORE

aloof ADVERB
away from other people or things
• *They stood a little aloof while he was talking to their niece.*—PRIDE AND PREJUDICE, JANE AUSTEN

alow (say uh-loh) ADVERB
below; down
USAGE *Alow* is often contrasted with *aloft* (meaning 'above' or 'up').
• *I was able to tell him that every man on board had done his duty, alow and aloft.*—TREASURE ISLAND, ROBERT LOUIS STEVENSON

ambuscade NOUN
1 an ambush
• *He got home pretty late that night, and when he climbed cautiously in at the window, he uncovered an ambuscade in the person of his aunt.*—THE ADVENTURES OF TOM SAWYER, MARK TWAIN
2 a hiding place
• *Newman ... darted out from his ambuscade to meet him.*—NICHOLAS NICKLEBY, CHARLES DICKENS

amend VERB
to put something right; to change your behaviour
• *Jane tells Mr Rochester that anyone who has done bad things should look to God 'for strength to amend'.*—JANE EYRE, CHARLOTTE BRONTË
➤ **amendment** NOUN • *If you, my dear father, will not take the trouble of checking her exuberant spirits ... she will soon be beyond the reach of amendment.*—PRIDE AND PREJUDICE, JANE AUSTEN

amend NOUN
something done to put things right
• *This was his plan of amends—of atonement—for inheriting their father's estate.*—PRIDE AND PREJUDICE, JANE AUSTEN

amenity NOUN
a pleasant feature or manner
• *Man-traps were not among the amenities of life.*—GREAT EXPECTATIONS, CHARLES DICKENS

amiable ADJECTIVE
1 friendly; cheerful; likeable
• *He had not a handsome face, but it was ... extremely amiable and cheerful.*—GREAT EXPECTATIONS, CHARLES DICKENS
2 adorable; beloved
• *Mr Collins was called from his amiable Charlotte by the arrival of Saturday.*—PRIDE AND PREJUDICE, JANE AUSTEN
➤ **amiably** ADVERB in a friendly, cheerful, or likeable way • *He smiled amiably and went out.*—THE WOMAN IN WHITE, WILKIE COLLINS

amity NOUN
friendship; being friendly
• *I yet lingered half-an-hour longer, hoping to see some sign of amity: but she gave none.*—JANE EYRE, CHARLOTTE BRONTË
🏛 French *amitié* meaning 'friendship'

amour propre (say am-oor prop-ruh) NOUN
self-esteem; pride
• *Shirley has hurt your amour propre.*—SHIRLEY, CHARLOTTE BRONTË

Foreign languages

Amour propre is French (meaning 'self-love' or 'love for yourself'). Speaking a foreign language such as French or German showed that a person was well educated. Authors used different languages in their writing and also gave their characters words or phrases to say. Sometimes these phrases are then explained in English but if not, you can often use the wider context to work out roughly what is meant—the quotation with *amour propre*, for instance, is part of a conversation about feelings.

In the following quotation, the French, Italian, and German words all refer to ladies.
• *I sought my ideal of a woman amongst English **ladies**, French **countesses**, Italian **signoras**, and German **gräfinnen**.*—JANE EYRE, CHARLOTTE BRONTË

amuse VERB
to cause time to pass in an enjoyable way
• *A walk to Meryton was necessary to amuse their morning hours and furnish conversation for the evening.*—PRIDE AND PREJUDICE, JANE AUSTEN

amusement NOUN
a hobby or entertainment; things done to pass the time pleasantly
• *Felix and Agatha spent more time in amusement and conversation.*—FRANKENSTEIN, MARY SHELLEY

anathematized (say uh-nath-uh-muh-tyzd) ADJECTIVE
detested; cursed
• *Governesses are referred to as 'the anathematised race' after Lady Ingram has said how much she detests them.*—JANE EYRE, CHARLOTTE BRONTË

anchorite (say ang-kuh-ryt) NOUN
a person who has withdrawn from society, often for religious reasons; a recluse
• *Mrs Sparsit has an 'anchorite turn of mind'.*—HARD TIMES, CHARLES DICKENS

andiron NOUN
a metal stand for holding up logs in a fireplace, usually one of a pair
• *The fireplace has 'well-polished andirons, and ... old brass tongs'.*—TESS OF THE D'URBERVILLES, THOMAS HARDY

animadversion to apace

animadversion NOUN
criticism; a critical remark
- You could hear *'the animadversions or commendations of Miss Scatcherd'*—her criticism or praise of each pupil.—JANE EYRE, CHARLOTTE BRONTË

animal ADJECTIVE
to do with the body rather than the soul; typical of animals rather than humans
- *The food contributed to the sense of animal comfort which I experienced.*—THE ISLAND OF DOCTOR MOREAU, H. G. WELLS
- *the animal instinct of self-preservation*—MARY BARTON, ELIZABETH GASKELL

➤ **animal spirits:** liveliness; exuberance; energy
- *She had high animal spirits.*—PRIDE AND PREJUDICE, JANE AUSTEN

animate VERB
1 to make someone feel lively or excited; to enliven or invigorate
- *The crisp air, the sunlight ... the moving river ... [seemed] to ... animate us, and encourage us.*—GREAT EXPECTATIONS, CHARLES DICKENS
2 to give life to a person or thing
- Victor aims *'to animate the lifeless clay'*.—FRANKENSTEIN, MARY SHELLEY

animation NOUN
1 liveliness; excitement
- *The conversation ... was at a high pitch of animation.*—SILAS MARNER, GEORGE ELIOT
2 life
- *I became myself capable of bestowing animation upon lifeless matter.*—FRANKENSTEIN, MARY SHELLEY

ankle-jacks NOUN
lace up ankle boots
- *He wore breeches and the laced-up shoes called ankle-jacks.*—FAR FROM THE MADDING CROWD, THOMAS HARDY

annex VERB
to attach something; to join something to something else
- *'We will not quarrel for the greater share of blame annexed to that evening,' said Elizabeth.*—meaning that they should not argue about who is most at fault.—PRIDE AND PREJUDICE, JANE AUSTEN

annul VERB
to stop something from existing; to reduce something to nothing
- *Maggie wonders if 'Stephen might have seen some possibilities that would alter everything, and annul the wretched facts'.*—THE MILL ON THE FLOSS, GEORGE ELIOT

anon ADVERB
1 soon
- *'Be silent, sir,' said Sir James, sternly. 'I will hear thee anon.'*—MEN OF IRON, HOWARD PYLE
2 now; then
- *The hours wore on;—Ahab now shut up within his cabin; anon, pacing the deck.*—MOBY DICK, HERMAN MELVILLE

➤ **ever and anon:** occasionally; every now and then
- *I went on with my day's business tranquilly; but ever and anon vague suggestions kept wandering across my brain.*—JANE EYRE, CHARLOTTE BRONTË

answer VERB
1 to be suitable or good enough
- *This is your bedroom; the furniture's hired for the occasion, but I trust it will answer the purpose.*—GREAT EXPECTATIONS, CHARLES DICKENS
- *Lakeman agrees that the lanyard (rope) looks odd 'but I think it will answer'.*—MOBY DICK, HERMAN MELVILLE
2 to meet someone's hopes, wishes, or expectations
- *Mr Bennet's expectations were fully answered.*—PRIDE AND PREJUDICE, JANE AUSTEN

anteroom (also **antechamber**) NOUN
a small room leading to a larger one
- *She sits in her own little office, and the ladies who are seeking employment wait in an anteroom.*—THE ADVENTURES OF SHERLOCK HOLMES, ARTHUR CONAN DOYLE

antimacassar NOUN
a small piece of cloth placed on the back or arm of a seat as protection or decoration
🏛 *anti* meaning 'against' + *Macassar*, a brand of hair oil

antipodes NOUN
the direct or complete opposite
- *The professor was the antipodes of Captain Swosser and ... Mr Badger is not in the least like either.*—BLEAK HOUSE, CHARLES DICKENS

antique ADJECTIVE
ancient; old
- *a very old woman, wearing a very antique peasant costume*—VILLETTE, CHARLOTTE BRONTË
USAGE In modern English, you might expect furniture to be *antique*, rather than clothes or buildings.

apace ADVERB
quickly
- *Morning drew on apace.*—OLIVER TWIST, CHARLES DICKENS

apartment to apprehension

apartment NOUN
a room or a set of rooms used for a particular purpose or by a particular person
• Bessie went into the housemaid's apartment.—JANE EYRE, CHARLOTTE BRONTË

aphorism NOUN
a short saying expressing a truth
• 'Character,' says Novalis, in one of his questionable aphorisms—'character is destiny.'—THE MILL ON THE FLOSS, GEORGE ELIOT

Apollyon NOUN
the Devil
• Apollyon came trailing his Hell behind him.—VILLETTE, CHARLOTTE BRONTË

apoplectic ADJECTIVE
causing, or likely to have, a stroke (in the medical sense)
• The news so shocked his mother that it brought on an apoplectic attack.—JANE EYRE, CHARLOTTE BRONTË
• a short-necked, apoplectic sort of fellow, [who …] would soon pop off—MANSFIELD PARK, JANE AUSTEN

apoplexy NOUN
a stroke (in the medical sense)
• Yes, he died of apoplexy nearly a year ago.—THE MILL ON THE FLOSS, GEORGE ELIOT

apostrophe NOUN
an exclamation or remark addressed to someone or something
• 'OH! you precious old thing, how I love you!' (this apostrophe was addressed to the quarto volume which she was now hugging rapturously).—CAPTAIN JANUARY, LAURA E. RICHARDS
➤ **apostrophize** VERB to address an exclamation to someone or something • 'What are you looking in at the door for?'—continued Walter, apostrophizing an old gentleman.—DOMBEY AND SON, CHARLES DICKENS

apothecary NOUN
a pharmacist. Apothecaries were often consulted instead of doctors.
• The apothecary came, and … examined his patient.—PRIDE AND PREJUDICE, JANE AUSTEN

appanage (also **apanage**) (say **ap-uh-nij**) NOUN
a benefit or allowance, or the person receiving it
• Captain Nevitt says he is 'an appanage of Nevitt Grange'—he will inherit it.—A LITTLE GIRL IN OLD PHILADELPHIA, AMANDA MINNIE DOUGLAS

apparel (also **wearing apparel**) NOUN
clothing
• The girls are not allowed to have 'braided hair and costly apparel'.—JANE EYRE, CHARLOTTE BRONTË
• the few articles of wearing apparel he had—OLIVER TWIST, CHARLES DICKENS

apparel VERB
to clothe or dress someone
• However, to please her, I allowed Sophie to apparel her in one of her short, full muslin frocks.—JANE EYRE, CHARLOTTE BRONTË

appellation NOUN
a name for someone; a way of referring to someone
• 'Now, George,' said Mrs. Bagnet briskly, 'here we are, Lignum and myself'—she often speaks of her husband by this appellation.—BLEAK HOUSE, CHARLES DICKENS

appertain VERB
to relate or belong to someone or something
• Not to me appertained that suit of wedding raiment.—JANE EYRE, CHARLOTTE BRONTË
• His inventory includes … the chattels and effects … appertaining to Mr Thomas Traddles, lodger.—DAVID COPPERFIELD, CHARLES DICKENS

appliance NOUN
a thing used for a particular purpose
• Wemmick [produced] a little kettle, a tray of glasses, and a black bottle. … With the aid of these appliances we all had something warm to drink.—GREAT EXPECTATIONS, CHARLES DICKENS

application NOUN
1 a request
• The surprise of such an application was great indeed.—PRIDE AND PREJUDICE, JANE AUSTEN
2 effort; concentration
• If your application equals your ability, I have no doubt of your success.—FRANKENSTEIN, MARY SHELLEY

apply VERB
1 to ask someone for something
• You are now the only one I can apply to for the truth.—MANSFIELD PARK, JANE AUSTEN
2 to apply yourself; to work hard
• As I applied so closely, it may be easily conceived that my progress was rapid.—FRANKENSTEIN, MARY SHELLEY
• Adèle was not easy to teach that day; she could not apply.—JANE EYRE, CHARLOTTE BRONTË

apprehend VERB
1 to expect something bad; to dread or fear something
• I trembled violently, apprehending some dreadful misfortune.—FRANKENSTEIN, MARY SHELLEY
2 to understand something
• I apprehend your meaning.—OLIVER TWIST, CHARLES DICKENS

apprehension NOUN
1 understanding
• Maggie has to explain because of Tom's lack of understanding, which is called his 'freedom from apprehension'.—THE MILL ON THE FLOSS, GEORGE ELIOT

apprehensive to arraign

2 a fear; anxiety
• When Elizabeth approaches Darcy's house, she finds that *'all her apprehensions of meeting its owner'* return.—PRIDE AND PREJUDICE, JANE AUSTEN

apprehensive ADJECTIVE
to do with understanding
• *His sensitiveness—that peculiar, apprehensive, detective faculty of his—felt in a moment the unspoken complaint.*—VILLETTE, CHARLOTTE BRONTË

apprentice NOUN
a person who worked for an employer in order to learn the skills of a trade or profession
• *the apothecary's apprentice*—OLIVER TWIST, CHARLES DICKENS

apprentice VERB
To be apprenticed was to have a position as an apprentice.
• *His most practical thought was getting Mary apprenticed to a dressmaker.*—MARY BARTON, ELIZABETH GASKELL
🏛 French *apprendre* meaning 'learn'

apprise (also apprize) VERB
to let someone know something
• *'But I apprised you that I was a hard man,'* said he.—JANE EYRE, CHARLOTTE BRONTË

approach VERB
to move something near to something else
• *I approached my cheek to her lips: she would not touch it.*—JANE EYRE, CHARLOTTE BRONTË

approbation NOUN
approval; praise
• *She liked him too little to care for his approbation.* —PRIDE AND PREJUDICE, JANE AUSTEN

appropriate VERB
to take something, often without permission, and often in order to use it for a particular purpose
• *So, she appropriated the greater part of the weekly stipend to her own use.*—OLIVER TWIST, CHARLES DICKENS
• *[They] seem to have a delight in appropriating precious articles to strange uses.*—DOMBEY AND SON, CHARLES DICKENS

approve VERB
to prove or show something
• *'But he had an approved tolerance for others.'*—his tolerance had been shown before.—THE STRANGE CASE OF DR JEKYLL AND MR HYDE, ROBERT LOUIS STEVENSON

appurtenances (say uh-pur-tin-uhn-siz) NOUN
accessories, equipment, or belongings
• *[The] tavern, with all its land … and appurtenances, … would be let to Elzevir Block.*—MOONFLEET, J. MEADE FALKNER

RELATED WORD *appertain* meaning 'relate to' or 'be appropriate'

arch ADJECTIVE
playful and defiant; mischievous
• *Elizabeth … turned to him with an arch smile.* —PRIDE AND PREJUDICE, JANE AUSTEN
➤ **archness** NOUN *'How could you be so treacherous!' said Tess, between archness and real dismay.*—TESS OF THE D'URBERVILLES, THOMAS HARDY

arch-fiend NOUN
the devil
• *I, like the arch-fiend, bore a hell within me.* —FRANKENSTEIN, MARY SHELLEY

ardent ADJECTIVE
passionate; enthusiastic
• *She thanked him in the most ardent terms.* —FRANKENSTEIN, MARY SHELLEY
• *I feel that burning hatred and ardent desire of revenge.*—FRANKENSTEIN, MARY SHELLEY
➤ **ardently** ADVERB • *You must allow me to tell you how ardently I admire and love you.*—PRIDE AND PREJUDICE, JANE AUSTEN

ardour NOUN
passion; great enthusiasm
• *I pursued my undertaking with unremitting ardour.* —FRANKENSTEIN, MARY SHELLEY

area NOUN
the piece of ground outside a basement, below street level
• *Or maybe he's got down some area and is in a coal cellar.*—DRACULA, BRAM STOKER

argosy (say ar-guh-si) NOUN
a large merchant ship
🏛 From the Italian port *Ragusa* (now Dubrovnik in Croatia). This word originally referred to a merchant ship from Ragusa or Venice.

aright ADVERB
correctly
• *God grant that we may be guided aright.*—DRACULA, BRAM STOKER

arouse VERB
to wake someone up or make them active again; to rouse someone
• *I mused over the fire … . The striking of the clock aroused me, but not from my dejection or remorse.* —GREAT EXPECTATIONS, CHARLES DICKENS

arraign VERB
1 to charge someone and take them to court
• *[Another man] was arraigned for killing a deer in the King's park.*—THE PRINCE AND THE PAUPER, MARK TWAIN

arrant to asperity

2 to complain about someone; to criticize something
- *I did not, in my heart, arraign the mercy or justice of God.*—VILLETTE, CHARLOTTE BRONTË

arrant ADJECTIVE
total; complete
- *an arrant traitor*—FAR FROM THE MADDING CROWD, THOMAS HARDY

array NOUN
1 an impressive display of things
- *They were looking at the table (which was spread out in great array).*—GREAT EXPECTATIONS, CHARLES DICKENS

2 a set of things arranged in a particular way
- *On the desk, among the neat array of papers, a large envelope was uppermost.*—THE STRANGE CASE OF DR JEKYLL AND MR HYDE, ROBERT LOUIS STEVENSON

3 clothing, especially an impressive outfit or uniform
- *I went out in my new array.*—GREAT EXPECTATIONS, CHARLES DICKENS

array VERB
1 to dress someone
- *She took off her pretty dress and arrayed herself in a plain one.*—THE MAYOR OF CASTERBRIDGE, THOMAS HARDY

2 to gather or line up soldiers or difficulties against someone or something
- *I thought faint-heartedly of the greatness of the risk, of the adverse chances arrayed against me.*—THE WOMAN IN WHITE, WILKIE COLLINS

3 to display or arrange things in a particular way
- *He bent forward ... with his teeth persuasively arrayed, in a ... smile.*—DOMBEY AND SON, CHARLES DICKENS

arrear NOUN
something that still needs to be done
- *My mother ... shuts the book, and lays it by as an arrear to be worked out when my other tasks are done.*—DAVID COPPERFIELD, CHARLES DICKENS

arrest VERB
1 to stop someone or something
- *Thought was arrested by utter bewilderment.*—SILAS MARNER, GEORGE ELIOT

2 to catch someone's attention
- *My attention was arrested by something that was moving rapidly down the opposite slope.*—THE WAR OF THE WORLDS, H. G. WELLS

art NOUN
1 a skill or talent; an area of expertise or activity
- *She had no means of ... freeing herself from [his] web ... ; for that would have required some art and knowledge of the world.*—DOMBEY AND SON, CHARLES DICKENS

2 a way of behaving or doing something, typically a bad or cunning one
- *Elizabeth's behaviour is described as 'a paltry device, a very mean art'.*—PRIDE AND PREJUDICE, JANE AUSTEN

artful NOUN
devious; scheming; cunning
- *an artful, noxious child*—JANE EYRE, CHARLOTTE BRONTË
- ➤ **artfully** ADVERB • *Well, sir! ... this woman was so very artfully dressed ... that she looked much slighter.*—GREAT EXPECTATIONS, CHARLES DICKENS

articles NOUN
a legal agreement or contract
- *Five thousand pounds was settled by marriage articles on Mrs Bennet and the children.*—PRIDE AND PREJUDICE, JANE AUSTEN
- *I signed articles to do my duty by the ship.*—THE CAPTAIN OF THE POLE-STAR, ARTHUR CONAN DOYLE

as PRONOUN
that
- *I know the chap as owns the ferrets.*—THE MILL ON THE FLOSS, GEORGE ELIOT

as CONJUNCTION
so that; in order that
- *There's a [conspiracy] to turn me out o' the choir, as I shouldn't share the Christmas money.*—SILAS MARNER, GEORGE ELIOT

ascetic ADJECTIVE
plain or severe; not having or allowing decoration or other unnecessary things
- *his gaunt, ascetic face*—THE RETURN OF SHERLOCK HOLMES, ARTHUR CONAN DOYLE
- *Maggie, in spite of her own ascetic wish to have no personal adornment, was obliged to give way to her mother about her hair.*—THE MILL ON THE FLOSS, GEORGE ELIOT
- *There was something ascetic in her look.*—JANE EYRE, CHARLOTTE BRONTË

ashen ADJECTIVE
covered or filled with ash
- *a scorched and blackened area, now cooling and ashen*—THE WAR OF THE WORLDS, H. G. WELLS

aslant ADVERB
at an angle; slanting
- *a wooden ceiling all aslant*—HARD TIMES, CHARLES DICKENS

aspect NOUN
1 the expression on someone's face
- *There was no misunderstanding her aspect and voice.*—SHIRLEY, CHARLOTTE BRONTË

2 the look or appearance of something
- *[The] windows ... gave it a church-like aspect.*—JANE EYRE, CHARLOTTE BRONTË

asperity NOUN
harshness; a sharp tone
- *Mrs Bennet ... assured him with some asperity that they were very well able to keep a good cook.*—PRIDE AND PREJUDICE, JANE AUSTEN

aspire *to* assuasive

aspire VERB
to rise up
- Sunflowers are a *'cheerful and aspiring plant'*.
—LITTLE WOMEN, LOUISA M. ALCOTT

assay VERB
to test or try something
- [Gabriel's] fist was raised and let fall as Thor might have done with his hammer in assaying it.—FAR FROM THE MADDING CROWD, THOMAS HARDY

assemblage NOUN
1 a group of people; a gathering
- A low buzz of admiration swept through the assemblage.—THE PRINCE AND THE PAUPER, MARK TWAIN
2 a collection or group of things
- a flag, on which was a singular assemblage of stars and stripes—RIP VAN WINKLE, WASHINGTON IRVING

assembly NOUN
1 a social gathering
- But you forget … that we shall meet him at the assemblies.—PRIDE AND PREJUDICE, JANE AUSTEN
2 a group of people
- The assembly was divided at this point.—HARD TIMES, CHARLES DICKENS

assent VERB
to agree to something
- Mr Collins readily assented.—PRIDE AND PREJUDICE, JANE AUSTEN

assent NOUN
agreement
- He nodded assent.—GREAT EXPECTATIONS, CHARLES DICKENS

asseverate VERB
to state something seriously and firmly
- But that he was not to be … mistaken for a gentleman, my father most strongly asseverates.
—GREAT EXPECTATIONS, CHARLES DICKENS
➤ **asseveration** NOUN • his solemn asseveration that he already considered the prisoner as good as dead—A TALE OF TWO CITIES, CHARLES DICKENS

assiduity (say ass-i-dyoo-it-i) NOUN
great care and persistence
- The Captain … went reading on with the greatest assiduity.—DOMBEY AND SON, CHARLES DICKENS

assiduous ADJECTIVE
showing great care and persistence
- [Stephen Guest's] attentions [to Lucy] were clearly becoming more assiduous.—THE MILL ON THE FLOSS, GEORGE ELIOT
➤ **assiduously** ADVERB • In your heart, you thoroughly despised the persons who so assiduously courted you.—PRIDE AND PREJUDICE, JANE AUSTEN

assign NOUN
a person given a legal right or responsibility
- Scrooge was [Marley's] sole executor, his sole administrator, his sole assign, his sole residuary legatee.—A CHRISTMAS CAROL, CHARLES DICKENS

assist VERB
to be present
- Mr Dick had regularly assisted at our councils.
—DAVID COPPERFIELD, CHARLES DICKENS
- I have a particular reason for wishing to assist at the ceremony.—THE MAYOR OF CASTERBRIDGE, THOMAS HARDY

assize NOUN
a county court
- Lawyer Empson says three of them will surely hang at next Assize.—MOONFLEET, J. MEADE FALKNER

associate NOUN
a person's colleague, companion, or friend
- He takes with him … a rather curious associate.
—THE SIGN OF FOUR, ARTHUR CONAN DOYLE

associate VERB
to make or have a connection with someone or something; to be involved with someone or something
- You are not to associate with servants.
—DAVID COPPERFIELD, CHARLES DICKENS

association NOUN
a connection, relationship, or involvement with someone or something
- Morstan was brought into close association with convicts.—THE SIGN OF FOUR, ARTHUR CONAN DOYLE
- I enjoyed friends, dear not only through habit and association, but from their own merits.—FRANKENSTEIN, MARY SHELLEY

assort VERB
1 to accompany something; to go with something
- His … low protruding forehead … assorted well with his harsh voice and coarse manner.—NICHOLAS NICKLEBY, CHARLES DICKENS
2 to group or classify something in a particular way
- Pip thinks Joe will not believe his story, but will *'assort it with the … dogs … as a monstrous invention'*.
—GREAT EXPECTATIONS, CHARLES DICKENS

assuagement NOUN
lessening of, or relief from, something
- I felt some assuagement of grief.—MOONFLEET, J. MEADE FALKNER

assuasive ADJECTIVE
soothing
- Bounderby [stared] with all his might at his so quiet and assuasive father-in-law.—HARD TIMES, CHARLES DICKENS

assume to aught

assume NOUN
1 to start to have, do, or use something
• *Anxious as ever to avoid discovery, I had before resolved to assume an alias.*—JANE EYRE, CHARLOTTE BRONTË
2 to deliberately adopt or put on a particular expression
• *Her countenance immediately assumed a knitted and intent expression.*—GREAT EXPECTATIONS, CHARLES DICKENS
3 to put on a particular set of clothes
• *Mrs Fairfax assumed her best black satin gown.*—JANE EYRE, CHARLOTTE BRONTË
➤ **assumed** ADJECTIVE put on; not genuine
• *waving his hand in assumed carelessness*—NICHOLAS NICKLEBY, CHARLES DICKENS

assumption NOUN
1 a deliberate expression; an act or pretence
• *'This is very curious!' said I, with the best assumption I could put on of its being nothing more to me.*—GREAT EXPECTATIONS, CHARLES DICKENS
2 the action of starting to have, do, or use something
• *I won him over to the assumption of a dress more like a prosperous farmer's.*—GREAT EXPECTATIONS, CHARLES DICKENS

asunder ADVERB
apart
• *He carried me about with him when I was quite a baby. We have never been asunder from that time.*—HARD TIMES, CHARLES DICKENS

athwart (say uh-thwort) PREPOSITION
across
• *some figure coming athwart the fields*—A DOG OF FLANDERS, OUIDA

atomy NOUN
a skeleton, or someone very thin
• *Who could have thought that little atomy had such an outrageous spirit!*—LORNA DOONE, R. D. BLACKMORE

atop (also **atop of**) PREPOSITION
on top of
• *There's lots o' loose stones about … and we might lay 'em atop of one another, and make a wall.*—SILAS MARNER, GEORGE ELIOT

atop ADVERB
on top
• *It was a most delectable cake, with a nosegay atop.*—AN OLD-FASHIONED GIRL, LOUISA M. ALCOTT

attainder NOUN
the process of sentencing someone to death, or of declaring them an outlaw, and confiscating their property
• *a bill of attainder*—A CHILD'S HISTORY OF ENGLAND, CHARLES DICKENS

attaint VERB
1 to accuse, condemn, or dishonour someone
• *Jem felt that his own character had been attainted.*—MARY BARTON, ELIZABETH GASKELL
2 to sentence someone to death or to being an outlaw, and to confiscate their property
• *Dost thou know that thy father is an attainted outlaw?*—MEN OF IRON, HOWARD PYLE

attend VERB
to accompany someone
• *[Jane's] mother attended her to the door.*—PRIDE AND PREJUDICE, JANE AUSTEN

attendant ADJECTIVE
accompanying; occurring with something or because of it
• *[The elders] shook their heads over the difficulties attendant on rearing children.*—SILAS MARNER, GEORGE ELIOT

attenuated ADJECTIVE
made weaker or less forceful
• *Through the door Bathsheba hears the children's 'little attenuated voices'.*—FAR FROM THE MADDING CROWD, THOMAS HARDY
➤ **attenuate** VERB to make something weaker or less forceful • *[The younger priests] are gradually attenuating the true doctrines.*—TESS OF THE D'URBERVILLES, THOMAS HARDY

attire VERB
to dress someone
• *I will attire my Jane in satin and lace.*—JANE EYRE, CHARLOTTE BRONTË

attitude NOUN
posture; position
• *Taking a walk is 'very refreshing after sitting so long in one attitude'.*—PRIDE AND PREJUDICE, JANE AUSTEN

auditor NOUN
a listener
• *I was not so attentive an auditor as I might have wished to be.*—BLEAK HOUSE, CHARLES DICKENS
➤ **auditress** NOUN a female auditor • *Mr Rochester asks Mrs Fairfax 'to serve [Adèle] as auditress and interlocutrice'.*—JANE EYRE, CHARLOTTE BRONTË

auditory NOUN
the audience, or the area for the audience
• *the younger portion of his auditory*—DAVID COPPERFIELD, CHARLES DICKENS

aught PRONOUN
anything
• *I thought he had not heard aught, so I told him the rumour.*—WUTHERING HEIGHTS, EMILY BRONTË

15

augur to azured

➤ **for aught I know:** for all I know • *For aught I knew, there might have been fifty of you.*—SHIRLEY, CHARLOTTE BRONTË

augur (say aw-guhr) VERB
to predict or be a sign of something
• *the sudden cloud, which augurs a coming tempest*—IVANHOE, WALTER SCOTT
➤ **augur** NOUN a sign; a prediction • *In spite of myself, he fills me with cheerful auguries.*—FRANKENSTEIN, MARY SHELLEY

auspice NOUN
a sign or omen
• *Maggie and Bob both laugh, and 'under these favouring auspices' he walks away.*—THE MILL ON THE FLOSS, GEORGE ELIOT

autograph NOUN
someone's handwriting
• *I have a document here in his handwriting … there it is … a murderer's autograph.*—THE STRANGE CASE OF DR JEKYLL AND MR HYDE, ROBERT LOUIS STEVENSON

automaton (PLURAL **automata**) NOUN
a moving mechanical toy or device, especially one made to look like a person
• *Mary … went about, where she was told, like an automaton.*—MARY BARTON, ELIZABETH GASKELL

avail VERB
to benefit someone or something; to be of help
• *Nor could it have availed her poor daughter.*—THE POMEGRANATE SEEDS, NATHANIEL HAWTHORNE
• *The circumstance which chiefly availed was the marriage of his daughter with a man of fortune.*—NORTHANGER ABBEY, JANE AUSTEN

avaricious ADJECTIVE
greedy for money or material things
• *And did you ever hear that my father was an avaricious, grasping man?*—JANE EYRE, CHARLOTTE BRONTË

avast EXCLAMATION
stop!
• *Come, come; avast with that story.*—MARY BARTON, ELIZABETH GASKELL

avaunt EXCLAMATION
used for telling someone to go away
• *He drew near and bent over her; she was obliged to look up, if it were only to bid him 'avaunt'.*—SHIRLEY, CHARLOTTE BRONTË

avidity NOUN
eagerness
• *I continued to read with the greatest avidity.*—FRANKENSTEIN, MARY SHELLEY

avocation NOUN
a task, occupation, or calling
• *The majority of the searchers had … gone back to their daily avocations.*—THE ADVENTURES OF TOM SAWYER, MARK TWAIN

avouch VERB
to state or swear that something is the case
• *Paulina and her friends being gone, I scarce could avouch that I had really seen them.*—VILLETTE, CHARLOTTE BRONTË

avow VERB
to admit or declare something
• *Marner was not justifiable in his wish to retain Eppie, after her real father had avowed himself.*—SILAS MARNER, GEORGE ELIOT

avowal NOUN
an act of admitting or declaring something
• *his shameless avowal of what he had done*—PRIDE AND PREJUDICE, JANE AUSTEN

awful ADJECTIVE
inspiring awe or wonder
• *[The mountain rose] above it … in awful majesty.*—FRANKENSTEIN, MARY SHELLEY

aye (also **ay**) (rhymes with **eye**) EXCLAMATION
yes
• *'Aye, aye,' said Dunstan, rising; 'all right.'*—SILAS MARNER, GEORGE ELIOT

aye ADVERB
always; still
• *If you in the morning / Throw minutes away / … You've lost them for ever, / For ever and aye.*—BLACK BEAUTY, ANNA SEWELL

azured ADJECTIVE
blue
• *the azured harebell*—RIP VAN WINKLE, WASHINGTON IRVING

Bb

BOZ

Boz is the pseudonym **Charles Dickens** used when he published his first novels *The Pickwick Papers* and *Oliver Twist*. At the time, many authors remained anonymous and used humorous nicknames to disguise their true identities. **Charlotte Brontë**, however, published *Jane Eyre* under the name **Currer Bell** because publishers did not want to publish women writers. **George Eliot** was the pen name adopted by the writer **Mary Anne Evans**.

babel NOUN
1 a noise of many people talking loudly; great confusion
• *Discipline prevailed: ... comparative silence quelled the Babel clamour of tongues.*—JANE EYRE, CHARLOTTE BRONTË
2 a tall building or structure
🏛 From the biblical story of the *Tower of Babel*, in which people trying build a tower to heaven were made to speak different languages by God, so that they could not understand each other.

bade VERB
commanded, invited, or wished (from the verb 'bid')
• *I ... bade farewell to my friend.*—FRANKENSTEIN, MARY SHELLEY

badinage NOUN (say ba-din-arjh)
witty conversation; teasing
• *I told her not to mind his badinage.*—JANE EYRE, CHARLOTTE BRONTË

baffle VERB
to foil an attempt; to frustrate someone's plans
• *I was baffled in every attempt.*—FRANKENSTEIN, MARY SHELLEY

baggage NOUN
a young woman or girl, often a bad one
• *'You saucy baggage!' retorted Mrs Pipchin.*—DOMBEY AND SON, CHARLES DICKENS

bailiff NOUN
1 the manager of a farm or estate
• *I shall have no bailiff; I shall continue to be my own manager.*—FAR FROM THE MADDING CROWD, THOMAS HARDY
2 an official
• *This bailiff was an important person, and his visits stood as events in village history.*—MOONFLEET, J. MEADE FALKNER

bailie NOUN
a magistrate or official, especially in Scotland

baldric NOUN
a diagonal belt in which a sword was worn
• *The Knight undid the clasp of the baldric.*—IVANHOE, WALTER SCOTT

balk (also **baulk**) VERB
to stop something; to deprive someone of something
• *You recollect how annoyed I was at being balked by so small a thing?*—THE SIGN OF FOUR, ARTHUR CONAN DOYLE

balk (also **baulk**) NOUN
a wooden beam
• *the old worm-eaten balk of timber which spanned the roof*—THE HOUND OF THE BASKERVILLES, ARTHUR CONAN DOYLE

Different spellings

Some words, like *balk*, have more than one way of being spelled. (In modern British English, *baulk* is more common.)

Sometimes words are spelled differently, although they are still easy to recognize.
• *The clanking of the engine-pumps, and the **spirting** and hissing of the water as it fell upon the blazing wood, added to the tremendous roar.*—OLIVER TWIST, CHARLES DICKENS

Sometimes these different spellings reflect dialect or accent.
• *'Show us where you live,' said the man. '**Pint** out the place!'*—GREAT EXPECTATIONS, CHARLES DICKENS

Sometimes these different spellings reflect a person's idiolect—their own particular way of speaking.
• *Joe tells Pip he thought 'a **wisit** at such a moment might not prove **unacceptabobble**'.*—GREAT EXPECTATIONS, CHARLES DICKENS

17

bandbox to bascinet

bandbox NOUN
a light decorative container for hats or other accessories
USAGE This word was often used figuratively. For instance, in the first quotation below, the reference is to being kept in a box, i.e. safe from harm. In the second quotation, the reference is to things being taken straight out of the box, i.e. to being brand new.
• [Mother would] shut us all up in bandboxes rather than have us associate with [Ned's friends].
—LITTLE WOMEN, LOUISA M. ALCOTT
• Mr Webster's clothes 'suggest the idea that a bandbox was his ... home'.—SAVED BY THE LIFEBOAT, ROBERT MICHAEL BALLANTYNE

baneful ADJECTIVE
harmful; dangerous
• a baneful monster—DREAM DAYS, KENNETH GRAHAME

bang NOUN
cannabis; bhang
• the yells and howls of the rebels, drunk with opium and with bang—THE SIGN OF FOUR, ARTHUR CONAN DOYLE

bantling NOUN
a young child
• a wife and a flock of bantlings—KITTY'S CLASS DAY AND OTHER STORIES, LOUISA M. ALCOTT

barbarous ADJECTIVE
uncivilized or cruel
• I ... have endured all the hardships which travellers in deserts and barbarous countries are wont to meet.
—FRANKENSTEIN, MARY SHELLEY
➤ **barbarously** ADVERB cruelly • Mrs Bennet felt 'that she herself had been barbarously used by them all'.—PRIDE AND PREJUDICE, JANE AUSTEN
➤ **barbarity** NOUN cruelty or lack of civilization
• [I] lay down happy to have found a shelter ... from the barbarity of man.—FRANKENSTEIN, MARY SHELLEY

bare VERB
bore (meaning 'carried' or 'gave birth to')
• And in time my wife bare me a child.—WESTWARD HO!, CHARLES KINGSLEY

bare ADJECTIVE
actual, sheer, or very; used for emphasis
• The bare idea!—GREAT EXPECTATIONS, CHARLES DICKENS
• I know what I feel, and how averse are my inclinations to the bare thought of marriage.—JANE EYRE, CHARLOTTE BRONTË

Barmecide NOUN
a person or thing offering imaginary food; an illusion
• the Barmecide supper of hot roast potatoes, or white bread and new milk—JANE EYRE, CHARLOTTE BRONTË

Capital letters

The word *Barmecide* comes from the name of a prince in the Arabian Nights stories.

Capital letters may alert you to the fact that a word is a proper noun, indicating a particular person, place, or institution. Proper nouns may refer to well-known people of the time or to characters from myths or religious stories. Even if you are not familiar with the person or place mentioned, the meaning can often be worked out from the rest of the sentence.

In these sentences we can work out that Chénier is a poet and that Hercules was a strong character.
• I looked up at him after repeating **Chénier's** poem.
—SHIRLEY, CHARLOTTE BRONTË
• He was a mild ... easy-going, foolish, dear fellow, —a sort of **Hercules** in strength, and also in weakness.
—GREAT EXPECTATIONS, CHARLES DICKENS

Capital letters were also used in places where they are not generally used in modern English, typically to indicate importance or to show that something was called a particular thing.
• There were more dances, and ... cake, and there was ... a great piece of **Cold Roast**, and there was a great piece of **Cold Boiled**.—A CHRISTMAS CAROL, CHARLES DICKENS

baronetcy NOUN
a position below that of baron
• Drummle ... was actually the next heir but one to a baronetcy.—GREAT EXPECTATIONS, CHARLES DICKENS

barouche NOUN
a carriage with four wheels, a seat in front for the driver (called the box), seats facing each other for the passengers, and a cover that could be pulled up over the back
• 'There is no hardship, I suppose ... ,' said Edmund, 'in going on the barouche box.'—MANSFIELD PARK, JANE AUSTEN

barton NOUN
a farmyard
• Then they drove the animals back to the barton.
—TESS OF THE D'URBERVILLES, THOMAS HARDY

bascinet (say bass-i-net) NOUN
a steel helmet
• Myles was polishing his bascinet with lard and wood-ashes.—MEN OF IRON, HOWARD PYLE

base *to* bedight

base ADJECTIVE
1 dishonourable
• *I had resolved ... that to create another ... fiend ... would be an act of the basest and most atrocious selfishness.*—FRANKENSTEIN, MARY SHELLEY
2 of a low social class
• *You reminded him that Quint was only a base menial?*—THE TURN OF THE SCREW, HENRY JAMES
3 not made of precious metal
• *a piece of base coin*—DOMBEY AND SON, CHARLES DICKENS

bashaw NOUN
a high-ranking official in the Ottoman empire (the former empire of Turkey); a pasha
USAGE In 19th century Western culture, pashas or bashaws were stereotypically known for having harems of many wives. A pasha's rank was signalled by the number of horse tails displayed on his standard, with three signifying the highest rank. Jane Eyre jokingly compares Mr Rochester to a *'three-tailed bashaw'* and threatens to *'stir up mutiny'* in his harem.

basin NOUN
a bowl from which you could eat or drink
• *He has just had a basin of beautiful strong broth, sir.*—OLIVER TWIST, CHARLES DICKENS

bate VERB
to lessen or lower something
• *He would not 'bate a jot of his dignity' by looking pleased at the thought of the marriage.*—SILAS MARNER, GEORGE ELIOT

battery NOUN
1 a platform or enclosure for cannons or other large guns
• *the mound of the Battery*—GREAT EXPECTATIONS, CHARLES DICKENS
2 a set of weapons; a group of soldiers
• *Every moment I expected the fire of some hidden battery to spring upon him.*—THE WAR OF THE WORLDS, H. G. WELLS

bauble NOUN
something that was attractive but without value
• *What are jewels to me ... ? Baubles and trash.*—LORNE DOONE, R.D. BLACKMORE

beacon VERB
to shine
• *At friendly meetings ... something eminently human beaconed from his eye.*—THE STRANGE CASE OF DR JEKYLL AND MR HYDE, ROBERT LOUIS STEVENSON

beadle NOUN
an official who kept order in the local community, in the church, or in an institution such as the workhouse
• *The master aimed a blow at Oliver's head ... and shrieked aloud for the beadle.*—OLIVER TWIST, CHARLES DICKENS

beast NOUN
an animal, rather than a human
• *Shall each man ... find a wife ... and each beast have his mate, and I be alone?*—FRANKENSTEIN, MARY SHELLEY

beau (say boh) (PLURAL beaux) NOUN
1 a suitor; a male admirer
• *Caroline Bingley hopes that the Bennet girls will have fun at Christmas 'and that your beaux will be ... numerous'.*—PRIDE AND PREJUDICE, JANE AUSTEN
2 a fashionable young man
• *I suppose your brother was quite a beau, Miss Dashwood, before he married.*—SENSE AND SENSIBILITY, JANE AUSTEN

beau-ideal (say boh-ee-day-al) NOUN
the most perfect possible example of something
• *My ... ambition is to give them a beau-ideal of a welcome when they come.*—JANE EYRE, CHARLOTTE BRONTË

beaver (also beaver bonnet, beaver hat) NOUN
a bonnet or hat made of felted beaver fur
• *We walked to town, my sister leading the way in a very large beaver bonnet.*—GREAT EXPECTATIONS, CHARLES DICKENS
• *the green veil which descended low from her beaver*—THE LAST OF THE MOHICANS, JAMES FENIMORE COOPER

beck NOUN
1 a gesture, for example, a nod, wave, or beckoning motion
• *Harriet was at the door; and the other [woman], rising from her seat at her beck, came ... towards her.*—DOMBEY AND SON, CHARLES DICKENS
2 a stream
• *the murmur of the beck*—WUTHERING HEIGHTS, EMILY BRONTË

become VERB
to suit someone; to give a good impression of someone
• *[The] threatening appearance in your manner ... does not become you.*—DOMBEY AND SON, CHARLES DICKENS
➤ **becoming** ADJECTIVE attractive; giving a good impression • *I thought Colonel Forster looked very becoming the other night.*—PRIDE AND PREJUDICE, JANE AUSTEN

bedew VERB
to make drops of liquid fall or form on a surface
• *Soft tears again bedewed my cheeks.*—FRANKENSTEIN, MARY SHELLEY

bedight ADJECTIVE
decorated
• *the pudding ... bedight with Christmas holly*—A CHRISTMAS CAROL, CHARLES DICKENS

beetle to belong

beetle NOUN
a tool with a heavy end, used for example, for beating something into place
• And now nothing was heard in the yard but the dull thuds of the beetle which drove in the spars, and the rustle of thatch in the intervals.—FAR FROM THE MADDING CROWD, THOMAS HARDY

beetling ADJECTIVE
overhanging
• We sat by our fire and gazed up at the beetling cliffs above us.—KING SOLOMON'S MINES, H. RIDER HAGGARD
• a low-browed, beetling shop—A CHRISTMAS CAROL, CHARLES DICKENS

befall VERB
to occur; to happen to someone
USAGE Unlike in modern English, the word 'befall' did not necessarily suggest something bad.
• This was no new arrangement, but a thing that had befallen many scores of times.—THE STRANGE CASE OF DR JEKYLL AND MR HYDE, ROBERT LOUIS STEVENSON
• Human beings never enjoy complete happiness … to imagine such a lot befalling me is a fairy tale—a day-dream.—JANE EYRE, CHARLOTTE BRONTË

before PREPOSITION
in front of
• an ample cushioned easy-chair … with a footstool before it—JANE EYRE, CHARLOTTE BRONTË

before ADVERB
in front
• Before and behind came other varieties.—FAR FROM THE MADDING CROWD, THOMAS HARDY

beforehand ADVERB
➣ **be beforehand with:** to act before someone else • The Sergeant was before-hand with me in opening the door for her.—THE MOONSTONE, WILKIE COLLINS

begad EXCLAMATION
a swear word used for showing surprise, anger, emphasis, etc.
• 'Begad!' he suddenly exclaimed, jumping up.—THE MAYOR OF CASTERBRIDGE, THOMAS HARDY

beget VERB
to cause or result in something
• Surely, in time, such deep love would beget love.—MARY BARTON, ELIZABETH GASKELL

beggar VERB
to cause someone to lose everything
• Many honest citizens … went forth beggared from their native town.—THE MILL ON THE FLOSS, GEORGE ELIOT
➣ **beggared** ADJECTIVE • Micawber signs his letter 'From the Beggared Outcast'.—DAVID COPPERFIELD, CHARLES DICKENS

beguile VERB
to pass time
• Scrooge … beguiled the rest of the evening with his banker's book.—A CHRISTMAS CAROL, CHARLES DICKENS

behindhand ADVERB & ADJECTIVE
not aware of the latest news
• But you are miserably behindhand. Mr Cole gave me a hint of it six weeks ago.—EMMA, JANE AUSTEN

behold VERB
to see something
• I suddenly beheld the figure of a man.—FRANKENSTEIN, MARY SHELLEY
➣ **beholder** NOUN an observer • A beholder was convinced that nothing on earth could be more hideous.—FAR FROM THE MADDING CROWD, THOMAS HARDY

behoof NOUN
benefit; advantage
• spending the money directly for his own behoof—SILAS MARNER, GEORGE ELIOT

behove (also **behoove**) VERB
➣ **it behoves you to do something:** you have a duty to do something • Then it behoves me to tell your fortune.—KIDNAPPED, ROBERT LOUIS STEVENSON

belated ADJECTIVE
later than expected; still out at nightfall
• Many a time he rode belated over the moors, moonlit or moonless as the case might be.—SHIRLEY, CHARLOTTE BRONTË

bellman NOUN
a person who rang a bell and made announcements; a town crier

bellows VERB
to use bellows to blow air on a fire
• Orlick prefers his new job to working at the forge because 'It's easier than bellowsing and hammering'.—GREAT EXPECTATIONS, CHARLES DICKENS

belong VERB
➣ **belong to something / someone:**
1 to be appropriate for something or someone
• She took care to express as much interest in the circumstance … as might naturally belong to their friendship.—EMMA, JANE AUSTEN
2 to be connected with someone; to be in the same circles or group
• We know very little of the inferior ranks. Post-captains may be very good sort of men, but they do not belong to us.—MANSFIELD PARK, JANE AUSTEN

bemired to bestow

bemired ADJECTIVE
dirty with mud; covered in mud
• Jane only has her *'damp and bemired apparel; in which [she] had slept on the ground and fallen in the marsh'.*—JANE EYRE, CHARLOTTE BRONTË

beneficent ADJECTIVE
kind; doing good
• *I could see his beneficent purpose.*—DRACULA, BRAM STOKER
➤ **beneficence** NOUN • *Her beneficence was the familiar topic of the poor.*—SHIRLEY, CHARLOTTE BRONTË

benevolence NOUN
the desire to do good; kindness or charity
• *the benevolence of her heart*—PRIDE AND PREJUDICE, JANE AUSTEN

benevolent ADJECTIVE
1 kind; wanting to do good
• *I saw the benevolent countenance of my father.*—FRANKENSTEIN, MARY SHELLEY
• *She was a benevolent, charitable, good woman.*—PERSUASION, JANE AUSTEN
2 charitable
• *Benevolent Societies*—THE MOONSTONE, WILKIE COLLINS
➤ **benevolently** ADVERB • *And yet ... you have benevolently restored me to life.*—FRANKENSTEIN, MARY SHELLEY

benignant (say bin-ig-nuhnt) ADJECTIVE
1 kind
• *Well might we like him ... when he could be so benignant and docile.*—VILLETTE, CHARLOTTE BRONTË
2 beneficial or favourable
• *[the Society's] benignant work*—SAVED BY THE LIFEBOAT, ROBERT MICHAEL BALLANTYNE
➤ **benignantly** ADVERB • *Mr Hall's eyes beamed benignantly through his spectacles.*—SHIRLEY, CHARLOTTE BRONTË
RELATED WORDS benign meaning 'gentle, mild, or harmless'

benignity (say bin-ig-nit-i) NOUN
kindness; goodness
• *that air of divine benignity*—FRANKENSTEIN, MARY SHELLEY

benison (say ben-i-suhn) NOUN
a blessing
• *Captain Cuttle '[received] the Manager's benison gravely and silently'.*—DOMBEY AND SON, CHARLES DICKENS

bent NOUN
a natural tendency or inclination
• *his bent for mischief*—VILLETTE, CHARLOTTE BRONTË
• *I felt daily more and more that I must disown half my nature, stifle half my faculties, wrest my tastes from their original bent.*—JANE EYRE, CHARLOTTE BRONTË

beset VERB (The word **beset** is also the past tense and past participle.)
1 to bother or trouble someone
• *all the dangers and difficulties which had so long beset us*—LORNA DOONE, R. D. BLACKMORE
2 to surround someone or something
• *We will beset the place so closely, that not so much as a fly shall carry news from thence.*—IVANHOE, WALTER SCOTT
➤ **besetting** ADJECTIVE continuing to cause worry or problems • *the cursed greed which has been my besetting sin through life*—THE SIGN OF FOUR, ARTHUR CONAN DOYLE

beset ADJECTIVE
1 surrounded by problems or people
• *We seem so beset with difficulties on every side.*—SENSE AND SENSIBILITY, JANE AUSTEN
2 covered or filled with something
• *cloth of gold and silver, all beset with jewels*—THE BLUE FAIRY BOOK, ANDREW LANG

besotted ADJECTIVE
not in a normal state of mind
• *I was so besotted with fright.*—MOONFLEET, J. MEADE FALKNER
🏛 From *sot*, meaning 'drunkard'

bespeak VERB
1 to ask someone for something; to order or reserve something
• *He's bespoke her for the first dance.*—SILAS MARNER, GEORGE ELIOT
2 to speak to someone
• *I would bespeak thee further.*—MEN OF IRON, HOWARD PYLE
3 to tell of something
• *He approached; his countenance bespoke bitter anguish.*—FRANKENSTEIN, MARY SHELLEY

best-born ADJECTIVE
born into a high social class
• *Jane reminds herself that the 'coarsely-clad little peasants' have hearts that are very similar to 'those of the best-born'.*—JANE EYRE, CHARLOTTE BRONTË

bestow VERB
1 to give or present something to someone
• *He stopped at the outer door to bestow the greetings of the season on the clerk.*—A CHRISTMAS CAROL, CHARLES DICKENS
2 to place something somewhere
• *[He] swept up ... the golden chain, and bestowed it in a pouch.*—IVANHOE, WALTER SCOTT

betake to blackaviced

betake
➤ **betake yourself to:** to go somewhere
• Mrs Gummidge ... betook herself to bed.
—DAVID COPPERFIELD, CHARLES DICKENS

bethink VERB
➤ **bethink you / yourself:** to think to yourself; to remind yourself • I bethought me of my dear Madam Mina.—DRACULA, BRAM STOKER

betimes ADVERB
early
• Milking was done betimes.—TESS OF THE D'URBERVILLES, THOMAS HARDY

betwixt PREPOSITION
between
• How dared you to come betwixt me and a young woman I liked?—GREAT EXPECTATIONS, CHARLES DICKENS

bevy NOUN
a group of people
• Tess and the other three were dressing themselves rapidly, the whole bevy having agreed to go together to Mellstock Church.—TESS OF THE D'URBERVILLES, THOMAS HARDY

beyond PREPOSITION
1 greater or better than; more than
• Elizabeth Bennet, whose friendship she valued beyond that of any other person—PRIDE AND PREJUDICE, JANE AUSTEN
2 outside the scope or limits of
• You have made me wretched beyond expression.—FRANKENSTEIN, MARY SHELLEY
3 other than; apart from
• Nothing of their conversation could be distinguished beyond a soothing murmur.—JANE EYRE, CHARLOTTE BRONTË

bide VERB
to wait or stay somewhere
• Can't we bide here?—TESS OF THE D'URBERVILLES, THOMAS HARDY

bier NOUN
a frame for carrying or displaying a coffin or body
• I followed the funeral into the church. The bier was placed in the centre aisle.—RIP VAN WINKLE, WASHINGTON IRVING

biffin NOUN
a type of apple for cooking
• Norfolk Biffins, squab and swarthy—A CHRISTMAS CAROL, CHARLES DICKENS

bijou NOUN
a jewel; a decorative trinket
• It would be pleasing to the saints if one used so fine a rosary as this, instead of wearing it as a vain bijou.—LITTLE MEN, LOUISA M. ALCOTT

bile NOUN
1 bad temper; anger
• Kate is described as full of 'bile and rancour'.—NICHOLAS NICKLEBY, CHARLES DICKENS
2 nausea; sickness
• 'The cramps was as common to her,' said Mrs Wickam, 'as biles is to yourself, Miss Berry.'—DOMBEY AND SON, CHARLES DICKENS

bilious ADJECTIVE
1 sick; nauseous
• He gorged himself habitually at table, which made him bilious.—JANE EYRE, CHARLOTTE BRONTË
2 bad-tempered or spiteful
• She happened this afternoon to be specially bilious and morose.—SHIRLEY, CHARLOTTE BRONTË

billet-doux NOUN
a love letter

billycock NOUN
a type of hat, similar to a bowler hat
• a battered billycock—THE ADVENTURES OF SHERLOCK HOLMES, ARTHUR CONAN DOYLE

bind VERB
1 to make someone agree to do something
• Pip speaks to Biddy 'after binding her to secrecy'.—GREAT EXPECTATIONS, CHARLES DICKENS
2 to make someone become an apprentice
• a handsome premium for binding me apprentice to some genteel trade—GREAT EXPECTATIONS, CHARLES DICKENS

bishop NOUN
mulled wine
• a Christmas bowl of smoking bishop—A CHRISTMAS CAROL, CHARLES DICKENS

bit NOUN
a piece or portion of food
• Silas and Eppie 'eat o' the same bit, and drink o' the same cup'.—SILAS MARNER, GEORGE ELIOT

black NOUN
a speck of dirt or soot
• I wondered ... why he stuck them on that dusty perch for the blacks and flies to settle on.—GREAT EXPECTATIONS, CHARLES DICKENS

blackaviced ADJECTIVE
dark-skinned; swarthy
• I would advise her blackaviced suitor to look out.—JANE EYRE, CHARLOTTE BRONTË

blackguard *to* blithe

blackguard (say **blag-uhd, blag-ard**) NOUN
a dishonourable or worthless man
• *This is a trick, you young blackguard.*—THE CORAL ISLAND, R. M. BALLANTYNE
➤ **blackguardly** ADJECTIVE • *Mr Guppy knows his insistence on speaking to Lady Dedlock 'does appear ... almost blackguardly'.*—BLEAK HOUSE, CHARLES DICKENS

black-hole NOUN
a room or cell where people were locked up as a punishment
• *The black-hole of that ship warn't a strong one ... I escaped to the shore.*—GREAT EXPECTATIONS, CHARLES DICKENS

blacking NOUN
a substance used for making something black, in particular black shoe polish
USAGE A well-known brand of blacking was made by Day and Martin.
• *'See there ... ,' he said, pointing ... to his top boots; 'not a drop of Day and Martin ... ; not a bubble of blacking!'*—OLIVER TWIST, CHARLES DICKENS

blade NOUN
a chap; a fellow
• *He forged wills, this blade did.*—GREAT EXPECTATIONS, CHARLES DICKENS

blanch VERB
to go white or pale, or to make this happen
• *My companion's face had blanched.*—THE TURN OF THE SCREW, HENRY JAMES
➤ **blanched** ADJECTIVE white; pale • *Here was the secret of her blanched face, her shaken nerves.*—THE MEMOIRS OF SHERLOCK HOLMES, ARTHUR CONAN DOYLE
• *Little birds were just twittering in the blossom-blanched orchard trees.*—JANE EYRE, CHARLOTTE BRONTË

blandishments NOUN
flattering or coaxing words
• *Miss Petowker had practised several blandishments, to soften the excellent old gentleman.*—NICHOLAS NICKLEBY, CHARLES DICKENS

blast VERB
to destroy; to ruin
• *Darcy says that Elizabeth accuses him of having 'blasted the prospects of Mr Wickham'.*—PRIDE AND PREJUDICE, JANE AUSTEN

blazon VERB
1 to paint or display a name or coat of arms on something
• *[Their names] shall be blazoned in letters of gold above my throne.*—ALLAN QUATERMAIN, H. RIDER HAGGARD

2 to show off or advertise something
• *Many a man would have even blazoned such irregularities.*—THE STRANGE CASE OF DR JEKYLL AND MR HYDE, ROBERT LOUIS STEVENSON

bleached ADJECTIVE
white; pale
• *The fronds [of the red weed] became bleached, and then shrivelled and brittle.*—THE WAR OF THE WORLDS, H. G. WELLS

bleared ADJECTIVE
blurred or dim
• *Beyond all this winked a few bleared lamplights.*—WESSEX TALES, THOMAS HARDY

blent VERB
blended
• *Presently a voice blent with the rich tones of the instrument.*—JANE EYRE, CHARLOTTE BRONTË

blight NOUN
something causing damage, destruction, or distress; a disease or fungus
• *But a blight had come over my existence.*—FRANKENSTEIN, MARY SHELLEY

blight VERB
to cause damage, destruction, or distress; to infect something with a disease or fungus
• *But don't blight our lives forever by a rash perversity that can answer no good purpose to any one, that can only create new evils.*—THE MILL ON THE FLOSS, GEORGE ELIOT
➤ **blighted** ADJECTIVE • *The whole place, with its scattered dirt-heaps and ill-grown shrubs, had a blighted, ill-omened look which harmonized with the black tragedy which hung over it.*—THE SIGN OF FOUR, ARTHUR CONAN DOYLE

blind VERB
to stop someone from knowing something
• *During my first experiment, a kind of enthusiastic frenzy had blinded me to the horror of my employment.*—FRANKENSTEIN, MARY SHELLEY

blind NOUN
something intended to stop someone from knowing something
• *The card is some hocus-pocus—a blind, as like as not.*—THE SIGN OF FOUR, ARTHUR CONAN DOYLE

blithe (also **blithesome**) ADJECTIVE
happy; cheerful
• *Scrooge said ... of all the blithe sounds he had ever heard, those were the blithest in his ears.*—A CHRISTMAS CAROL, CHARLES DICKENS
➤ **blithely** ADVERB • *singing blithely over her work*—THE WOMAN IN WHITE, WILKIE COLLINS

blockhead to boon

blockhead NOUN
a stupid person
• *You know that, you blockhead.*—NICHOLAS NICKLEBY, CHARLES DICKENS

blockhouse NOUN
a low building made of logs, used as a shelter or fort

blond (also **blonde**) NOUN
a type of lace, originally made from undyed silk, but often also black in the 19th century
• *the square of unembroidered blond I had myself prepared as a covering for my ... head*—JANE EYRE, CHARLOTTE BRONTË

blowsy (also **blowzy**) (say **blow-zi**) ADJECTIVE
1 rough; red-faced
• *a face made blowsy by cold and damp*—SILAS MARNER, GEORGE ELIOT
2 untidy; scruffy
• *Her hair so untidy, so blowsy!* —PRIDE AND PREJUDICE, JANE AUSTEN

blunderbuss NOUN
1 a type of gun which could fire a lot of ammunition over a short distance
• *'Tis but a lad scaring rooks with a blunderbuss.* —MOONFLEET, J. MEADE FALKNER
2 a clumsy person; an idiot
• *'Oh dear! what a blunderbuss I am!' exclaimed Jo.* —LITTLE WOMEN, LOUISA M. ALCOTT

blusterous ADJECTIVE
aggressive; rough
• *Joe says Pumblechook's 'manners is given to blusterous'*—meaning he tends to be aggressive. —GREAT EXPECTATIONS, CHARLES DICKENS

boat-cloak NOUN
a large cloak worn by a sailor, especially a naval officer
• *He had his boat-cloak on him, and looked, as I have said, a natural part of the scene.*—GREAT EXPECTATIONS, CHARLES DICKENS

boatswain (say **boh-sun**) NOUN
a ship's officer in charge of rigging, boats, and anchors
• *a virtuous boatswain in His Majesty's service* —GREAT EXPECTATIONS, CHARLES DICKENS

bob NOUN
a shilling (5p)
• *I had to pay five bob, ... and then a young man ... thieved another five while I was asleep and another boy ... thieved ninepence.*—BLEAK HOUSE, CHARLES DICKENS

bodkin NOUN
a pointed instrument, for example, a needle
• *He ... strung [his papers] together with a bodkin and a piece of string.*—THE WOMAN IN WHITE, WILKIE COLLINS

body NOUN
➤ **in a body**: all together; as one group
• *We moved in a body to old Dr Denman's surgical theatre.*—THE STRANGE CASE OF DR JEKYLL AND MR HYDE, ROBERT LOUIS STEVENSON

bogle NOUN
a monster or spirit; a scarecrow or scary person
• *Paul looked upon [her] ... as a kind of learned Guy Fawkes, or artificial Bogle, stuffed full of scholastic straw.*—DOMBEY AND SON, CHARLES DICKENS

bogy (also **bogie, bogey**) NOUN
a monster or scary spirit
• *a most dreadful bogy, all teeth, horns, and tail* —WATER BABIES, CHARLES KINGSLEY

bole NOUN
a tree trunk or stem
• *the rough boles of a great oak*—JANE EYRE, CHARLOTTE BRONTË

bombazeen (also **bombazine**) NOUN
a type of fabric. Black bombazeen was often used for mourning clothes.
• *Mrs Pipchin ... looms dark in her black bombazeen skirts, black bonnet, and shawl.*—DOMBEY AND SON, CHARLES DICKENS

bonnet NOUN
1 a wide-brimmed hat for women and girls, tied under the chin
2 a hat without a brim for women and girls
3 a hat without a brim for a man or boy, like a beret or beanie

booby NOUN
a foolish person
• *Pip describes Drummle as 'a contemptible, clumsy, sulky booby'.*—GREAT EXPECTATIONS, CHARLES DICKENS

book-learned ADJECTIVE
educated
• *'Are you book-learned?' she inquired presently.* —JANE EYRE, CHARLOTTE BRONTË

boon NOUN
1 a request; a favour
• *Laurie ... clasped his hands imploringly, as if begging some boon.*—LITTLE WOMEN, LOUISA M. ALCOTT
2 something good
• *The money Jane is left by her uncle 'was a grand boon doubtless; and independence would be glorious'.* —JANE EYRE, CHARLOTTE BRONTË

boot-black to brace

➢ **boon companion:** a very close friend • *He had three or four boon companions.*—THE LEGEND OF SLEEPY HOLLOW, IRVING WASHINGTON

boot-black *NOUN*
a person who polished other people's boots and shoes

bootless *ADJECTIVE*
useless; fruitless
• *I had spent some time in this bootless search.*
—MOONFLEET, J. MEADE FALKNER

booty *NOUN*
valuable goods
• *The thief 'made off with his booty'.*—THE MEMOIRS OF SHERLOCK HOLMES, ARTHUR CONAN DOYLE
➢ **play booty:** to join forces with the enemy; to let the other side win • *Don't play booty with me.*
—OLIVER TWIST, CHARLES DICKENS

borough *NOUN*
a town or district, often one with its own Member of Parliament
• *Thomas Gradgrind ... of Stone Lodge, M.P. for that borough*—HARD TIMES, CHARLES DICKENS

bosky *ADJECTIVE*
covered in bushes or small trees
• *the more distant bosky shades*—THE MERRY ADVENTURES OF ROBIN HOOD, HOWARD PYLE

bosom *NOUN*
1 a person's chest, often as the centre of emotions
• *He had retired with a lighter heart in his bosom.*
—UNCLE TOM'S CABIN, HARRIET BEECHER STOWE
• *[His] left arm, the mutilated one, he kept hidden in his bosom.*—JANE EYRE, CHARLOTTE BRONTË
• *But the young man caught her to his bosom.*
—OLIVER TWIST, CHARLES DICKENS
2 loving care
• *[He] might return to the bosom of his family.*
—GREAT EXPECTATIONS, CHARLES DICKENS
3 the heart or midst of something
• *deep in the bosom of the hills*—SILAS MARNER, GEORGE ELIOT

bossed *ADJECTIVE*
(said about metal) decorated with a raised pattern or design; embossed
• *The tankards are on the side-table still, but the bossed silver is undimmed by handling.*—SILAS MARNER, GEORGE ELIOT

boudoir *NOUN*
a small private room
• *I have a nice little boudoir and bedroom.*—THE WOMAN IN WHITE, WILKIE COLLINS

bound *ADJECTIVE*
1 apprenticed (from the verb 'bind')
• *This boy must be bound.*—GREAT EXPECTATIONS, CHARLES DICKENS
2 obliged (from the verb 'bind')
• *The landlord [was] under the habitual sense that he was bound to keep his house open to all company.*
—SILAS MARNER, GEORGE ELIOT
➢ **I'll be bound:** I'm sure • *We shall hear of him soon enough, I'll be bound.*—SILAS MARNER, GEORGE ELIOT

bound *VERB*
to form the boundary or limit of something
• *I thought the continent of Europe had bounded his wanderings; till now I had never heard ... of visits to more distant shores.*—JANE EYRE, CHARLOTTE BRONTË

bounden *ADJECTIVE*
➢ **your bounden duty:** your responsibility; something to be done without fail • *I owe that to you. It is my bounden duty to you.*—DOMBEY AND SON, CHARLES DICKENS

bounteous *ADJECTIVE*
plentiful; generous
• *your most bounteous gift*—IVANHOE, WALTER SCOTT

bourne (also **bourn**) *NOUN*
1 a destination
• *I could only think of the bourne of my travels.*
—FRANKENSTEIN, MARY SHELLEY
2 a small stream; a brook. This is related to the modern dialect word *burn*, meaning 'stream'.

bower *NOUN*
1 a cottage or summer house
• *Then, he conducted me to a bower ... and in this retreat our glasses were already set forth.*
—GREAT EXPECTATIONS, CHARLES DICKENS
2 a woman's bedroom or private room
• *his lady's bower*—IVANHOE, Sir Walter Scott
3 a pleasant shady place under trees
• *nooks and bowers in the grounds*—SHIRLEY, CHARLOTTE BRONTË

box-place (also **box seat**) *NOUN*
the driver's seat on a coach or carriage, or a passenger's seat beside this
• *I had secured my box-place by to-morrow's coach.*
—GREAT EXPECTATIONS, CHARLES DICKENS

brace *VERB*
to strengthen something or someone; to give someone courage
• *I feel a cold northern breeze play upon my cheeks, which braces my nerves.*—FRANKENSTEIN, MARY SHELLEY

brace to brig

➤ **brace up:** to make someone or yourself feel strong or brave enough in preparation for something • *She was bracing herself up to refuse him, for once and for all.*—MARY BARTON, ELIZABETH GASKELL
• *I got to tell the truth, and you want to brace up, Miss Mary, because it's a bad kind.*—THE ADVENTURES OF HUCKLEBERRY FINN,

brace NOUN
a rope attached to a ship's yard (a rod across a mast, for hanging a sail)
• *Man the braces!*—MOBY DICK, HERMAN MELVILLE

brain fever NOUN
illness said to be caused by inflammation of the brain
• *[She] was temporarily insane from an acute attack of brain-fever.*—THE MEMOIRS OF SHERLOCK HOLMES, ARTHUR CONAN DOYLE
• *He has been … suffering from a violent brain fever.*—DRACULA, BRAM STOKER

brand NOUN
1 a piece of burning wood
• *I waved my brand … and … fired the straw.*—FRANKENSTEIN, MARY SHELLEY
2 a piece of hot metal used for burning an identifying mark onto an animal or person
• *Pain and fear and grief [were] written on her as with a brand.*—THE WOMAN IN WHITE, WILKIE COLLINS
3 a mark or sign of something
• *She had been … called 'quick' all her little life, and now … this quickness was the brand of inferiority.*—THE MILL ON THE FLOSS, GEORGE ELIOT

brand VERB
to burn a mark onto an animal or person
• *a … branded convict*—MOONFLEET, J. MEADE FALKNER
🏛 Old English *brand* meaning 'burning'
RELATED WORD *brand* meaning 'identifying mark' is related to the modern sense of a product sold under a particular name

brave ADJECTIVE
looking very good; splendid
• *Belinda Cratchit, second of her daughters, also brave in ribbons*—A CHRISTMAS CAROL, CHARLES DICKENS

bravo NOUN
a thug; a killer
• *Men have before hired bravos to transact their crimes.*—THE STRANGE CASE OF DR JEKYLL AND MR HYDE, ROBERT LOUIS STEVENSON

brawl VERB
(said about water) to flow or move noisily
• *the brawling waves*—FRANKENSTEIN, MARY SHELLEY

brawn NOUN
cooked meat from the head of an animal, chopped and pressed into a mould

brazen ADJECTIVE
made of brass
• *the black door with the brazen door-plate*—HARD TIMES, CHARLES DICKENS

bread-poultice NOUN
a soft substance made with soaked bread, applied to the skin as a remedy for boils, bruises, inflammation, etc.

breast NOUN
a person's chest, often as the centre of emotions or thoughts
• *If you have a suspicion in your own breast, keep that suspicion in your own breast.*—GREAT EXPECTATIONS, CHARLES DICKENS
• *I beheld tears trickle fast from between his fingers; a groan burst from his heaving breast.*—FRANKENSTEIN, MARY SHELLEY
• *But that she ever thought of it, or watched it, was a secret which she kept within her own young breast.*—DOMBEY AND SON, CHARLES DICKENS
➤ **make a clean breast of it:** to confess everything • *You must make a clean breast of it, for if you do I hope that I may be of use to you.*—THE SIGN OF FOUR, ARTHUR CONAN DOYLE

breastpin NOUN
a brooch, often used as a fastener

breeches NOUN
trousers that ended just below the knee
• *He wore breeches and the laced-up shoes called ankle-jacks.*—FAR FROM THE MADDING CROWD, THOMAS HARDY

brethren NOUN
1 brothers
• *Angel often felt that he was nearer to his father … than was either of his brethren.*—TESS OF THE D'URBERVILLES, THOMAS HARDY
2 the members of a church congregation or community, especially the men
• *the younger brethren or sisters*—SILAS MARNER, GEORGE ELIOT

bride-cake NOUN
wedding cake
• *Miss Havisham's room contains a 'rotten bride-cake that was hidden in cobwebs'.*—GREAT EXPECTATIONS, CHARLES DICKENS

brig NOUN
a ship with two masts
• *Next day we were picked up by the brig Hotspur.*—THE MEMOIRS OF SHERLOCK HOLMES, ARTHUR CONAN DOYLE

brigand to brooklet

brigand NOUN
a member of a band of robbers; a bandit
• *You spoke like a brigand who demanded my purse rather than like a lover who asked my heart.*—SHIRLEY, CHARLOTTE BRONTË

brimstone NOUN
sulphur

USAGE Brimstone, or sulphur, was used in various medicines.
• *Mrs Squeers stood ... over an immense basin of brimstone and treacle, of which delicious compound she administered a large instalment to each boy in succession.*—NICHOLAS NICKLEBY, CHARLES DICKENS
Because of sulphur's flammable properties, the word 'brimstone' was often used with reference to fire or flames.
• *Stockdale produced a spark, and was kindling the brimstone.*—WESSEX TALES, THOMAS HARDY
Sometimes, as in modern English, 'brimstone' referred to the fire of hell.
• *a murderer who ... saw ... brimstone flames around him*—TESS OF THE D'URBERVILLES, THOMAS HARDY

brine NOUN
➢ **the brine:** the sea • *where the brine lies fathoms deep and emerald clear*—SHIRLEY, CHARLOTTE BRONTË

bringing-up NOUN
education or upbringing; background
• *But, your bringing-up was different from mine.*—HARD TIMES, CHARLES DICKENS

brink NOUN
the edge
• *I felt that I had come to the brink of my grave.*—GREAT EXPECTATIONS, CHARLES DICKENS

broadcloth NOUN
good-quality cloth, mainly used for men's clothes
• *dressed in good broadcloth*—THE MILL ON THE FLOSS, GEORGE ELIOT

broadside NOUN
1 (also **broadsheet**)
a newspaper printed on one side only
• *halfpenny broadsides, giving an account of the bloody murder*—MARY BARTON, ELIZABETH GASKELL
2 a confrontation in which a ship fires all the guns on one side
• *The same broadside I lost my leg.*—TREASURE ISLAND, ROBERT LOUIS STEVENSON

broider VERB
to decorate cloth with embroidery
• *screens broidered with parrots and peacocks*—THE BIRTHDAY OF THE INFANTA, OSCAR WILDE

Prefixes and suffixes

Some do not use the prefix found in modern English. An example is 'broider' instead of 'embroider' or 'prisoned' instead of 'emprisoned'.
• *Jane does not want her bones to '***be prisoned** *in a workhouse coffin'.*—JANE EYRE, CHARLOTTE BRONTË

Other words have a prefix which is absent in modern English, such as 'befooled' instead of 'fooled'.
• *the men whom he had robbed and **befooled***—THE SIGN OF FOUR ARTHUR, CONAN DOYLE

Recognizing prefixes and suffixes can help you to unravel the meaning of words.
• *I could not **unlove** him now, merely because I found that he had ceased to notice me.*—JANE EYRE, CHARLOTTE BRONTË
• *I said to myself there was something thundery and **changeful** in the weather.*—KIDNAPPED, ROBERT LOUIS STEVENSON

You may not realize immediately that something is a prefix and it may help to re-read a section in order to understand it.
• *His hard features were revealed all agrin and **ashine** with glee.*—SHIRLEY, CHARLOTTE BRONTË
• *Often ... a slight cloud would **bedim** the sky.*—FRANKENSTEIN, MARY SHELLEY

---

broil NOUN
an argument or fight; a disturbance
• *Never ... did I know any ... squires ... get himself into so many broils as thou.*—MEN OF IRON, HOWARD PYLE

brood VERB
to lean or hover over something
• *He was obliged to sit close to [the fire], and brood over it, before he could extract the least sensation of warmth from such a handful of fuel.*—A CHRISTMAS CAROL, CHARLES DICKENS

brook VERB
to tolerate or permit something
• *I have not been in the habit of brooking disappointment.*—PRIDE AND PREJUDICE, JANE AUSTEN

brooklet NOUN
a small stream
• *A little brooklet ... had overflowed after a rapid thaw.*—JANE EYRE, CHARLOTTE BRONTË

brougham to burthen

> ### Similes
>
> Here, the word *brooklet* is used in a simile.
> - [Her] hair ripples as obstinately as a brooklet under the March breeze.—SILAS MARNER, GEORGE ELIOT
>
> Figurative language from the 19th century includes references to things that were familiar (for example nature and the countryside, food, jobs, everyday objects, and customs) as well as to things that were unknown and new. Here are some more examples of similes from this period.
> - They must have bolted as blindly *as a flock of sheep*.
> —THE WAR OF THE WORLDS, H. G. WELLS
> - You thought you were *as dead as a herring* two hours since.—JANE EYRE, CHARLOTTE BRONTË
> - He was as black *as a sweep with the black dust*.—THE WAR OF THE WORLDS, H. G. WELLS
> - I was as flat *as a warming-pan*.—HARD TIMES, CHARLES DICKENS,
> - They would be obliged to 'run away'—a course *as dark and dubious as a balloon journey*.—SILAS MARNER, —GEORGE ELIOT,
> - It was as still *as a church on a week-day*.
> —JANE EYRE, CHARLOTTE BRONTË,

brougham NOUN (say **broo-um**)
a four-wheeled horse-drawn carriage with the driver's seat outside at the front
- A brougham was waiting at our door.—THE MEMOIRS OF SHERLOCK HOLMES, ARTHUR CONAN DOYLE

brownie NOUN
a friendly or helpful elf or goblin with shaggy hair
- Jane asks Mr Rochester for a comb, saying he is 'like a brownie'.—JANE EYRE, CHARLOTTE BRONTË

browse VERB
to graze on grass or on the shoots, leaves, etc. of trees; to trim trees by grazing on them
- fields, where no cattle now browsed—JANE EYRE, CHARLOTTE BRONTË
- The trees bore evident marks of having been browsed by the horses.—THE LAST OF THE MOHICANS, JAMES FENIMORE COOPER

buckler NOUN
a small shield
- to fight this battle out ... with sword and buckler and bascinet—MEN OF IRON, HOWARD PYLE

buckram NOUN
a kind of stiff fabric
- a woman in large buckram sleeves—THE MILL ON THE FLOSS, GEORGE ELIOT

buffet NOUN
a punch or hit
- I began ... to rain kicks and buffets on the door.
—KIDNAPPED, ROBERT LOUIS STEVENSON

bull's-eye NOUN
1 a lantern with a round piece of glass
- 'Lend me your bull's-eye, sergeant,' said my companion.—THE SIGN OF FOUR, ARTHUR CONAN DOYLE
2 a round window or piece of glass
- The carpenter's work includes *'inserting bull's eyes in the [ship's] deck'*.—MOBY DICK, HERMAN MELVILLE

bulwark (say **buul-wuhk**) NOUN
➤ **bulwarks**
1 the side of a ship, above the deck
- I was cast clean over the bulwarks into the sea.
—KIDNAPPED, ROBERT LOUIS STEVENSON
2 a defence or protector
- He thought ... Great Britain the ... bulwark of Protestantism.—THE MILL ON THE FLOSS, GEORGE ELIOT

bumper NOUN
a large cup or glass of alcoholic drink, especially one drunk as a toast
- I begged Mr Micawber to fill us bumpers, and proposed the toast in due form.—DAVID COPPERFIELD, CHARLES DICKENS

burgess NOUN
1 a citizen of a town or borough
- burgesses with rights and privileges—THE MAYOR OF CASTERBRIDGE, THOMAS HARDY
2 a councillor, M.P., or official

burgh (say **burr-uh**) NOUN
a borough
- a fairly built burgh, the houses of good stone
—KIDNAPPED, ROBERT LOUIS STEVENSON

burgher (say **bur-guhr**) NOUN
a citizen of a town or borough
- He spoke to the princes, the nobles ... and the burghers, with just the same ease.—VILLETTE, CHARLOTTE BRONTË

burthen NOUN
1 a burden; a heavy load
- This fellow carried all our luggage ... trotting along under the burthen.—KIDNAPPED, ROBERT LOUIS STEVENSON
2 the load a ship could carry
- She was a brig of some 120 tons burthen.
—MOONFLEET, J. MEADE FALKNER

burthen VERB
to burden someone; to weigh someone down
- *The other men were variously burthened; some carrying picks and shovels ... others laden with pork, bread, and brandy.*—TREASURE ISLAND, ROBERT LOUIS STEVENSON

burthensome ADJECTIVE
burdensome; causing difficulty or weighing someone down
- *To be immortal would not be so burthensome.*—THE MORTAL IMMORTAL, MARY SHELLEY

bushel NOUN
a measure for grain or fruit, equal to 8 gallons (36.4 litres); a large amount
- *a bushel of coal-dust*—GREAT EXPECTATIONS, CHARLES DICKENS

busk VERB
to prepare someone or something
- *busking the [ship] for sea*—KIDNAPPED, ROBERT LOUIS STEVENSON

busk NOUN
one of the strips that stiffened a corset

but ADVERB
only
- *I was but ten.*—JANE EYRE, CHARLOTTE BRONTË

➤ **not but:** only • *Elizabeth could not but be pleased, could not but triumph.*—PRIDE AND PREJUDICE, JANE AUSTEN

but CONJUNCTION
➤ **but that:**
1 that • *I did not doubt but that the monster followed me.*—FRANKENSTEIN, MARY SHELLEY
2 if it was not for the fact that • *I might have become sullen in my study ... but that she was there to subdue me.*—FRANKENSTEIN, MARY SHELLEY
3 used with 'not so ...' to say that something was not enough to prevent another thing • *an old wall; not so high but that I could struggle up and ... look over it*—GREAT EXPECTATIONS, CHARLES DICKENS

butter-fingers NOUN
someone who dropped or failed to catch something
➤ **butter-fingered** ADJECTIVE • *He ... called his rescuers 'butter-fingered land-lubbers'.*—THE STORY OF A BAD BOY, THOMAS BAILEY ALDRICH

by ADVERB
nearby
- *I could no longer talk or laugh freely when he was by.*—JANE EYRE, CHARLOTTE BRONTË

byre NOUN
a cowshed
- *And ... the cattle in the byres, and the horses from the stable, and the men from cottage-door, each has had his rest and food.*—LORNA DOONE, R. D. BLACKMORE

Cc

CRYSTAL PALACE

The **Crystal Palace** was a huge building built in London's Hyde Park to house the **Great Exhibition** of **1851**. This huge event brought together inventions, products, and materials from all around the world. It was visited by over six million people. Designed by Joseph Paxton and built from iron and glass, the Crystal Palace resembled a giant greenhouse and housed more than 13,000 exhibits including the Koh-i-Noor, which was then the largest diamond in the world.

c ABBREVIATION
➢ **& c.:** etc.; etcetera
• I had read Goldsmith's History of Rome, and had formed my opinion of Nero, Caligula, & c. —JANE EYRE, CHARLOTTE BRONTË

cab NOUN
a horse-drawn vehicle that could be hired like a taxi
• I want you … to take a cab [and] drive straight to my house.—THE STRANGE CASE OF DR JEKYLL AND MR HYDE, ROBERT LOUIS STEVENSON
➢ **cabman** NOUN the driver of a cab
• For cabmen and cabmen's horses [Christmas] is no holiday.—BLACK BEAUTY, ANNA SEWELL

cabin-boy NOUN
a boy who worked as a servant to a ship's officers or passengers
• all [the crew], from the black-bearded captain down to the tiniest cabin-boy—CAPTAIN JANUARY, LAURA E. RICHARDS

COMPOUND WORDS Many words, like 'cabin-boy', consist of two or more words joined together. It is often easy to guess their meaning from the context.

• A stable-boy had run out to the horse's head. —THE ADVENTURES OF SHERLOCK HOLMES, ARTHUR CONAN DOYLE
• The newsboys … were crying themselves hoarse along the footways: 'Special edition. Shocking murder of an M.P.'—THE STRANGE CASE OF DR JEKYLL AND MR HYDE, ROBERT LOUIS STEVENSON

cabriolet (say kab-ree-uh-lay, kab-ree-oh-lay) NOUN
a light carriage with a hood and two wheels, pulled by one horse
• I hurried into a cabriolet, and bade farewell to my friend.—FRANKENSTEIN, MARY SHELLEY

cad NOUN
a man who behaved badly, especially towards women
• And if you are a girl, you can't knock people down when they are cads.—HILDEGARDE'S NEIGHBORS, LAURA E. RICHARDS

cadence NOUN
the tone, pitch, or rhythm of speech, music, or another sound, especially when rising and falling away
• She sang, and her voice flowed in a rich cadence, swelling or dying away like a nightingale.—FRANKENSTEIN, MARY SHELLEY

cadet NOUN
1 a younger or youngest son
• John was an old servant, and had known his master when he was the cadet of the house.—JANE EYRE, CHARLOTTE BRONTË
2 a younger section of a family; a member of this section
• His branch was a cadet one.—THE MEMOIRS OF SHERLOCK HOLMES, ARTHUR CONAN DOYLE

Cain NOUN
used with reference to the Bible story in which Cain killed his brother, Abel, and was then banished
• He would slouch out, like Cain … as if he had no idea where he was going and no intention of ever coming back.—GREAT EXPECTATIONS, CHARLES DICKENS
• 'Sons,' said he, 'one of you must leave my roof if this occurs again. I will have no Cain and Abel strife here.' —SHIRLEY, CHARLOTTE BRONTË
➢ **mark of Cain:** a sign of evil or of being a murderer

caitiff NOUN
a cowardly or worthless person
• Thou art a coward caitiff!—MEN OF IRON, HOWARD PYLE

cake to cantonment

cake NOUN
a small flattened loaf
• *There was a little shop with some cakes of bread in the window.*—JANE EYRE, CHARLOTTE BRONTË

calculate VERB
to plan; to intend
• *[I was] calculating to build a palace and sell it.*
—THE ADVENTURES OF HUCKLEBERRY FINN, MARK TWAIN
➤ **calculated** ADJECTIVE right for something; likely to do something • *The ladies are very fond of him; though you would not think his appearance calculated to recommend him particularly in their eyes.*—JANE EYRE, CHARLOTTE BRONTË

caleche (also **calèche**) (say kuh-lesh) NOUN
1 a light carriage with low wheels and a hood that could be folded or removed
2 a woman's loose-fitting hood or bonnet, with hoops to keep it away from her hair

calico NOUN
cotton cloth, often considered of low quality
• *[Tom] might as well have calico as linen.*—THE MILL ON THE FLOSS, GEORGE ELIOT

callosity NOUN
an area of thick hard skin; a callus
• *the callosities of his forefinger and thumb*—A STUDY IN SCARLET, ARTHUR CONAN DOYLE

callous ADJECTIVE
with thickened or hardened skin; calloused
• *callous palms*—SILAS MARNER, GEORGE ELIOT

callow ADJECTIVE
young; not fully mature
• *a little callow gosling*—VILLETTE, CHARLOTTE BRONTË

cambric NOUN
a type of delicate cotton or linen fabric
• *a wisp of cambric for a neckcloth*—DOMBEY AND SON, CHARLES DICKENS
• *fine cambric handkerchiefs*—VILLETTE, CHARLOTTE BRONTË

cameo NOUN
a carved portrait; an oval brooch containing this
• *this cameo head*—JANE EYRE, CHARLOTTE BRONTË

canister NOUN
a small, usually metal container, for holding something such as loose tea leaves
• *[He took] down the tin canister in which he kept his cash.*—DOMBEY AND SON, CHARLES DICKENS

canker NOUN
something harmful; something that destroyed something
• *The real care and canker was that I was going away from Grace Maskew.*—MOONFLEET, J. MEADE FALKNER

canker VERB
to spoil something; to rot something
• *A few pounds got by selling a good old servant into hard work, and misery, would canker all the rest of his money.*—BLACK BEAUTY, ANNA SEWELL
➤ **cankering** ADJECTIVE • *A cankering evil sat at my heart and drained my happiness at its source.*
—JANE EYRE, CHARLOTTE BRONTË

cannikin NOUN
a small container for drink
• *He drew some cognac from the cask into a tin cannikin.*—TREASURE ISLAND, ROBERT LOUIS STEVENSON

cannonade NOUN
repeated firing of guns or cannons
• *[There] was a fitful cannonade far away in the southwest ...*—THE WAR OF THE WORLDS, H. G. WELLS

canst VERB
a form of 'can' used with 'thou'
• *Still thou canst listen to me and grant me thy compassion.*—FRANKENSTEIN, MARY SHELLEY

cant NOUN
hypocrisy; insincere talk
• *I am not writing to flatter parental egotism, to echo cant, or prop up humbug.*—JANE EYRE, CHARLOTTE BRONTË

cant ADJECTIVE
slang
• *Sheep was a cant word of the time for a spy.*
—A TALE OF TWO CITIES, CHARLES DICKENS

cant VERB
to tilt; to tip
• *[The Hispaniola] canted over to the port side, till the deck stood at an angle of forty-five degrees.*
—TREASURE ISLAND, ROBERT LOUIS STEVENSON

canting ADJECTIVE
using whining, pleading, or hypercritical language
• *a hundred canting speeches full of oily words*
—NICHOLAS NICKLEBY, CHARLES DICKENS

cantonment NOUN
a military camp, or a military settlement in British India

canula to career

canula NOUN
a cannula (a tube used in surgery)
• On the further side ... there [were] forceps ... saws, canulas, and trocars.—HIS FIRST OPERATION, ARTHUR CONAN DOYLE

canvass VERB
1 to discuss something in detail
• The whole [story] was now openly acknowledged and publicly canvassed.—PRIDE AND PREJUDICE, JANE AUSTEN
2 to try to get support or business
• one of those miserable apothecaries who canvass for practice in strange neighbourhoods—SILAS MARNER, GEORGE ELIOT
USAGE In modern English, you might expect to canvass political opinion or voters.

capacity NOUN
1 ability
• I never saw such capacity, and taste, and application, and elegance.—PRIDE AND PREJUDICE, JANE AUSTEN
2 a role or function; a position
• Moreover ... how came Mr Dowlas to be so eager to act in that capacity?—SILAS MARNER, GEORGE ELIOT

capital ADJECTIVE
1 very great; significant or particular
• Five minutes afterwards ... you will have understood that these arrangements are of capital importance.—THE STRANGE CASE OF DR JEKYLL AND MR HYDE, ROBERT LOUIS STEVENSON
2 excellent
• Her performance was pleasing, though by no means capital.—PRIDE AND PREJUDICE, JANE AUSTEN

capon NOUN
a male chicken
• roasted capons—THE MERRY ADVENTURES OF ROBIN HOOD, HOWARD PYLE

caprice NOUN
a whim or impulse; a sudden feeling or change of mood
• She had taken an amiable caprice to me.—JANE EYRE, CHARLOTTE BRONTË

capstan NOUN
a rotating cylinder on a ship for winding a rope
• Stubb eats his meal of whale steak on the top of the capstan, 'as if that capstan were a sideboard'.—MOBY DICK, ROBERT LOUIS STEVENSON

captious ADJECTIVE
likely to point out faults; critical
• Georgiana ... had ... a captious and insolent carriage.—JANE EYRE, CHARLOTTE BRONTË

car NOUN
1 a carriage or cart
• He fastened the car door, climbed to his own seat outside, and we set off.—JANE EYRE, CHARLOTTE BRONTË
2 a train carriage
• the fancy car of an excursion train—ROSE IN BLOOM, LOUISA M. ALCOTT
3 the passenger compartment of a hot-air balloon
• The ropes which held the car were cut, and the balloon ... mounted 2,000 feet.—THE MYSTERIOUS ISLAND, JULES VERNE
4 a chariot
• So she ... got into her car drawn by a pair of winged dragons.—TANGLEWOOD TALES, NATHANIEL HAWTHORNE

carbine NOUN
a short rifle
• He put his carbine to his shoulder.—THE SIGN OF FOUR, ARTHUR CONAN DOYLE

carboy NOUN
a large, rounded glass bottle with a narrow neck, for holding dangerous chemicals or making beer or wine
• The carboy has been cracked, you see, and the stuff has leaked out.—THE SIGN OF FOUR, ARTHUR CONAN DOYLE

carbuncle NOUN
1 a red gemstone, in particular a garnet, or a mythical stone said to glow in the dark
• The fog [lay] above the drowned city, where the lamps glimmered like carbuncles.—THE STRANGE CASE OF DR JEKYLL AND MR HYDE, ROBERT LOUIS STEVENSON
2 a large boil or abscess on the skin

carcanet (say kar-kuh-net) NOUN
a necklace or jewelled collar
• On her dress was no ornament ... neither was there a ring on her hand, or a necklace or carcanet about her neck.—THE PRINCESS AND THE GOBLIN, GEORGE MACDONALD

carcass (also **carcase**) NOUN
an insulting or humorous way of referring to a person's body, dead or alive
• For what would they risk their rascal carcases but money?—TREASURE ISLAND, ROBERT LOUIS STEVENSON

career NOUN
1 a rapid course of movement
• a monstrous tripod, higher than many houses, striding over the young pine trees, and smashing them aside in its career—THE WAR OF THE WORLDS, H. G. WELLS
2 a course of action; the course of someone's life
• His career depends entirely upon my treatment of him.—FAR FROM THE MADDING CROWD, THOMAS HARDY

careless to catalepsy

- *It seems her career there was very honourable: from a pupil, she became a teacher.*—JANE EYRE, CHARLOTTE BRONTË

➤ **in full career:** at full speed; with maximum force • *The trumpets sounded, and the knights charged each other in full career.*—IVANHOE, WALTER SCOTT

careless ADJECTIVE
1 free from worry; carefree
- *this land ... where men lived in careless abundance*—SILAS MARNER, GEORGE ELIOT

2 not caring about something
- *I threw myself into the carriage ... hardly knowing whither I was going, and careless of what was passing around.*—FRANKENSTEIN, MARY SHELLEY
- *He tried to speak in a cool, careless way, but his eyes were shining with excitement and greed.*—THE SIGN OF FOUR, ARTHUR CONAN DOYLE

➤ **carelessly** ADJECTIVE without showing concern; deliberately not looking worried • *'Oh, there was a little account between us,' said Dunsey, carelessly.*—SILAS MARNER, GEORGE ELIOT

➤ **carelessness** NOUN • *She tossed her head with affected carelessness.*—OLIVER TWIST, CHARLES DICKENS

carking ADJECTIVE
worrying; causing anxiety or distress
- *the carking accidents of her daily existence*—THE MAYOR OF CASTERBRIDGE, THOMAS HARDY

carlot NOUN
a peasant; a country person
- *And when he passed through the villages ... the carlots would not suffer him even to sleep in the byres.*—THE STAR-CHILD, OSCAR WILDE

carriage NOUN
1 a horse-drawn four-wheeled vehicle
- *Mr Darcy handed the ladies into the carriage.*—PRIDE AND PREJUDICE, JANE AUSTEN

2 a person's posture
- *She was very pale, but she walked with a firm step, and her carriage was full of grace and gentle dignity.*—THE PRINCE AND THE PAUPER, MARK TWAIN

carronade NOUN
a short, wide cannon fired from a ship

carry VERB
➤ **carry your point:** to get your own way; to win an argument • *I hoped to find you reasonable; but depend upon it I will carry my point.*—PRIDE AND PREJUDICE, JANE AUSTEN

carven ADJECTIVE
carved
- *massive carven furniture*—LITTLE LORD FAUNTLEROY, FRANCES HODGSON BURNETT

case-knife NOUN
a dagger with a sheath

casement NOUN
a window, especially one opening with a hinge, like a door
- *[The full moon] came ... to that space in the sky opposite my casement.*—JANE EYRE, CHARLOTTE BRONTË

cassino (also casino) NOUN
a card game
- *Miss De Bourgh chose to play at cassino.*—PRIDE AND PREJUDICE, JANE AUSTEN

cassone NOUN
an Italian chest, intricately carved, used for a bride's clothes and belongings
- *an old Italian cassone*—THE PICTURE OF DORIAN GRAY, OSCAR WILDE

cast NOUN
1 the appearance, form, or features of something
- *She ... dislikes your cast of character.*—JANE EYRE, CHARLOTTE BRONTË

2 a slight squint; a look in a particular direction
- *a fellow with a cast in his eye*—SILAS MARNER, GEORGE ELIOT

caste NOUN
social class
- *the prejudices of creed and caste*—JANE EYRE, CHARLOTTE BRONTË

castor (also caster) NOUN
1 a small container for sprinkling salt, pepper, or sugar. A *set of castors* typically included other things, for example, a vinegar bottle.
- *The waiter laid a cloth ... for me, and put a set of castors on it.*—DAVID COPPERFIELD, CHARLES DICKENS

2 a hat
- *Michael [arrived] hatless, in his shirt-sleeves—his coat and castor having been detained at the public-house in pledge.*—SHIRLEY, CHARLOTTE BRONTË

casualty NOUN
a chance event
- *No! he would rather trust to casualties.*—SILAS MARNER, GEORGE ELIOT

catalepsy NOUN
a seizure causing someone to become rigid and unconscious
- *He was arrested ... by the invisible wand of catalepsy, and stood like a graven image, with wide but sightless eyes.*—SILAS MARNER, GEORGE ELIOT

➤ **cataleptic** ADJECTIVE *He has been for some years a victim to cataleptic attacks.*—THE MEMOIRS OF SHERLOCK HOLMES, ARTHUR CONAN DOYLE

cataract to chandler

cataract NOUN
a large waterfall; a rushing mass of water
• They were about to be swept within the vortex at the foot of the cataract.—THE LAST OF THE MOHICANS, JAMES FENIMORE COOPER

catholicity NOUN
the quality of being wide-ranging or including everything
• Mr Utterson is said to be friendly to everyone, showing his *'catholicity of good-nature'*.—THE STRANGE CASE OF DR JEKYLL AND MR HYDE, ROBERT LOUIS STEVENSON

caul NOUN
the membrane around a fetus
USAGE It was thought to be lucky if a baby was born with part of the *caul* covering its head, and this caul could be bought as a lucky charm, especially by sailors.
• I was born with a caul, which was advertised for sale, in the newspapers, at the low price of fifteen guineas. —DAVID COPPERFIELD, CHARLES DICKENS

cavil VERB
to quibble; to raise trivial objections
➤ **caviller** NOUN a person who raised trivial objections • I don't like cavillers or questioners. —JANE EYRE, CHARLOTTE BRONTË

cavil NOUN
raising trivial objections; a trivial objection
• I will listen to no cavil.—SENSE AND SENSIBILITY, JANE AUSTEN

celerity NOUN
speed
• [This] could only be some new device for making his fortune with unusual celerity.—DOMBEY AND SON, CHARLES DICKENS

cell NOUN
a small room, storeroom, or dwelling
• a solitary chamber, or rather cell, at the top of the house—FRANKENSTEIN, MARY SHELLEY
• a goblin's cell—JANE EYRE, CHARLOTTE BRONTË

certes (say **sur-tiz**) ADVERB
certainly
• Certes this is a serious matter.—THE PRINCE AND THE PAUPER, MARK TWAIN

chafe VERB
1 to rub something in order to warm it
• Holding my hand in both his own, he chafed it. —JANE EYRE, CHARLOTTE BRONTË
2 to irritate or frustrate someone
• It chafed me that this grasping fellow should be always shouting to me.—MOONFLEET, J. MEADE FALKNER
3 to feel impatient or frustrated
• [I] knew how his keen spirit was chafing against this involuntary inaction.—THE SIGN OF FOUR, ARTHUR CONAN DOYLE

chaff VERB
to tease or mock someone
• He said that … he would be chaffed by all the other clerks about having letters from a lady.—THE ADVENTURES OF SHERLOCK HOLMES, ARTHUR CONAN DOYLE

chaff NOUN
1 husks of grain, separated from the seed; used for referring to worthless or unwanted people or things
• Drummle … informed our host that … he could scatter us like chaff.—GREAT EXPECTATIONS, CHARLES DICKENS
2 mockery; teasing
• He is ever ready with a reply to any piece of chaff which may be thrown at him by the passers-by.—THE ADVENTURES OF SHERLOCK HOLMES, ARTHUR CONAN DOYLE

chagrin NOUN
annoyance, disappointment, or embarrassment
• In … the unhappy defects of her family [there was] a subject of yet heavier chagrin.—PRIDE AND PREJUDICE, JANE AUSTEN

chaise (say **shayz**) NOUN
1 a horse-drawn carriage for one or two people
• 'Mrs Long says that … he came down on Monday in a chaise and four'—with four horses.—PRIDE AND PREJUDICE, JANE AUSTEN
2 a post-chaise (a carriage for passengers and mail)
• At length the chaise arrived.—PRIDE AND PREJUDICE, JANE AUSTEN

chamber NOUN
a room
• He lived in chambers which had once belonged to his deceased partner.—A CHRISTMAS CAROL, CHARLES DICKENS

champaign NOUN
flat, open countryside
• [Below us] lay league on league of the most lovely champaign country.—KING SOLOMON'S MINES, H. RIDER HAGGARD

chancel NOUN
the part of a church for the vicar or priest and the choir, sometimes separated from the rest of the church by steps or a screen
• [They] went up the chancel steps.—FAR FROM THE MADDING CROWD, THOMAS HARDY

chandler NOUN
1 someone who sold groceries and household items
• She kept a chandler's shop.—HARD TIMES, CHARLES DICKENS

'Change to charity

2 a merchant; a dealer
• *Uncle Pumblechook ... was a well-to-do cornchandler in the nearest town.*—GREAT EXPECTATIONS, CHARLES DICKENS
3 someone who made or sold candles

'Change NOUN
the stock exchange
• *Scrooge's name was good upon 'Change.*—A CHRISTMAS CAROL, CHARLES DICKENS

changeling NOUN
a child who was believed to have been put in the place of another child by fairies
• *You mocking changeling—fairy-born and human-bred!*—JANE EYRE, CHARLOTTE BRONTË

chany (say chain-ey) NOUN
china; crockery
• *It drives me past patience to hear you all talking o' ... buying in this, that, and the other, such as silver and chany.*—THE MILL ON THE FLOSS, GEORGE ELIOT

Local accents

Chany is a dialect form of the word 'china'.

Characters may speak in dialect or with a local accent. When their speech is written to reflect this, it can be easier to understand it by saying it aloud. The context of the sentence can also help you to understand the vocabulary.

• *If she ben't one o' th' handsomest, she's noan faal and varry good-natured; and i' his een she's fair beautiful, onybody may see that.*—JANE EYRE, CHARLOTTE BRONTË

---

chap VERB
to knock
• *Ay ... he'll be dead, no doubt; and that'll be what brings ye chapping to my door.*—KIDNAPPED, ROBERT LOUIS STEVENSON

chapbook NOUN
a booklet containing popular tales or songs or religious writing, sold by travelling sellers
• *[There] was an entry on the fly-leaf of a chap-book ... plainly written by my father's hand.*—KIDNAPPED, ROBERT LOUIS STEVENSON

chaplet NOUN
1 a garland or tiara worn on someone's head
• *Hilda has a 'green chaplet crowning her fair locks'.*—HILDEGARDE'S NEIGHBORS, LAURA E. RICHARDS
2 a string of beads, used as rosary beads or as a necklace
• *See that chaplet dipped with pearls.*—THE SIGN OF FOUR, ARTHUR CONAN DOYLE

character NOUN
a good reputation
• *He is now perhaps sorry for what he has done, and anxious to re-establish a character.*—PRIDE AND PREJUDICE, JANE AUSTEN

charge NOUN
1 a child or other person being looked after by someone
• *My charge lay fast asleep.*—GREAT EXPECTATIONS, CHARLES DICKENS
2 the responsibility of looking after someone
• *I always thought they were very unfit to have the charge of her.*—PRIDE AND PREJUDICE, JANE AUSTEN
3 an instruction or task given to someone
• *Mr Wopsle, Joe, and I, received strict charge to keep in the rear.*—GREAT EXPECTATIONS, CHARLES DICKENS
• *The boy was proud of his charge, and undertook it in all seriousness.*—PRIDE AND PREJUDICE, JANE AUSTEN
4 an accusation
• *The justice of the charge struck her too forcibly for denial.*—PRIDE AND PREJUDICE, JANE AUSTEN
➤ **lay something to someone's charge:** to accuse someone of something • *Two offences of a very different nature ... you last night laid to my charge.*—PRIDE AND PREJUDICE, JANE AUSTEN

charge VERB
to give someone a task or instruction
• *Mr Lloyd 'charged [Bessie] to be very careful that I was not disturbed during the night'.*—JANE EYRE, CHARLOTTE BRONTË
• *Miss Smith ... was charged with the care of the linen and the inspection of the dormitories.*—JANE EYRE, CHARLOTTE BRONTË

charity NOUN
1 love or generosity towards other people; kindness
• *Sir John [begged] in the name of charity, that they would all dine with Lady Middleton that day, as ... she would otherwise be quite alone.*—SENSE AND SENSIBILITY, JANE AUSTEN
2 dutiful or organized care, rather than compassion
• *You would not like to be long dependent on our hospitality—you would wish ... to dispense ... with my sisters' compassion, and, above all, with my charity.*—JANE EYRE, CHARLOTTE BRONTË
3 charitable organizations
• *a charity school*—NICHOLAS NICKLEBY, CHARLES DICKENS
➤ **charity-boy** NOUN a boy attending a charity school • *Noah was a charity-boy, but not a workhouse orphan.*—OLIVER TWIST, CHARLES DICKENS

charivari to chicken-hearted

charivari NOUN
the noise of things being banged together in a mockery of a musical performance, intended to show contempt
• [We] played a charivari with the ruler and desk, the fender and fire-irons.—JANE EYRE, CHARLOTTE BRONTË

charlatan NOUN
a person making claims about their own or their medicine's abilities; a con man
• I got this cordial at Rome, of an Italian charlatan—a fellow you would have kicked, Carter.—JANE EYRE, CHARLOTTE BRONTË

charnel-house (also **charnel**) NOUN
1 a place where the bones or bodies of dead people were kept
• I collected bones from charnel-houses.—FRANKENSTEIN, MARY SHELLEY
2 a place of death
• My heart was a sort of charnel; it will now be a shrine.—JANE EYRE, CHARLOTTE BRONTË

charwoman NOUN
a woman employed to clean someone's house
• Through a partly-opened door the noise of a scrubbing-brush led up to the charwoman.—FAR FROM THE MADDING CROWD, THOMAS HARDY

chasten (say chay-suhn) VERB
to make someone reflect, learn, and change his or her behaviour
• Durbeyfield is told to 'chasten yourself with the thought of "how are the mighty fallen".'—TESS OF THE D'URBERVILLES, THOMAS HARDY
➤ **chastened** ADJECTIVE • [He] eventually changed for the better, and appeared as a chastened and thoughtful man.—WESSEX TALES, THOMAS HARDY

chastise VERB
1 to punish
• [The dog's] master was in the frequent habit of chastising her violently.—SHIRLEY, CHARLOTTE BRONTË
2 to control; to make something or someone more disciplined
• Godfrey's home was one 'where the daily habits were not chastised by the presence of household order'.—SILAS MARNER, GEORGE ELIOT

chattel NOUN
something owned by someone; a possession
• You [were] without a chattel to your name, and I was the master of the house in Corn Street.—THE MAYOR OF CASTERBRIDGE, THOMAS HARDY
• the chattels of the ploughman—TESS OF THE D'URBERVILLES, THOMAS HARDY

chaw NOUN
something chewed, especially tobacco; an act of chewing
• Some of them kinds of loafers never has a cent in the world, nor a chaw of tobacco of their own.—THE ADVENTURES OF HUCKLEBERRY FINN, MARK TWAIN

chaw VERB
to chew
• Don't ye chaw quite close, shepherd, for I let the bacon fall in the road … and may be 'tis rather gritty.—FAR FROM THE MADDING CROWD, THOMAS HARDY

check VERB
to stop or curtail something; to stop someone from doing something
• Elizabeth … checked her laugh.—PRIDE AND PREJUDICE, JANE AUSTEN
➤ **check yourself**: to stop yourself from speaking or from doing something • Godfrey checked himself. It had been agreed … [the topic] should be approached very carefully.—SILAS MARNER, GEORGE ELIOT

check NOUN
something that stops something from happening; a restraint
• He was forever busy, and the only check to his enjoyments was my sorrowful and dejected mind.—FRANKENSTEIN, MARY SHELLEY

check-rein NOUN
a strap running from a horse's back over its head to a bit in its mouth, stopping the horse from putting its head down too far
• [The horse] cannot use all his power with his head held back as it is with that check-rein.—BLACK BEAUTY, ANNA SEWELL

cheer NOUN
food and drink offered to someone
• [They availed] themselves of the good cheer which was so liberally supplied.—IVANHOE, WALTER SCOTT
➤ **of good cheer**: cheerful • I was weak and weary, but he bade me be of good cheer.—THE PRISONER OF ZENDA, ANTHONY HOPE
➤ **what cheer?**: how are you? • 'My pretty,' said the Captain, knocking at the door, 'what cheer?'—DOMBEY AND SON, CHARLES DICKENS

chemise NOUN
a loose-fitting dress, over-garment, or nightdress

cheval-glass (say shuh-val-glaass) NOUN
a tall mirror attached to a stand with hinges, allowing it to be tilted

chicken-hearted ADJECTIVE
cowardly
• Frank calls Bathsheba 'a chicken-hearted creature … under all [her] boldness'.—FAR FROM THE MADDING CROWD, THOMAS HARDY

chidden to Christmas

chidden *VERB*
scolded
• *Helen ... was chidden for the triviality of the inquiry.* —JANE EYRE, CHARLOTTE BRONTË

chide *VERB*
to scold
• *Elzevir took the candle, chiding me a little for being late.* —MOONFLEET, J. MEADE FALKNER

chief *NOUN*
➢ **the chief of something:** most of something
• *Elizabeth passed the chief of the night in her sister's room.* —PRIDE AND PREJUDICE, JANE AUSTEN

chiffonier (also **chiffonnier**) (say shif-on-ee-uhr) *NOUN*
a low cupboard or cabinet; a sideboard

childer *NOUN*
children
• *We're like childer, ever wanting what we han not got.* —MARY BARTON, ELIZABETH GASKELL

chimera (say ky-meer-uh, kim-eer-uh) *NOUN*
an illusion; something imaginary
• *Modern scientists 'know ... that the elixir of life is a chimera'.* —FRANKENSTEIN, MARY SHELLEY

chine *NOUN*
1 the backbone
• *The captain's blow 'would certainly have split him to the chine had it not been intercepted'.* —TREASURE ISLAND, ROBERT LOUIS STEVENSON
2 a piece of meat including part of a backbone
• *Mr Osgood offers his guests 'hams and chines'.* —SILAS MARNER, GEORGE ELIOT

chit *NOUN*
an insignificant young woman
• *Alec asks Tess, 'what am I, to be repulsed so by a mere chit like you?'—meaning rejected by her.* —TESS OF THE D'URBERVILLES, THOMAS HARDY

chivalry *NOUN*
1 bravery, nobility, and adventurousness, like that of knights in the middle ages
• *the wild spirit of chivalry which so often impelled his master upon dangers which he might easily have avoided* —IVANHOE, WALTER SCOTT
2 polite and protective behaviour by men towards women
• *Bob does not want to intrude because of his 'chivalry toward dark-eyed Maggie'.* —THE MILL ON THE FLOSS, GEORGE ELIOT

chloral *NOUN*
a name for a chemical used as a sedative or anaesthetic
• *If I do not [sleep], I shall tomorrow night get them to give me a dose of chloral.* —DRACULA, BRAM STOKER

choler (sounds like **collar**) *NOUN*
anger; an angry temperament
• *[My] choler rose, and I nearly gave him back an angry word.* —MOONFLEET, J. MEADE FALKNER
➤ **choleric** *ADJECTIVE* • *'You villain!' said the choleric Major, 'where's the breakfast?'* —DOMBEY AND SON, CHARLES DICKENS
USAGE In the past, *choler*, also known as *yellow bile*, was one of the four *humours* that were believed to make up the human body and influence personality.

cholera *NOUN*
an infectious and often fatal disease causing severe vomiting and diarrhoea
• *After a while, the cholera came, and Captain Stuart died.* —UNCLE TOM'S CABIN, HARRIET BEECHER STOWE

chop-house *NOUN*
a restaurant, usually one serving mainly meat, cooked and presented simply

chord *NOUN*
an emotion; a feeling
• *Troy found unexpected chords of feeling to be stirred again within him.* —FAR FROM THE MADDING CROWD, THOMAS HARDY
USAGE In this meaning, *chord* is often used to compare the human mind or heart and its emotions to a musical instrument.
• *He had struck so successfully on one of those little jarring chords in the human heart.* NICHOLAS NICKLEBY —CHARLES DICKENS,

chrisen *VERB*
to christen someone; to give someone a first name
• *I know'd my name to be Magwitch, chrisen'd Abel.* —GREAT EXPECTATIONS, CHARLES DICKENS

Christmas

The 19th century saw the creation of Christmas as we know it. At the start of the century, most businesses made employees work over Christmas, but Christmas Day was made a national holiday in 1834, followed by Boxing Day in 1871.

Queen Victoria helped to popularize the Christmas tree when the royal family was pictured around theirs in the *Illustrated London News* in 1848.

The first Christmas card was sold in 1843 and the Christmas cracker was invented by Tom Smith in 1848.

At the Christmas dinner table, roast beef and goose were gradually replaced by turkey as the century wore on.

chronometer to clem

chronometer NOUN
1 an instrument for measuring time accurately in all conditions, especially at sea
• *His watch exactly agreed with the ship's chronometers.*—AROUND THE WORLD IN EIGHTY DAYS, JULES VERNE
2 a clock or watch
• *Solomon has 'his spectacles on his forehead and the great chronometer in his pocket'.*—DOMBEY AND SON, CHARLES DICKENS

Church Militant NOUN
all Christian believers as a group, seen as struggling against evil on earth
• *that church-militant of whose humblest members he is one*—JANE EYRE, CHARLOTTE BRONTË

churl NOUN
a rude or unkind person
• *I've been blaming you, threatening you, behaving like a churl to you.*—FAR FROM THE MADDING CROWD, THOMAS HARDY

cicatrised (say **sik-uh-tryzd**) ADJECTIVE
scarred
• *I thought you would be revolted, Jane, when you saw … my cicatrised visage.*—JANE EYRE, CHARLOTTE BRONTË

cipher (also **cypher**) NOUN
1 a code or symbol; something written in code or secret symbols
• *The clue was found to the cipher, and the secret [was] out.*—MOONFLEET, J. MEADE FALKNER
2 someone's initials; a monogram
• *There was the cipher 'L. L. B.' formed in gold beads.*—VILLETTE, CHARLOTTE BRONTË
3 a person of no importance
• *Fanny and Eliza became ciphers in the sick-room.*—SHIRLEY, CHARLOTTE BRONTË

cipher VERB
to add, subtract, etc.; to do sums
• *Mrs Pegler says her son Josiah could 'write and cipher beautiful'.*—HARD TIMES, CHARLES DICKENS
➢ **cipher out:** to work something out • *When he had ciphered it out, he told me how we was to do.*—THE ADVENTURES OF HUCKLEBERRY FINN, MARK TWAIN

circlet NOUN
a ring
• *the circlet of gold which marked her as having been a bride*—A STUDY IN SCARLET, ARTHUR CONAN DOYLE
• *She rose … leaving a little circlet of flowers.*—RUPERT OF HENTZAU, ANTHONY HOPE

circumambient ADJECTIVE
surrounding
• *When Ella finds herself staying in the poet Trewe's house surrounded by his things, she feels as if he himself is all around her: he is described as 'this circumambient, unapproachable master'.*—WESSEX TALES, THOMAS HARDY

circumjacent ADJECTIVE
surrounding; around something
• *Sir Leicester [glanced] at the circumjacent cousins on sofas and ottomans.*—BLEAK HOUSE, CHARLES DICKENS

circumstanced ADJECTIVE
in a particular situation or position
• *[He was] without envy or hatred of those more happily circumstanced than himself.*—SHIRLEY, CHARLOTTE BRONTË
USAGE *Circumstanced* is usually used with an adverb, as in 'similarly circumstanced' or 'comfortably circumstanced'.

circumvent VERB
to outwit
• *I rather relish the notion of circumventing my mother and that ogress old Horsfall.*—SHIRLEY, CHARLOTTE BRONTË
USAGE In modern English, you might expect to *circumvent* a difficulty or a rule, rather than a person.

clangour NOUN
a continuous loud or clanging noise
• *the clangour of the machinery*—THE WAR OF THE WORLDS, H. G. WELLS

clear ADJECTIVE
1 light, bright, or fresh in appearance
• *Her face and brow were clear, her eyes of the darkest gray.*—SHIRLEY, CHARLOTTE BRONTË
2 free of worry or guilt
• *After Rudolf's difficult decision 'his face was calm and clear'.*—RUPERT OF HENTZAU, ANTHONY HOPE

clear VERB
to look happier; to brighten
• *Then suddenly we both jumped off the fence together, our faces clearing.*—DREAM DAYS, KENNETH GRAHAME

cleave VERB
to split something in two
• *And away went the [boat], cleaving the water like an arrow.*—DOMBEY AND SON, CHARLES DICKENS
➢ **cleave to:** to cling to; to stick to • *[He] tried to speak, but his tongue seemed to cleave to the roof of his mouth.*—A HOUSE OF POMEGRANATES, OSCAR WILDE

clem VERB
to starve
• *I've seen a father who [would have] killed his child rather than let it clem before his eyes.*—MARY BARTON, ELIZABETH GASKELL
➤ **clemmed** ADJECTIVE starving; extremely hungry
• *Folk do say one mustn't give clemmed people much to eat.*—MARY BARTON, ELIZABETH GASKELL

clerical to cogitate

clerical ADJECTIVE
to do with the clergy or with being a priest
• *a clerical friend*—THE MILL ON THE FLOSS, GEORGE ELIOT

clerk (also **clark**) NOUN
1 someone whose job was to keep records, copy documents, etc.
• *[Scrooge kept] his eye upon his clerk, who … was copying letters.*—A CHRISTMAS CAROL, CHARLES DICKENS
2 a person who could read and write; a scholar
• *[Oliver] had been studying the subject under the able tuition of the village clerk … who was a gardener by trade.*—OLIVER TWIST, CHARLES DICKENS
3 a clergyman or monk
• *St Dunstan, when he lived as a hermit is referred to as 'the poor Clerk of Saint Dunstan's cell'.*—IVANHOE, WALTER SCOTT
RELATED WORD *cleric* meaning 'priest or religious leader'; *clerical* meaning either 'relating to administrative work' or 'relating to the clergy'

clew NOUN
1 a clue
• *Mr Deane was rather puzzled, and suspected that there had been something 'going on' among the young people to which he wanted a clew.*—THE MILL ON THE FLOSS, GEORGE ELIOT
2 a ball of string; a thread
USAGE This word was often used figuratively, with reference to the Greek myth in which Theseus used a ball of string to find his way through a maze.
• *[The waiter] pulled out a napkin, as if it were a magic clew without which he couldn't find the way up stairs.*—GREAT EXPECTATIONS, CHARLES DICKENS

clinker NOUN
coal or a brick hardened by being burnt, for example in a furnace; hardened lava
• *rusty and blackened clinkers*—THE WAR OF THE WORLDS, H. G. WELLS

cloaca NOUN
a sewer
• *After [digging] an hour I began to speculate on the distance one had to go before the cloaca was reached.*—THE WAR OF THE WORLDS, H. G. WELLS

clod-hopping ADJECTIVE
clumsy; awkward
• *What a mercy you are shod with velvet, Jane! —a clod-hopping messenger would never do at this juncture.*—JANE EYRE, CHARLOTTE BRONTË

clodpole NOUN
a stupid, clumsy person
• *'Thou fightest like a clodpole,' said the old man.*—MEN OF IRON, HOWARD PYLE

clothier NOUN
a manufacturer or seller of clothes or cloth
• *John Gale, a small clothier*—SHIRLEY, CHARLOTTE BRONTË

cloud-castle NOUN
an unrealistic fantasy
• *[Their plots] are … a mere enchanter's cloud-castle.*—WESTWARD HO!, CHARLES KINGSLEY

club-walking NOUN
a festival or parade organized by a local club
• *Then she put upon her the white frock that Tess had worn at the club-walking.*—TESS OF THE D'URBERVILLES, THOMAS HARDY

clumb VERB
climbed
• *I clumb up the shed and crept into my window just before day was breaking.*—THE ADVENTURES OF HUCKLEBERRY FINN, MARK TWAIN

coadjutor (say koh-aj-uh-tuhr) NOUN
an assistant; a helper
• *I will, while in town, speak to a married missionary, whose wife needs a coadjutor.*—JANE EYRE, CHARLOTTE BRONTË

coeval (say koh-ee-vuhl) ADJECTIVE
of the same age or period
• *The church was surrounded by yew trees, which seemed almost coeval with itself.*—RIP VAN WINKLE, WASHINGTON IRVING

coeval NOUN
a person of the same age or period; a contemporary
• *[They] were held by their coevals to have had dealings with the Evil One.*—DRACULA, BRAM STOKER

coffee-room NOUN
a dining room in an inn or hotel
• *I got back to my breakfast in the Boar's coffee-room.*—GREAT EXPECTATIONS, CHARLES DICKENS

cogitate VERB
to think deeply about something; to turn something over in your mind
• *Arthur Gride was cogitating in the parlour upon what had taken place last night.*—NICHOLAS NICKLEBY, CHARLES DICKENS
• *Mr Gamfield, chimney-sweep, went his way down the High Street, deeply cogitating in his mind his ways and means of paying certain arrears of rent.*—OLIVER TWIST, CHARLES DICKENS
➤ **cogitation** NOUN • *'Well,' said Joe, with the same appearance of profound cogitation.*—GREAT EXPECTATIONS, CHARLES DICKENS

cognizance to commend

cognizance (say **kog**-niz-uhnss, kon-iz-uhnss) NOUN
a heraldic emblem of a noble family
• *You might see that cognizance carved on the manor, and on the stonework and woodwork of the church.*
—MOONFLEET, J. MEADE FALKNER
➤ **take cognizance of:** to notice; to be aware of • *[He] stares at objects without taking cognizance thereof.*—DOMBEY AND SON, CHARLES DICKENS

cognomen NOUN
a name or nickname
• *'The cognomen of Crane' is appropriate because Ichabod Crane is tall and thin.*—THE LEGEND OF SLEEPY HOLLOW, WASHINGTON IRVING

coincidence NOUN
the fact of two things being the same
• *Our coincidence of feeling was soon discovered.*
—PRIDE AND PREJUDICE, JANE AUSTEN

coiner NOUN
someone who made coins; a forger of coins
• *The coiner of a bad shilling was put to Death.*
—A TALE OF TWO CITIES, CHARLES DICKENS

collateral ADJECTIVE
additional; secondary
• *opinions of collateral importance*—SILAS MARNER, GEORGE ELIOT
RELATED WORD *lateral* meaning 'on the side'

collation NOUN
a meal, usually of several cold dishes
• *The party go into 'the appointed dining-parlour, where a collation was prepared'.*—MANSFIELD PARK, JANE AUSTEN

collect VERB
to conclude or infer something
• *From all that I can collect by your manner of talking, you must be two of the silliest girls in the country.*
—PRIDE AND PREJUDICE, JANE AUSTEN
➤ **collect yourself:** to get your thoughts or emotions under control • *I paused to collect myself.*
—FRANKENSTEIN, MARY SHELLEY

collogue (say kol-ohg) VERB
to talk secretly or privately
• *The Squire says Godfrey has 'collogue[d] with [Dunsey] to embezzle my money'.*—SILAS MARNER, GEORGE ELIOT

collop NOUN
a slice of meat
• *Alan was ... looking pleasantly forward to a dram and a dish of hot collops.*—KIDNAPPED, ROBERT LOUIS STEVENSON

colloquy (say kol-uh-kwee) NOUN
a conversation
• *Lucy has an 'anxious colloquy with aunt Pullet'.*
—THE MILL ON THE FLOSS, GEORGE ELIOT
➤ **colloquise** VERB to talk; to converse • *All I had now to do was to obey him in silence: no need for me to colloquise further.*—JANE EYRE, CHARLOTTE BRONTË

colly VERB
to blacken someone with coal dust
• *Being in the coal-hole 'was enough to colly him all over'.*—SILAS MARNER, GEORGE ELIOT

collyrium NOUN
eye lotion
• *Emanuel's thoughts are said to be 'collyrium to the spirit's eyes', making 'inward sight [grow] clear and strong'.*—VILLETTE, CHARLOTTE BRONTË

come VERB
➤ **come down:** an informal phrase meaning 'to give or provide with money' • *Dickens uses this phrase in a pun: 'The heaviest rain, and snow, and hail, and sleet, ... often "came down" handsomely, and Scrooge never did.'*—A CHRISTMAS CAROL, CHARLES DICKENS

comely ADJECTIVE
pleasant-looking; attractive
• *a comely lass*—MOONFLEET, J. MEADE FALKNER
• *[his] broad, comely face*—THE ADVENTURE OF THE DANCING MEN, ARTHUR CONAN DOYLE
➤ **comeliness** NOUN • *[He had] all the grace of youth and comeliness.*—NICHOLAS NICKLEBY, CHARLES DICKENS

comfit NOUN
a sweet made with a nut, seed, or dried fruit covered with sugar or chocolate
• *[Alice] pulled out a box of comfits ... and handed them round as prizes.*—ALICE'S ADVENTURES IN WONDERLAND, LEWIS CARROLL

comforter NOUN
a wool scarf
• *[Scrooge's] clerk put on his white comforter.*
—A CHRISTMAS CAROL, CHARLES DICKENS

comical ADJECTIVE
odd; strange
• *It looks comical to me.*—SILAS MARNER, GEORGE ELIOT

commend VERB
1 to praise
• *I believe that Mrs Pipchin's management of children is quite astonishing. I have heard it commended in private circles.*—DOMBEY AND SON, CHARLES DICKENS

commendation *to* compassionate

2 to recommend
• *'I commend that fact very carefully to your attention,'* said Holmes to [his] colleague.—THE ADVENTURE OF THE DANCING MEN, ARTHUR CONAN DOYLE
3 to entrust
• *[He] led her from the room and commended her to Helga's care.*—RUPERT OF HENTZAU, ANTHONY HOPE
➤ **commendatory** ADJECTIVE expressing praise
• *every commendatory remark*—THE MAYOR OF CASTERBRIDGE, THOMAS HARDY

commendation NOUN
praise
• *I am flattered by his commendation.*—SENSE AND SENSIBILITY, JANE AUSTEN

commiserate VERB
to feel pity for; to express sympathy for
• *[When] you have heard [my tale], abandon or commiserate me, as you shall judge that I deserve.*—FRANKENSTEIN, MARY SHELLEY
• *Susan Nipper could only commiserate Mr Toots's unfortunate condition.*—DOMBEY AND SON, CHARLES DICKENS
USAGE In modern English, you usually *commiserate with* someone, rather than *commiserate* someone.

commission VERB
to give someone a task
• *Calling back the servant, ... she commissioned him ... to fetch his master and mistress home instantly.*—PRIDE AND PREJUDICE, JANE AUSTEN

commission NOUN
a task or errand
• *Jane goes to town 'to perform some small commissions for myself and one or two of my fellow-teachers'.*—JANE EYRE, CHARLOTTE BRONTË
➤ **be in commission (of the peace):** to be a Justice of the Peace (a magistrate) • *Though this great lady was not in commission of the peace of the county, she was a most active magistrate in her own parish.*—PRIDE AND PREJUDICE, JANE AUSTEN

commodious ADJECTIVE
1 useful or convenient
• *A small cupboard held a diminutive but commodious set of earthenware.*—VILLETTE, CHARLOTTE BRONTË
2 pleasant or comfortable
• *The church [was] most commodious to sit in.*—MOONFLEET, J. MEADE FALKNER
3 spacious; roomy
• *The room is 'of a commodious, well-proportioned size'.*—NORTHANGER ABBEY, JANE AUSTEN

commons NOUN
1 rations or provisions; an amount or portion. The phrase *short commons* meant 'a small ration'.
• *The gruel was served out; and a long grace was said over the short commons.*—OLIVER TWIST, CHARLES DICKENS
2 the Commons / Doctors' Commons
a society of lawyers in London; their place or type of business
• *the great expense of a suit in Doctors' Commons*—OLIVER TWIST, CHARLES DICKENS

commonweal NOUN
the common good; the good of everyone
• *the conception of the commonweal of mankind*—THE WAR OF THE WORLDS, H. G. WELLS

commune VERB
➤ **commune with:** to consult or discuss closely with someone • *After more communing with herself next day, she arrived at the desperate conclusion of consulting Harry.*—OLIVER TWIST, CHARLES DICKENS

compact NOUN
a contract or agreement
• *You shall ... judge whether or not I had a right to break the compact.*—JANE EYRE, CHARLOTTE BRONTË

compact VERB
to form something by putting things together
• *Eppie was an object compacted of changes and hopes.*—SILAS MARNER, GEORGE ELIOT

compass VERB
1 to surround
• *We were compassed round by a very thick fog.*—FRANKENSTEIN, MARY SHELLEY
2 to be able to achieve something; to manage
• *If you can compass it, do cure the younger girls of running after the officers.*—PRIDE AND PREJUDICE, JANE AUSTEN

compass NOUN
1 the limits or boundaries of a place
• *three passengers shut up in the narrow compass of one lumbering old mail coach*—A TALE OF TWO CITIES, CHARLES DICKENS
2 the scope or range of something
• *Her father ... had never denied her anything that lay within the compass of human possibility.*—UNCLE TOM'S CABIN, HARRIET BEECHER STOWE

compassionate VERB
to feel pity or sympathy for someone
• *I persuaded myself that ... they would compassionate me and overlook my personal deformity.*—FRANKENSTEIN, MARY SHELLEY

compeers *to* conceive

compeers NOUN
people of a similar status or situation; companions
• Paul's attempts to be like other children *'only showed again the difference between himself and his compeers'.*—DOMBEY AND SON, CHARLES DICKENS

compel VERB
to cause something by force or great pressure
• *The same power that compels her silence may compel her speech.*—DRACULA, BRAM STOKER

competence (also **competency**) NOUN
an income, usually not from work; a living
• *With the small competence he possessed, eked out by such employment as he could pick up, he travelled from town to town.*—A STUDY IN SCARLET, ARTHUR CONAN DOYLE

complacency NOUN
pleasure
• *Their brother, indeed, was the only one of the party whom she could regard with any complacency.*
—PRIDE AND PREJUDICE, JANE AUSTEN

complacent ADJECTIVE
1 happy; showing pleasure
• *But happily for her, she was quite complacent again now and beamed with nods and smiles.*—BLEAK HOUSE, CHARLES DICKENS
2 willing; complaisant
• *a complacent listener to her talk*—SHIRLEY, CHARLOTTE BRONTË

complaisance NOUN
obliging, agreeable behaviour; willingness to agree
• *Sir William says of Mr Darcy's willingness to dance with Elizabeth 'we cannot wonder at his complaisance; for who would object to such a partner?'*—PRIDE AND PREJUDICE, JANE AUSTEN
➤ **complaisant** ADJECTIVE • *Henery continued in a more complaisant mood.*—FAR FROM THE MADDING CROWD, THOMAS HARDY

comport VERB
➤ **comport with:** to be compatible with; to fit in with or be suitable for • *Mr Toots was more aggressive 'than comported with a professor of the peaceful art of self-defence'.*—DOMBEY AND SON, CHARLES DICKENS

composition NOUN
1 character
• *[The princess] had no shyness in her composition.*
—THE LIGHT PRINCESS, GEORGE MACDONALD
2 a mixture; a preparation
• *Rosanna had taken out a spot [on] my coat, with a new composition, warranted to remove anything.*
—THE MOONSTONE, WILKIE COLLINS

compound NOUN
a mixture
• *[He] had become quite renowned as a compound of pride, avarice, brutality, and meanness.*—GREAT EXPECTATIONS, CHARLES DICKENS

compound VERB
1 to make something by mixing things together
• *I once again compounded and swallowed the transforming draught.*—THE STRANGE CASE OF DR JEKYLL AND MR HYDE, ROBERT LOUIS STEVENSON
• *an immense fire, compounded of coal, peat, and wood*—WUTHERING HEIGHTS, EMILY BRONTË
2 to settle a debt or dispute; to bargain or agree terms
• *Some of his rich relations might have paid his debts or compounded for 'em.*—BLEAK HOUSE, CHARLES DICKENS
➤ **compound for:** to accept or settle for something • *I was glad to compound for an affectionate hug.*—DAVID COPPERFIELD, CHARLES DICKENS

comprehend VERB
to include something or someone
• *In this danger Kitty is also comprehended. She will follow wherever Lydia leads.*—PRIDE AND PREJUDICE, JANE AUSTEN

compute VERB
to estimate; to calculate
• *He computes the value of the jewels at not less than half a million sterling.*—THE SIGN OF FOUR, ARTHUR CONAN DOYLE
➤ **computation** NOUN • *There had come many [shots] from the north—seven, by the squire's computation; eight or nine, according to Gray.*
—TREASURE ISLAND, ROBERT LOUIS STEVENSON

con VERB
to study hard; to learn something by heart
• *It was the hour of study; they were engaged in conning over their to-morrow's task.*—JANE EYRE, CHARLOTTE BRONTË

concealment NOUN
something hidden or not revealed; a secret
• *We had no concealments from each other.*
—THE WOMAN IN WHITE, WILKIE COLLINS

conceive VERB
1 to form an opinion
• *[She recognised] a certain Mr Hyde ... for whom she had conceived a dislike.*—THE STRANGE CASE OF DR JEKYLL AND MR HYDE, ROBERT LOUIS STEVENSON
• *Judge Thatcher had conceived a great opinion of Tom.*—THE ADVENTURES OF TOM SAWYER, MARK TWAIN
2 to imagine; to think of something
• *No one can conceive the anguish I suffered.*
—FRANKENSTEIN, MARY SHELLEY
• *I tried in vain to conceive some plan of escape.*
—THE WAR OF THE WORLDS, H. G. WELLS

concentre to confidence

concentre VERB
to bring or turn things towards a central point; to concentrate things in one place
• Firm fields of ice ... concentre the multiplied rigours of extreme cold.—JANE EYRE, CHARLOTTE BRONTË

conception NOUN
idea; understanding
• Charlotte's kindness extended farther than Elizabeth had any conception of.—PRIDE AND PREJUDICE, JANE AUSTEN

concern NOUN
1 a matter; a situation
• [They] betrayed their close interest in the concern by the anxious furtive glance they cast.—NICHOLAS NICKLEBY, CHARLES DICKENS
2 a business
• [He] had just bought the concern.—THE ADVENTURES OF HUCKLEBERRY FINN, MARK TWAIN

conciliate VERB
to make someone less angry or upset
• Mr Dombey tells Mrs Dombey, 'you will not conciliate me ... by this course of conduct.'—DOMBEY AND SON, CHARLES DICKENS
➤ **conciliating** ADJECTIVE • His manners are so conciliating and gentle.—FRANKENSTEIN, MARY SHELLEY

concourse NOUN
a crowd; a crowded place
• There was a concourse of people in one spot.—BLEAK HOUSE, CHARLES DICKENS

concussion NOUN
a violent movement or sound
• a sound like the distant concussion of a gun—THE WAR OF THE WORLDS, H. G. WELLS

condescend VERB
1 to bother to do something beneath your dignity
• Twice has she condescended to give me her opinion.—PRIDE AND PREJUDICE, JANE AUSTEN
2 to stoop or lower yourself to do something bad
• I condescended to ... conceal from him your sister's being in town.—PRIDE AND PREJUDICE, JANE AUSTEN

condescension NOUN
1 the graciousness to bother to do something beneath your dignity
• I hope you will believe us grateful for the condescension.—PRIDE AND PREJUDICE, JANE AUSTEN
2 the fact of stooping or lowering yourself to do something bad
• I at last fell before the assaults of temptation ... and this brief condescension to my evil finally destroyed the balance of my soul.—THE STRANGE CASE OF DR JEKYLL AND MR HYDE, ROBERT LOUIS STEVENSON

condition NOUN
someone's social position
• Could you expect me ... to congratulate myself on the hope of relations, whose condition in life is so decidedly beneath my own?—PRIDE AND PREJUDICE, JANE AUSTEN

condole VERB
to express sympathy
• Lady Lucas ... walked here on Wednesday morning to condole with us.—PRIDE AND PREJUDICE, JANE AUSTEN

conduct VERB
to lead someone somewhere
• 'Spirit!' said Scrooge, 'show me no more! Conduct me home.'—A CHRISTMAS CAROL, CHARLES DICKENS

conductor NOUN
someone leading another person to a place
• I followed my conductor in silence.—FRANKENSTEIN, MARY SHELLEY
➤ **conductress** NOUN a female conductor
• My young conductress locked the gate, and we went across the courtyard.—GREAT EXPECTATIONS, CHARLES DICKENS

confabulate VERB
to have a conversation
• The two proud dowagers, Lady Lynn and Lady Ingram, confabulate together.—JANE EYRE, CHARLOTTE BRONTË
➤ **confabulation** NOUN • [She] had a long confabulation with Mrs Crump.—AT THE BACK OF THE NORTH WIND, GEORGE MACDONALD

confederate NOUN
an ally or accomplice
• By the way ... you see that they had ... a confederate in the house.—THE SIGN OF FOUR, ARTHUR CONAN DOYLE

conference NOUN
a conversation; a discussion
• Mr Franklin and I had a private conference on the subject of the Moonstone.—THE MOONSTONE, WILKIE COLLINS

confide VERB
to leave something or someone in someone's care
• I slipped off my ring and confided it to the Lascar.—THE ADVENTURES OF SHERLOCK HOLMES, ARTHUR CONAN DOYLE

confidence NOUN
1 complete trust
• My sweet cousin, there must be perfect confidence between us.—FRANKENSTEIN, MARY SHELLEY
2 the fact of sharing secrets with someone
• The spy [dropped] his soft voice to a tone that invited confidence.—A TALE OF TWO CITIES, CHARLES DICKENS

3 a secret confided to someone
• *Joe imparted a confidence to me.*
—GREAT EXPECTATIONS, CHARLES DICKENS

confine VERB
➢ **be confined:** (of a mother) to be in bed during and after labour and birth • Mr Jarndyce talks about *'the announcement in the newspapers when [Mr Skimpole's] mother was confined'*—meaning when he was born.—BLEAK HOUSE, CHARLES DICKENS
➢ **confinement** NOUN • Perch asks for a jar of preserved ginger for Mrs Perch's *'recovery from her next confinement'.*—DOMBEY AND SON, CHARLES DICKENS

confine NOUN
a border; a limit
• *I arrived on the confines of Switzerland.*
—FRANKENSTEIN, MARY SHELLEY

confound VERB
1 to confuse something; to mix something up
• *[The old woman] fell into the habit of confounding the names of her two sons-in-law.*—DOMBEY AND SON, CHARLES DICKENS
2 to surprise or confuse someone
• *[Paul] sometimes quite confounded Mrs Pipchin.*
—DOMBEY AND SON, CHARLES DICKENS
3 to defeat someone
• *Here is to good King Richard ... may all enemies to him be confounded.*—THE MERRY ADVENTURES OF ROBIN HOOD, HOWARD PYLE
➢ **confound it / you / him:** used to express annoyance • *Confound you, hold your tongue!*—SILAS MARNER, GEORGE ELIOT

confounded ADJECTIVE
1 confused or surprised
• *The master seemed confounded a moment.*
—WUTHERING HEIGHTS, EMILY BRONTË
2 used for expressing annoyance
• *As it is, you have wasted the best part of my day with your confounded imagination.*—THE ISLAND OF DOCTOR MOREAU, H. G. WELLS

confute VERB
to prove a person or argument wrong
• *I will assume that ... the false testimony ... might be confuted.*—THE WOMAN IN WHITE, WILKIE COLLINS

conjecture VERB
to guess something
• *If they saw him depart, they could not fail to conjecture his design.*—PRIDE AND PREJUDICE, JANE AUSTEN

conjunction NOUN
the coming together of people or things in one place
• *And now by an odd conjunction she found herself in the rooms of Robert Trewe.*—WESSEX TALES, THOMAS HARDY

conjuration NOUN
1 a spell or magic trick
• *When he heard a horse approaching ... he felt as if his conjuration had succeeded.*—SILAS MARNER, GEORGE ELIOT
2 an appeal to someone to do something
• *This vehement conjuration the old gentleman accompanies with such a thrust at his granddaughter that it is too much for his strength.*—BLEAK HOUSE, CHARLES DICKENS

conjure VERB
1 to beg someone to do something
• *I conjure you, Louisa, tell me what is the matter.*
—HARD TIMES, CHARLES DICKENS
2 to think of something; to call something to mind
• *[The youth] had been trying to invent a remarkable comment upon the affair. He could conjure nothing of sufficient point.*—THE RED BADGE OF COURAGE, STEPHEN CRANE

connubial ADJECTIVE
between or relating to a married couple
• *Mr Toots says he and his wife 'were sitting in the enjoyment of connubial bliss'.*—DOMBEY AND SON, CHARLES DICKENS

conscious ADJECTIVE
self-conscious; uncomfortably aware of something
• *Mr Dombey looked into his plate with a conscious air.*
—DOMBEY AND SON, CHARLES DICKENS

consequence NOUN
importance; a high social position
• *The world is blinded by his fortune and consequence.*—PRIDE AND PREJUDICE, JANE AUSTEN

consideration NOUN
importance
• *But it must ... lessen their chance of marrying men of any consideration in the world.*—PRIDE AND PREJUDICE, JANE AUSTEN

console VERB
to comfort an unhappy or distressed person; to take away someone's sadness
• *In Marianne he was consoled for every past affliction.*—SENSE AND SENSIBILITY, JANE AUSTEN

console to conventual

➤ **consolation** NOUN • *I can offer you no consolation, my friend.*—FRANKENSTEIN, MARY SHELLEY
➤ **consolatory** ADJECTIVE offering comfort
• *an absence of consolatory gentleness*—JANE EYRE, CHARLOTTE BRONTË

console NOUN
a shelf or table fixed to the wall by an ornamental bracket

constable NOUN
➣ **outrun the constable:** to spend too much money; to live beyond your means • *I shall … check your bills, and … pull you up if I find you outrunning the constable.*—GREAT EXPECTATIONS, CHARLES DICKENS

constitutional NOUN
a healthy walk
• *'Now, Dombey,' said Miss Blimber, 'I am going out for a constitutional.'*—DOMBEY AND SON, CHARLES DICKENS

construction NOUN
an interpretation
• *Elizabeth … gave them to understand … that … his actions were capable of a very different construction.*—PRIDE AND PREJUDICE, JANE AUSTEN

construe VERB
1 to interpret something in a particular way
• *She's an excitable, nervous person: she construed her dream into an apparition.*—JANE EYRE, CHARLOTTE BRONTË
2 to grammatically analyse a text or sentence, for example in Latin
• *Henry confesses to his tutor 'I have not construed a line'.*—SHIRLEY, CHARLOTTE BRONTË

consumption NOUN
tuberculosis
• *The Martians have never suffered 'all the fevers and contagions of human life, consumption, cancers, tumours'.*—THE WAR OF THE WORLDS, H. G. WELLS

contagion NOUN
an infectious disease
USAGE This word was often used figuratively to refer to something spreading quickly.
• *the contagion of suspicion and fear*—THE HAUNTED HOUSE, CHARLES DICKENS

contemn VERB
to feel contempt for
• *Bois-Guilbert tells Rebecca they should not 'endure the scorn of the bigots whom we contemn'.*—IVANHOE, WALTER SCOTT

contingent ADJECTIVE
likely to happen, but not certain
• *The results of confession were not contingent, they were certain.*—SILAS MARNER, GEORGE ELIOT

contrition NOUN
a feeling of guilt or sorrow for having done something bad
• *She felt for Harriet, with pain and with contrition.*—EMMA, JANE AUSTEN

contrivance NOUN
1 a device or scheme; a means of making something happen
• *Pip compliments Wemmick on 'his ingenious contrivance for announcing himself'.*—GREAT EXPECTATIONS, CHARLES DICKENS
2 plotting
• *And this … is the end … of all his sister's falsehood and contrivance!*—PRIDE AND PREJUDICE, JANE AUSTEN

contrive VERB
to manage to do something; to cleverly make something happen
• *How can you contrive to write so even?*—PRIDE AND PREJUDICE, JANE AUSTEN
• *Mr Carson … let scarcely a day pass without contriving a meeting with the beautiful little milliner.*—MARY BARTON, ELIZABETH GASKELL

contumacy (say kon-tyuh-muh-si) NOUN
stubborn refusal to obey
• *Mr Carker says he has been sent to Edith by Mr Dombey, 'because he intends that I shall be a punishment for your contumacy'.*—DOMBEY AND SON, CHARLES DICKENS
➤ **contumacious** ADJECTIVE stubbornly disobedient • *She sat still, looking a little contumacious, and very much indisposed to stir.*—SHIRLEY, CHARLOTTE BRONTË

contumely NOUN
contempt
• *The grocer had offered his hand in marriage which 'Mrs Pipchin had, with contumely and scorn, rejected'.*—DOMBEY AND SON, CHARLES DICKENS
➤ **contumelious** ADJECTIVE contemptuous
• *Miss Ingram would '[push Adèle] away with some contumelious epithet if she happened to approach her'.*—JANE EYRE, CHARLOTTE BRONTË

conventual ADJECTIVE
belonging or relating to a convent
• *a group of conventual buildings*—FAR FROM THE MADDING CROWD, THOMAS HARDY

conversable to coronal

conversable (also **conversible**) ADJECTIVE
pleasant to talk to; full of pleasant conversation
• *If I find him conversable, I shall be glad of his acquaintance.*—EMMA, JANE AUSTEN

converse NOUN
conversation
• *Donald ... stood in animated converse with his friends a few yards off.*—THE MAYOR OF CASTERBRIDGE, THOMAS HARDY

convey VERB
to take or accompany someone somewhere; to take something somewhere
• *She began to speak of [Mr Knightley's] kindness in conveying the aunt and niece.*—EMMA, JANE AUSTEN

conveyance NOUN
a method of transport; a vehicle
• *Clare stopped the conveyance and said to Tess that ... it was here that he would leave her.*—TESS OF THE D'URBERVILLES, THOMAS HARDY

convict-barracks NOUN
housing for convicted criminals who had been sent to a penal colony in another country

convivial ADJECTIVE
sociable and lively
• *Mr Weston was chatty and convivial.*—EMMA, JANE AUSTEN
➤ **conviviality** NOUN friendliness; being sociable
• *The party composed themselves for conviviality.*—NICHOLAS NICKLEBY, CHARLES DICKENS
• *Squire Cass frequently enjoyed the double pleasure of conviviality and condescension.*—SILAS MARNER, GEORGE ELIOT

convoy VERB
to take or accompany someone somewhere
• *Caroline is 'convoyed home by Robert'.*—SHIRLEY, CHARLOTTE BRONTË

cookshop NOUN
a shop selling cooked food
• *a window above a cookshop*—THE PRISONER OF ZENDA, ANTHONY HOPE

cooper NOUN
a barrel maker or repairer
• *The stalls of tailors, hosiers, coopers ... and other such trades had almost disappeared.*—THE MAYOR OF CASTERBRIDGE, THOMAS HARDY

copper NOUN
a container in which clothes were washed or food was cooked. Originally these containers were made of copper.
• *The master, in his cook's uniform, stationed himself at the copper.*—OLIVER TWIST, CHARLES DICKENS

copybook NOUN
a book with model handwriting for students to copy as practice
• *a children's schoolroom—containing globes ... and copybooks*—THE WAR OF THE WORLDS, H. G. WELLS

coquet VERB
to flirt
• *She was only showing a little womanly fondness for coquetting.*—MARY BARTON, ELIZABETH GASKELL

coquetry NOUN
flirting; flirtation
• *Do you think Miss Ingram will not suffer from your dishonest coquetry?*—JANE EYRE, CHARLOTTE BRONTË

coquette NOUN
a flirtatious woman
• *[Miss Price] was pretty, and a coquette.*—NICHOLAS NICKLEBY, CHARLES DICKENS
➤ **coquettish** ADJECTIVE • *[Miss Oliver] was coquettish but not heartless.*—JANE EYRE, CHARLOTTE BRONTË

cordial ADJECTIVE
1 warm and friendly; hearty
• *Their reception from Mr Bennet ... was not quite so cordial.*—PRIDE AND PREJUDICE, JANE AUSTEN
• *We exchanged a cordial good-night.*—GREAT EXPECTATIONS, CHARLES DICKENS
2 strongly felt; heartfelt
• *Both, though hating each other, were joined in one mind by a no less cordial hatred of Tom.*—UNCLE TOM'S CABIN, HARRIET BEECHER STOWE

cordial NOUN
a comforting drink, often alcoholic; a liquid medicine
• *I will give her a cordial, and it will pass.*—VILLETTE, CHARLOTTE BRONTË

corn-factor NOUN
someone whose job was to buy and sell corn
• *The workhouse 'contracted ... with a corn-factor to supply periodically small quantities of oatmeal'.*—OLIVER TWIST, CHARLES DICKENS

coronal NOUN
a small crown
• *a little coronal of sparkling blue stones*—VILLETTE, CHARLOTTE BRONTË

coronal ADJECTIVE
relating to the top of the head
• *[his] coronal locks*—THE MILL ON THE FLOSS, GEORGE ELIOT

corporation to country

corporation NOUN
1 a city or town council
• *a veritable town, with a real mayor and corporation*—WESSEX TALES, THOMAS HARDY
2 a large belly
• The rector is a large man, with *'an ample corporation'.*—SHIRLEY, CHARLOTTE BRONTË

corporeal ADJECTIVE
bodily; physical
• The pain of disillusionment was like *'that of a corporeal wound'.*—DREAM DAYS, KENNETH GRAHAME

corpse candle NOUN
a candle used during a vigil for a dead person
• *I ... guessed ... that ... the light moving in the churchyard ... was no corpse-candle, but a lantern of smugglers.*—MOONFLEET, J. MEADE FALKNER

cortege NOUN
a procession; a group of people accompanying someone
• *It was said that the Royal cortege approached.*—THE MAYOR OF CASTERBRIDGE, THOMAS HARDY

coster NOUN
a costermonger
• *a coster's orange barrow*—THE ADVENTURES OF SHERLOCK HOLMES, ARTHUR CONAN DOYLE

costermonger NOUN
someone who sold fruit and vegetables in the street
• *the jingling costermonger's cart*—THE STREETS-MORNING, CHARLES DICKENS

cottager NOUN
a person living in a cottage; in the feudal system, a tenant of a cottage on a lord's land
• *Some of my own cottagers live in wretched circumstances.*—SHIRLEY, CHARLOTTE BRONTË

couch VERB
to lie
• *[His dog] Tartar ... had followed him, and he couched across his feet.*—SHIRLEY, CHARLOTTE BRONTË

couch NOUN
a bed; a place to sleep
• *I made a couch with furs.*—DRACULA, BRAM STOKER

council NOUN
a meeting; a consultation
• *Herbert had come in, and we held a very serious council by the fire.*—GREAT EXPECTATIONS, CHARLES DICKENS

counsel NOUN
1 advice
• *I have attended to ... the counsels of reason.*—JANE EYRE, CHARLOTTE BRONTË
2 a lawyer

counsel VERB
to advise someone
• *I counsel you to resist firmly every temptation.*—JANE EYRE, CHARLOTTE BRONTË
➢ **keep your own counsel:** to say nothing; to keep your thoughts or opinions to yourself
➢ **take counsel:** to consult with someone; to have a discussion • *Three men ... stopped to take counsel together.*—OLIVER TWIST, CHARLES DICKENS

counsellor NOUN
1 an adviser
• *I could have wished my wife had been my counsellor; had had more character.*—DAVID COPPERFIELD, CHARLES DICKENS
2 a lawyer
• *the counsellor for Compeyson*—GREAT EXPECTATIONS, CHARLES DICKENS

countenance NOUN
1 someone's face; someone's expression
• *As the trial had proceeded, her countenance had altered.*—FRANKENSTEIN, MARY SHELLEY
2 a calm expression; composure
• *Mr Raymond could hardly keep his countenance.*—AT THE BACK OF THE NORTH WIND, GEORGE MACDONALD
• *She came up to me, claimed me as an acquaintance, stared me out of countenance.*—MANSFIELD PARK, JANE AUSTEN
3 support
• *Elizabeth praises her aunt and uncle for 'affording [Lydia] their personal protection and countenance'.*—PRIDE AND PREJUDICE, JANE AUSTEN

counterpane NOUN
a bedspread
• *The bed 'was covered with a patchwork counterpane'.*—THE BLACK VEIL, CHARLES DICKENS

countersign NOUN
a sign or password given as a reply to a guard on duty
• *'Nine to seven', cried the sentinel. 'Seven to five', returned Jefferson Hope promptly, remembering the countersign which he had heard in the garden.*—A STUDY IN SCARLET, ARTHUR CONAN DOYLE

counting-house NOUN
a room or building where a person or business kept money and where accounts were done
• *The door of Scrooge's counting-house was open, that he might keep his eye upon his clerk.*—A CHRISTMAS CAROL, CHARLES DICKENS

country NOUN
an area or region
• *Silas has arrived from 'an unknown country'.*—SILAS MARNER, GEORGE ELIOT

coupé to crave

coupé NOUN
a closed horse-drawn carriage for two passengers, with four wheels and an outside seat for the driver
• *When he reached his own house there was a coupé standing before the door.*—LITTLE LORD FAUNTLEROY, FRANCES HODGSON BURNETT

courser NOUN
a fast horse
• *One of the Emperor's huntsmen was riding 'on a large courser'.*—THE BLUE FAIRY BOOK, ANDREW LANG

court NOUN
a courtyard
• *Jane sits in the orchard because it is private*—'A VERY HIGH WALL SHUT IT OUT FROM THE COURT'.—JANE EYRE, CHARLOTTE BRONTË

court VERB
1 to try to get someone's attention and approval
• *But how that money caused us to be honoured, feared, respected, courted, and admired.*—DOMBEY AND SON, CHARLES DICKENS
2 to become romantically involved with someone; to try to win someone's love
• *His gallantry to my Lady … has never changed since he courted her.*—BLEAK HOUSE, CHARLES DICKENS
3 to encourage or seek something
• *Florence, though she wept … courted the remembrance.*—meaning that she actively tried to remember.—DOMBEY AND SON, CHARLES DICKENS

court-suit NOUN
a man's best or most formal clothes
• *As he thought his court-suit necessary to the occasion, it was not for me to tell him that he looked far better in his working-dress.*—GREAT EXPECTATIONS, CHARLES DICKENS

cove NOUN
a slang word for a man; a chap
• *I've seen many a drunk chap in my time … but never anyone so cryin' drunk as that cove.*—A STUDY IN SCARLET, ARTHUR CONAN DOYLE

cover NOUN
1 deceitful behaviour
• *She's an underhand little thing: I never saw a girl of her age with so much cover.*—JANE EYRE, CHARLOTTE BRONTË
2 bushes, trees, and undergrowth providing shelter for birds and animals that were hunted
• *His father had purchased the estate for the sake of the game covers.*—JANE EYRE, CHARLOTTE BRONTË

coverlet (also **coverlid**) NOUN
a bed cover
• *[The old man] had not been in bed on the previous night, but had merely lain down on the coverlet.*—DOMBEY AND SON, CHARLES DICKENS

covert (say **kuv-uht**) NOUN
an area of thick vegetation, suitable for animals to hide in
• *Out he burst from the covert … a shower of little broken twigs falling about him.*—THE MERRY ADVENTURES OF ROBIN HOOD, HOWARD PYLE

covetous ADJECTIVE
wanting to have something belonging to someone else
• *[Scrooge was] a squeezing, wrenching, grasping, scraping, clutching, covetous, old sinner!*—A CHRISTMAS CAROL, CHARLES DICKENS

covey NOUN
a group of partridges or other birds
• *I beg you will … shoot as many as you please. … [Mr Bennet] will … save all the best of the covies for you.*—PRIDE AND PREJUDICE, JANE AUSTEN

coxcomb NOUN
a vain, silly man
• *He is the greatest coxcomb I ever saw, and amazingly disagreeable.*—NORTHANGER ABBEY, JANE AUSTEN
From *cock's-comb*, referring to the red crest of a cockerel, and to the jester's hat shaped like this. The hat of the jester, or fool, is where the idea of foolishness comes from.

cozen VERB
to deceive someone; to get something by cheating
• *He's a treacherous old goat … and cozened me with cunning tricks and lying promises.*—NICHOLAS NICKLEBY, CHARLES DICKENS

cracksman NOUN
a burglar; someone who broke into safes
• *Beddington, the famous forger and cracksman*—THE MEMOIRS OF SHERLOCK HOLMES, ARTHUR CONAN DOYLE

crape NOUN
another spelling of 'crêpe', a thin wrinkled fabric
• *[Miss Ingram] wore a morning robe of sky-blue crape.*—JANE EYRE, CHARLOTTE BRONTË
USAGE Veils, hat bands, arm bands, etc. made of black crêpe were worn for several months or even years by people who were in mourning.
• *Cousin Abbott may go, and we can't think o' wearing crape less nor half a year for him.*—THE MILL ON THE FLOSS, GEORGE ELIOT

crave VERB
to ask respectfully for something; to beg
• *But when my friend Dombey, Sir … talks to you of Major Bagstock, I must crave leave to set him and you right.*—DOMBEY AND SON, CHARLES DICKENS

crazy ADJECTIVE
damaged or likely to collapse; dilapidated
• *the crazy little box of a cottage*—GREAT EXPECTATIONS, CHARLES DICKENS

creature NOUN
a being created by or completely dependent on another person
• *For the first time ... I felt what the duties of a creator towards his creature were.*—FRANKENSTEIN, MARY SHELLEY

credential NOUN
a document proving someone's identity or qualifications
• *[Miss Halcombe] furnished herself with the Count's letter ... as a species of credential which might be useful to her.*—THE WOMAN IN WHITE, WILKIE COLLINS

credulity NOUN
readiness to believe something; gullibility
• *What use were anger and protestations against her silly credulity?*—WUTHERING HEIGHTS, EMILY BRONTË

credulous ADJECTIVE
gullible; ready to believe something
• *[They] considered the other side a muddle-headed and credulous set.*—SILAS MARNER, GEORGE ELIOT

creeps NOUN
➢ **the creeps:** a feeling of fear or disgust; the shivers • *She was constantly complaining of the cold, and of its occasioning a visitation in her back which she called 'the creeps'.*—DAVID COPPERFIELD, CHARLES DICKENS

creosote (also **creasote**) NOUN
a liquid used for treating wood and as an antiseptic
• *the pungent smell of the creosote*—THE SIGN OF FOUR, ARTHUR CONAN DOYLE

cresset NOUN
a metal container, usually on a pole, with wood, oil, etc. inside that was burned as a light
• *At nightfall ... the Danes lit cressets of tar and hemp.*—THE DRAGON AND THE RAVEN, G. A. HENTY

crib NOUN
1 a very small place to live or sleep
• *a mean little airless lodging, a mere closet for one, a mere crib for two*—HARD TIMES, CHARLES DICKENS
2 an advantageous situation
• *... here's a nice little crib all ready for me to step into*—THE ADVENTURES OF SHERLOCK HOLMES, ARTHUR CONAN DOYLE
3 a translation of a classic book used by students as a cheat
• *I flung aside a crib of Horace I had been reading.*—THE ISLAND OF DOCTOR MOREAU, H. G. WELLS

➢ **crack a crib:** to break into a house • *He'll crack a crib in Scotland one week, and be raising money to build an orphanage in Cornwall the next.*—THE ADVENTURES OF SHERLOCK HOLMES, ARTHUR CONAN DOYLE

crib VERB
to steal; to rob
• *[The money] was soon all gone; and then she looked around the room to crib it of its few remaining ornaments.*—MARY BARTON, ELIZABETH GASKELL

crier NOUN
someone who called out public announcements in a town or market
• *Edith says that, in order to marry her off, her qualities have 'been paraded ... to enhance my value, as if the common crier had called [them] through the streets'.*—DOMBEY AND SON, CHARLES DICKENS

crisis NOUN
a turning point; a change of fortunes
• *The crisis of the disease was safely past.*—OLIVER TWIST, CHARLES DICKENS
• *that crisis in our affairs*—GREAT EXPECTATIONS, CHARLES DICKENS

cross VERB
to thwart someone; to get in the way of someone's wishes
• *He must have been crossed in love, father, when he was a young man.*—THE MOONSTONE, WILKIE COLLINS

cross-grained ADJECTIVE
bad-tempered; stubborn and difficult
• *I never met with such a cross-grained old savage.*—NICHOLAS NICKLEBY, CHARLES DICKENS

crown-piece NOUN
a coin worth a crown (five shillings)
• *One of the young dancers 'had recklessly handed a new crown-piece to the musicians, as a bribe to keep going'.*—WESSEX TALES, THOMAS HARDY

crucible NOUN
a melting pot for metals
• *The sea was as a crucible of molten gold.*—MOBY DICK, HERMAN MELVILLE
• *these philosophers, whose hands seem only made to dabble in dirt, and their eyes to pore over the microscope or crucible*—FRANKENSTEIN, MARY SHELLEY

cruet (say **kroo-it**) NOUN
a small bottle or container for vinegar, sauce, etc.
• *a mustard-pot ... and a vinegar-cruet*—MOBY DICK, HERMAN MELVILLE

crupper NOUN
a strap attached to the back of a saddle, with a loop around the horse's tail to keep the saddle in place

crutched *to* cut

crutched (also **crutch-headed**) ADJECTIVE
with a handle or cross-piece at the top to support someone when walking
• *[Miss Havisham was] stabbing with her crutched stick at the pile of cobwebs.*—GREAT EXPECTATIONS, CHARLES DICKENS

crystalline ADJECTIVE
very clear
• *A calm day had settled into a crystalline evening.*—SHIRLEY, CHARLOTTE BRONTË

cui bono PHRASE
a Latin phrase meaning 'who benefits' or 'to whose benefit'
• *When Jane offers to paint a portrait of Rosamund for St John, he replies, 'Cui bono? No.'*—meaning 'what would be the good of that?'—JANE EYRE, CHARLOTTE BRONTË

cuirass (say kwi-rass) NOUN
1 a piece of armour consisting of a breastplate joined to a plate protecting the back
2 a tight-fitting bodice

cultivate VERB
to develop a person or thing
• *I ... cultivated the acquaintance of the men of science of the university.*—FRANKENSTEIN, MARY SHELLEY
➤ **cultivated** ADJECTIVE well developed; refined and well educated • *He is so gentle, yet so wise; his mind is so cultivated.*—FRANKENSTEIN, MARY SHELLEY

cumber VERB
1 to burden someone; to slow someone down or get in their way • *Bear in mind that he was cumbered with a great-coat.*—KIDNAPPED, ROBERT LOUIS STEVENSON
RELATED WORD In current English, *encumber* is used with the same meaning.
2 to litter an area; to be scattered somewhere
• *[Holmes] peered keenly at the house, and at the great rubbish-heaps which cumbered the grounds.*—THE SIGN OF FOUR, ARTHUR CONAN DOYLE

cumber NOUN
a burden
• *What with illness and bad luck, I've been nothing but cumber all my life.*—THE MILL ON THE FLOSS, GEORGE ELIOT

cumbrous ADJECTIVE
1 large and heavy
• *the cumbrous seats of oak*—MOONFLEET, J. MEADE FALKNER
2 awkward
• *Mr Dombey speaks to Mrs Granger 'with cumbrous gallantry'.*—DOMBEY AND SON, CHARLES DICKENS

Cupid NOUN
1 the god of love, represented as a naked baby boy with wings, and a bow and arrows which he uses to make people fall in love
2 a beautiful baby or boy
• *Miss Tox says of baby Paul, 'Is he not beautiful Mr Dombey! Is he not a Cupid, Sir!'*—DOMBEY AND SON, CHARLES DICKENS

cupidity NOUN
greed or lust, especially for money or possessions
• *Dunstan ... saw ... the means of gratifying at once his jealous hate and his cupidity.*—SILAS MARNER, GEORGE ELIOT

curate NOUN
a priest or assistant priest
• *He is the curate of the parish.*—SENSE AND SENSIBILITY, JANE AUSTEN

curacy NOUN
a curate's position
• *a large ... town where his curacy was situated*—JANE EYRE, CHARLOTTE BRONTË

curl-paper NOUN
a small piece of soft paper twisted into the hair and left overnight to make it curl
• *Teachers and pupils descended to breakfast in dressing-gowns and curl-papers.*—VILLETTE, CHARLOTTE BRONTË

curricle NOUN
a small, light, open carriage with two large wheels, pulled by two horses
• *It was a gentleman's carriage, a curricle.*—PERSUASION, JANE AUSTEN

cushat NOUN
a wood pigeon; a dove

cut VERB
1 to be insulting or hurtful
• *Now ... the accusation cut me to the heart.*—JANE EYRE, CHARLOTTE BRONTË
2 to beat a person or animal with a cane or whip
• *It was only a moment that I stopped him, for he cut me heavily an instant afterwards.*—DAVID COPPERFIELD, CHARLES DICKENS
3 to snub or deliberately ignore someone
• *Sir John ... had cut me ever since my marriage.*—SENSE AND SENSIBILITY, JANE AUSTEN
➤ **cut someone off**: to not allow someone to have or inherit something • *[He] was so irritated at her disobedience, he cut her off without a shilling.*—JANE EYRE, CHARLOTTE BRONTË

50

cut NOUN
1 an act of deliberately ignoring someone; a snub
• *I ... still pretended not to know him. 'Is this a cut?' said Mr Drummle.*—GREAT EXPECTATIONS, CHARLES DICKENS
2 a hurtful or insulting remark
• *This was a cut, of course, at me.*—LORNA DOONE, R. D. BLACKMORE

'cute ADJECTIVE
clever; sharp
• *It 'ud take a 'cute man to make a tale like that.*
—SILAS MARNER, GEORGE ELIOT

cynosure NOUN
1 the centre of attention
• *I thought of Eliza and Georgiana; I beheld one the cynosure of a ball-room, the other the inmate of a convent cell.*—JANE EYRE, CHARLOTTE BRONTË
2 a leader or guiding influence
• *[He] held Frank in high honor, and considered him a very oracle and cynosure of fashion and chivalry.*
—WESTWARD HO!, CHARLES KINGSLEY,

daemon to **debasement**

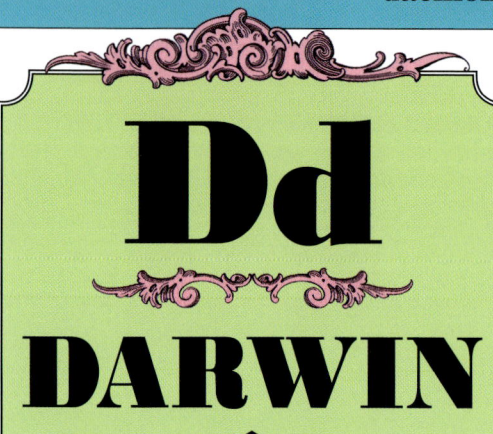

Dd

DARWIN

Charles Darwin was one of the most prominent scientists of the 19th century. Inspired by his voyages on board the H.M.S. Beagle and the birds and animals he observed in the Galapágos Islands, Darwin published *On the Origin of Species by Means of Natural Selection* in **1859** which set out his **theory of evolution.** Darwin's theories were controversial but they gave a scientific basis to our understanding of the natural world.

daemon NOUN
a demon or devil; a supernatural spirit or godlike being
• *It was the wretch, the filthy daemon, to whom I had given life.*—FRANKENSTEIN, MARY SHELLEY

daguerreotype (say duh-gerr-uh-typ) NOUN
a kind of photograph
➤ **daguerreotype** VERB to make a daguerreotype photograph of something • *a head, that, daguerreotyped ... with that expression, would have been lovely*—SHIRLEY, CHARLOTTE BRONTË

Photography

In the 1830s, the Frenchman Louis Daguerre developed the daguerreotype, a process which captured images on a silvered copper plate. Each one was unique, but in 1841 the British scientist and inventor Henry Fox Talbot patented the process of developing multiple prints from a single negative. Photographic studios sprang up, allowing ordinary people to be photographed. In 1888, George Eastman introduced the Kodak box camera, which turned photography into a leisure activity accessible to all.

damask NOUN
a type of heavy patterned fabric
• *heavy damask curtains*—TESS OF THE D'URBERVILLES, THOMAS HARDY
🏛 From the city *Damascus*, in Syria, where the fabric was originally made

darkling ADJECTIVE
dark or growing dark
• *The Martians seemed in solitary possession of the darkling night.*—THE WAR OF THE WORLDS, H. G. WELLS

dastard (also **dastardly**) ADJECTIVE
wicked and cruel
• *the treachery of this dastard scheme*—LORNA DOONE, R. D. BLACKMORE

daw NOUN
a jackdaw
• *the circling flocks of rooks and daws*—OTTO OF THE SILVER HAND, HOWARD PYLE

deacon NOUN
a church official or an assistant priest
• *The second day ... the minister and one of the deacons came.*—SILAS MARNER, GEORGE ELIOT

dead ADJECTIVE
(said about goods, stock, or money) not able to be sold; not making any money
• *What's Christmas time to you but ... a time for balancing your books, and having every item in 'em ... presented dead against you?*—A CHRISTMAS CAROL, CHARLES DICKENS

deal NOUN
fir or pine wood
• *the old deal table*—GREAT EXPECTATIONS, CHARLES DICKENS
➤ **a deal: a lot** • *Sir, I've a deal to thank you for.*—SILAS MARNER, GEORGE ELIOT

dearth (rhymes with **birth**) NOUN
lack
• *Thou art as one who in time of dearth pours water into a broken vessel.*—THE FISHERMAN AND HIS SOUL, OSCAR WILDE

debar VERB
to prevent someone from doing something; to deprive someone of something
• *The sick man [was] debarred from any change of position save the mere turning of his head from side to side.*—NICHOLAS NICKLEBY, CHARLES DICKENS

debasement NOUN
a loss of quality, dignity, or virtue
• *Mr Knightley and Harriet Smith!—such an elevation on her side! such a debasement on his!*—EMMA, JANE AUSTEN

debauch to defile

debauch NOUN
an instance of immoral behaviour, for example, involving alcohol, other drugs, or overeating
• *a debauch of opium*—THE MOONSTONE, WILKIE COLLINS

decease NOUN
a person's death
• *the expected decease of her mother*—JANE EYRE, CHARLOTTE BRONTË

declension NOUN
a decline; a reduction
• *Bob has 'a sudden declension in his high spirits'* when he thinks that Martha is not coming.
—A CHRISTMAS CAROL, CHARLES DICKENS

decline VERB
1 (said about a day) to draw to an end
• *But, what with loitering on the way ... the day had quite declined when I came to the place.*
—GREAT EXPECTATIONS, CHARLES DICKENS
2 be declined
(said about the sun) to go down or start to go down
• *The sun is already far declined.*—FRANKENSTEIN, MARY SHELLEY

decline NOUN
1 the lowering or setting of the sun
• *the slow decline of the sun*—THE MAYOR OF CASTERBRIDGE, THOMAS HARDY
2 a disease such as tuberculosis that led to death; the end of someone's life
• *He was in a Decline, and was a shadow to look at.*
—GREAT EXPECTATIONS, CHARLES DICKENS

decorum NOUN
what is appropriate in terms of rank, situation, or behaviour
• *Elizabeth is told that 'honour [and] decorum ... forbid' her marriage to Darcy.*—PRIDE AND PREJUDICE, JANE AUSTEN

deed NOUN
1 a thing done
• *I look on the hands which executed the deed.*
—FRANKENSTEIN, MARY SHELLEY
2 a legal document showing ownership or other rights
• *[Marley's] chain ... was made ... of cash-boxes, keys, padlocks, ledgers, deeds, and heavy purses wrought in steel.*—A CHRISTMAS CAROL, CHARLES DICKENS

deep ADJECTIVE
cunning; sly
• *'You're a deep little puss, you are,' said Silas.*
—SILAS MARNER, GEORGE ELIOT

defect NOUN
a character flaw; a fault
• *I am perfectly convinced ... that Mr Darcy has no defect.*—PRIDE AND PREJUDICE, JANE AUSTEN

Familiar words with similar meanings

You will find familiar words being used in different ways from modern English. Sometimes, as with *defect*, they may have a similar meaning to the modern sense. Although in modern English we often associate 'defect' with faulty goods it is easy to understand the meaning here.

Sometimes words are combined differently from in modern English. In the sentence below we would say 'found guilty'.
• *Was the woman **brought in** guilty? No; she was acquitted.*—GREAT EXPECTATIONS, CHARLES DICKENS

Sometimes words are simply in a different order to modern English.
• *On each side stood a ... **bush-holly** or yew.*—JANE EYRE, CHARLOTTE BRONTË

---

defection NOUN
the act of abandoning someone or something for another person, place, etc.
• *Elizabeth says she is not too upset by Wickham pursuing another woman: 'Kitty and Lydia take his defection much more to heart than I do.'*—PRIDE AND PREJUDICE, JANE AUSTEN

defective ADJECTIVE
faulty; flawed
• *I am a defective being, with many faults and few redeeming points.*—JANE EYRE, CHARLOTTE BRONTË
USAGE In modern English, you might expect goods to be *defective*, rather than people.

defile VERB
to move along a narrow track or passage; to move in single file
• *Instantly the regiments began to defile through the ... gateway.*—KING SOLOMON'S MINES, H. RIDER HAGGARD

defile NOUN
a narrow track or passage
• *All night their course lay through intricate defiles and over ... rock-strewn paths.*—A STUDY IN SCARLET, ARTHUR CONAN DOYLE
RELATED WORD *file* as a noun meaning 'a line of people' and as a verb meaning 'to walk somewhere in a line'

defray to depose

defray VERB
to provide the money for something
• *I am prepared to defray all charges.*—BLEAK HOUSE, CHARLES DICKENS

deglutition (say dee-gloo-tish-uhn) NOUN
swallowing
• *too bitter … a morsel for human deglutition*—JANE EYRE, CHARLOTTE BRONTË

degree NOUN
1 rank; position
• *men, women, and children of the lowest and poorest degree*—THE PRINCE AND THE PAUPER, MARK TWAIN
➢ **by degrees:** gradually • *I grew by degrees cold as a stone.*—JANE EYRE, CHARLOTTE BRONTË
➢ **by slow / rapid degrees:** used for saying how quickly something happened • *By slow degrees he recovered and ate a little soup.*—FRANKENSTEIN, MARY SHELLEY
➢ **to a degree:**
1 to a great extent
• *I felt desolate to a degree.*—JANE EYRE, CHARLOTTE BRONTË
2 to some extent
• *To a degree, I know it is the same with them all.*—PERSUASION, JANE AUSTEN
3 used for saying to what extent something happened
• *Miss Nancy's mind resembled her aunt's to a degree that everybody said was surprising.*—SILAS MARNER, GEORGE ELIOT

delf (say delft) NOUN
glazed dishes, tiles, etc. with a blue and white painted pattern
• *a set of tea-things in delf*—JANE EYRE, CHARLOTTE BRONTË

deliberate ADJECTIVE
resulting from careful consideration
• *'And that,' said I, 'is your deliberate opinion, Mr Wemmick?'*—GREAT EXPECTATIONS, CHARLES DICKENS
➤ **deliberately** ADVERB in a careful or considered way • *He deliberately scrutinised each sketch and painting.*—JANE EYRE, CHARLOTTE BRONTË

delicate ADJECTIVE
considerate; tactful; sensitive to others' needs
• *Felix was too delicate to accept this offer.*—FRANKENSTEIN, MARY SHELLEY
➤ **delicacy** NOUN consideration for others; sensitivity • *With their true natural delicacy, they abstained from comment.*—JANE EYRE, CHARLOTTE BRONTË

deliver VERB
to save or rescue someone from something
• *He felt a reformed man, delivered from temptation.*—SILAS MARNER, GEORGE ELIOT

dell NOUN
a small valley or hollow, with trees or plants
• *the dells full of ferns and bluebells*—LITTLE LORD FAUNTLEROY, FRANCES HODGSON BURNETT

demean VERB
➢ **demean yourself:** to behave in a particular way
• *He would have made the pupils 'demean themselves with heroism'.*—VILLETTE, CHARLOTTE BRONTË
USAGE In modern English, you would expect *demean yourself* to suggest undignified behaviour.

demeanour NOUN
a person's behaviour or manner
• *The girl was young and of gentle demeanour.*—FRANKENSTEIN, MARY SHELLEY

demesne (say dim-ayn, dim-een) NOUN
1 the land belonging to an estate or manor, or one part of it
• *a view of the Parsonage and all its demesnes*—MANSFIELD PARK, JANE AUSTEN
2 an area or field of activity
• *the still demesne of nature*—SHIRLEY, CHARLOTTE BRONTË

demoiselle (say dem-waa-zel) NOUN
a young woman
• *the sharp-eyed demoiselles*—LITTLE WOMEN, LOUISA M. ALCOTT

demoralize VERB
to make someone lose their morals
• *For surely so much pleasure will demoralize them.*—A LITTLE GIRL IN OLD PHILADELPHIA, AMANDA MINNIE DOUGLAS

denizen (say den-iz-uhn) NOUN
a person or thing living in a place
• *the denizens of the lane*—THE MAYOR OF CASTERBRIDGE, THOMAS HARDY

denominate VERB
to refer to a person or thing in a particular way
• *a house about a mile from Meryton, denominated … Lucas Lodge*—PRIDE AND PREJUDICE, JANE AUSTEN

depose VERB
1 to give evidence; to state something in evidence
• *A woman deposed that she … saw a boat … push off from that part of the shore.*—FRANKENSTEIN, MARY SHELLEY
• *[He feared] he should be called upon to depose about this … child.*—GREAT EXPECTATIONS, CHARLES DICKENS

depositary to despond

2 to remove someone from their post; to take over from someone
• *I knocked, and an elderly woman ... responded. She was immediately deposed, however, by Herbert.* —GREAT EXPECTATIONS, CHARLES DICKENS
3 to put something down somewhere

depositary NOUN
a person to whom something was entrusted
• *I expected to be made the depositary of some extraordinary confidence.* —THE WOMAN IN WHITE, WILKIE COLLINS

deprecate (say dep-rik-ayt) VERB
1 to dislike or disapprove of something; to show dislike or disapproval
• *I learned ... to deprecate the vices of mankind.* —FRANKENSTEIN, MARY SHELLEY
2 to ask for something not to happen; to say that something should not happen
• *'Why should we put an end to all that's sweet and lovely!' she deprecated.* —TESS OF THE D'URBERVILLES, THOMAS HARDY
➤ **deprecatingly** ADVERB • *The little man waved his hand deprecatingly.* —THE SIGN OF FOUR, ARTHUR CONAN DOYLE
➤ **deprecation** NOUN • *He pursued his theme ... without noticing my deprecation.* —JANE EYRE, CHARLOTTE BRONTË

depression NOUN
a shallow hollow in the ground; a sunken area
• *Before her, in a slight depression, were the remains of a village.* —TESS OF THE D'URBERVILLES, THOMAS HARDY

depute VERB
to pass a job on to someone
• *Larry and Bunco were deputed to fish for trout.* —OVER THE ROCKY MOUNTAINS, R. M. BALLANTYNE

deputy NOUN
someone acting on behalf of a person or group
• *He went as the deputy of some missionary society to preach ... forty miles from here.* —TESS OF THE D'URBERVILLES, THOMAS HARDY

derbies NOUN
a slang word for handcuffs
• *Just hold out while I fix the derbies.* —THE ADVENTURES OF SHERLOCK HOLMES, ARTHUR CONAN DOYLE

descant VERB
to talk for a long time or in a boring manner
• *He ... descanted at some length upon the merits of his company.* —NICHOLAS NICKLEBY, CHARLES DICKENS
• *Mrs Snevellicci ... was ... descanting to Nicholas upon the manifold accomplishments and merits of her daughter.* —NICHOLAS NICKLEBY, CHARLES DICKENS

description NOUN
a type; a kind
• *It was a fiery West Indian night; one of the description that frequently precede the hurricanes of those climates.* —JANE EYRE, CHARLOTTE BRONTË

descry (say diss-kry) VERB
to see someone or something
• *At length we descried a light and a roof.* —GREAT EXPECTATIONS, CHARLES DICKENS

desert (also deserts) NOUN
what someone deserved
• *You ... do not intend to pursue my enemy with the punishment which is his desert.* —FRANKENSTEIN, MARY SHELLEY

design NOUN
a plan, scheme, or intention
• *'I see your design, Bingley,' said his friend. 'You dislike an argument, and want to silence this.'* —PRIDE AND PREJUDICE, JANE AUSTEN
• *'[Jane] is not acting by design'—she is not acting with a particular motive.* —PRIDE AND PREJUDICE, JANE AUSTEN

design VERB
to intend or be determined to do something; to plan or scheme
• *So, designing to cross the Great North Road, they went on.* —THE WAR OF THE WORLDS, H. G. WELLS
• *You have a curious, designing mind, Mr Rochester.* —JANE EYRE, CHARLOTTE BRONTË

desire VERB
to ask or tell someone to do something
• *I have written to Colonel Forster to desire him to find out [about Wickham].* —PRIDE AND PREJUDICE, JANE AUSTEN

desolate VERB
1 to make someone feel terribly sad or utterly forlorn
• *a fiend whose unparalleled barbarity had desolated my heart* —FRANKENSTEIN, MARY SHELLEY
2 to empty a place of people or life
• *the charred and desolated area* —THE WAR OF THE WORLDS, H. G. WELLS

desperado NOUN
a reckless or desperate person
• *The children peep at their 'desperado brother'.* —DOMBEY AND SON, CHARLES DICKENS

despond VERB
to despair
• *Don't despond, but hope and keep happy.* —LITTLE WOMEN, LOUISA M. ALCOTT

despond to diffidence

➤ **desponding** ADJECTIVE despairing • *Elizabeth was sad and desponding.*—FRANKENSTEIN, MARY SHELLEY

despond NOUN
➤ **the Slough of Despond:** hopelessness; depression • *Mrs Sparsit [had] fallen from her pinnacle of exultation into the Slough of Despond.*—HARD TIMES, CHARLES DICKENS

despondence NOUN
despondency; despair
• *I was filled with the bitterest sensations of despondence and mortification.*—FRANKENSTEIN, MARY SHELLEY

destitute ADJECTIVE
living in extreme poverty without the basic necessities
• *What could [she] do, I asked, left destitute and penniless?*—JANE EYRE, CHARLOTTE BRONTË
➤ **destitute of:** without • *His face appeared to me to be quite destitute of colour.*—BLEAK HOUSE, CHARLES DICKENS

detain VERB
to delay someone
• *I will not detain you a minute.*—PRIDE AND PREJUDICE, JANE AUSTEN

detect VERB
to find, see, or notice something
• *I detected the footsteps of two persons.*—THE WOMAN IN WHITE, WILKIE COLLINS

determine VERB
to decide something
• *Wednesday being so close upon us, we determined to go back to London that night.*—GREAT EXPECTATIONS, CHARLES DICKENS

deuce NOUN
➤ **the deuce:** used instead of 'the devil', for showing annoyance, shock, or emphasis • *'What the deuce is the matter with the dog?' growled Holmes.*—THE SIGN OF FOUR, ARTHUR CONAN DOYLE
➤ **deuced** ADJECTIVE & ADVERB great; extremely
• *There was a deuced lot of mystery about nothing.*—RUPERT OF HENTZAU, ANTHONY HOPE
• *It would be a deuced fine match for her.*—THE MILL ON THE FLOSS, GEORGE ELIOT

device NOUN
a scheme or plot; a way of achieving something
• *I resolved to alight as soon as we touched the town, and put myself out of his hearing. This device I executed successfully.*—GREAT EXPECTATIONS, CHARLES DICKENS

➤ **follow your own devices:** to act freely
• *We are not free to follow our own devices, you and I.*—GREAT EXPECTATIONS, CHARLES DICKENS

devilish ADVERB
extremely
• *She was a devilish lively woman.*—DOMBEY AND SON, CHARLES DICKENS

devoir NOUN
duty
• *The Grand Master … commanded the herald to … do his devoir.*—IVANHOE, WALTER SCOTT
🏛 Latin *debere*, meaning 'to owe', and French *devoir*, meaning 'duty'

dexter NOUN
used for talking about the right-hand side. (On a shield, this was from the point of view of the person holding the shield, i.e. on the left as you looked at it.) The word for the other side was *sinister*.
• *the lower dexter*—LORNA DOONE, R. D. BLACKMORE
🏛 Latin *dexter*, meaning 'on the right' or 'skilful'. The word **dexterous** has the same origin: the right hand was considered stronger, or more skilful, than the left.

dexterous ADJECTIVE
skilful, especially with the hands
• *I was secretly afraid of him when I saw him so dexterous.*—GREAT EXPECTATIONS, CHARLES DICKENS
➤ **dexterously** ADVERB • *I saw him dexterously tear a narrow slip from the margin [of the page].*—JANE EYRE, CHARLOTTE BRONTË
➤ **dexterity** NOUN skill • *a great show of dexterity*—GREAT EXPECTATIONS, CHARLES DICKENS

diablerie (say dee-aa-bluh-ree) NOUN
witchcraft; sorcery
• *Jane thinks 'there is diablerie in the business after all'.*—JANE EYRE, CHARLOTTE BRONTË
🏛 French *diable*, meaning 'devil'

dickens NOUN
➤ **the dickens:** used instead of 'the devil', for showing annoyance, shock, or emphasis
• *What the dickens does the fellow expect?*—LITTLE WOMEN, LOUISA M. ALCOTT
🏛 The exact origin is unclear, but it existed long before the 19th century and the fame of Charles Dickens.

diffidence NOUN
lack of self-confidence; shyness; hesitation
• *The first feelings of diffidence overcome, Caroline soon felt glad to talk.*—SHIRLEY, CHARLOTTE BRONTË
➤ **diffident** ADJECTIVE shy; hesitant • *[He] was a diffident man and slow to offer his own opinions.*—LITTLE MEN, LOUISA M. ALCOTT

diffuse to disclaim

diffuse ADJECTIVE
not concise or focused; using many words
• *I began to fear as I wrote in this book that I was getting too diffuse.*—DRACULA, BRAM STOKER

diggings NOUN
lodgings
• *I was in diggings out Hampstead way.*—THE MEMOIRS OF SHERLOCK HOLMES, ARTHUR CONAN DOYLE
RELATED WORD digs, also meaning 'lodgings'

dignity NOUN
a person of high social rank; a dignitary
• *It was the place where he was likely to find the powers and dignities of Raveloe.*—SILAS MARNER, GEORGE ELIOT

dike (also **dyke**) NOUN
a long ditch, wall, or embankment to prevent flooding
• *Down banks and up banks, and over gates, and splashing into dikes, ... no man cared where he went.*—GREAT EXPECTATIONS, CHARLES DICKENS

dilate VERB
to expand; to make something grow larger
• *This [terror] dilated until it filled the room.*—GREAT EXPECTATIONS, CHARLES DICKENS

diligence NOUN
a stagecoach
• *Having ... secured a seat in the diligence, I departed.*—VILLETTE, CHARLOTTE BRONTË

dimity NOUN
a type of strong patterned fabric
• *dimity curtains*—THE MAYOR OF CASTERBRIDGE, THOMAS HARDY
🏛 Greek *dimitos*, from *di-* 'twice' + *mitos* 'warp thread'

dint
a dent or hollow
• *Polly ... smoothed out a slight dint.*—AN OLD-FASHIONED GIRL, LOUISA M. ALCOTT
➤ **by dint of:** by means of • *By dint of these encouragements, he was persuaded to move.*—NICHOLAS NICKLEBY, CHARLES DICKENS

dip (also **dip-candle**) NOUN
a candle made by dipping a wick in melted tallow (animal fat)
• *It was pretty dark with Scrooge's dip.*—A CHRISTMAS CAROL, CHARLES DICKENS

directly ADVERB
1 immediately
• *I must have the money directly.*—SILAS MARNER, GEORGE ELIOT
2 soon
• *She will be home directly.*—A TALE OF TWO CITIES, CHARLES DICKENS

directly CONJUNCTION
as soon as
• *Directly I came home again, I travelled down into Yorkshire.*—NICHOLAS NICKLEBY, CHARLES DICKENS

direful ADJECTIVE
dreadful
• *accidents of the most direful nature*—LIFE AT PLUMFIELD WITH JO'S BOYS, LOUISA M. ALCOTT

disapprobation NOUN
disapproval; criticism
• *His disapprobation was expressed, but apparently very little regarded.*—PERSUASION, JANE AUSTEN

discern VERB
to find, see, or notice something; to perceive something
• *Bending forward, he could just discern the marks made by the little feet on the virgin snow.*—SILAS MARNER, GEORGE ELIOT

discharge VERB
1 to carry out a duty or task
• *I was invested with the office of teacher; which I discharged with zeal for two years.*—JANE EYRE, CHARLOTTE BRONTË
2 to pay a debt
• *[Wickham] had left many debts behind him, which Mr Darcy afterwards discharged.*—PRIDE AND PREJUDICE, JANE AUSTEN
3 to order or allow someone to leave; to dismiss someone
• *[I le] discharged the servant.*—NICHOLAS NICKLEBY, CHARLES DICKENS
4 to fire or release a weapon
• *A fresh canister of the black vapour was discharged.*—THE WAR OF THE WORLDS, H. G. WELLS

discharge NOUN
1 the carrying out of a duty or task
• *It is also a duty ... to yourself, for excessive sorrow prevents ... the discharge of daily usefulness.*—FRANKENSTEIN, MARY SHELLEY
2 the payment of a debt
• *the discharge of dishonouring debts*—SHIRLEY, CHARLOTTE BRONTË
3 the firing or release of a weapon
• *discharges of cannon*—GREAT EXPECTATIONS, CHARLES DICKENS

disclaim VERB
to deny or reject a compliment, suggestion, etc.
• *Miss Bennet eagerly disclaimed all extraordinary merit, and threw back the praise on her sister.*—PRIDE AND PREJUDICE, JANE AUSTEN
USAGE In modern English, you might expect someone to *disclaim* knowledge or responsibility, rather than a compliment or accusation.

discompose to disinclination

discompose VERB
to distress someone, or make them feel awkward or uncomfortable
- Such doings discomposed Mr Bennet exceedingly.—PRIDE AND PREJUDICE, JANE AUSTEN
➤ **discomposed** ADJECTIVE • He certainly is greatly, very greatly discomposed.—NORTHANGER ABBEY, JANE AUSTEN

discomposure NOUN
distress or upset; an awkward or uncomfortable feeling
- The discomposure of spirits ... could not be easily overcome.—PRIDE AND PREJUDICE, JANE AUSTEN

discourse NOUN
1 conversation
- She then changed the discourse to one ... on which there could be no difference of sentiment.—PRIDE AND PREJUDICE, JANE AUSTEN
2 a speech on a topic; a sermon
- You are capable of profiting by this discourse which I now deliver for your good.—BLEAK HOUSE, CHARLES DICKENS

discourse VERB
to have a conversation
- Silas and Eppie were seated on the bank discoursing in the ... shade of the ash tree.—SILAS MARNER, GEORGE ELIOT

discover VERB
to reveal something to someone
- I did not doubt ... the monster ... would discover himself to me.—FRANKENSTEIN, MARY SHELLEY

discretion NOUN
good judgment; wisdom
- She had even [advised] him to marry as soon as he could, provided he chose with discretion.—PRIDE AND PREJUDICE, JANE AUSTEN

discriminate VERB
to distinguish one thing from another
- I discovered that my ear was ... trying to discriminate amidst the confusion of accents those of Mr Rochester.—JANE EYRE, CHARLOTTE BRONTË
- The drug had no discriminating action; it was neither diabolical nor divine.—THE STRANGE CASE OF DR JEKYLL AND MR HYDE, ROBERT LOUIS STEVENSON

discrimination NOUN
the ability to recognize the difference between things
- 'I said he wasn't mad,' cried a third, feeling that his discrimination deserved approval.—UNDER THE LILACS, LOUISA M. ALCOTT

disdain NOUN
a feeling of scorn or contempt
- 'It would do,' I affirmed with some disdain, 'perfectly well.'—JANE EYRE, CHARLOTTE BRONTË

disdain VERB
to treat someone with scorn or contempt; to refuse out of pride to do something
- My Lady, you may have some ... reasons for disdaining to utter something that you know.—BLEAK HOUSE, CHARLES DICKENS

disengage VERB
to release someone or something
- Florence disengaged herself ... from the ministration of Mrs Pipchin and her attendants.—DOMBEY AND SON, CHARLES DICKENS

disengaged ADJECTIVE
1 free; available
- I am always disengaged after four or five o'clock.—DAVID COPPERFIELD, CHARLES DICKENS
- Then taking the disengaged arm of Mr Darcy, she left Elizabeth to walk by herself.—PRIDE AND PREJUDICE, JANE AUSTEN
2 emotionally detached
- [Elizabeth] presently answered the question in a tolerably disengaged tone.—PRIDE AND PREJUDICE, JANE AUSTEN

disfigure VERB
to spoil the appearance of a person or thing
- My right arm was tolerably restored; disfigured, but fairly serviceable.—GREAT EXPECTATIONS, CHARLES DICKENS

disgust VERB
to make someone feel that something is unpleasant; to annoy someone
- There was nothing ... in Bingley, that could provoke [Mr Bennet's] ridicule, or disgust him into silence.
➤ **disgusting** ADJECTIVE unpleasant or annoying; distasteful • Such weather makes every thing and every body disgusting.—SENSE AND SENSIBILITY, JANE AUSTEN

disgust NOUN
unpleasantness; annoyance
- Tom had felt some disgust on learning that Hector and Achilles might possibly never have existed.—THE MILL ON THE FLOSS, GEORGE ELIOT

disinclination NOUN
reluctance; unwillingness
- Moreover, she had a strong disinclination to speak on the terrible subject.—MARY BARTON, ELIZABETH GASKELL
➤ **disincline** VERB to make someone reluctant to do something • Their conversation the preceding evening did not disincline him to seek her again.—PERSUASION, JANE AUSTEN

disinterested to dissever

➤ **disinclined** ADJECTIVE reluctant; unwilling; not in favour of something • *Mr Lorry and Defarge were rather disinclined to this course.*—A TALE OF TWO CITIES, CHARLES DICKENS

disinterested ADJECTIVE
not motivated by hope of personal gain
• *His choice is disinterested at least, for he must know my father can give her nothing.*—PRIDE AND PREJUDICE, JANE AUSTEN
➤ **disinterestedness** NOUN • *'My dear Jane!' exclaimed Elizabeth, 'you are too good. Your sweetness and disinterestedness are really angelic.'* —PRIDE AND PREJUDICE, JANE AUSTEN

USAGE You might expected *disinterested* to mean 'uninterested', and therefore to have a negative connotation, but in the sense shown here, being *disinterested*, or *disinterestedness*, is a good thing.

dismals NOUN
low mood; depression
• *Myra's dismals and Jane's lectures have made her [feel] blue.*—EIGHT COUSINS, LOUISA M. ALCOTT

dispensation NOUN
an act of God's goodness
• *a blessed dispensation*—HARD TIMES, CHARLES DICKENS

dispense VERB
to say that someone need not or must not do something
• *Me, she had dispensed from joining the group.*—JANE EYRE, CHARLOTTE BRONTË

dispirited ADJECTIVE
discouraged; depressed
• *She seldom went away without leaving them more dispirited than she found them.*—PRIDE AND PREJUDICE, JANE AUSTEN

disposal NOUN
the organization or arrangement of something
• *Sir Thomas helps Mrs Price with the 'disposal of her sons'*—with finding a position for them.—MANSFIELD PARK, JANE AUSTEN

dispose VERB
1 to make someone feel inclined to do something
• *She had received ideas which disposed her to be courteous.*—PERSUASION, JANE AUSTEN
2 to place something somewhere
• *He ... laid him down on the ground ... disposing himself upon his back.*—THE ADVENTURES OF TOM SAWYER, MARK TWAIN
➤ **dispose of:** to organize, arrange, or deal with something • *She has been allowed to dispose of her time in the most idle and frivolous manner.*—PRIDE AND PREJUDICE, JANE AUSTEN

disposed ADJECTIVE
1 inclined; willing
• *The butcher ... was not disposed to answer rashly.*—SILAS MARNER, GEORGE ELIOT
2 used for describing a person's attitude towards someone or something
• *You are always ... anxious to help the oppressed ... so you will be favourably disposed towards him, I know.*—NICHOLAS NICKLEBY, CHARLES DICKENS

disposition NOUN
1 a tendency or inclination; a person's character
• *a disposition to think a little too well of herself*—EMMA, JANE AUSTEN
• *Miss Nipper was of a resolute disposition.*—DOMBEY AND SON, CHARLES DICKENS
2 the way that something was organized, arranged, or dealt with
• *The disposition of everything in the rooms, from the largest object to the least ... [was] so pleasant.*—A TALE OF TWO CITIES, CHARLES DICKENS

disquietude NOUN
anxiety; unease
• *The lawyer stood a while when Mr Hyde had left him, the picture of disquietude.*—THE STRANGE CASE OF DR JEKYLL AND MR HYDE, ROBERT LOUIS STEVENSON

disquisition NOUN
1 a long or complicated written or spoken account of something
• *fierce theological disquisitions*—DOMBEY AND SON, CHARLES DICKENS
2 research; investigation
• *Creating a female monster would require 'profound study and laborious disquisition'.*—FRANKENSTEIN, MARY SHELLEY

disrelish NOUN
dislike; distaste
• *Mrs Blimber speaks 'with a great disrelish'.*—DOMBEY AND SON, CHARLES DICKENS

disremember VERB
to forget something
• *I disremember her name.*—THE ADVENTURES OF HUCKLEBERRY FINN, MARK TWAIN

dissertation NOUN
a speech, lecture, or sermon
• *Tom ... was delivering all around (but especially to Annie, who was wondering at his learning) a dissertation on precious stones.*—LORNA DOONE, R.D. BLACKMORE

dissever VERB
to separate or divide people or things
• *Henchard's wife was dissevered from him by death.*—THE MAYOR OF CASTERBRIDGE, THOMAS HARDY

dissertation to dog-cart

➤ **disseverment** NOUN • Jane thinks morbidly about death and executions, *'of the disseverment of bone and vein'.*—JANE EYRE, CHARLOTTE BRONTË

dissertation NOUN
a speech, lecture, or sermon
• *Tom ... was delivering all around ... a dissertation on precious stones.*—LORNA DOONE, R. D. BLACKMORE

dissipate VERB
to make something disappear
• *Presently a breeze dissipated the cloud.*
—FRANKENSTEIN, MARY SHELLEY

dissipation NOUN
pleasure; indulgence
• *It was Christmas week: we took to no settled employment, but spent it in a sort of merry domestic dissipation.*—JANE EYRE, CHARLOTTE BRONTË
• *They all went out for a walk before tea. Even Briggs ... partook of this dissipation.*—DOMBEY AND SON, CHARLES DICKENS

dissolute ADJECTIVE
immoral
• *[They] were of a dissolute and wasteful disposition.*
—THE ADVENTURES OF SHERLOCK HOLMES, ARTHUR CONAN DOYLE

dissolution NOUN
1 the process of being dissolved
• *the dissolution of the sugar*—NICHOLAS NICKLEBY, CHARLES DICKENS
2 the breaking up or ending of something
• *A dissolution of partnership*—DAVID COPPERFIELD, CHARLES DICKENS
3 death
• *I will dog thee till the very instant of dissolution!*
—IVANHOE, WALTER SCOTT
USAGE Robert Louis Stevenson uses this word to talk about what happens to Dr Jekyll before he is transformed into Mr Hyde.
• *I once more prepared and drank the cup, once more suffered the pangs of dissolution, and came to myself once more with the character, the stature and the face of Henry Jekyll.*—THE STRANGE CASE OF DR JEKYLL AND MR HYDE, ROBERT LOUIS STEVENSON

distinguish VERB
to pay particular attention to someone; to single someone out
• *The rest of the evening passed with ... no farther attempt to distinguish Elizabeth.*—PRIDE AND PREJUDICE, JANE AUSTEN

distracted ADJECTIVE
mad; deranged
• *Oh, Lord ! What will become of me. I shall go distracted.*—PRIDE AND PREJUDICE, JANE AUSTEN

➤ **distractedly** ADVERB • *I should certainly be a more interesting object to all my acquaintance, were I distractedly in love with him.*—PRIDE AND PREJUDICE, JANE AUSTEN

distrain VERB
to seize someone's property because they owed rent or other money
• *I must hand over that rent of Fowler's to the Squire ... for he's threatening to distrain for it.*—SILAS MARNER, GEORGE ELIOT

distrait ADJECTIVE
absent-minded; distracted
• *Holmes was curiously distrait.*—THE RETURN OF SHERLOCK HOLMES, ARTHUR CONAN DOYLE

divers ADJECTIVE
various; several different
• *He was soon attended by divers surgeons, who arrived in quick succession from all parts.*—DOMBEY AND SON, CHARLES DICKENS

divert VERB
to entertain someone; to give someone enjoyment
• *'Are you not diverted?' 'Oh! yes. Pray read on.'*
—PRIDE AND PREJUDICE, JANE AUSTEN
➤ **diversion** NOUN entertainment; enjoyment
• *Sir William, to Elizabeth's high diversion, was stationed in the doorway ... constantly bowing whenever Miss de Bourgh looked that way.*—PRIDE AND PREJUDICE, JANE AUSTEN

divine VERB
to discover something, often (but not necessarily) by supernatural means
• *a secret which I desired to divine*—FRANKENSTEIN, MARY SHELLEY

divine ADJECTIVE
godly, holy, or sacred; from or like God
• *Divine justice pursued its course; disasters came thick on me ... I began to see and acknowledge the hand of God in my doom.*—JANE EYRE, CHARLOTTE BRONTË

divine NOUN
a priest or clergyman
• *So the professor and the divine met at dinner that evening.*—THE WATER-BABIES, CHARLES KINGSLEY

dog-cart NOUN
1 an open carriage with two seats back to back; originally, the rear seat could be converted to a box for carrying a dog
• *He met me with the dog-cart at the station.*—THE MEMOIRS OF SHERLOCK HOLMES, ARTHUR CONAN DOYLE
2 a two-wheeled cart with a box for a hunter's dogs
3 a small cart drawn by a dog. In 1854 the use of dogs to pull carts became illegal in England.

dog-days *to* drayman

dog-days NOUN
the hottest part of summer
• Scrooge is so cold that he makes his office icy *'in the dog-days'.*—A CHRISTMAS CAROL, CHARLES DICKENS

doit NOUN
a coin, especially an old Dutch coin worth half a farthing
USAGE The word 'doit' was used meaning 'a very small amount'.
• *I have told ye, sir ... that not one doit of it belongs to me.*—KIDNAPPED, ROBERT LOUIS STEVENSON

dolorous ADJECTIVE
sad; distressed or distressing
• *wretched dolorous dreams*—TESS OF THE D'URBERVILLES, THOMAS HARDY

domestic NOUN
a household servant
• *Our plain manner of living, our small rooms, and few domestics ... must make Hunsford extremely dull to a young lady like yourself.*—PRIDE AND PREJUDICE, JANE AUSTEN

domiciliation NOUN
a place to live; the time spent living somewhere
• *Newson was her 'father in early domiciliation'*—she lived with him when she was young.—THE MAYOR OF CASTERBRIDGE, THOMAS HARDY

dotard (say doh-tuhd) NOUN
someone who was old and/or foolish
• *Have fools ... have boys, have dotards ... one by one rejected me?*—DOMBEY AND SON, CHARLES DICKENS

doubloon NOUN
a gold coin from Spain
• *The coins are 'doubloons ... and guineas ... all shaken together'.*—TREASURE ISLAND, ROBERT LOUIS STEVENSON
🏛 A doubloon was worth *double* another gold coin called a pistole.

doubt VERB
to fear or suspect something bad
• *You've been naughty to her, I doubt, Tom?*—THE MILL ON THE FLOSS, GEORGE ELIOT

doughty ADJECTIVE
brave; formidable
• *doughty warriors*—IVANHOE, WALTER SCOTT

dower NOUN
the money or property received by a husband from his wife's family when they married; a dowry
• *[Nicholas] took to wife the daughter of a neighbouring gentleman with a dower of one thousand pounds.*—NICHOLAS NICKLEBY, CHARLES DICKENS

➤ **dowerless** ADJECTIVE without a dowry; poor
• *a dowerless girl*—A CHRISTMAS CAROL, CHARLES DICKENS

drab NOUN
1 dull brown fabric
• *a long drab greatcoat*—WESSEX TALES, THOMAS HARDY
2 a dull brown colour
• *Every leaf ... having already been consumed, the whole field was ... a desolate drab.*—TESS OF THE D'URBERVILLES, THOMAS HARDY

draggled ADJECTIVE
wet and dirty because of trailing across wet ground
• *She was so draggled with the stream.*—THE PRINCESS AND THE GOBLIN, GEORGE MACDONALD
➤ **draggle** VERB to trail along • *a girl who wore a triangular shawl, its corner draggling on the stubble*—TESS OF THE D'URBERVILLES, THOMAS HARDY

draggle-tailed ADJECTIVE
with your skirt trailing along the ground; scruffy
• *thy ... draggle-tailed dress*—MARY BARTON, ELIZABETH GASKELL

draper NOUN
a person whose job was to sell cloth
• *She bought nothing whatever at any of the other drapers' shops, or at any milliners' or tailors' shops.*—THE MOONSTONE, WILKIE COLLINS

drapery NOUN
draped or hanging cloth, for example, covers or curtains
• *a bay window, about which hung some heavy drapery*—NICHOLAS NICKLEBY, CHARLES DICKENS

draught (rhymes with **craft**) NOUN
1 a liquid medicine
• *a sedative draught*—JANE EYRE, CHARLOTTE BRONTË
2 a drink; an act of drinking
• *Mr Crackit stopped to take a draught of spirits and water.*—OLIVER TWIST, CHARLES DICKENS

drawing room NOUN
a sitting room; the room to which ladies withdrew after dinner
• *When the ladies returned to the drawing room, there was little to be done but to hear Lady Catherine talk.*—PRIDE AND PREJUDICE, JANE AUSTEN

dray NOUN
a cart with flat sides, used, for instance, for transporting beer barrels
• *A brewer's dray rumbled by.*—THE WAR OF THE WORLDS, H. G. WELLS

drayman NOUN
a man who drove a dray; a beer delivery man
• *The drayman was ... very drunk ... and the brewer had to pay damages.*—BLACK BEAUTY, ANNA SEWELL

dreadnought to dyspeptic

dreadnought NOUN
a thick woollen fabric; a heavy weatherproof garment made from this
• *his dreadnought coat*—THE CRICKET ON THE HEARTH, CHARLES DICKENS

drench VERB
to make an animal drink medicine
• *Well, it's the cow as I drenched.*—SILAS MARNER, GEORGE ELIOT

dressing-case NOUN
a box for holding toiletries
• *His dressing-case, brushes, and so forth, all of quite an elegant kind, lay about.*—BLEAK HOUSE, CHARLES DICKENS

dressing-glass NOUN
a mirror used when getting ready
• *Mr Shelby was standing before his dressing-glass, sharpening his razor.*—UNCLE TOM'S CABIN, HARRIET BEECHER STOWE

drive VERB
➢ **drive at something / drive away**: to work hard at something • *He was on his stool in a jiffy; driving away with his pen.*—A CHRISTMAS CAROL, CHARLES DICKENS

drop VERB
to mention something; to let something slip
• *Why Jane—you never dropt a word of this; you sly thing!*—PRIDE AND PREJUDICE, JANE AUSTEN

USAGE In modern English, you might expect someone to *drop* a hint, but not a word, remark, or general piece of information.
The spelling of *dropt* is an example of a different spelling from modern English, but which is still easy to understand.

drover NOUN
a person who herded cattle or sheep
• *the drover's track*—A TRADITION OF EIGHTEEN HUNDRED AND FOUR, THOMAS HARDY

drubbing NOUN
a beating
• *He at once gave him a drubbing.*—OLIVER TWIST, CHARLES DICKENS

drudge VERB
to do hard or boring work such as housework
• *Now, while a servant must often drudge and be dirty … a dressmaker's apprentice must … never soil her hands.*—MARY BARTON, ELIZABETH GASKELL

drugget NOUN
1 a rough fabric; a rug made of drugget
• *a threadbare drugget in the middle of the floor*—THE MOONSTONE, WILKIE COLLINS
2 a thick fabric used for clothing

druggist NOUN
a person who sold medicines; a pharmacist
• *He reached a druggist's shop, and entered.*—MARY BARTON, ELIZABETH GASKELL

dudgeon NOUN
resentment; indignation; a feeling of being offended
• *[Mr Rochester] retired, in dudgeon, quite to the other end of the room.*—JANE EYRE, CHARLOTTE BRONTË

dull ADJECTIVE
1 slow to learn; unintelligent
• *Joe warns Pip that if he plans to teach him to read 'I tell you beforehand I am awful dull, most awful dull'.*—GREAT EXPECTATIONS, CHARLES DICKENS
2 gloomy; feeling low
• *The loss of her daughter made Mrs Bennet very dull for several days.*—PRIDE AND PREJUDICE, JANE AUSTEN

dumb-waiter NOUN
a table or trolley for food or drink. Some dumb-waiters had circular shelves which could be turned around.
• *The table was comfortably laid … and at the side of his chair was a capacious dumb-waiter, with a variety of bottles and decanters on it.*—GREAT EXPECTATIONS, CHARLES DICKENS

dunderhead NOUN
a stupid person
• *If I used my own [name], some of these dunderheads would recognize it and want to meddle in the affair.*—A STUDY IN SCARLET, ARTHUR CONAN DOYLE
➢ **dunder-headed** ADJECTIVE • *the dunder-headed king of the noodles*—GREAT EXPECTATIONS, CHARLES DICKENS

duteous ADJECTIVE
dutiful; respectful
• *[He] made a duteous pilgrimage to his mother.*—LIFE AT PLUMFIELD WITH JO'S BOYS, LOUISA M. ALCOTT

duty NOUN
respects
• *The young ladies go 'to pay their duty to their aunt'.*—PRIDE AND PREJUDICE, JANE AUSTEN

DV ABBREVIATION
an abbreviation for the Latin, *deo volente* meaning 'God willing'—a way of expressing a wish
• *They would be far on their road to London: and so should I (D.V.),—or rather not I, but one Jane Rochester.*—JANE EYRE, CHARLOTTE BRONTË

dyspeptic ADJECTIVE
suffering from *dyspepsia* (indigestion); irritable
• *a nervous, dyspeptic, unhappy old woman*—EIGHT COUSINS, LOUISA M. ALCOTT

Ee

ELEPHANT MAN

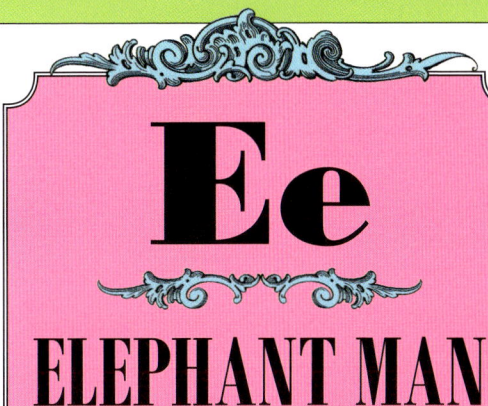

Born in Leicester in **1862**, **Joseph Merrick** developed severe deformities in childhood. Unable to find employment, he was exhibited as the **'Elephant Man'** in freak shows which travelled the country. These were a popular form of entertainment in which the public observed people with unusual conditions. Rescued by a surgeon named Frederick Treves, Merrick lived in the London Hospital until his death at the age of twenty-seven.

ear-drop (also **ear-dropper**) NOUN
a drop earring
• *a pair of coral ear-drops*—UNCLE TOM'S CABIN, HARRIET BEECHER STOWE

earnest NOUN
1 a sign or declaration
• *The joyful surprise that lighted up their faces … was the first pleasing earnest of their welcome.*—PRIDE AND PREJUDICE, JANE AUSTEN
2 a first payment; an initial amount
• *I had promised to pay for his information and given him an earnest.*—DRACULA, BRAM STOKER

easeful ADJECTIVE
relaxed or relaxing
• *Tess enjoys whistling to the bullfinches 'in easeful grace'.*—TESS OF THE D'URBERVILLES, THOMAS HARDY
➤ **easefully** ADVERB in a relaxed manner; comfortably • *[She was] standing with her hands on her hips, easefully looking at the preparations.*—THE MAYOR OF CASTERBRIDGE, THOMAS HARDY

eating-house NOUN
a shop selling cooked meals; a restaurant
• *The sailor stopped at an eating-house in the neighbourhood, and went in.*—THE MOONSTONE, WILKIE COLLINS

ebon ADJECTIVE
ebony; dark brown or black
• *The cabinet was topped with 'an ebon crucifix'.*—JANE EYRE, CHARLOTTE BRONTË

ebullition NOUN
1 boiling; bubbling
• *Suddenly … the ebullition ceased and the compound changed to a dark purple.*—THE STRANGE CASE OF DR JEKYLL AND MR HYDE, ROBERT LOUIS STEVENSON
2 an outburst of strong feeling
• *'I wish half the women in England were as respectable as you,' he said, in an ebullition of bitterness against womankind in general.*—TESS OF THE D'URBERVILLES, THOMAS HARDY

ecclesiastic NOUN
a priest
• *The aged ecclesiastic had turned his face towards me.*—THE MEMOIRS OF SHERLOCK HOLMES, ARTHUR CONAN DOYLE

éclat NOUN
very obvious success; distinction; brilliance
• *the éclat of a proverb*—PRIDE AND PREJUDICE, JANE AUSTEN

ecod EXCLAMATION
a swear word used for showing surprise, anger, emphasis, etc.
• *'What's that to you? Ecod!' growled Mr Cruncher.*—A TALE OF TWO CITIES, CHARLES DICKENS

Exclamations

Emotions were expressed in different ways in the 19th century. *Ecod*, *egad*, and *begad* are all expressions used in the 19th century which are derived from the word 'god'.
• *Begad, I nearly forgot myself just now!*—THE MAYOR OF CASTERBRIDGE, THOMAS HARDY

ecstasy NOUN
a frenzy or trance-like state
• *In what ecstasy of unhappiness I got these broken words out of myself, I don't know.*—GREAT EXPECTATIONS, CHARLES DICKENS

een NOUN
eyes
• *Miss Helstone 'has gentle blue een, wi' long lashes'.*—SHIRLEY, CHARLOTTE BRONTË

e'er to embrowned

e'er ADVERB
ever or any (used for emphasis)
• George was *'walking as slow as e'er he could'*.
—MARY BARTON, ELIZABETH GASKELL

efface VERB
to cause a memory or feeling to disappear
• *But joy soon effaced every other feeling.*—JANE EYRE, CHARLOTTE BRONTË

effluvia NOUN
unpleasant fumes or smells
• Residents *'observed the foetid effluvia'* coming from the deceased person's house.—BLEAK HOUSE, CHARLES DICKENS

effulgent ADJECTIVE
shining; radiant
• *the effulgent Antarctic skies*—MOBY DICK, HERMAN MELVILLE
➤ **effulgence** NOUN • *In the moonlight London has a 'pale effulgence'.*—BLEAK HOUSE, CHARLES DICKENS

eft NOUN
a newt

egad EXCLAMATION
a swear word used for showing surprise, anger, emphasis, etc.
• *'Egad!' said Mr Carker, shaking his head, 'Time flies!'*—DOMBEY AND SON, CHARLES DICKENS

ejaculate VERB
to exclaim something
• *'What, me!' I ejaculated.*—JANE EYRE, CHARLOTTE BRONTË
➤ **ejaculation** NOUN an exclamation • *I uttered an ejaculation of discontent.*—WUTHERING HEIGHTS, EMILY BRONTË

eke VERB
➤ **eke something out:** to make something last longer or go further • *Eked out by apple sauce and mashed potatoes, it was a sufficient dinner for the whole family.*—A CHRISTMAS CAROL, CHARLES DICKENS

eke ADJECTIVE
also
• *an old-fashioned old gentleman, attorney-at-law and eke solicitor of the High Court of Chancery*—BLEAK HOUSE, CHARLES DICKENS

elate ADJECTIVE
very happy; elated
• *And now my heart is elate because I find you perfect.*—SHIRLEY, CHARLOTTE BRONTË

elate VERB
to make someone proud, happy, or excited
• *Yes, only ten days ago had he elated her by his pointed regard.*—NORTHANGER ABBEY, JANE AUSTEN

eld NOUN
old age
• The woman's hand was not *'the withered limb of eld … it was a rounded supple member'*.—JANE EYRE, CHARLOTTE BRONTË

election NOUN
1 choice
• *Alfred … has of his own election joined the [society called] Infant Bonds of Joy.*—BLEAK HOUSE, CHARLES DICKENS
2 being chosen by God
• *[William] had dreamed that he saw the words 'calling and election sure' standing by themselves on a white page in the open Bible.*—SILAS MARNER, GEORGE ELIOT

elephantiasis NOUN
an infection causing extreme swelling

eloquent ADJECTIVE
expressing something; indicative of something
• *His whole bearing was eloquent of satisfaction.*
—THE PRISONER OF ZENDA, ANTHONY HOPE

elude VERB
to escape from someone or something
• *I darted towards the spot … but the devil eluded my grasp.*—FRANKENSTEIN, MARY SHELLEY
• *He had eluded pursuit.*—DAVID COPPERFIELD, CHARLES DICKENS

elysium (say il-iz-ee-uhm) NOUN
a place of perfect happiness; a paradise
• Members of the board claimed the workhouse was *'a brick and mortar elysium, where it was all play and no work'.*—OLIVER TWIST, CHARLES DICKENS
🏛 In Greek mythology, *Elysium* was a place where heroes and others chosen by the gods lived a happy afterlife.

embalm VERB
1 to preserve
• *the secret … which the old Musgraves had thought it necessary to embalm in so curious a fashion*—THE MEMOIRS OF SHERLOCK HOLMES, ARTHUR CONAN DOYLE
2 to perfume; to give a pleasant scent to
• *A forest of flowering shrubs embalmed the climate of this spot.*—VILLETTE, CHARLOTTE BRONTË

embosom VERB
to surround and protect
• *such deep and leafy seclusion as ought to embosom a religious house*—VILLETTE, CHARLOTTE BRONTË

embrowned ADJECTIVE
turned brown; darkened
• *It was a fine autumn morning; the early sun shone serenely on embrowned groves and still green fields.*
—JANE EYRE, CHARLOTTE BRONTË

embruted *to* engage

embruted ADJECTIVE
brutish; rough and animal-like
• Rochester is *'already bound to a bad, mad, and embruted partner'*.—JANE EYRE, CHARLOTTE BRONTË

emergence NOUN
an unexpected urgent problem; an emergency
• Colonel Brandon is *'a person ... well able to assist or advise Miss Dashwood in any emergence'*.—SENSE AND SENSIBILITY, JANE AUSTEN

eminence NOUN
a rising piece of ground; a hill
• *They ... found themselves at the top of a considerable eminence.*—PRIDE AND PREJUDICE, JANE AUSTEN

employment NOUN
activity that kept someone busy
• *Elizabeth ... chose for her employment the examination of all the letters which Jane had written to her.*—PRIDE AND PREJUDICE, JANE AUSTEN

empressement NOUN
eagerness; insistent friendliness
• *Madame always received him with the same empressement.*—VILLETTE, CHARLOTTE BRONTË

emulous ADJECTIVE
wanting to do as well as someone else
• *He is not envious, but emulous of your attainments.*—WUTHERING HEIGHTS, EMILY BRONTË
➤ **emulously** ADVERB • *The inhabitants were all doing well, it seemed and all emulously hoping to do better still.*—THE STRANGE CASE OF DR JEKYLL AND MR HYDE, ROBERT LOUIS STEVENSON
RELATED WORD emulate, meaning 'copy someone'

enchain VERB
to imprison or enslave someone
• *Louis Moore writes about how Shirley's features and qualities 'hopelessly ... enchain me'.*—in modern English, he might say that he is captivated by her.—SHIRLEY, CHARLOTTE BRONTË

enclosure (also **inclosure**) NOUN
1 a document inside an envelope
• *The lawyer unsealed it, and several enclosures fell to the floor.*—THE STRANGE CASE OF DR JEKYLL AND MR HYDE, ROBERT LOUIS STEVENSON
2 an envelope containing a document
• *On the outside I wrote this direction: 'Keep the enclosure unopened until nine o'clock to-morrow morning.'*—THE WOMAN IN WHITE, WILKIE COLLINS

encomium NOUN
a remark, piece of writing, etc. that praises someone or something highly
• *Lavish encomiums on 'Dombey's sister' reached his ears from all the boys.*—DOMBEY AND SON, CHARLES DICKENS

encumber VERB
to burden or hamper someone
• *Downe descended, but being encumbered with his bag and umbrella, his foot slipped.*—WESSEX TALES, THOMAS HARDY

encumbrance NOUN
a burden
• *I am aware that they may be ... some encumbrance to you.*—EMMA, JANE AUSTEN

end NOUN
an aim
• *I fancy we can attain our end in a simpler way.*—THE RETURN OF SHERLOCK HOLMES, ARTHUR CONAN DOYLE

endue (also **indue**) VERB
to give someone or something a quality
• *Frankenstein's monster is 'A being whom I myself had formed, and endued with life'.*—FRANKENSTEIN, MARY SHELLEY

enforce VERB
to express something forcibly; to reinforce an idea
• *Elinor, having once delivered her opinion ... did not see the necessity of enforcing it by any farther assertion.*—SENSE AND SENSIBILITY, JANE AUSTEN
USAGE In modern English, you might expect a law or rule to be *enforced*, rather than an opinion.

engage VERB
1 to reserve accommodation
• *Sherlock Holmes and I had no difficulty in engaging a bedroom and sitting-room at the Crown Inn.*—THE ADVENTURES OF SHERLOCK HOLMES, ARTHUR CONAN DOYLE
2 to promise to do something; to commit to something
• *I think that I can engage to clear you of the charge.*—THE SIGN OF FOUR, ARTHUR CONAN DOYLE
3 to ask or invite someone to commit to something
• *I hope to engage you to be serious likewise.*—PRIDE AND PREJUDICE, JANE AUSTEN
4 to ask someone to dance
• *She had fully proposed being engaged by Mr Wickham for those very dances.*—PRIDE AND PREJUDICE, JANE AUSTEN
➤ **engage for something**: to promise or commit to something • *She ventured to engage for her attendance.*—PRIDE AND PREJUDICE, JANE AUSTEN
➤ **engagement** NOUN a commitment; an arrangement • *We were all under engagement to dine at Mr Badger's house.*—BLEAK HOUSE, CHARLES DICKENS

engender to envenomed

engender VERB
to cause something
• Florence 'did not dare to venture [into Edith's rooms], lest she should unconsciously engender new trouble'.
—DOMBEY AND SON, CHARLES DICKENS

engraver NOUN
someone who job was to engrave pictures on metal or wood in order to create printed images, maps, etc.
• Lizzie Small is an engraver, and designs the most delightful little pictures.—AN OLD FASHIONED GIRL, LOUISA M. ALCOTT

enigmatical ADJECTIVE
mysterious; enigmatic
• My companion smiled an enigmatical smile.
—A STUDY IN SCARLET, ARTHUR CONAN DOYLE

enkindle VERB
to inspire something or someone; to arouse an emotion
• I [felt] the spirit of revenge enkindled in my heart.
—FRANKENSTEIN, MARY SHELLEY

enlighten VERB
to shine light on something
• [The moon] enlightened my path.—FRANKENSTEIN, MARY SHELLEY

ennui NOUN
lack of enthusiasm; boredom
• If I was ever overcome by ennui, the sight of what is beautiful in nature ... could always interest my heart.
—FRANKENSTEIN, MARY SHELLEY

enounce VERB
to pronounce; to say something
• Mr Rochester spoke 'in the tone one might fancy a speaking automaton to enounce its single words'
—meaning that he spoke in a robotic way.—JANE EYRE, CHARLOTTE BRONTË

enow ADJECTIVE
enough
• 'That's fair enow,' said the old man Morgan.
—TREASURE ISLAND, ROBERT LOUIS STEVENSON

enshroud VERB
to cover and make invisible
• Whether these creatures faded into mist, or mist enshrouded them, he could not tell.—A CHRISTMAS CAROL, CHARLES DICKENS

ensign NOUN
1 a military or naval flag
• We buried him the same afternoon with the ship's ensign around him.—THE CAPTAIN OF THE POLE-STAR, ARTHUR CONAN DOYLE
2 a low-ranking officer; a flag bearer
• His name was entered at the Horse Guards as an applicant for an ensign's commission.—BLEAK HOUSE, CHARLES DICKENS
3 a sign or symbol
• [The apron] was the ensign of a good housewife.
—SHIRLEY, CHARLOTTE BRONTË

entail VERB
1 to leave property to members of the same family over a number of generations
• 'Mr Bennet's property ... unfortunately for his daughters, was entailed, in default of heirs male, on a distant relation.'—meaning that if there were no sons in a generation, a distant relation would inherit.
—PRIDE AND PREJUDICE, JANE AUSTEN
2 to cause something to happen to someone
• Mr Carker says he is glad of the opportunity to approach Mrs Dombey, 'even if it has entailed upon me the penalty of her temporary displeasure'.—DOMBEY AND SON, CHARLES DICKENS

entail NOUN
a legal arrangement entailing property; property or land that was entailed
• I'd have you to remember, sir, my property's got no entail on it.—SILAS MARNER, GEORGE ELIOT

entreat VERB
to ask someone very insistently to do something; to beg
• He entreated me to write often.—FRANKENSTEIN, MARY SHELLEY

entreaty NOUN
a plea; a fervent request
• The old girl promptly makes a sign of entreaty to him to say nothing.—BLEAK HOUSE, CHARLES DICKENS

entresol NOUN
an extra storey built between the ground and the first floor; a mezzanine
• My bedroom was on the first floor, above an entresol.—A TERRIBLY STRANGE BED, WILKIE COLLINS

enumerate VERB
to count things; to mention things one by one
• Lydia ... was enumerating the various pleasures of the morning to any body who would hear her.—PRIDE AND PREJUDICE, JANE AUSTEN

envenomed ADJECTIVE
poisoned; poisonous
• Philip felt Tom's casual insult as if it had been inflicted with 'the most envenomed spite'.—THE MILL ON THE FLOSS, GEORGE ELIOT

environ to essay

environ VERB
to surround someone or something
• *The trees environing the old chateau ... moved in a rising wind.*—A TALE OF TWO CITIES, CHARLES DICKENS

environs (say in-vy-ruhnz) NOUN
surrounding areas
• *It was completely dark when I arrived in the environs of Geneva.*—FRANKENSTEIN, MARY SHELLEY

epaulet (also **epaulette**) NOUN
an ornamental flap on the shoulder of a garment, especially one on an officer's uniform
• *Most of them had, hanging up among their stock, an officer's coat or two, epaulettes and all.*—DAVID COPPERFIELD, CHARLES DICKENS

epistolary ADJECTIVE
relating to letter-writing
• *I wonder what she thought of my correspondence? What estimate did she form of [my] epistolary powers?*—VILLETTE, CHARLOTTE BRONTË

epitome (say i-pit-uh-mi) NOUN
a perfect example of something
• *Mr Oak appeared ... looking altogether an epitome of the world's health and vigour.*—FAR FROM THE MADDING CROWD, THOMAS HARDY

equal ADJECTIVE
able to deal or cope with something
• *Elizabeth found herself quite equal to the scene, and could observe the three ladies before her composedly.*—PRIDE AND PREJUDICE, JANE AUSTEN

equipage (say ek-wip-ij) NOUN
1 a carriage and its horses, driver, etc.
• *'The equipage did not answer to that of any of their neighbours.'*—meaning that it did not look like any of their neighbours' carriages.—PRIDE AND PREJUDICE, JANE AUSTEN
2 an outfit including any accessories or equipment
• *Rather than Matthew at the door, Martin would rather have seen the Devil, 'in full equipage of horns, hoofs, and tail'.*—SHIRLEY, CHARLOTTE BRONTË

ere (say air) PREPOSITION & CONJUNCTION
before
• *'I am very ill, I know,' she said ere long.*—JANE EYRE, CHARLOTTE BRONTË
• *A quarter of an hour had elapsed ere she returned downstairs.*—NORTHANGER ABBEY, JANE AUSTEN

erection NOUN
a building or structure
• *It was a windowless erection used for storage.*—TESS OF THE D'URBERVILLES, THOMAS HARDY

erethism (say err-ith-iz-uhm) NOUN
an abnormally sensitive or over-excited state
• *The intense excitement of the events had no doubt left my perceptive powers in a state of erethism.*—THE WAR OF THE WORLDS, H. G. WELLS

erewhile ADVERB
a while ago; some time before
• *Shirley's song, erewhile somewhat full and thrilling, had become delicately faint.*—SHIRLEY, CHARLOTTE BRONTË

errant ADJECTIVE
1 misbehaving; not following accepted rules
• *[He] had a vague longing for some discipline that would have checked his own errant weakness.*—SILAS MARNER, GEORGE ELIOT
2 wandering; straying
• *a long tethering chain, used to prevent the escape of errant horses*—FAR FROM THE MADDING CROWD, THOMAS HARDY
USAGE In modern English, you usually use *errant* to describe an unfaithful spouse or naughty child.

erst ADVERB
in the past; long ago
• *And the child lulled the parent, as the parent had erst lulled the child.*—SHIRLEY, CHARLOTTE BRONTË

espial NOUN
spying
• *[The Captain] cut a small hole of espial in the wall.*—DOMBEY AND SON, CHARLES DICKENS

espy VERB
to spot something; to notice something
• *Beth looked up, [and] espied the wistful face behind the birches.*—LITTLE WOMEN, LOUISA M. ALCOTT

esquire NOUN
1 a young nobleman who attended a knight
• *His lance, shield, and sword ... were borne by his two esquires behind him.*—IVANHOE, WALTER SCOTT
2 a landowner; a country squire
• *I am indeed no longer a girl, but quite a woman and something more. I am an esquire!*—SHIRLEY, CHARLOTTE BRONTË
USAGE Esquire, or Esq., was written after a man's name on letters and documents when there was no other title, such as, for example, 'Sir' or 'Dr'.
• *Oliver glanced at [the letter], and saw that it was directed to Harry Maylie, Esquire.*—OLIVER TWIST, CHARLES DICKENS

essay VERB
to try
• *Mrs. Corney twice essayed to speak: and twice failed.*—OLIVER TWIST, CHARLES DICKENS

essay to evince

essay NOUN
1 an attempt; a try
• *He had often seen children lose courage in making their first essay at riding.*—LITTLE LORD FAUNTLEROY, FRANCES HODGSON BURNETT
2 a piece of writing on a particular topic
• *Darwin's essay on 'Climbing Plants'*—OUTLINES OF LESSONS IN BOTANY, JANE H. NEWELL

establishment NOUN
1 a marriage
• *Miss Lucas, who accepted him solely from the pure and disinterested desire of an establishment, cared not how soon that establishment were gained.*—PRIDE AND PREJUDICE, JANE AUSTEN
2 a household
• *As chief of my lady's establishment, I couldn't allow this sort of loose talk about a servant of ours.*—THE MOONSTONE, WILKIE COLLINS

estate NOUN
1 a condition, state, or category; a class or rank
• *ancient, handsome houses, now for the most part decayed from their high estate*—THE STRANGE CASE OF DR JEKYLL AND MR HYDE, ROBERT LOUIS STEVENSON
• *a man of his low estate*—RIP VAN WINKLE, WASHINGTON IRVING
2 a property; land with one or more buildings
• *a small estate of two or three farms*—JANE EYRE, CHARLOTTE BRONTË
3 a person's wealth
• *Four thousand a year is a pretty estate.*—MANSFIELD PARK, JANE AUSTEN

esteem VERB
1 to respect and admire someone
• *I know that you could be neither happy nor respectable, unless you truly esteemed your husband.*—PRIDE AND PREJUDICE, JANE AUSTEN
2 to have a particular opinion of something
• *I do not know whether I ever before mentioned to you my feelings on this subject, but … I trust you will not esteem them unreasonable.*—PRIDE AND PREJUDICE, JANE AUSTEN
➤ **estimation** NOUN • *an opinion I am very far from agreeing with you in your estimation of ladies in general*—PRIDE AND PREJUDICE, JANE AUSTEN

estrange VERB
to separate people or cause them to be no longer friendly
• *He is estranged from our eldest son and daughter.*—DAVID COPPERFIELD, CHARLES DICKENS

Etiquette

Etiquette guides detailed how men and women were expected to behave and gave advice on the correct ways to dress on different occasions, how to entertain guests, and how to greet people. At social functions, men and women who had not previously met had to be formally introduced by a mutual acquaintance before they could dance together. Anyone breaking the rules of etiquette could find themselves excluded from polite society. One of the bestselling etiquette guides, *Mrs Beeton's Book of Household Management*, sold two million copies in the decade following its publication in 1861.

---

evanescent ADJECTIVE
quickly fading or disappearing; fleeting
• *The passion usually called [love] is evanescent as steam.*—FAR FROM THE MADDING CROWD, THOMAS HARDY

Eve NOUN
➢ **daughter of Eve**: a woman or girl, often (but not necessarily) a morally weak one

evenfall NOUN
the start of the evening; dusk
• *Having sufficiently rested they proceeded on their way at evenfall.*—THE MAYOR OF CASTERBRIDGE, THOMAS HARDY

eventide NOUN
the end of the day; evening
• *The overshadowing trees and the approach of eventide enveloped them in gloom.*—FAR FROM THE MADDING CROWD, THOMAS HARDY

ever ADVERB (see also **anon**)
always
• *But he was ever ready to listen to me.*—GREAT EXPECTATIONS, CHARLES DICKENS

evils NOUN
➢ **have the evils**: to be unwell • *Mary had her evils; but upon the whole, as was evident by her staying so long, she had found more to enjoy than to suffer.*—PERSUASION, JANE AUSTEN

evince VERB
to show a quality or feeling
• *After eating and drinking, Susan 'evinced a disposition to swear eternal friendship'.*—DOMBEY AND SON, CHARLES DICKENS
• *Catherine evinced a child's annoyance at this neglect.*—WUTHERING HEIGHTS, EMILY BRONTË

ewer NOUN
a large water jug
• *a washing-stand, with ewers and basins, and soap and brushes, and towels*—WATER BABIES, CHARLES KINGSLEY

exaction NOUN
the demanding of something, especially a payment, from someone
• *[Caroline] mused over the mystery of 'business,' tried ... to understand its perplexities, liabilities, duties, exactions.*—SHIRLEY, CHARLOTTE BRONTË

exceeding ADVERB
extremely
• *We came at last to the foot of an exceeding steep wood.*—KIDNAPPED, ROBERT LOUIS STEVENSON

exceeding ADJECTIVE
very great
• *'You will be better presently, Lucretia!' repeated Mrs Chick, with exceeding scorn.*—DOMBEY AND SON, CHARLES DICKENS

excellence NOUN
an excellent feature or quality
• *A beadle can be said to be 'possessed of all the excellences and best qualities of humanity'.*—OLIVER TWIST, CHARLES DICKENS

except CONJUNCTION
unless
• *[He was] promised arrest as a vagrant except he moved on promptly.*—THE PRINCE AND THE PAUPER, MARK TWAIN

excessive ADJECTIVE
extreme; very great
• *The cold is excessive.*—FRANKENSTEIN, MARY SHELLEY
➤ **excessively** ADVERB • *Well, how excessively charming that is!*—DOMBEY AND SON, CHARLES DICKENS

exchequer NOUN
the money belonging to a person or group
• *'[Mr Kidderminster] presided on this occasion over the exchequer'—meaning he was in charge of taking money at the door.*—HARD TIMES, CHARLES DICKENS

excise NOUN
1 tax charged on particular goods
• *Surely good liquor would never be stored in so shy a place if it ever had paid the excise.*—MOONFLEET, J. MEADE FALKNER
2 a government organization responsible for collecting tax on particular goods
• *Some of the Excise had got wind of our whereabouts.*—MOONFLEET, J. MEADE FALKNER

exciseman NOUN
an official whose job was to make sure people did not avoid excise (tax on goods), especially by smuggling
• *Under the site of the tree a square hole was revealed, and an exciseman went and looked down.*—WESSEX TALES, THOMAS HARDY

excite VERB
1 to agitate or upset someone
• *She continued either delirious or lethargic; and the doctor forbade everything which could painfully excite her.*—JANE EYRE, CHARLOTTE BRONTË
2 to cause or stir up a feeling
• *He excites at once my admiration and my pity.*—FRANKENSTEIN, MARY SHELLEY
➤ **excitement** ADJECTIVE agitation • *'I'm glad to hear it, sir,' said Marner, with gathering excitement.*—SILAS MARNER, GEORGE ELIOT

excrescence NOUN
1 a growth on someone's body or on a plant
• *the gentleman with the excrescence on his nose*—A CHRISTMAS CAROL, CHARLES DICKENS
2 an unpleasant additional thing
• *I was an excrescence on the entertainment.*—GREAT EXPECTATIONS, CHARLES DICKENS

execrate VERB
to express hatred for someone; to curse someone
• *Yet she appeared confident ... and did not tremble, although gazed on and execrated by thousands.*—FRANKENSTEIN, MARY SHELLEY

execration NOUN
hatred and cursing; an expression of hatred; a curse
• *a shower of mingled threats and execrations*—OLIVER TWIST, CHARLES DICKENS

execute VERB
to perform something; to carry something out
• *Now was the moment for her resolution to be executed.*—PRIDE AND PREJUDICE, JANE AUSTEN
➤ **execution** NOUN • *Your defects in writing ... you consider ... as proceeding from a rapidity of thought and carelessness of execution.*—PRIDE AND PREJUDICE, JANE AUSTEN

executor (say ig-zek-yuh-tuhr, eg-zek-yuh-tuhr) NOUN
the person legally responsible for making sure that a dead person's will was carried out
• *Scrooge knew he was dead? Of course he did. ... Scrooge was his sole executor.*—A CHRISTMAS CAROL, CHARLES DICKENS

exercise to express

exercise VERB
to make use of a power, right, or ability
• [Mr Collins] was at the same time exercising great self-denial.—PRIDE AND PREJUDICE, JANE AUSTEN

exhort VERB
to urge or encourage someone to do something
• He was then exhorted not to hide his sin, but to confess.—SILAS MARNER, GEORGE ELIOT
• Startop … exhorted him to be a little more agreeable.—GREAT EXPECTATIONS, CHARLES DICKENS
➤ **exhortation** NOUN • [Agatha was] more cheerful after having listened to the exhortations of her father.—FRANKENSTEIN, MARY SHELLEY
• Dolly's exhortation … was uttered in the soothing persuasive tone with which she would have tried to prevail on a sick man to take his medicine.—SILAS MARNER, GEORGE ELIOT

exigency NOUN
urgency; an urgent need or emergency
• The exigency of affairs was helping her to forget for a time the terrible experience of the night.—DRACULA, BRAM STOKER
• I … offered her a purse for immediate exigencies.—JANE EYRE, CHARLOTTE BRONTË

exiguity (say eg-zig-yoo-it-i) NOUN
a small amount; scarcity
• an exiguity of cloth—SILAS MARNER, GEORGE ELIOT

exordium NOUN
the introductory part of a speech or piece of writing
• The Captain asked for attention 'in a short complimentary exordium, [then] narrated the whole history of Uncle Sol's departure'.—DOMBEY AND SON, CHARLES DICKENS

exotic NOUN
a tropical or foreign plant
• He strove to shelter her, as a fair exotic is sheltered by the gardener.—FRANKENSTEIN, MARY SHELLEY

expatiate VERB
to speak or write in detail about something
• Ralph proceeded to expatiate on … the case.—NICHOLAS NICKLEBY, CHARLES DICKENS

expectations NOUN
the prospect of inheriting wealth
• I am the daughter of a gentleman … and though my father is not rich, I have expectations from an uncle.—VILLETTE, CHARLOTTE BRONTË
USAGE The title of Charles Dickens' novel *Great Expectations* refers to this meaning of the word, as well as to the more general meaning that is still used today.

expedite VERB
to make something happen more quickly
• It only remained … to secure and expedite a marriage.—PRIDE AND PREJUDICE, JANE AUSTEN

expedition NOUN
speed; promptness
• Miss La Creevy finished her breakfast with great expedition.—NICHOLAS NICKLEBY, CHARLES DICKENS

expiate VERB
to make amends for something bad you have done, especially by suffering
• Will she forget what she knows of … my sordid schemes? Will she let me expiate these things?—SHIRLEY, CHARLOTTE BRONTË
➤ **expiation** NOUN • Caroline had to repair stockings every day 'by way of penance for the expiation of her sins'.—SHIRLEY, CHARLOTTE BRONTË

expose VERB
➤ **expose yourself:**
1 to make yourself look foolish
Elizabeth [trembled] lest her mother should be exposing herself again.—PRIDE AND PREJUDICE, JANE AUSTEN
2 to make yourself vulnerable to something
I reflect that you are … exposing yourself to the same dangers which have rendered me what I am.—FRANKENSTEIN, MARY SHELLEY
3 to reveal your presence
I'll be very careful not to expose myself.—THE CORAL ISLAND, R. M. BALLANTYNE

exposition NOUN
an explanation
• Dolly's exposition of her simple … theology fell rather unmeaningly on Silas's ears.—SILAS MARNER, GEORGE ELIOT

expostulation NOUN
the expression of strong disapproval
• I could hear Mrs Hudson, our landlady, raising her voice in a wail of expostulation and dismay.—THE SIGN OF FOUR, ARTHUR CONAN DOYLE
• [I disregarded] her expostulations at my rudeness.—WUTHERING HEIGHTS, EMILY BRONTË

express NOUN
1 a messenger that delivered a message very quickly; the message delivered
• An express came at twelve last night.—PRIDE AND PREJUDICE, JANE AUSTEN
2 a type of rifle
• [He] had an express … in his hand.—KING SOLOMON'S MINES, H. RIDER HAGGARD

express ADJECTIVE
1 exact; precise
- *his son ... who was his express image*—A TALE OF TWO CITIES, CHARLES DICKENS

2 special; particular
- *At present, the Squire had only given an express welcome to the heads of families.*—SILAS MARNER, GEORGE ELIOT

express ADVERB
especially
- *Had it made for me, express!*—GREAT EXPECTATIONS, CHARLES DICKENS

extemporized ADJECTIVE
done or made without planning or preparation; improvised
- *Tufts and garlands of green foliage decorated the walls, beams, and extemporized chandeliers.*—FAR FROM THE MADDING CROWD, THOMAS HARDY

extenuation NOUN
the lessening or partial excusing of a crime or bad behaviour
- *[Ginevra] may justly proffer the plea of ignorance in extenuation of most of her faults.*—VILLETTE, CHARLOTTE BRONTË

extinguisher NOUN
a conical device for snuffing out a candle, lamp, or torch
- *The Spirit has 'a bright clear jet of light' from its head, and 'a great extinguisher for a cap ... held under its arm'.*—A CHRISTMAS CAROL, CHARLES DICKENS

extort VERB
to extract or get information from someone or something
- *She did at last extort from her father an acknowledgement that the horses were engaged.*—PRIDE AND PREJUDICE, JANE AUSTEN

USAGE In modern English, you might expect money, rather than information or a promise, to be *extorted* from someone.

Ff

FAMINE

In **1815**, Parliament passed the Corn Laws to protect British farmers from cheaper imports of grain from overseas. This pushed up the prices of staple foods like bread and led to food shortages and outbreaks of starvation. The **1840s** became known as the 'Hungry Forties'. In Ireland between 1845 and 1852, failures of the potato crop and poor management led to the death from starvation of more than one million people. This period is now known as the **Great Famine**.

fable NOUN
an untrue story
• *They have written to me that you are to marry Kenn. As if I should believe that! Perhaps they have told you some such fables about me.*—THE MILL ON THE FLOSS, GEORGE ELIOT

factious ADJECTIVE
showing, resulting from, or causing division or disagreement
• *your factious purposes*—A CHRISTMAS CAROL, CHARLES DICKENS

faculty NOUN
a mental power
• *I ardently desired to understand them, and bent every faculty towards that purpose.*—FRANKENSTEIN, MARY SHELLEY

fag VERB
to work hard at something tiring or boring
• *I fagged away at German.*—JANE EYRE, CHARLOTTE BRONTË
➤ **fagged** ADJECTIVE exhausted • *Every body seemed rather fagged after the morning's party.*—EMMA, JANE AUSTEN

➤ **fagging** NOUN tiring or boring work • *[I was] accustomed ... to a life of ceaseless reprimand and thankless fagging.*—JANE EYRE, CHARLOTTE BRONTË
USAGE The words *fag* and *fagging* were also used with reference to the practice in boarding schools of younger boys doing jobs for older pupils.

faggot (also **fagot**) NOUN
a bundle of sticks tied together
• *[He saw] an old woman with a heavy bundle of faggots on her back.*—THE PINK FAIRY BOOK, ANDREW LANG

fain ADJECTIVE
1 wanting to do something; willing
• *[He played] tunes of my own south country that made me fain to be home from my adventures.*—KIDNAPPED, ROBERT LOUIS STEVENSON
2 obliged; forced
• *But the room was dark; and as she made no answer to his call, he was fain to go back for the lamp.*—DOMBEY AND SON, CHARLES DICKENS

fain ADVERB
willingly; gladly
• *I've never spoken a word to him, or set eyes on him; though I'd fain have done so.*—MARY BARTON, ELIZABETH GASKELL

fair ADJECTIVE
1 beautiful
• *It was as sweet and fair a view as I have ever seen.*—THE TIME MACHINE, H. G. WELLS
2 favourable
• *[The couple] entered the neighbourhood with the usual fair report of being very respectable, agreeable people.*—MANSFIELD PARK, JANE AUSTEN
➤ **by fair means**: without violence • *If a horse 'can't be broken in by fair means, she will never be good for anything'.*—BLACK BEAUTY, ANNA SEWELL
➤ **in a fair way**: seeming likely to do something; well on the way to something • *[If] we could find that spot, we should be in a fair way towards finding what the secret was.*—THE MEMOIRS OF SHERLOCK HOLMES, ARTHUR CONAN DOYLE
USAGE *Fair* is often contrasted with *foul*.
• *For thirty years ... I've sailed the seas, and seen good and bad ... fair weather and foul.*—TREASURE ISLAND, ROBERT LOUIS STEVENSON

fair ADVERB
1 simply; truly—used for emphasis
• *I cannae draw [a sword] upon ye, David. It's fair murder.*—KIDNAPPED, ROBERT LOUIS STEVENSON
• *I fair hate pride.*—SHIRLEY, CHARLOTTE BRONTË
2 favourably; pleasantly
• *And when they were through, the king ... spoke them fair and gave each man three guineas.*—KIDNAPPED, ROBERT LOUIS STEVENSON

fair-spoken *to* faugh

fair-spoken ADJECTIVE
polite and pleasant
• *Well, sir, you have been very fair-spoken to me.*
—THE SIGN OF FOUR, ARTHUR CONAN DOYLE

Fairy Tales

In Germany in the early 1800s, the Brothers Grimm published traditional folk stories and fairy tales, establishing the versions of stories such as *Cinderella* and *Hansel and Gretel* that we know today. They were translated into English in 1823, followed later by translations of fairy tales by the Danish author Hans Christian Andersen including *The Little Mermaid*. Although the cautionary tales collected by the Brothers Grimm were not originally intended for young readers, Hans Christian Andersen's stories were expressly written for children, which helped to create today's view of fairy tales as children's stories.

---

fakir NOUN
a Muslim or Hindu holy man who lived as a beggar

fancy VERB
to think or imagine something
• *It isn't what you fancy; it is not as bad as that.*
—THE STRANGE CASE OF DR JEKYLL AND MR HYDE, ROBERT LOUIS STEVENSON

fancy NOUN
1 imagination
• *Scrooge had as little of what is called fancy about him as any man in the City of London.*—A CHRISTMAS CAROL, CHARLES DICKENS
2 an idea, often a foolish one
• *I read and studied the wild fancies of these writers with delight.*—FRANKENSTEIN, MARY SHELLEY
➤ **the fancy**: boxers or boxing enthusiasts
• *The prize-fighter compliments Sherlock Holmes's punch and tells him, 'You might have aimed high, if you had joined the fancy'.*—THE SIGN OF FOUR, ARTHUR CONAN DOYLE
➤ **to my fancy**: in my opinion • *To my fancy, it is only because he does not rattle away like other young men.*—PRIDE AND PREJUDICE, JANE AUSTEN

fancy ADJECTIVE
created from someone's imagination
• *Eliza, such as we have described her, is not a fancy sketch, but taken from remembrance.*—UNCLE TOM'S CABIN, HARRIET BEECHER STOWE

fantastic (also **fantastical**) ADJECTIVE
strange or unreal; seeming to be from fantasy rather than reality
• *I don't think I could rest until I know more of this fantastic business.*—THE SIGN OF FOUR, ARTHUR CONAN DOYLE
➤ **fantastically** ADVERB • *masked figures fantastically dressed*—THE STORY OF A BAD BOY, THOMAS BAILEY ALDRICH

farthing NOUN
a coin worth a quarter of an old penny
USAGE The word *farthing* was used meaning 'the smallest amount'.
• *He left me without a farthing.*—WESSEX TALES, THOMAS HARDY

farthingale NOUN
hoops or a pad of fabric worn under a skirt to give it a wider shape
• *A banner 'depicted Queen Elizabeth herself … in ample ruff and farthingale'.*—WESTWARD HO!, CHARLES KINGSLEY

fasces (say **fass-eez**) NOUN
a bundle of sticks or a symbol like a bundle of sticks

fastness NOUN
a secure place well protected by natural features
• *great jagged mountain fastnesses*—DRACULA, BRAM STOKER

fatal ADJECTIVE
to do with destiny; fateful
• *That night I had come to the fatal cross-roads.*
—THE STRANGE CASE OF DR JEKYLL AND MR HYDE, ROBERT LOUIS STEVENSON
➤ **fatality** NOUN fate or destiny; a twist of fate
• *The same fatality which had made me just one day too late in calling on Sergeant Cuff, made me again one day too late in calling on Godfrey.*—THE MOONSTONE, WILKIE COLLINS

Fata Morgana NOUN
a mirage
🏛 Italian *fata*, meaning 'fairy' + *Morgana*, the sister of King Arthur, who was said to have seen a mirage near Sicily

fatigue NOUN
a tiring experience
• *My father [was] fearful that I could not sustain the fatigues of a journey.*—FRANKENSTEIN, MARY SHELLEY

faugh EXCLAMATION
an exclamation of disgust
• *Faugh! It sickens me to think of it.*—DRACULA, BRAM STOKER

fealty to ferule

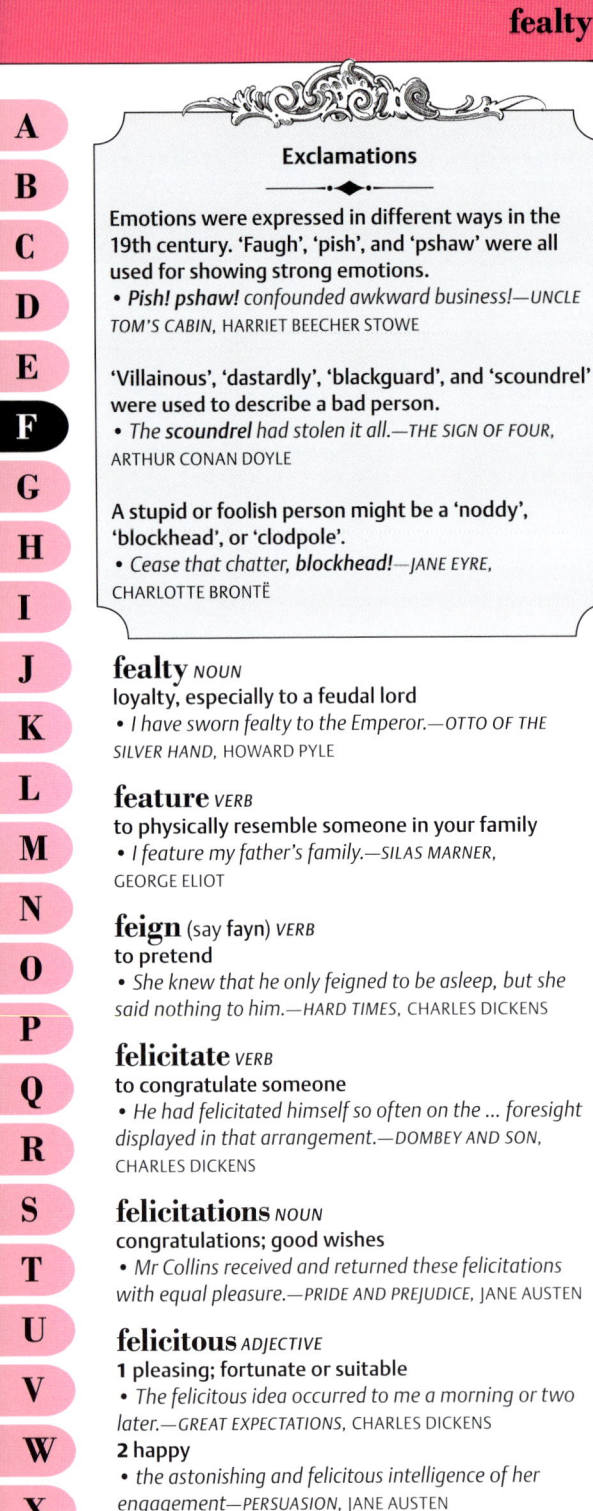

> ### Exclamations
>
> Emotions were expressed in different ways in the 19th century. 'Faugh', 'pish', and 'pshaw' were all used for showing strong emotions.
> - *Pish! pshaw!* confounded awkward business!—UNCLE TOM'S CABIN, HARRIET BEECHER STOWE
>
> 'Villainous', 'dastardly', 'blackguard', and 'scoundrel' were used to describe a bad person.
> - The *scoundrel* had stolen it all.—THE SIGN OF FOUR, ARTHUR CONAN DOYLE
>
> A stupid or foolish person might be a 'noddy', 'blockhead', or 'clodpole'.
> - Cease that chatter, *blockhead!*—JANE EYRE, CHARLOTTE BRONTË

fealty NOUN
loyalty, especially to a feudal lord
- I have sworn fealty to the Emperor.—OTTO OF THE SILVER HAND, HOWARD PYLE

feature VERB
to physically resemble someone in your family
- I feature my father's family.—SILAS MARNER, GEORGE ELIOT

feign (say fayn) VERB
to pretend
- She knew that he only feigned to be asleep, but she said nothing to him.—HARD TIMES, CHARLES DICKENS

felicitate VERB
to congratulate someone
- He had felicitated himself so often on the … foresight displayed in that arrangement.—DOMBEY AND SON, CHARLES DICKENS

felicitations NOUN
congratulations; good wishes
- Mr Collins received and returned these felicitations with equal pleasure.—PRIDE AND PREJUDICE, JANE AUSTEN

felicitous ADJECTIVE
1 pleasing; fortunate or suitable
- The felicitous idea occurred to me a morning or two later.—GREAT EXPECTATIONS, CHARLES DICKENS
2 happy
- the astonishing and felicitous intelligence of her engagement—PERSUASION, JANE AUSTEN

felicity NOUN
1 happiness
- Have you any thing else to propose for my domestic felicity?—PRIDE AND PREJUDICE, JANE AUSTEN
2 a fortunate or pleasing thing
- So often … she had heard them wish for a ball at home as the greatest of all felicities.—MANSFIELD PARK, JANE AUSTEN

fell ADJECTIVE
deadly; ferocious; evil
- [He] twisted innocent events and things, and wrenched them to the same fell purpose.—DOMBEY AND SON, CHARLES DICKENS

felon NOUN
an abscess next to a fingernail or toenail
- I had a felon on my thumb.—FAR FROM THE MADDING CROWD, THOMAS HARDY

felon ADJECTIVE
wicked; cruel
- 'That was a felon stroke!' exclaimed the Black Knight.—IVANHOE, WALTER SCOTT

feminity NOUN
1 the fact of being female. The modern word 'femininity' has an extra syllable.
- Bathsheba 'strove miserably against this feminity which would insist upon supplying unbidden emotions'—meaning she felt emotions she did not want to feel.—FAR FROM THE MADDING CROWD, THOMAS HARDY
2 women
- Moore keeps his own supplies of food and drink so as 'not to be dependent on the feminity in the cottage yonder'.—SHIRLEY, CHARLOTTE BRONTË

fend NOUN
to care for or support someone
- I've always thought of a little home where he'd sit i' the corner, and I should fend and do everything for him.—SILAS MARNER, GEORGE ELIOT

fender NOUN
1 a frame around a fireplace
- She took her feet off the fender.—OLIVER TWIST, CHARLES DICKENS
2 a piece of rope or other material protecting the side of a boat from knocks
- the clearer river, where the ships' boys might take their fenders in—GREAT EXPECTATIONS, CHARLES DICKENS

ferule NOUN
a ruler with a wide end, used for punishing schoolchildren
- Mr Hall says 'Henry, you merit the ferule.'—meaning he deserves to be hit with it.—SHIRLEY, CHARLOTTE BRONTË

🏛 Latin *ferula*, meaning 'giant fennel', whose stalk was used in Roman times to beat people

fervid *to* filmy

fervid ADJECTIVE
very enthusiastic; passionate
• *'I do love you, Tess … !' he said, tightening his arms round her with fervid pressure.*—TESS OF THE D'URBERVILLES, THOMAS HARDY

fess VERB
to confess
• *I shall tell them, myself, all about it, and 'fess' to Mother how silly I've been.*—LITTLE WOMEN, LOUISA M. ALCOTT

festal ADJECTIVE
relating to a celebration; festive
• *One day the Boy, on walking in to the village, found everything wearing a festal appearance.*—DREAM DAYS, KENNETH GRAHAME

festoon NOUN
a curved decoration of flowers, draped fabric, etc.
• *The walls and ceilings were gilded and painted … crimson drapery hung in festoons from window, door, and mirror.*—DOMBEY AND SON, CHARLES DICKENS

fetch VERB
to give a sigh or take a breath
• *He … fetched a deep breath, and sat down in a chair with his hand before his face.*—DOMBEY AND SON, CHARLES DICKENS
➤ **fetch your breath:** to catch your breath; to get your breath back • *Mrs MacStinger stopped to fetch her breath.*—DOMBEY AND SON, CHARLES DICKENS

fetid ADJECTIVE
smelling unpleasant
• *The air of the room was fetid with stale tobacco smoke.*—THE RETURN OF SHERLOCK HOLMES, ARTHUR CONAN DOYLE

fetishism NOUN
worship of objects, called *fetishes*, believed to have magical or spiritual powers; belief in these powers
• *Eliot refers to the belief in 'the gods of the hearth' as 'that fetishism'.*—SILAS MARNER, GEORGE ELIOT
➤ **fetishistic** ADJECTIVE • *A curious fetishistic fear of this grimy [book] … prevented her ever allowing it to stay in the house all night.*—TESS OF THE D'URBERVILLES, THOMAS HARDY

fetter NOUN
1 a chain put on a prisoner, usually around the ankle
• *Afterwards the heavy fetters that were put about our ankles set up sores.*—MOONFLEET, J. MEADE FALKNER
2 a restriction on someone's freedom
• *At school on Mondays, Tom felt the weekend 'made the going into captivity and fetters again so much more odious'.*—THE ADVENTURES OF TOM SAWYER, MARK TWAIN

fetter VERB
1 to put someone in chains
• *Scrooge says to the chained spectre, 'You are fettered. … Tell me why?'*—A CHRISTMAS CAROL, CHARLES DICKENS
2 to restrict; to confine
• *The footprints show 'toes never fettered by boots, naked feet'.*—THE SIGN OF FOUR, ARTHUR CONAN DOYLE

feverish ADJECTIVE
agitated; excited
• *The lawyer listened gloomily; he did not like his friend's feverish manner.*—THE STRANGE CASE OF DR JEKYLL AND MR HYDE, ROBERT LOUIS STEVENSON
➤ **feverishly** ADVERB • *He walked feverishly up and down the platform.*—AROUND THE WORLD IN EIGHTY DAYS, JULES VERNE

fey ADJECTIVE
1 mysterious; with supernatural or clairvoyant powers
2 close to death

fiacre (say fee-aa-kruh) NOUN
a small horse-drawn carriage with four wheels, that could be hired
• *Between us we procured a fiacre and brought you here.*—VILLETTE, CHARLOTTE BRONTË

fie EXCLAMATION
an expression of strong disapproval or disagreement
• *Pooh, pooh, Madam! Fie for shame! You're absurd.*—DOMBEY AND SON, CHARLES DICKENS

fiend NOUN
a demon, monster, or wicked person
• *Mrs Reed … gazed at me as if she really did not know whether I were child or fiend.*—JANE EYRE, CHARLOTTE BRONTË
➤ **the fiend:** the devil • *I tell thee, the fiend can impose diseases … in order to bring into credit some diabolical fashion of cure.*—IVANHOE, WALTER SCOTT

filbert NOUN
a type of hazelnut; a cob nut
• *the Sunday dessert … of fresh filberts, apples, and pears*—SILAS MARNER, GEORGE ELIOT

fillip NOUN
a push; a boost
• *Socially he had received a startling fillip downwards.*—THE MAYOR OF CASTERBRIDGE, THOMAS HARDY

filmy ADJECTIVE
1 covered with a thin film
• *On the table 'stood the two full glasses of untasted wine, now flat and filmy'.*—TESS OF THE D'URBERVILLES, THOMAS HARDY

fingerpost to flip

2 vague; insubstantial
• Mr Toots had a filmy something in his mind, which led him to conclude that … he would be fortunate and blest.—DOMBEY AND SON, CHARLES DICKENS

fingerpost NOUN
a signpost on a road pointing in the direction of nearby places
• And there was a finger-post at the corner, … 'To St. Ogg's, 2 miles.'—THE MILL ON THE FLOSS, GEORGE ELIOT

finished ADJECTIVE
accomplished; perfect; excellent
• She was, at such crises, sadly deficient in finished manner.—SHIRLEY, CHARLOTTE BRONTË

fire VERB
to suddenly become very angry or excited; to flush with anger or excitement
• She fired when she asked the last question, and she slapped my face … when I answered it.—GREAT EXPECTATIONS, CHARLES DICKENS
➢ **fire up:** to become flushed with emotion • I felt my face fire up as I looked at Joe.—GREAT EXPECTATIONS, CHARLES DICKENS

fire-irons NOUN
tools including a poker, tongs, and a shovel, kept near a fireplace
• The floor was spotless; the grate and fire-irons were burnished bright.—JANE EYRE, CHARLOTTE BRONTË

firelock NOUN
a musket (an old-fashioned gun with a long barrel) which fired using sparks
• One of them snatched my firelock up and levelled it at my head.—THE SIGN OF FOUR, ARTHUR CONAN DOYLE

firmament NOUN
the sky; the heavens
• The desert looks 'as alien to man as the star-studded firmament above'.—KING SOLOMON'S MINES, H. RIDER HAGGARD

fix VERB
1 to win someone's affection or loyalty; to win a man as a husband
• If a woman conceals her affection … from the object of it, she may lose the opportunity of fixing him.—PRIDE AND PREJUDICE, JANE AUSTEN
2 to stare at someone
• He continued to fix me.—THE TURN OF THE SCREW, HENRY JAMES
3 to take revenge on someone; to kill someone
• I'll fix you!—TRUE TO HIMSELF; OR, ROGER STRONG'S STRUGGLE FOR PLACE, EDWARD STRATEMEYER

flag NOUN
a flat paving stone; a flagstone
• Poole stamped on the flags of the corridor.—THE STRANGE CASE OF DR JEKYLL AND MR HYDE, ROBERT LOUIS STEVENSON

flagstaff NOUN
a flagpole

flambeau NOUN (PLURAL flambeaux)
a burning torch

flaxen ADJECTIVE
1 blonde
• Tom had 'flaxen hair, blue eyes, … and fair complexion'.—AGNES GREY, ANNE BRONTË
2 made from the flax plant
• The shepherd believed 'the bag held nothing but flaxen thread'.—SILAS MARNER, GEORGE ELIOT

fleckered ADJECTIVE
with uneven patches of colour or light; streaked or dappled
• the fleckered shade of the ash tree—SILAS MARNER, GEORGE ELIOT

flexuous ADJECTIVE
curving; bending
• Miss Templeman deposited herself on the sofa in her former flexuous position.—THE MAYOR OF CASTERBRIDGE, THOMAS HARDY

flight NOUN
1 the act of fleeing; escape
• As yet my flight, I was sure, was undiscovered.—JANE EYRE, CHARLOTTE BRONTË
2 used for talking about the rapid passing of time
• He took no note of the flight of time, but worked tranquilly on.—THE PRINCE AND THE PAUPER, MARK TWAIN

flinders NOUN
➢ **all to flinders:** into many small pieces
• You mean to say our old raft warn't smashed all to flinders?—THE ADVENTURES OF HUCKLEBERRY FINN, MARK TWAIN

flint NOUN
a piece of rock used with a metal rod (called a 'steel') to produce sparks for making a fire
• Scrooge is described as 'Hard and sharp as flint, from which no steel had ever struck out generous fire'.—A CHRISTMAS CAROL, CHARLES DICKENS

flip NOUN
a hot sweetened alcoholic drink
• We had a hot supper … and we had some flip to finish with.—GREAT EXPECTATIONS, CHARLES DICKENS

flog to forelock

flog VERB
to beat or whip a person or animal
- *A private [in the regiment] had been flogged.*
—PRIDE AND PREJUDICE, JANE AUSTEN
- *But then it seems disgraceful to be flogged.*
—JANE EYRE, CHARLOTTE BRONTË

floor-cloth NOUN
fabric used as a floor covering
- *the squares and diamonds of the floor-cloth*
—DOMBEY AND SON, CHARLES DICKENS

florin NOUN
an old British coin or a foreign gold or silver coin
- *[The old man] only left his widow and son two hundred florins.*—THE YELLOW FAIRY BOOK, ANDREW LANG

USAGE A *florin* can refer to various specific coins, for example the Dutch guilder or the British two-shilling coin. It was often used in fairy tales with a foreign or historical setting.

fluttered ADJECTIVE
flustered; agitated
- *He was so fluttered and so glowing with his good intentions, that his broken voice would scarcely answer to his call.*—A CHRISTMAS CAROL, CHARLES DICKENS

fly NOUN (PLURAL flys)
a carriage, typically one drawn by a single horse and hired out; when first introduced, flys were pulled or pushed by men
- *I ... hired a fly to take me to the town.*—THE WOMAN IN WHITE, WILKIE COLLINS

fob NOUN
a small pocket for a watch
- *Nickleby replaced his watch in his fob.*—NICHOLAS NICKLEBY, CHARLES DICKENS

foot NOUN
➢ **on foot:** under way; in progress • *May I ask whether you have any professional inquiry on foot at present?*—THE SIGN OF FOUR, ARTHUR CONAN DOYLE

foot VERB
➢ **foot it:**
1 to walk; to go on foot
- *[I] was resolved to give up further inquiry and foot it home.*—MOONFLEET, J. MEADE FALKNER
2 to dance; to perform dance steps
- *The boy danced a hornpipe, 'snapping his fingers in the air and footing it right cleverly'.*—KIDNAPPED, ROBERT LOUIS STEVENSON

footman NOUN
a male servant wearing a special uniform, who let in visitors and served meals in a home
- *Mrs Bennet was prevented replying by the entrance of the footman with a note for Miss Bennet.*—PRIDE AND PREJUDICE, JANE AUSTEN

COMPOUND WORDS Many words, like 'footman', consist of two or more words joined together. Sometimes you can guess the meaning from the context.
- *The coachman mounted his box and drove slowly off.*
—NICHOLAS NICKLEBY, CHARLES DICKENS

Sometimes you may need to look up the first word.
- *But the turnpike-man gave him a meal.*—OLIVER TWIST, CHARLES DICKENS

footpad NOUN
a highwayman who robbed people on foot rather than riding a horse
- *The lanes and fields ... were at that time ... infested with footpads and with highwaymen.*—LORNA DOONE, R. D. BLACKMORE

forbye ADVERB
in addition; as well
- *To be sure there are fords, and a bridge forbye.*
—KIDNAPPED, ROBERT LOUIS STEVENSON

forebode VERB
to sense something bad; to have a premonition of something
- *'Well!' asked Cornelius, foreboding some mischief.*
—THE BLACK TULIP, ALEXANDRE DUMAS

forecastle (also fo'csle) (say fohk-suhl) NOUN
1 the front part of a ship below the deck, where the crew slept
- *Down into the forecastle then, down with ye, I'll keep ye there till ye're sick of it.*—MOBY DICK, HERMAN MELVILLE
2 in the past, a raised deck at the front of a ship
- *As the Danes approached, the archers on the forecastle opened a destructive fire upon them.*
—THE DRAGON AND THE RAVEN, G. A. HENTY

foredoomed ADJECTIVE
fated; doomed in advance
- *They were foredoomed to die, and they knew the truth.*—KING SOLOMON'S MINES, H. RIDER HAGGARD

forego (also forgo) VERB
to do without something; to give something up
- *[The idea] that he should forego any enjoyment on her account gave her pain.*—MANSFIELD PARK, JANE AUSTEN

forelock NOUN
a lock of hair falling over a person's or horse's forehead
- *The figure seized the horse by the forelock, and led it to the corner of the field.*—FAR FROM THE MADDING CROWD, THOMAS HARDY

USAGE Men would *touch their forelock* as a sign of respect to a person of high social standing.

form *to* frock

• 'Please, sir,' he said, touching his forelock, 'I have the cab downstairs.'—A STUDY IN SCARLET, ARTHUR CONAN DOYLE

form NOUN
a bench
• lines of plain deal forms and desks —A CHRISTMAS CAROL, CHARLES DICKENS
➢ **in due form / in form:** according to a rule or custom • The visit was returned in due form. —PRIDE AND PREJUDICE, JANE AUSTEN

forth ADVERB
forwards; out from somewhere
• [Catherine's] fingers grasped the handle of a drawer and drew it forth.—NORTHANGER ABBEY, JANE AUSTEN

forthwith ADVERB
at once; immediately
• The Captain ... disappearing for a few moments, forthwith returned in the blue suit.—DOMBEY AND SON, CHARLES DICKENS

fortin NOUN
a fortune
• Why, old Mr Lammeter had a pretty fortin, didn't they say, when he come into these parts?—SILAS MARNER, GEORGE ELIOT

fosse NOUN
a long, narrow trench, usually dug as a defence
• [The] fosse is spanned by a primitive drawbridge, which was let down by the guard to allow us to pass in. —KING SOLOMON'S MINES, H. RIDER HAGGARD

foul ADJECTIVE
filthy; polluted
• The ways were foul and narrow; the shops and houses wretched.—A CHRISTMAS CAROL, CHARLES DICKENS
USAGE Foul is often contrasted with *fair*.
• For thirty years ... I've sailed the seas, and seen good and bad ... fair weather and foul.—TREASURE ISLAND, ROBERT LOUIS STEVENSON

foul VERB
to make something dirty; to pollute something
• Scamp that I was to foul that innocent life!—TESS OF THE D'URBERVILLES, THOMAS HARDY

fount NOUN
1 a source of something good
• The school at Casterbridge is referred to as a 'fount of knowledge'.—WESSEX TALES, THOMAS HARDY
2 a water source; a spring
• Water from the town pump 'was purer from that original fount than from their own wells'.—THE MAYOR OF CASTERBRIDGE, THOMAS HARDY

fountain-head NOUN
the original source of something
• Why not question the housekeeper? ... Why not go ... to the fountain-head of information at once? —THE WOMAN IN WHITE, WILKIE COLLINS

frame NOUN
1 a person's body
• The human frame could no longer support the agonies that I endured.—FRANKENSTEIN, MARY SHELLEY
2 a person's mood or mindset
• And ... you shall say that we have sent him to you in the best health and in the happiest frame.—A TALE OF TWO CITIES, CHARLES DICKENS

fratch NOUN
a quarrel; a disagreement
• I ha' never had no fratch afore, sin ever I were born, wi' any o' my like.—HARD TIMES, CHARLES DICKENS

freak NOUN
a whim; a tendency to think or act strangely
• What do you mean by such freaks, young fellow? —SILAS MARNER, GEORGE ELIOT

free ADJECTIVE
➢ **make free:** to behave in an over-familiar or disrespectful manner; to help yourself too freely to something • You'll excuse my takin' the liberty, Miss,—I thought I'd make free to buy it for you. —THE MILL ON THE FLOSS, GEORGE ELIOT

French plum NOUN
a prune
• The French plums blushed in modest tartness from their highly-decorated boxes.—A CHRISTMAS CAROL, CHARLES DICKENS

fretted ADJECTIVE
patterned, especially with patterns cut through or into a surface
• a fretted screen—SILAS MARNER, GEORGE ELIOT

frieze NOUN
thick woollen cloth
• a cloak of grey frieze—JANE EYRE, CHARLOTTE BRONTË

frightfully ADVERB
1 horribly; frighteningly
• The Magician stamped loudly with his feet, glared frightfully out of his green eyes.—THE GREEN FAIRY BOOK, ANDREW LANG
2 extremely
• I am frightfully confused regarding time and place. —A TALE OF TWO CITIES, CHARLES DICKENS

frock NOUN
1 a dress
• My darling ... you wear that pretty black frock in remembrance of your Mama.—DOMBEY AND SON, CHARLES DICKENS

frock coat to futurity

USAGE Frocks were worn by young children of both sexes, sometimes over trousers.
• *Is there any one who can recover the experience of his childhood ... of what he liked and disliked when he was in frock and trousers?* —THE MILL ON THE FLOSS, GEORGE ELIOT
2 a smock worn by a farm worker
• *the countryman in his clay-stained frock* —PAVED WITH GOLD, AUGUSTUS MAYHEW

frock coat NOUN
a long, double-breasted man's coat
• *The man wears 'a very shiny hat and oppressively respectable frock-coat'.* —THE ADVENTURES OF SHERLOCK HOLMES, ARTHUR CONAN DOYLE

frogged ADJECTIVE
with frogging (a fastening or decoration with toggles and loops)
• *A tall, stout official ... in a peaked cap and frogged jacket* —THE ADVENTURES OF SHERLOCK HOLMES, ARTHUR CONAN DOYLE

front NOUN
1 a person's face or forehead
• *Anger crosses her front.* —SHIRLEY, CHARLOTTE BRONTË
2 (also **false front**)
a hairpiece worn by women at the front of their head
• *a crisp and glossy front* —THE MILL ON THE FLOSS, GEORGE ELIOT

froward ADJECTIVE
difficult in behaviour; stubborn or awkward
• *'Everybody knows how much I hate him.—Yes.' repeated the froward young person, 'HATE him!'* —FAR FROM THE MADDING CROWD, THOMAS HARDY

frowzy (also **frowsy**) ADJECTIVE
scruffy; looking neglected
• *There were frowzy fields, and cow-houses, and dunghills, and dustheaps.* —DOMBEY AND SON, CHARLES DICKENS

fuddled ADJECTIVE
confused; not thinking clearly
• *Myles [was] still fuddled with the fumes of sleep.* —MEN OF IRON, HOWARD PYLE

fugitive ADJECTIVE
quick to disappear; fleeting; elusive; transient
• *How evanescent, fugitive, fitful she looked.* —SHIRLEY, CHARLOTTE BRONTË

fugitive NOUN
someone who had escaped or was in hiding
• *Felix conducted the fugitives through France.* —FRANKENSTEIN, MARY SHELLEY

fugleman (say **fyoo**-guhl-muhn) NOUN
a soldier leading and keeping time in drilling exercises
• *In leading the crowd in cheering 'Slackbridge acted as fugleman, and gave the time'.* —HARD TIMES, CHARLES DICKENS

fulgent (say **ful**-juhnt) ADJECTIVE
shining brightly
• *When angry, Shirley's eyes are 'fulgent with quick-flashing fire'.* —SHIRLEY, CHARLOTTE BRONTË

functionary NOUN
a person with a particular function or post; a worker or an official
• *In her inexperience she knew little about jail functionaries.* —WESSEX TALES, THOMAS HARDY

funk NOUN
fear; a coward
• *What is he but funk and precautions?* —THE WAR OF THE WORLDS, H. G. WELLS

funk VERB
to avoid something because of fear
• *There's no sense in funking. If you don't go to-day, you must to-morrow.* —HIS FIRST OPERATION, ARTHUR CONAN DOYLE

furbish VERB
➢ **furbish up:** to make something old look newer; to polish something • *[Meg] fell to snipping and spoiling her clothes, in her attempts to furbish them up.* —LITTLE WOMEN, LOUISA M. ALCOTT

furnish VERB
to provide something for someone
• *A walk to Meryton was necessary to ... furnish conversation for the evening.* —PRIDE AND PREJUDICE, JANE AUSTEN
• *Silas, furnished with some old coverings, turned out with his two companions into the rain again.* —SILAS MARNER, GEORGE ELIOT

furze NOUN
gorse (a wild prickly bush with yellow flowers)
• *The furze bush was still there.* —SILAS MARNER, GEORGE ELIOT

fustian NOUN
a thick, hard-wearing cloth
• *The beer-drinkers were 'chiefly men in fustian jackets and smock-frocks'.* —SILAS MARNER, GEORGE ELIOT

futurity NOUN
future time; the future
• *Anne Elliot has 'a cheerful confidence in futurity'.* —PERSUASION, JANE AUSTEN

gage to gambling-house

Gg

GOTHIC

Gothic was a popular fiction genre in the early 1800s, with stories of innocent heroes or heroines finding themselves in strange places, plagued by sinister and supernatural events. This genre, with its elements of horror and death, increased in popularity in the late 1800s with **Robert Louis Stevenson's** *The Strange Case of Dr Jekyll and Mr Hyde* and **Bram Stoker's** *Dracula*.

gage NOUN
something given as a pledge; a token or sign
• *a gage of their reconciliation*—FAR FROM THE MADDING CROWD, THOMAS HARDY

gaiety NOUN
1 cheerfulness; happiness or fun
• *the lighthearted gaiety of boyhood*—FRANKENSTEIN, MARY SHELLEY
2 gaieties
entertainments; festivities
• *Flower-shows, operas, balls—there was a whole round of gaieties in prospect.*—THE MOONSTONE, WILKIE COLLINS

gall VERB
to make someone feel bitter, resentful, or irritated
• *I desire you to ... divert my thoughts, which are galled with dwelling on one point.*—JANE EYRE, CHARLOTTE BRONTË

gall NOUN
bitterness, resentment, or irritation; bile
• *Many times ... the bitter gall of envy rose within me.*—FRANKENSTEIN, MARY SHELLEY

gallant ADJECTIVE
impressive
• *a gallant sight*—THE MERRY ADVENTURES OF ROBIN HOOD, HOWARD PYLE
➤ **gallantly** ADVERB • *Peter Cratchit ... rejoiced to find himself so gallantly attired.*—A CHRISTMAS CAROL, CHARLES DICKENS

galley NOUN
1 a ship with sails and oars whose oarsmen were usually slaves or criminals. Being sent to the galleys was a known punishment.
• *The ... judge ... sentenced us to the galleys for life.*—MOONFLEET, J. MEADE FALKNER
2 a large rowing boat
• *I was taken on board the galley.* GREAT EXPECTATIONS, CHARLES DICKENS
3 a ship's kitchen

gallipot NOUN
a small pot or jar
🏛 Probably *galley* + *pot*, because gallipots were brought from the Mediterranean on board ships

gallows NOUN
a structure on which criminals were executed by hanging
• *I cared nothing for the law,—nothing for the gallows.*—THE SIGN OF FOUR, ARTHUR CONAN DOYLE

galvanic ADJECTIVE
1 produced by galvanism; electrical
• *a galvanic battery*—OLIVER TWIST, CHARLES DICKENS
2 shaking; twitchy
• *Don't be galvanic, sir!*—DAVID COPPERFIELD, CHARLES DICKENS

galvanism NOUN
electricity produced by a chemical reaction; the use of electrical stimulation
• *Perhaps a corpse would be re-animated; galvanism had given token of such things.*—INTRODUCTION TO FRANKENSTEIN, MARY SHELLEY
🏛 From the Italian scientist *Luigi Galvani*, who discovered that dead frogs' leg muscles twitched when stimulated by an electric current.

galvanize VERB
to use galvanism on someone
• *Sherlock Holmes sprang out of his chair as if he had been galvanized.*—THE ADVENTURES OF SHERLOCK HOLMES, ARTHUR CONAN DOYLE

gambling-house NOUN
a place where gambling took place
• *The regular attendants at the gambling-house were considered 'suspicious'.*—A TERRIBLY STRANGE BED, WILKIE COLLINS

game to geniality

game VERB
to gamble
• Compeyson betted and gamed.—GREAT EXPECTATIONS, CHARLES DICKENS
➤ **gaming** NOUN • [Wickham] had left gaming debts behind him.—PRIDE AND PREJUDICE, JANE AUSTEN

gamin NOUN
a child who lived on the streets; an urchin

gammon VERB
to deceive someone
• Larry O'Ale [invented] it all to gammon us.—OVER THE ROCKY MOUNTAINS, R. M. BALLANTYNE

gammon EXCLAMATION
nonsense
• 'Gammon!' said one. 'He's a humbug,' said another.—BLACK BEAUTY, ANNA SEWELL

Exclamations

Emotions were expressed in different ways in the 19th century.
• 'Oh, **botheration**!' returned Sydney, with a ... good-humoured laugh.—A TALE OF TWO CITIES, CHARLES DICKENS
• **Pshaw**, my dear boy! it was simplicity itself.—THE SIGN OF FOUR, ARTHUR CONAN DOYLE

---

garb NOUN
clothing
• Yet she was meanly dressed, a coarse blue petticoat and a linen jacket being her only garb.—FRANKENSTEIN, MARY SHELLEY
• He was an aged man, clad in seafaring garb.—THE SIGN OF FOUR, ARTHUR CONAN DOYLE

garland NOUN
a collection of writings; an anthology
• black-letter garlands—IVANHOE, WALTER SCOTT

garner VERB
to gather in and store a harvest
• The corn ... was garnered by farmers ... in ... Durnover.—THE MAYOR OF CASTERBRIDGE, THOMAS HARDY

garner NOUN
a place to store grain
• [They] met the winter with empty garners.—VILLETTE, CHARLOTTE BRONTË

garnish VERB
to decorate or equip something with something
• a ready-garnished home—SILAS MARNER, GEORGE ELIOT
USAGE In modern English, you might expect a dish, rather than a room or building, to be garnished.

garret NOUN
a small room on the top floor, under the roof; an attic
• I ... proceeded to descend the narrow garret staircase.—JANE EYRE, CHARLOTTE BRONTË

gas NOUN
gas lamps
• The gloom augments; the bright gas springs up in the streets.—BLEAK HOUSE, CHARLES DICKENS

gaud NOUN
something that is showy and bright
• dressing ... her up in some gaud or other—DOMBEY AND SON, CHARLES DICKENS
RELATED WORDS gaudy, meaning extravagantly showy or bright

gauntlet NOUN
the part of a glove covering your wrist
• sheepskin gloves with gauntlets—TESS OF THE D'URBERVILLES, THOMAS HARDY

gay ADJECTIVE
happy; bright and cheerful
• Safie was always gay and happy.—FRANKENSTEIN, MARY SHELLEY
• The sun shone in between the gay blue chintz window curtains.—JANE EYRE, CHARLOTTE BRONTË
➤ **gaily** ADVERB • All the family members are 'decked out gaily in their holiday attire'.—A CHRISTMAS CAROL, CHARLES DICKENS

genial ADJECTIVE
1 friendly, kind, or cheerful
• The spirit has a 'genial face'.—A CHRISTMAS CAROL, CHARLES DICKENS
2 pleasantly warm
• The pleasant showers and genial warmth of spring greatly altered the aspect of the earth.—FRANKENSTEIN, MARY SHELLEY
3 natural
• It seemed natural: it seemed genial to be so well loved, so caressed by him.—JANE EYRE, CHARLOTTE BRONTË
➤ **genially** ADVERB • 'Oh, yes you do, McMurdo,' cried Sherlock Holmes, genially.—THE SIGN OF FOUR, ARTHUR CONAN DOYLE

geniality NOUN
friendliness, kindness, or cheerfulness
• The geniality ... was somewhat theatrical to the eye.—THE STRANGE CASE OF DR JEKYLL AND MR HYDE, ROBERT LOUIS STEVENSON

gentle to gladsome

gentle ADJECTIVE
noble; of good character
• *O God bless this gentle Christian man!*—GREAT EXPECTATIONS, CHARLES DICKENS

gentlefolk NOUN
people with a high social position
• *the greatest gentlefolk in the whole county*—TESS OF THE D'URBERVILLES, THOMAS HARDY

gentleman NOUN
a man with a high social position
• *True. You are a gentleman's daughter. But who was your mother?*—PRIDE AND PREJUDICE, JANE AUSTEN

gentlewoman NOUN
a woman with a high social position
• *I was rather astonished to find her so very lady-like! But she is really quite the gentlewoman.*—EMMA, JANE AUSTEN

gentry NOUN
people of high social position, especially those next below the nobility
• *[Was he] likely to receive many cards of invitation from the nobility and gentry in the neighbourhood?*—NICHOLAS NICKLEBY, CHARLES DICKENS
• *an article much in vogue among the nobility and gentry*—GREAT EXPECTATIONS, CHARLES DICKENS

germ NOUN
a seed; an early stage that could develop or grow into something
• *My wife was mad—her excesses had prematurely developed the germs of insanity.*—JANE EYRE, CHARLOTTE BRONTË

gewgaw (say **gyoo-gaw**) NOUN
a useless showy ornament or person
• *a glittering gewgaw*—THE LAST OF THE MOHICANS, JAMES FENIMORE COOPER

gibbet (say **jib-it**) NOUN
a structure on which criminals were executed by hanging; a post on which their corpses were left hanging

giddy ADJECTIVE
foolish
• *I felt how giddy and how wrong it was.*—THE CRICKET ON THE HEARTH, CHARLES DICKENS

gig NOUN
a light carriage with two wheels
• *Farfrae ... had ... put the horse into the gig.*—THE MAYOR OF CASTERBRIDGE, THOMAS HARDY

gillie NOUN
1 a highland chief's attendant
2 a man with the job of helping landowners and their guests to fish and hunt

girandole (say **ji-run-dole**) NOUN
a branched candle holder
• *the light of the girandoles on the mantelpiece*—JANE EYRE, CHARLOTTE BRONTË

gird VERB
1 to surround something
• *the ring of low white vapour girding all the verge of sky*—LORNA DOONE, R. D. BLACKMORE
2 to tie a garment with a belt; to fasten a sword on with a band
• *Girded round its middle was an antique scabbard; but no sword was in it.*—A CHRISTMAS CAROL, CHARLES DICKENS
3 to say unpleasant things to someone
• *He has learned that way of girding at us.*—THE MOONSTONE, WILKIE COLLINS

girdle NOUN
1 a belt
• *In his girdle he wore a long and double-edged dagger.*—IVANHOE, WALTER SCOTT
2 a metal plate for cooking on; a griddle
• *Mr Sympson walks like 'a hen treading a hot girdle'.*—SHIRLEY, CHARLOTTE BRONTË

girt VERB
1 surrounded; girded
• *Pondicherry Lodge stood in its own grounds, and was girt round with a very high stone wall topped with broken glass.*—THE SIGN OF FOUR, ARTHUR CONAN DOYLE
2 tied or fastened; girded
• *[He] took up his hat and pistols, girt on a cutlass ... and with a musket over his shoulder, ... set off briskly through the trees.*—TREASURE ISLAND, ROBERT LOUIS STEVENSON

Past tense and past participles

Some verb forms, like 'girt', are different from modern English. Other examples are 'spake' instead of 'spoke', 'dropt' instead of 'dropped', and 'blent' instead of 'blended'.

---

gladsome ADJECTIVE
joyful; cheerful
• *Nobody ever stopped him in the street to say, with gladsome looks, 'My dear Scrooge, how are you?'*—A CHRISTMAS CAROL, CHARLES DICKENS

glance to grateful

glance VERB
to gleam; to shine suddenly
• *a bright glancing light*—SILAS MARNER, GEORGE ELIOT

glance NOUN
a gleam or flash
• *the transient glance of this February sun*—THE MILL ON THE FLOSS, GEORGE ELIOT

gloaming NOUN
twilight; the dim light after sunset or before sunrise
• *the first gloaming of the night*—KIDNAPPED, ROBERT LOUIS STEVENSON

glut VERB
to fully satisfy someone's appetite
• *I do not destroy the lamb and the kid to glut my appetite.*—FRANKENSTEIN, MARY SHELLEY

gnome NOUN
a mythical dwarf-like creature that guarded underground treasures
• *Hitherto [Silas] had been treated very much as if he had been a useful gnome or brownie ... seeing that without him there was no getting the yarn woven.*—SILAS MARNER, GEORGE ELIOT

gonoph NOUN
a pickpocket
• *He's as obstinate a young gonoph as I know.*—BLEAK HOUSE, CHARLES DICKENS
From *gannabh*, the Hebrew word for 'thief'. The earliest recorded usage of the word in English seems to be in Charles Dickens' novels.

goodly ADJECTIVE
good; substantial or admirable
• *a goodly sum of money*—BLEAK HOUSE, CHARLES DICKENS

goodman NOUN
the man in charge of a household or establishment; a way of addressing or referring to a man who was not of the upper classes
• *'Alack, goodman!' she murmured, 'have we not children enough of our own?'*—THE STAR-CHILD, OSCAR WILDE

goodwife NOUN
the woman in charge of a household or establishment; a way of addressing or referring to a woman who was not of the upper classes
• *Loose thy hold from the boy, goodwife.*—THE PRINCE AND THE PAUPER, MARK TWAIN

goose VERB
to hiss at a performer
• *He was goosed last night.*—HARD TIMES, CHARLES DICKENS

gorgeous ADJECTIVE
brightly coloured; richly decorated
• *gorgeous yellow stockings*—CIRCE'S PALACE, NATHANIEL HAWTHORNE
➤ **gorgeously** ADVERB • *gorgeously robed priests*—THE PRISONER OF ZENDA, ANTHONY HOPE

gorget (say gor-jit) NOUN
1 a piece of throat armour
• *The other two [arrows] were averted by the gorget.*—IVANHOE, WALTER SCOTT
2 something worn around your neck or over your throat, for example, a scarf, collar, or necklace
3 a coloured section on the throat of a bird or animal
French *gorge*, meaning 'throat'

gormandizer NOUN
someone who ate a lot of good food or who overate
• *Ah, the gluttons and gormandizers!*—CIRCE'S PALACE, NATHANIEL HAWTHORNE

gout NOUN
a drop or splash of liquid; a clot
• *a gout of ink*—THE WAR OF THE WORLDS, H. G. WELLS

governess NOUN
a woman who lived with a family as their children's teacher
• *Five daughters brought up at home without a governess!—I never heard of such a thing.*—PRIDE AND PREJUDICE, JANE AUSTEN

graminivorous ADJECTIVE
feeding on grass
• *A Gradgrind child 'had only been introduced to a cow as a graminivorous ruminating quadruped with several stomachs'.*—HARD TIMES, CHARLES DICKENS

grasping ADJECTIVE
greedy
• *And did you ever hear that my father was an avaricious, grasping man?*—JANE EYRE, CHARLOTTE BRONTË

grass-plot (also **grass-plat**) NOUN
a piece of land covered in turf; a lawn
• *There were no flowers, no garden-beds; only a broad gravel-walk girdling a grass-plat.*—JANE EYRE, CHARLOTTE BRONTË

grateful ADJECTIVE
welcome; causing gratitude
• *The blended scents of tea and coffee were so grateful to the nose.*—A CHRISTMAS CAROL, CHARLES DICKENS
USAGE In modern English, you might expect a person to be *grateful*, rather than a sight or smell.

grave to groom

grave VERB
to engrave
• *Was it round? ... and had it letters ... graved upon it?* —THE PRINCE AND THE PAUPER, MARK TWAIN
➤ **graved** ADJECTIVE • *a ring of graved jasper* —THE STAR-CHILD, OSCAR WILDE

graven VERB
engraved
➤ **a graven image:** a statue or a carved image of a god; an idol • *He ... stood like a graven image.* —SILAS MARNER, GEORGE ELIOT

graver NOUN
a tool for cutting or engraving
• *[He was] lettering a tombstone with a mallet and graver.* —MOONFLEET, J. MEADE FALKNER

gravity NOUN
seriousness
• *a tone of gentle gravity* —SILAS MARNER, GEORGE ELIOT

greensward NOUN
grassy ground
• *The cows are heard 'on the lower levels of greensward'.* —WESSEX TALES, THOMAS HARDY

gride NOUN
a harsh grating sound
• *the gride of many wheels* —THE WAR OF THE WORLDS, H. G. WELLS

grig NOUN
a small creature, for example, a small eel or a cricket
➤ **as lively / merry as a grig:** very lively or merry • *Tom was swimming about in the river ... as lively as a grig.* —THE WATER BABIES, CHARLES KINGSLEY

grind VERB
1 to crush something into tiny pieces or powder
• *We were ... obliged to grind our corn at his mill.* —A TALE OF TWO CITIES, CHARLES DICKENS
2 to sharpen or smooth something by rubbing it on a rough surface
• *Gabriel Oak [was] ... grinding his shears for the sheep-shearing.* —FAR FROM THE MADDING CROWD, THOMAS HARDY
3 to turn the handle of a machine or of a barrel organ; to play music on a barrel organ
• *[He] was grinding an organ before the shop, and a miserable little shrivelled monkey was sitting on the instrument.* —THE WOMAN IN WHITE, WILKIE COLLINS
4 to work or study hard for a long time
• *Grind away over your old Greek as much as you like, but don't bother me.* —JACK AND JILL, LOUISA M. ALCOTT
5 to make students work hard; to teach in a dull way
USAGE Dickens uses this word in a pun (with the word 'blade' referring both to a young man and to a knife).
• *After grinding a number of dull blades ... he had wearied of that poor work.* —GREAT EXPECTATIONS, CHARLES DICKENS
RELATED WORD To *keep your nose to the grindstone* is to work hard for a long time.

grinder NOUN
1 a person whose job was to grind or sharpen tools
• *the knife-grinder* —SILAS MARNER, GEORGE ELIOT
2 a person playing a barrel organ
• *The organ-grinder ... put in his claim to a penny.* —THE WOMAN IN WHITE, WILKIE COLLINS
3 a tutor
• *Mr Pocket had ... taken up the calling of a Grinder.* —GREAT EXPECTATIONS, CHARLES DICKENS
4 a tooth, especially a molar
• *Rob (also known as 'the Grinder') begins to 'use his own personal grinders'*—i.e. to eat.— DOMBEY AND SON, CHARLES DICKENS
USAGE In *Dombey and Sons*, character Rob the Grinder, and his school 'the Charitable Grinders', are named with reference to the workhouse job of grinding bones (to make fertilizer).

gripe NOUN
grasp; grip
• *[He] held them in a gripe like that of an iron vice.* —THE GOLDEN FLEECE, NATHANIEL HAWTHORNE

gripe VERB
to seize someone; to cause someone pain
• *I can't abide new [food] nor new faces ... you [never] know but what they'll gripe you.* —THE MILL ON THE FLOSS, GEORGE ELIOT

groat NOUN
a coin, especially an old English silver coin worth four old pence
USAGE The word *groat* was used meaning 'a very small amount'.
• *I have not so much as a single groat in my purse.* —THE MERRY ADVENTURES OF ROBIN HOOD, HOWARD PYLE

grog NOUN
a mixture of rum another strong alcoholic drink) and water
• *They wished each other Merry Christmas in their can of grog.* —A CHRISTMAS CAROL, CHARLES DICKENS

groom NOUN
a person employed to look after horses
• *Why, my grandfather made the grooms' livery.* —SILAS MARNER, GEORGE ELIOT

gross to guy

gross *ADJECTIVE*
very large and obvious
• *This must be the grossest falsehood!*—PRIDE AND PREJUDICE, JANE AUSTEN

gruel *NOUN*
a liquid food like very watery porridge
• *a basin of gruel for which he had no appetite*—SILAS MARNER, GEORGE ELIOT

guerdon (say **gur-duhn**) *NOUN*
a reward; something received as payment
• *They receive a somewhat larger guerdon for their toil.*—THE DRAGON AND THE RAVEN, G. A. HENTY

guinea *NOUN*
a gold coin with a value of £1.05
• *the iron pot that contained his guineas and silver coins*—SILAS MARNER, GEORGE ELIOT

gutter *VERB*
1 to flicker, as if about to go out
• *a guttering candle*—THE ADVENTURES OF SHERLOCK HOLMES, ARTHUR CONAN DOYLE
2 to drip or stream somewhere
• *Angel [looked] at the flames, and at the grease guttering down the sides.*—TESS OF THE D'URBERVILLES, THOMAS HARDY

guy *NOUN*
a person who looked dreadful, often because of the way they were dressed
• *What a guy you were, father!*—SHIRLEY, CHARLOTTE BRONTË

guy *VERB*
1 to secure something somewhere by tying it
• *The settles on which they sat down were thin and tall, their tops being guyed by pieces of twine to hooks in the ceiling.*—THE MAYOR OF CASTERBRIDGE, THOMAS HARDY
2 to mock or ridicule someone
• *I'm guyed at by the children.*—THE SIGN OF FOUR, ARTHUR CONAN DOYLE

Hh

HOLMES

The fictional detective **Sherlock Holmes** first appeared in 1887, in the novel *A Study in Scarlet* by Arthur Conan Doyle. Holmes, with his powers of deduction, became a bestselling sensation and appeared in dozens of short stories published in the *Strand* magazine. Although killed off by his creator in the short story *The Final Problem* in 1893, the enduring popularity of the great detective led to his eventual return in further stories and novels.

habit NOUN
1 clothing
• *The Jester wore his usual fantastic habit.*—IVANHOE, WALTER SCOTT
2 a woman's outfit for horse riding
• *She is never wilder than when equipped in her habit and hat.*—SHIRLEY, CHARLOTTE BRONTË
➤ **habited** ADJECTIVE dressed • *He was mighty plainly habited, with a knitted nightcap drawn over his ears.*—KIDNAPPED, ROBERT LOUIS STEVENSON

habituate VERB
to get someone used to something
• *an irksome struggle with difficulties in habituating myself to new rules and unwonted tasks*—JANE EYRE, CHARLOTTE BRONTË
➤ **habituated** ADJECTIVE accustomed • *The action was more frank and fearless than any I was habituated to indulge in.*—JANE EYRE, CHARLOTTE BRONTË

hack NOUN
1 a horse
• *He'll keep no more hacks at my expense.*—SILAS MARNER, GEORGE ELIOT
2 a hackney coach
• *A hack now drove to the door.*—UNCLE TOM'S CABIN, HARRIET BEECHER STOWE

hackney NOUN
1 a horse used for general riding and for pulling carriages
• *Mr Moore ... , after stabling his dray-horses, had saddled his hackney.*—SHIRLEY, CHARLOTTE BRONTË
2 a hackney coach

hackney coach (also hackney carriage) NOUN
a horse-drawn carriage that could be hired like a taxi
• *I never pay a hackney coach, ma'am; I never hire one.*—NICHOLAS NICKLEBY, CHARLES DICKENS
➤ **hackney coachman** NOUN • *A hackney-coachman ... packed me up in his coach.*—GREAT EXPECTATIONS, CHARLES DICKENS

haggard ADJECTIVE
looking ill or tired, and worried or afraid
• *My haggard and wild appearance awoke intense alarm.*—FRANKENSTEIN, MARY SHELLEY

hail VERB
1 to call out or wave to someone
• *Voices hailed us out of the darkness.*—THE SIGN OF FOUR, ARTHUR CONAN DOYLE
2 to welcome or recognize someone or something
• *[They] would hail with obvious relief the appearance of a friend.*—THE STRANGE CASE OF DR JEKYLL AND MR HYDE, ROBERT LOUIS STEVENSON
• *You were hereafter to be hailed as the benefactors of your species.*—FRANKENSTEIN, MARY SHELLEY

hail NOUN
a call or wave; a greeting
• *At our hail the man in the [boat] sprang up from the deck and shook his ... fists at us.*—THE SIGN OF FOUR, ARTHUR CONAN DOYLE
➤ **within hail**: within earshot; very close to something • *a respectable lodging-house ... almost within hail of my windows*—GREAT EXPECTATIONS, CHARLES DICKENS

halberd (also halbert) NOUN
a weapon that was a combination of a spear and an axe
• *At the door stand tall guards ... bearing halberds.*—THE PRINCE AND THE PAUPER, MARK TWAIN

half-holiday NOUN
a half-day off work
• *I ... retired to my own room, and there spent ... the half-holiday granted in honour of the occasion.*—JANE EYRE, CHARLOTTE BRONTË

halter to harlequinade

halter NOUN
1 a rope for hanging someone; a noose
• *He did not wish to put his head in a halter.*—THE SIGN OF FOUR, ARTHUR CONAN DOYLE
2 a rope or strap put round a horse's head so it could be led or fastened to something
• *Robert came into the field with a halter, which he slipped over my head, and led me away.*—BLACK BEAUTY, ANNA SEWELL

hamadryad (say ham-uh-dry-uhd, ham-uh-dry-ad) NOUN
in Greek and Roman mythology, a nymph who lived in a tree

hammercloth NOUN
a cloth covering the box (driver's seat) of a coach
• *[He got] on his box, which I remember to have been decorated with an old weather-stained pea-green hammercloth.*—GREAT EXPECTATIONS, CHARLES DICKENS

handmaid NOUN
a female servant; a maid
• *the little orphan who serves me as a handmaid*—JANE EYRE, CHARLOTTE BRONTË

handsome ADJECTIVE
1 attractive; good-looking (used of women and men)
• *The lady was young, engaging, and handsome.*—A TALE OF TWO CITIES, CHARLES DICKENS
2 gracious; generous
• *It was really a very handsome thought.*—PRIDE AND PREJUDICE, JANE AUSTEN
➤ **handsomely** ADVERB
1 in an attractive and high-quality way
• *a lady very handsomely and becomingly dressed*—DOMBEY AND SON, CHARLES DICKENS
2 graciously; generously
• *He very handsomely hopes they will be happy together.*—PERSUASION, JANE AUSTEN

handspike NOUN
a wooden or metal rod, used for example as a crowbar
• *Then he rapped on the door with a bit of stick like a handspike that he carried.*—TREASURE ISLAND, ROBERT LOUIS STEVENSON

hansom (also **hansom cab**) NOUN
a two-wheeled cab (a carriage for hire) pulled by a horse, with space for two passengers inside and a driver outside
• *I rose ... from table, got into a hansom, and drove straight to Jekyll's house.*—THE STRANGE CASE OF DR JEKYLL AND MR HYDE, ROBERT LOUIS STEVENSON

hap VERB
happen
• *It remains but to name a fitting place of combat, and, if it so hap, also of execution.*—IVANHOE, WALTER SCOTT

hap NOUN
1 luck; fortune
• *Then abruptly she turned and went in, leaving my cousins side by side wishing me good hap.*—THE WAR OF THE WORLDS, H. G. WELLS
2 a chance occurrence; a piece of bad luck
• *I let it be known, by some hap, that I was [his] cousin.*—LORNA DOONE, R. D. BLACKMORE

haply ADVERB
perhaps; by any chance
• *[They] would look for news, and ... get none, but, haply, tidings of his death.*—MARY BARTON, ELIZABETH GASKELL
• *Keep your guns pointing to heaven, lest haply we shoot one another.*—LORNA DOONE, R. D. BLACKMORE

happen ADVERB
perhaps
• *But happen somebody can tell me which is the way.*—SILAS MARNER, GEORGE ELIOT

happy ADJECTIVE
fortunate
• *Mr Wickham is blessed with such happy manners as may ensure his making friends.*—PRIDE AND PREJUDICE, JANE AUSTEN

hard by PREPOSITION & ADVERB
very near to something; nearby or right beside
• *Hard by the top of Putney Hill I came upon another skeleton.*—THE WAR OF THE WORLDS, H. G. WELLS
• *Hard by was a small stone-quarry.*—GREAT EXPECTATIONS, CHARLES DICKENS

hardihood NOUN
daring; courage
• *I was meditating an escape ... without having the hardihood to slip away.*—DAVID COPPERFIELD, CHARLES DICKENS

hardy ADJECTIVE
bold; daring or courageous
• *What makes you so venturesome and hardy?*—JANE EYRE, CHARLOTTE BRONTË
USAGE In modern English, you might expect a plant to be *hardy*, rather than a person.

harlequinade NOUN
a traditional pantomime; also used to mean a ridiculous performance
• *Henchard does not suspect that Jopp is involved 'in the night's harlequinade'.*—THE MAYOR OF CASTERBRIDGE, THOMAS HARDY

harp to Hercules

harp VERB
➢ **harp on something:** to keep talking or thinking about a subject • *[She] harped so long on the subject ... that at last he let himself be talked over.*—THE RED FAIRY BOOK, ANDREW LANG

hasp NOUN
a hinge, lock, or latch
• *The hasp sprang open with a loud snap.*—THE SIGN OF FOUR, ARTHUR CONAN DOYLE

hauteur (say oh-tur) NOUN
a proud, distant manner; haughtiness
• *In a changed Mr Darcy, Elizabeth 'heard an accent ... far removed from hauteur or disdain of his companions'.*—PRIDE AND PREJUDICE, JANE AUSTEN

hawser NOUN
a heavy rope for tying up or towing a ship
• *The hawser was as taut as a bowstring, and the current so strong she pulled upon her anchor.*—TREASURE ISLAND, ROBERT LOUIS STEVENSON

hazard NOUN
1 a risk
• *'[I saw] the urgent necessity of quieting her at any hazard'*—meaning whatever the risk.—THE WOMAN IN WHITE, WILKIE COLLINS
2 a gambling game played with dice
• *Life is like a game of hazard, and surely none ever flung worse throws ... as I.*—MOONFLEET, J. MEADE FALKNER
➢ **at hazard:** randomly • *I know nothing ... I spoke at hazard.*—SHIRLEY, CHARLOTTE BRONTË

head NOUN
➢ **on this / that head:** on this (or that) topic
• *Dolly [was] rather startled by Silas's knowledge on this head.*—SILAS MARNER, GEORGE ELIOT
• *On that head, therefore, I shall be uniformly silent.*—PRIDE AND PREJUDICE, JANE AUSTEN

headsman NOUN
1 an executioner who beheaded people
• *The headsman might inflict more than one stroke.*—THE BLACK TULIP, ALEXANDRE DUMAS
2 the person in charge of a whaling boat
• *The whale-boat pushes off from the ship, with the headsman or whale-killer as temporary steersman.*—MOBY DICK, HERMAN MELVILLE

heath-bell NOUN
heather, or another moorland plant, with bell-shaped flowers

hebdomadal ADJECTIVE
weekly
• *The girls have a 'hebdomadal treat' of a whole slice of bread and butter.*—JANE EYRE, CHARLOTTE BRONTË

heel VERB
to lean over to one side
• *their heeling, pitching boat*—THE WAR OF THE WORLDS, H. G. WELLS

heliograph NOUN
a signalling device that used a mirror to reflect flashes of light from the sun
• *'What is that flicker in the sky?' he asked abruptly. I told him it was the heliograph signalling.*—THE WAR OF THE WORLDS, H. G. WELLS

helpmate (also **helpmeet**) NOUN
a helpful partner, especially a wife or husband
• *Mr Bumble ... followed his helpmate downstairs.*—OLIVER TWIST, CHARLES DICKENS

hem VERB
to clear your throat
• *The Doctor, having taken a glass of port wine ... hemmed twice or thrice.*—DOMBEY AND SON, CHARLES DICKENS

hem EXCLAMATION
the sound of someone clearing their throat
• *I heard a hem close at my elbow: I turned, and saw Sam.*—JANE EYRE, CHARLOTTE BRONTË
• *'Hem!' said Miss La Creevy, coughing delicately behind her black silk mitten.*—NICHOLAS NICKLEBY, CHARLES DICKENS

hempen ADJECTIVE
made from hemp, a strong plant fibre
• *hempen rope*—OTTO OF THE SILVER HAND, HOWARD PYLE

hence ADVERB
1 so; for this reason
• *They moved at little more than a foot pace; and hence it was quite dark when he was brought home.*—DOMBEY AND SON, CHARLES DICKENS
2 from now
• *I wonder how you will answer me a year hence.*—JANE EYRE, CHARLOTTE BRONTË
3 away from here
• *Go away! Get hence quickly.*—THE JUNGLE BOOK, RUDYARD KIPLING

henceforth (also **henceforward**) ADVERB
from now on, or from that time onwards
• *You will, I hope, acquit me henceforth of cruelty towards Mr Wickham.*—PRIDE AND PREJUDICE, JANE AUSTEN

Hercules NOUN
in mythology, a hero who had superhuman strength
• *The carriage road was such as no carriage ... could possibly have passed along, without Hercules to assist in lifting it out of the deep clay ruts.*—MARY BARTON, ELIZABETH GASKELL

herein to hoard

herein ADVERB
1 in this respect; with regard to this
• 'I find the shock ... very heavy indeed.' She could give him no comfort herein.—HARD TIMES, CHARLES DICKENS
2 in this place, document, or thing
• The Reader is informed how he liked Nicholas, who is herein introduced.—NICHOLAS NICKLEBY, CHARLES DICKENS

heretofore (say heer-tuh-for) ADVERB
until now or until that time; previously
• [She] said in a more sympathetic tone than she had heretofore used, 'Do tell me, Mary, what's fretting you so?'—MARY BARTON, ELIZABETH GASKELL

hereupon ADVERB
at that point
• [They] went on to Miss Havisham's, where they lost me. Hereupon they went back to the hotel.
—GREAT EXPECTATIONS, CHARLES DICKENS

heyday EXCLAMATION
used showing surprise, happiness, or cheerfulness; hey!
• 'Heyday!' said Bryce ... 'you're on your brother's horse to-day: how's that?'—SILAS MARNER, GEORGE ELIOT

hie VERB
to go somewhere quickly
• I hied me to the window-recess.—JANE EYRE, CHARLOTTE BRONTË
• And so it goes on; and ... every one must hie to work.—LORNA DOONE, R. D. BLACKMORE

hierophant NOUN
a priest who interpreted mysteries

high ADJECTIVE
1 noble; virtuous
• I was nourished with high thoughts of honour and devotion.—FRANKENSTEIN, MARY SHELLEY
2 arrogant; with an air of superiority
• So high and so conceited that there was no enduring him!—PRIDE AND PREJUDICE, JANE AUSTEN
➤ **high words:** an argument or angry conversation • I had quite high words with him last night.—THE SIGN OF FOUR, ARTHUR CONAN DOYLE

high ADVERB
➤ **play high:** to gamble for high stakes (i.e. for a lot of money) • On entering the drawing-room she found the whole party [playing cards], and was immediately invited to join them; but suspecting them to be playing high she declined it.—PRIDE AND PREJUDICE, JANE AUSTEN

hilarious ADJECTIVE
full of laughter, fun, or good cheer; boisterous
• Miss Eliott found them a most hilarious set, for it was impossible to control entirely the merriment which possessed them.—LITTLE MEN, LOUISA M. ALCOTT

hilarity NOUN
lively fun; boisterousness
• After a short silence on both sides, Mrs Jennings, with all her natural hilarity, burst forth again.—SENSE AND SENSIBILITY, JANE AUSTEN

hindforemost ADVERB
backwards; back to front
• The tall girl snatched the bonnet and put it on her own head hind-foremost with a grin.—THE MILL ON THE FLOSS, GEORGE ELIOT
• I'll pull you through hindforemost.—WATER BABIES, CHARLES KINGSLEY

hindmost ADJECTIVE
furthest back
• Angel's eye at last fell upon Tess, the hindmost of the four.—TESS OF THE D'URBERVILLES, THOMAS HARDY

hint VERB
to suggest something
• 'Couldn't I take 'em all at once, and have it over, Jacob?' hinted Scrooge.—A CHRISTMAS CAROL, CHARLES DICKENS
USAGE In modern English, you would expect *hint* to mean 'suggest something in an indirect way'.

histrionic ADJECTIVE
relating to acting and the theatre; theatrical
• '[He] said he had played ... on the histrionic boards.'—meaning on the stage.—THE ADVENTURES OF HUCKLEBERRY FINN, MARK TWAIN
🏛 Latin *histrion* meaning 'actor'

hither (also **hitherward**) ADVERB
to or towards this place; here
• Come, Jane—come hither.—JANE EYRE, CHARLOTTE BRONTË

hitherto ADVERB
until now; until this time
• I had hitherto attended the schools of Geneva.
—FRANKENSTEIN, MARY SHELLEY

hoar (also **hoar frost**) NOUN
frost covering surfaces, leaves, etc. in a silvery-white layer
• The cold hoar frost glistened on the tombstones.
—THE STORY OF THE GOBLINS WHO STOLE A SEXTON, CHARLES DICKENS

hoard VERB
to be kept safe
• He sat down to the dinner that had been hoarding for him by the fire.—A CHRISTMAS CAROL, CHARLES DICKENS
USAGE In modern English, you would expect people to *hoard* things, rather than things to be *hoarding*.

hocus to house

hocus VERB
1 to trick someone
• *I thought maybe you was trying to hocus me again.*
—THE ADVENTURES OF HUCKLEBERRY FINN, MARK TWAIN
2 to drug someone in order to steal from them

hogshead NOUN
a large barrel, used as a unit of measurement; the amount it contained
• *three hogsheads of ale*—IVANHOE, WALTER SCOTT

holland NOUN
linen fabric
• *[The girls] were uniformly dressed in brown stuff frocks of quaint fashion, and long holland pinafores.*
—JANE EYRE, CHARLOTTE BRONTË

Hollands NOUN
Dutch gin
• *We'll find you a glass of Hollands to keep out autumn chills.*—MOONFLEET, J. MEADE FALKNER

holm (also **holme**) NOUN
1 a piece of flat ground near a river, sometimes flooded
• *Mists ... rolled down ... [the] holm till they blended with the frozen fog of the beck.*—JANE EYRE
2 a small island, especially in a river or lake

holograph ADJECTIVE
handwritten by its author
• *The will was holograph, for Mr Utterson ... had refused to lend the least assistance in the making of it.*—THE STRANGE CASE OF DR JEKYLL AND MR HYDE, ROBERT LOUIS STEVENSON

holt NOUN
hold
• *Tom, something's always told me we'd never get holt of that swag.*—THE ADVENTURES OF TOM SAWYER, MARK TWAIN

holus-bolus ADVERB
all at once; all in one go
• *[She made] a sudden snatch at the heap of silver, put it back, holus-bolus, in her pocket.*—THE MOONSTONE, WILKIE COLLINS

homily NOUN
a sermon or lecture
• *Mr Wopsle ... considered the subject of the day's homily, ill chosen.*—GREAT EXPECTATIONS, CHARLES DICKENS

hook VERB
➢ **hook it:** to disappear; to go away • *I hated to leave him; but I did. I hooked it one dark night.*—UNDER THE LILACS, LOUISA M. ALCOTT

hookah NOUN
a pipe for smoking tobacco through a long tube passing through water, originally used in the Middle East
• *The little man stopped to relight his hookah and puffed thoughtfully for a few moments.*—THE SIGN OF FOUR, ARTHUR CONAN DOYLE

hopeless ADJECTIVE
without hope
• *They were hopeless of remedy.*—PRIDE AND PREJUDICE, JANE AUSTEN

horn-book NOUN
a sheet of stiffened or covered paper showing the alphabet, for teaching children

horrors NOUN
an attack of severe shaking or nervousness
• *Arthur [was] shivering dreadful with the horrors.*
—GREAT EXPECTATIONS, CHARLES DICKENS

horse-block NOUN
a block for standing on when getting onto or off a horse
• *She would have persuaded her father to go round to the horse-block instead of alighting at the door-steps.*
—SILAS MARNER, GEORGE ELIOT

hosier NOUN
a maker or seller of stockings and socks, or of men's clothing
• *I went to the hatter's, and the bootmaker's, and the hosier's.*—GREAT EXPECTATIONS, CHARLES DICKENS

houri NOUN
a beautiful young woman, especially in the Muslim Paradise

house NOUN
1 an inn or pub
• *He's perhaps gone to pay a visit at the Three Crowns, by Whitbridge—I know he's fond of the house.*—SILAS MARNER, GEORGE ELIOT
2 a company or institution
• *Many a year went round before I was a partner in the House.*—GREAT EXPECTATIONS, CHARLES DICKENS
➢ **the house:** the workhouse • *So, they established the rule, that all poor people should have the alternative ... of being starved by a gradual process in the house, or by a quick one out of it.*—OLIVER TWIST, CHARLES DICKENS

house EXCLAMATION
used for getting the attention of the landlord or serving staff in an inn or pub
• *'House, house, house!' cried Mr Folair.*—NICHOLAS NICKLEBY, CHARLES DICKENS

house of correction *to* hyperborean

house of correction NOUN
a place where homeless people and minor criminals were kept and made to work
• *a miserable shoeless criminal, who had been taken up for playing the flute, and … committed … to the House of Correction for one month*—OLIVER TWIST, CHARLES DICKENS

house-place NOUN
the main living area of a cottage or farmhouse, usually the kitchen
• *She was startled by a man speaking in the house-place below.*—MARY BARTON, ELIZABETH GASKELL

hulk NOUN
1 an old ship used as a prison or for storage
• *People are put in the Hulks because they murder, and because they rob … and do all sorts of bad.*—GREAT EXPECTATIONS, CHARLES DICKENS
2 a large structure, especially a ship or the hull of a ship
• *The huge ship rolled up more and more, like a dying whale, exposing all her long black hulk.*

humbug NOUN
1 hypocritical or false behaviour
• *There was no humbug or hypocrisy about Mr Glegg; his eyes would have watered with true feeling over the sale of a widow's furniture.*—THE MILL ON THE FLOSS, GEORGE ELIOT
2 a hypocrite
• *He's a humbug … preaching to us and then doing the same himself.*—BLACK BEAUTY, ANNA SEWELL

humbug EXCLAMATION
used showing irritation or disbelief
• *'Bah!' said Scrooge. 'Humbug!'*—A CHRISTMAS CAROL, CHARLES DICKENS
USAGE Although the character Scrooge is famous for saying 'Bah, humbug', he does not actually say these words together as a phrase in the novel *A Christmas Carol*.
• *Scrooge having no better answer ready on the spur of the moment, said, 'Bah!' again; and followed it up with 'Humbug.'*—A CHRISTMAS CAROL, CHARLES DICKENS

humour NOUN
1 an inclination or mood
• *I have the humour, sir, to marry a young wife, and a pretty wife.*—THE CRICKET ON THE HEARTH, CHARLES DICKENS
2 one of the substances that were believed in the past to make up the human body and to influence personality
• *We will see if that fare will not cool thy hot humors.*—MEN OF IRON, HOWARD PYLE
USAGE The four humours were *blood*, *phlegm*, *choler* (or *yellow bile*), and *melancholy* (or *black bile*).

hurdle NOUN
1 a wooden frame with woven sticks, used as a temporary fence
• *Instead of gates of wrought iron, a pair of hurdles were tied across with a straw rope.*—KIDNAPPED, ROBERT LOUIS STEVENSON
2 a frame or sledge for carrying a person, especially for carrying a condemned criminal to be executed

hurry VERB
to transport something, especially coal in a mine
• *I hurry for my brother.*—TESTIMONY OF MARY BARRETT, GATHERED BY ASHLEY'S MINES COMMISSION, 1842

husband NOUN
someone who managed money, land, or other resources
• *I trust you will be a good husband of your money.*—KIDNAPPED, ROBERT LOUIS STEVENSON
➤ **husbandry** NOUN the management of money, land, or other resources • *extravagant habits and bad husbandry*—SILAS MARNER, GEORGE ELIOT

husband VERB
to use or manage something carefully and not waste it
• *[She] made up her mind to husband her physical strength.*—MARY BARTON, ELIZABETH GASKELL

husbandman NOUN
someone who farmed land; a farmer
• *The husbandmen plowed and planted as usual.*—THE POMEGRANATE SEEDS, NATHANIEL HAWTHORNE

huzza EXCLAMATION
hooray
• *Huzza! cried the Court.*—THE REMARKABLE ROCKET, OSCAR WILDE

hydrophobia NOUN
rabies (a serious disease causing madness and fear of water)
• *Do you truly expect that you will be seized with hydrophobia, and die raving mad?*—SHIRLEY, CHARLOTTE BRONTË

hymeneal (say hy-mi-**nee**-uhl, hy-muh-**nee**-uhl) ADJECTIVE
relating to marriage
• *Cornelia, in a new pair of spectacles, was waiting to be led to the hymeneal altar.*—DOMBEY AND SON, CHARLES DICKENS

hyperborean (say high-puh-**bor**-i-uhn, high-puh-**bor**-ree-uhn) ADJECTIVE
from or relating to the far north
• *Other fish are found exceedingly brisk in those Hyperborean waters.*—MOBY DICK, HERMAN MELVILLE

Ii

INDUSTRY

Although the **Industrial Revolution** began in the late **1700s**, it reached its peak in the 19th century. Steam power and machinery enabled goods and materials to be mass produced in factories, and people worked long hours in harsh conditions. The British parliament passed **Factory Acts** to improve working conditions. Engineers such as **Isambard Kingdom Brunel** built bridges and tunnels that transformed the British landscape. Many of these are still used today.

ideal ADJECTIVE
imaginary rather than real
• This is solid, an affair of the actual world, nothing ideal about it.—JANE EYRE, CHARLOTTE BRONTË

idiot NOUN
a person of low intelligence
• an idiot child—SILAS MARNER, GEORGE ELIOT

if CONJUNCTION
to the extent that
• If in our trio there was a superior and a leader, it was Diana.—JANE EYRE, CHARLOTTE BRONTË

ignis fatuus (say ig-niss fat-yoo-uhss) NOUN
a flickering light seen at night over marshy ground, also called a will-o'-the-wisp
🏛 Latin, meaning 'foolish fire'

ignominious ADJECTIVE
shameful; humiliating
• The punishment seemed to me in a high degree ignominious.—JANE EYRE, CHARLOTTE BRONTË
➤ **ignominiously** ADVERB in a humiliating or shameful manner • And I soon found myself ... having my face ignominiously shoved against the kitchen wall.—GREAT EXPECTATIONS, CHARLES DICKENS

➤ **ignominy** NOUN disgrace; humiliation
• This preparation for bonds [i.e. being tied to the chair], and the additional ignominy it inferred, took a little of the excitement out of me.—JANE EYRE, CHARLOTTE BRONTË

ill ADVERB
badly
• Well or ill done, excusably or inexcusably, it was done.—GREAT EXPECTATIONS, CHARLES DICKENS

ill ADJECTIVE
bad
• How very ill Miss Eliza Bennet looks this morning, Mr Darcy ... She is grown so brown and coarse!—PRIDE AND PREJUDICE, JANE AUSTEN
➤ **take something ill:** to be offended by something; to resent something • I took it ill that he should be brought here to pester me with his company.—GREAT EXPECTATIONS, CHARLES DICKENS

illiberal ADJECTIVE
1 ungenerous; small in amount
• He judged that ... irregular meals, and illiberal measures of sleep would be bad for his crazed mind.—THE PRINCE AND THE PAUPER, MARK TWAIN
2 uncultured; not well-educated
• Mrs Bennet's 'weak understanding and illiberal mind, had very early in their marriage put an end to all real affection for her'.—PRIDE AND PREJUDICE, JANE AUSTEN

illumine VERB
to light something up
• [The sun's] light illumined the wreathed and dewy orchard trees.—JANE EYRE, CHARLOTTE BRONTË

imbrue VERB
to stain something, especially with blood
• Pip says the convict who has threatened to eat his heart and liver wants to '[imbrue] his hands in me'.—GREAT EXPECTATIONS, CHARLES DICKENS

immaterial ADJECTIVE
spiritual or abstract rather than physical; insubstantial
• our mental existences, which are immaterial and have no dimensions—THE TIME MACHINE, H. G. WELLS
➤ **immateriality** NOUN • I began to perceive more deeply ... the trembling immateriality, the mistlike transience, of [our] seemingly so solid body.—THE STRANGE CASE OF DR JEKYLL AND MR HYDE, ROBERT LOUIS STEVENSON

immitigable ADJECTIVE
impossible to reduce or make less serious
• Her main fault was a brooding, eternal, immitigable suspicion of all men.—SHIRLEY, CHARLOTTE BRONTË

impalpable *to* imposture

impalpable ADJECTIVE
1 impossible to grasp, physically or mentally
• *Only the spark of the spirit will remain,—the impalpable principle of light and thought.*—JANE EYRE, CHARLOTTE BRONTË
2 not seen, heard, or felt
• *As he swept his long arms, as though brushing aside some impalpable obstacle, the wolves fell back.*—DRACULA, BRAM STOKER

impassible ADJECTIVE
not showing any emotion
• *Even though the ship is in serious trouble, the Captain 'preserves the same impassible countenance'.*—THE CAPTAIN OF THE POLE-STAR, ARTHUR CONAN DOYLE

impeachment NOUN
a question or doubt over something
• *Sir Leicester would do anything 'rather than give occasion for the least impeachment of his integrity'.*—BLEAK HOUSE, CHARLES DICKENS

impend VERB
to be about to happen; to threaten
• *If I [broke my promise], what manifold miseries might not impend over me and my devoted family!*—FRANKENSTEIN, MARY SHELLEY

imperious ADJECTIVE
haughty; behaving like a superior
• *I felt at times as if he were my relation rather than my master: yet he was imperious sometimes still.*—JANE EYRE, CHARLOTTE BRONTË

impetuosity NOUN
a tendency to speak or act hastily, without thinking first
• *He looked and spoke with eagerness: his old impetuosity was rising.*—JANE EYRE, CHARLOTTE BRONTË

impetuous ADJECTIVE
speaking or acting hastily, without thinking first
• *Her pale face and impetuous manner made him start.*—PRIDE AND PREJUDICE, JANE AUSTEN
• *When I did speak, it was only to express an impetuous wish that I had never been born.*—JANE EYRE, CHARLOTTE BRONTË
➤ **impetuously** ADVERB • *'Confound you, hold your tongue!' said Godfrey, impetuously.*—SILAS MARNER, GEORGE ELIOT

implacable ADJECTIVE
not easy to stop, calm down, or make less angry
• *The old Squire was an implacable man: he made resolutions in violent anger, and he was not … moved from them after his anger had subsided.*—SILAS MARNER, GEORGE ELIOT

➤ **implacably** ADVERB • *Mrs Chadband folds her arms and looks implacably at Mr Bucket.*—BLEAK HOUSE, CHARLES DICKENS

import VERB
to mean something; to have a particular meaning
• *[His words] seemed to imply that it imported something to him whether I forgot him or not.*—JANE EYRE, CHARLOTTE BRONTË

import NOUN
meaning; significance
• *I read these words over and over again: I … was unable fully to penetrate their import.*—JANE EYRE, CHARLOTTE BRONTË

important ADJECTIVE
with an air of self-importance; pompous
• *With a most important aspect he protested that he had never in his life witnessed such behaviour in a person of rank.*—PRIDE AND PREJUDICE, JANE AUSTEN
• *The servant who stood at the horse's head was bid in an important voice 'to let him go.'*—NORTHANGER ABBEY, JANE AUSTEN

importunate ADJECTIVE
demanding attention or an answer; persistent
• *On these subjects her thirst for information was still very importunate.*—DOMBEY AND SON, CHARLES DICKENS

importune VERB
to harass or bother someone
• *I must beg, therefore, to be importuned no farther on the subject.*—PRIDE AND PREJUDICE, JANE AUSTEN

importunity NOUN
1 persistence
• *[Linton] implored her to accompany him, with a frantic importunity that admitted no denial.*—WUTHERING HEIGHTS, EMILY BRONTË
2 a persistent demand
• *I had little heart to eat, but took what he gave me to save myself from his importunities.*—MOONFLEET, J. MEADE FALKNER

impose VERB
➤ **impose on:** to deceive someone • *I know not in what manner, under what form of falsehood he had imposed on you; but his success is not perhaps to be wondered at.*—PRIDE AND PREJUDICE, JANE AUSTEN

imposture NOUN
a deception; dishonesty
• *'Good heavens!' cried the Colonel, laughing, 'do you mean to say all our sympathy was wasted and your fit an imposture?'*—THE MEMOIRS OF SHERLOCK HOLMES, ARTHUR CONAN DOYLE

imprecate to inaptitude

imprecate VERB
to utter a curse
• How often did I imprecate curses on the cause of my being!—FRANKENSTEIN, MARY SHELLEY

imprecation NOUN
a curse
• [He] muttered dreadful imprecations on her head.—DOMBEY AND SON, CHARLES DICKENS

impress VERB (say im-press)
1 to form a lasting impression; to strike someone in a particular way
• [My friends' story] was one which could not fail to impress itself deeply on my mind.—FRANKENSTEIN, MARY SHELLEY
• Still the fact impressed him as strange.—WESSEX TALES, THOMAS HARDY
2 to have a particular effect or influence
• [Hortense's] formal and self-important character … impressed her manners and moulded her countenance.—SHIRLEY, CHARLOTTE BRONTË

impress NOUN (say im-press)
1 a mark made by pressing an object into something soft; an impression
• Dr Watson wrote about 'the uses of plaster of Paris as a preserver of impresses'.—THE SIGN OF FOUR, ARTHUR CONAN DOYLE
2 a distinctive quality or sign
• Not one face 'bore the impress of pity or compassion'.—NICHOLAS NICKLEBY, CHARLES DICKENS

impressible VERB
easily influenced; impressionable
• Marner had one of those impressible self-doubting natures.—SILAS MARNER, GEORGE ELIOT

impressive ADJECTIVE
emphatic; insistent
• My manner as I thus addressed him was impressive but calm.—FRANKENSTEIN, MARY SHELLEY

impropriety (say im-pruh-**pry**-uh-ti) NOUN
inappropriate or incorrect behaviour; an inappropriate or incorrect action
• Catherine … thought there could be no impropriety in her going with Mr Thorpe.—NORTHANGER ABBEY, JANE AUSTEN
• He seemed to think I had committed an impropriety in proposing to accompany him unmarried.—JANE EYRE, CHARLOTTE BRONTË

improvident ADJECTIVE
not planning for the future; wasteful; reckless
• He had suffered from the scanty living consequent upon bad times and improvident habits.—MARY BARTON, ELIZABETH GASKELL

imprudent ADJECTIVE
foolish; rash
• Oh … how imprudent he has been!—DAVID COPPERFIELD, CHARLES DICKENS
➤ **imprudently** ADVERB • I had certainly acted imprudently.—FRANKENSTEIN, MARY SHELLEY
➤ **imprudence** NOUN rashness; foolishness
• Elizabeth had frequently united with Jane in an endeavour to check the imprudence of Catherine and Lydia.—PRIDE AND PREJUDICE, JANE AUSTEN

impulse NOUN
1 a thought or feeling; an inclination
• My first impulse was to rise and fasten the bolt.—JANE EYRE, CHARLOTTE BRONTË
2 something causing another thing to happen
• The little outward impulse of her father's speech gave Mary the push which she … required.—MARY BARTON, ELIZABETH GASKELL
3 a push or sudden movement
• [The soldier] sent her reeling back whence she came with a vigorous impulse from his strong arm.—THE PRINCE AND THE PAUPER, MARK TWAIN
➤ **with / as / by one (or a common) impulse:** together; at the same time • By a common impulse we clambered higher.—THE WAR OF THE WORLDS, H. G. WELLS

imputation NOUN
an accusation; a claim that someone had done something wrong
• If his reply agrees with your statement, you shall be publicly cleared from every imputation.—JANE EYRE, CHARLOTTE BRONTË

impute VERB
to say that something had a particular cause, or was someone's fault
• Mr Darcy '[imputed] his visit to a wish of hearing that she were better'—meaning he claimed that was the reason.—PRIDE AND PREJUDICE, JANE AUSTEN

inanition NOUN
exhaustion caused by lack of food
• I was now nearly sick from inanition, having taken so little the day before.—JANE EYRE, CHARLOTTE BRONTË

inappreciable ADJECTIVE
too precious to put a value on; priceless
• Louisa talks about 'all the inappreciable things' that make life worth living.—HARD TIMES, CHARLES DICKENS

inaptitude NOUN
unsuitability; lack of ability
• In simplicity … and a fine guileless inaptitude for all worldly affairs, he is a perfect child.—BLEAK HOUSE, CHARLES DICKENS

inclination *to* indignity

inclination NOUN
a bending of the head or body; a nod or bow
• *Elizabeth ... answered only by a slight inclination of the head.*—PRIDE AND PREJUDICE, JANE AUSTEN

incommode VERB
to inconvenience, trouble, or burden someone
• *I wouldn't have incommoded none of you, if I'd had my way.*—GREAT EXPECTATIONS, CHARLES DICKENS

incommodious ADJECTIVE
uncomfortable, inconvenient, or unpleasant
• *[The house] was antique, rambling, and incommodious.*—SHIRLEY, CHARLOTTE BRONTË
➤ **incommodiousness** NOUN • *The partners in the House were proud of its smallness, proud of its darkness, proud of its ugliness, proud of its incommodiousness.*—A TALE OF TWO CITIES, CHARLES DICKENS

incontinently (also **incontinent**) ADVERB
immediately; at once
• *[As] soon as I struck a match in order to see them, they fled incontinently.*—THE TIME MACHINE, H. G. WELLS

incorporate VERB
1 to make someone or something a part of something
• *At an early age, he was 'incorporated in a narrow religious sect'.*—SILAS MARNER, GEORGE ELIOT
2 to express or embody something
• *the forms in which their religious feeling has incorporated itself*—SILAS MARNER, GEORGE ELIOT
USAGE Robert Louis Stevenson uses this word to talk literally about taking over the body of another person, after Dr Jekyll wakes up to find he has the body of Mr Hyde.
• *I was slowly losing hold of my original and better self, and becoming slowly incorporated with my second and worse.*—THE STRANGE CASE OF DR JEKYLL AND MR HYDE, ROBERT LOUIS STEVENSON
🏛 Latin *in* meaning 'into' + *corporare* meaning 'form into a body'

incorrigible ADJECTIVE
impossible to change for the better
• *He was an incorrigible tease.*—LITTLE WOMEN, LOUISA M. ALCOTT

incubus NOUN
1 an evil spirit that visited people while they were asleep
• *While lying down on a hot afternoon ... the incubus oppressed her.*—WESSEX TALES, THOMAS HARDY
2 a problem or worry
• *It was unlikely that the miller's savings 'could remove the hateful incubus of debt'.*—THE MILL ON THE FLOSS, GEORGE ELIOT

incumbrance NOUN
a burden; an encumbrance
• *I was left helpless, with the prospect of a coming incumbrance in the shape of a child.*—THE WOMAN IN WHITE, WILKIE COLLINS

indefatigable ADJECTIVE
never becoming tired; tireless
• *The indefatigable bell now sounded for the fourth time.*—JANE EYRE, CHARLOTTE BRONTË
➤ **indefatigably** ADVERB • *He played whist indefatigably, for he had found partners as enthusiastic in the game as himself.*—AROUND THE WORLD IN EIGHTY DAYS, JULES VERNE

indenture (also **indentures**) NOUN
a contract, especially one binding an apprentice to an employer
• *My indentures were duly signed and attested, and I was 'bound'.*—GREAT EXPECTATIONS, CHARLES DICKENS

independence (also **independency**) NOUN
an inheritance; an income which meant that someone did not need to rely on anyone else
• *The independence she settled on Robert ... has put it in his power to make his own choice.*—SENSE AND SENSIBILITY, JANE AUSTEN
• *I must tell you that I possess a small independency, arising partly from my own savings, and partly from a legacy.*—SHIRLEY, CHARLOTTE BRONTË

india-rubber NOUN
natural rubber
• *Jumping from their horses, the Miss Applewhites 'bounced on the ground as if they were made of india-rubber'.*—THE MOONSTONE, WILKIE COLLINS
🏛 The natural substance *rubber* was called this because it was used for rubbing out or erasing pencil marks. India was one of the countries where the trees grew from which the substance was taken.

indifferent ADJECTIVE
not very good; fairly bad
• *She hated having visitors in the house while her health was so indifferent.*—PRIDE AND PREJUDICE, JANE AUSTEN

indigence NOUN
poverty; need
• *a life of indigence and suffering*—OLIVER TWIST, CHARLES DICKENS
➤ **indigent** ADJECTIVE poor; needy • *an indigent niece*—MANSFIELD PARK, JANE AUSTEN

indignity NOUN
treatment or circumstances causing shame or loss of dignity
• *There is no indignity so abhorrent to their feelings!*—PRIDE AND PREJUDICE, JANE AUSTEN

indite VERB
to write
• [Joe] proceeded to indite a note to Biddy.
—GREAT EXPECTATIONS, CHARLES DICKENS

indolent ADJECTIVE
lazy
• He was an indolent man, who lived only to eat, drink, and play at cards.—PRIDE AND PREJUDICE, JANE AUSTEN
➤ **indolence** NOUN • She ... lingered on the road, inclined by her indolence to believe that if she waited under a warm shed the snow would cease to fall.
—SILAS MARNER, GEORGE ELIOT

induct VERB
1 to install a clergyman in a paid position
• They were married under the happiest auspices, Mr Sweeting having been just inducted to a comfortable living.—SHIRLEY, CHARLOTTE BRONTË
2 to introduce someone to something
• Jack was being rapidly inducted into the wisdom of the world.—HOPE MILLS, AMANDA MINNIE DOUGLAS
3 to install someone in a chair
• Caroline looks at 'a large arm-chair, into which she at length recollected she ought to induct Mrs Sykes'.
—SHIRLEY, CHARLOTTE BRONTË

indulge VERB
to allow yourself to freely express a feeling or impulse
• His sisters ... indulged their mirth for some time at the expense of their dear friend's vulgar relations.
—PRIDE AND PREJUDICE, JANE AUSTEN

indurated ADJECTIVE
hardened
• Every nerve and muscle appeared ... indurated by unremitted exposure and toil.—THE LAST OF THE MOHICANS, JAMES FENIMORE COOPER

industry NOUN
hard work; effort
• Joe had a strong sense of the virtue of industry.
—GREAT EXPECTATIONS, CHARLES DICKENS

ineligible ADJECTIVE
unsuitable
• He is a respectable young man, and one whose acquaintance will not be ineligible.—SENSE AND SENSIBILITY, JANE AUSTEN

inequality NOUN
unevenness; lack of regularity
• [The wagon] swept from side to side, like a dog's tail wagging, with each ... inequality of the road.—DRACULA, BRAM STOKER

inestimable ADJECTIVE
too great or valuable to calculate
• 'If your friend,' she said, 'would be good enough to stop, he might be of inestimable service to me.'
—THE SIGN OF FOUR, ARTHUR CONAN DOYLE

inexorable ABBREVIATION
impossible to stop, prevent, or persuade
• I read an inexorable purpose in his gray eyes.—THE RETURN OF SHERLOCK HOLMES, ARTHUR CONAN DOYLE
➤ **inexorably** ADVERB • He inexorably refuses to give any explanation.—DAVID COPPERFIELD, CHARLES DICKENS

inextricable ADJECTIVE
impossible to disentangle or escape from
• The English archers were defeated and their horsemen in inextricable confusion.—IN FREEDOM'S CAUSE, G. A. HENTY
• They ran to and fro; they crowded together: some sobbed, some stumbled: the confusion was inextricable.—JANE EYRE, CHARLOTTE BRONTË
➤ **inextricably** ADVERB • It is as if I had a string ... under my left ribs, tightly and inextricably knotted to a similar string ... in ... your little frame.—JANE EYRE, CHARLOTTE BRONTË

infamous ADJECTIVE
wicked; disgraceful
• George Wickham has treated Mr Darcy in a most infamous manner.—PRIDE AND PREJUDICE, JANE AUSTEN

infamy NOUN
1 great wickedness; evil
• Have you seen that awful den of hellish infamy, with the very moonlight alive with grisly shapes?—DRACULA, BRAM STOKER
2 disgrace
• Elizabeth knows that Darcy has saved Lydia 'from irremediable infamy'.—PRIDE AND PREJUDICE, JANE AUSTEN

infantine ADJECTIVE
relating to babies or young children
• Miss Tox describes a school for young children as 'an infantine Boarding-House of a very select description'.
—DOMBEY AND SON, CHARLES DICKENS

inferior ADJECTIVE
1 of a low standard; poor
• a shepherd of inferior morals and dreadful temper
—FAR FROM THE MADDING CROWD, THOMAS HARDY
2 of a lower standard, rank, or quality than others
• a young woman of inferior birth—PRIDE AND PREJUDICE, JANE AUSTEN
• Her air was not conciliating, nor was her manner of receiving them, such as to make her visitors forget their inferior rank.—PRIDE AND PREJUDICE, JANE AUSTEN
• the inferior classes—DOMBEY AND SON, CHARLES DICKENS

inferior to insatiate

➤ **inferiority** NOUN the fact of being or feeling inferior to others • *There she felt her own inferiority very keenly.*—PERSUASION, JANE AUSTEN

inferior NOUN
a person of lower rank, position, or quality
• *[Mr Martin] is undoubtedly her inferior as to rank in society.*—EMMA, JANE AUSTEN

infernal ADJECTIVE
1 relating to or similar to hell
• *a red-hot wind, driving straight from the infernal regions*—A TALE OF TWO CITIES, CHARLES DICKENS
2 used for expressing annoyance
• *'I could not sleep,' he answered. 'This infernal problem is consuming me.'*—THE SIGN OF FOUR, ARTHUR CONAN DOYLE

information NOUN
education, knowledge, or learning
• *She was a woman of mean understanding, little information, and uncertain temper.*—PRIDE AND PREJUDICE, JANE AUSTEN

infusoria NOUN
a name given to various single-cell organisms
• *the infusoria under the microscope*—THE WAR OF THE WORLDS, H. G. WELLS

ing NOUN
a Northern English word for a meadow, especially one by a river
• *John discusses 'the farming of certain "crofts" and "ings"'.*—SHIRLEY, CHARLOTTE BRONTË

injected ADJECTIVE
bloodshot
• *He ... clutched at the table and held on, staring with injected eyes.*—THE STRANGE CASE OF DR JEKYLL AND MR HYDE, ROBERT LOUIS STEVENSON

injunction NOUN
an instruction; a command
• *Elizabeth would not oppose such an injunction.*—PRIDE AND PREJUDICE, JANE AUSTEN

injure VERB
1 to harm someone, especially by damaging their reputation
• *Lucetta reproaches Henchard for calling on her after ten: 'It is too late for propriety, and might injure me'.*—THE MAYOR OF CASTERBRIDGE, THOMAS HARDY
2 to be unfair to someone; to do someone an injustice
• *With respect to that ... accusation, of having injured Mr Wickham, I can only refute it by laying before you the whole of his connection with my family.*—PRIDE AND PREJUDICE, JANE AUSTEN

USAGE In modern English, you might expect a person or part of their body to be *injured*, rather than their reputation.

injurious ADJECTIVE
1 harmful
• *Jane's regrets over Bingley 'must have been injurious to her own health'.*—PRIDE AND PREJUDICE, JANE AUSTEN
2 insulting; harmful to someone's reputation
• *[He] protested against her suspicion as most injurious.*—EMMA, JANE AUSTEN
➤ **injuriously** ADVERB • *Why do you injuriously introduce the name of my mother by adoption?*—GREAT EXPECTATIONS, CHARLES DICKENS

inkhorn NOUN
a small container for ink
• *A clerk sat at the other end of the same table, with inkhorn in one hand and pen in the other.*—MEN OF IRON, HOWARD PYLE

inkstand NOUN
a holder or tray for ink bottles
• *Here is an inkstand, here are pens and paper.*—BLEAK HOUSE, CHARLES DICKENS

inmate NOUN
one of the occupants of a house
• *She wrote also with great pleasure of her brother's being an inmate of Mr Darcy's house.*—PRIDE AND PREJUDICE, JANE AUSTEN

USAGE In modern English, you would talk about the *inmates* of a prison or other institution, rather than of a home.

inn NOUN
a house where travellers could eat, drink, and stay the night
• *I put up at an inn of minor reputation down the town, and ordered some dinner.*—GREAT EXPECTATIONS, CHARLES DICKENS

inroad NOUN
1 an unwanted or forced entrance; an invasion
• *During Silas's absence in the daytime the door had been locked, and there had been no marks of any inroad on his return.*—SILAS MARNER, GEORGE ELIOT
2 an attack by something unwanted
• *[Elizabeth] was filled with disquiet at the idea of my suffering, away from her, the inroads of misery and grief.*—FRANKENSTEIN, MARY SHELLEY

insatiate (say in-say-shi-uht) ADJECTIVE
never satisfied; insatiable
• *I shuddered to think who might be the next victim sacrificed to his insatiate revenge.*—FRANKENSTEIN, MARY SHELLEY

inscrutable *to* intelligence

inscrutable ADJECTIVE
mysterious; impossible to understand or interpret
• *that ghastly, inscrutable smile*—THE SIGN OF FOUR, ARTHUR CONAN DOYLE
• *It was vain to try to read with such an inscrutable fixture before me.*—JANE EYRE, CHARLOTTE BRONTË
➤ **inscrutably** ADVERB • *[She was] so inscrutably embarrassed that I came again to her aid.*—THE TURN OF THE SCREW, HENRY JAMES

insensate ADJECTIVE
lacking any feeling or compassion
• *A stick used to beat someone 'had broken in the middle under the stress of this insensate cruelty'.*—THE STRANGE CASE OF DR JEKYLL AND MR HYDE, ROBERT LOUIS STEVENSON

insensibility NOUN
1 unconsciousness
• *Susan Nipper ... falls into a state of insensibility, and is taken into a baker's shop to recover.*—DOMBEY AND SON, CHARLES DICKENS
2 insensitivity
• *The elder Miss Bennets alone were still able to eat, drink, and sleep ... Very frequently were they reproached for this insensibility by Kitty and Lydia.*—PRIDE AND PREJUDICE, JANE AUSTEN
3 lack of awareness or interest
• *With Mr Weston's ball in view ... there had been a great deal of insensibility to other things.*—EMMA, JANE AUSTEN

insensible ADJECTIVE
1 unconscious
• *She dropped insensible in his arms.*—A TALE OF TWO CITIES, CHARLES DICKENS
2 unaware
• *Mrs Nickleby [was] quite insensible to the sarcastic tone of Ralph's last remark.*—NICHOLAS NICKLEBY, CHARLES DICKENS
3 insensitive
• *After what you have just said to me, I should be insensible indeed if I didn't respect and admire you.*—THE MOONSTONE, WILKIE COLLINS

insensibly ADVERB
1 without being aware of something; unknowingly
• *[He was] insensibly influenced ... by Mary's sweet, earnest, lovely countenance.*—MARY BARTON, ELIZABETH GASKELL
2 gradually, imperceptibly
• *And then insensibly there came the strange change which I had noticed in the night.*—DRACULA, BRAM STOKER
3 involving unconsciousness
• *Here's the cook lying insensibly drunk on the kitchen floor.*—GREAT EXPECTATIONS, CHARLES DICKENS

insinuate VERB
1 to position something somewhere; to sneak something into a place
• *She took his hand, opened the unresisting fingers, insinuated into them the handkerchief, and closed them upon it one by one.*—VILLETTE, CHARLOTTE BRONTË
2 to drop something into a conversation; to add a comment
• *In the course of much verbal meandering he insinuated [this] information.*—SHIRLEY, CHARLOTTE BRONTË
➤ **insinuate yourself into something:** to get yourself into a particular place; to manoeuvre yourself into a particular position • *Fagin walked straight upstairs, and ... softly insinuating himself into the chamber, looked anxiously about.*—OLIVER TWIST, CHARLES DICKENS

inspirit VERB
to give someone energy or encouragement
• *During the day I was sustained and inspirited by the hope of night.*—FRANKENSTEIN, MARY SHELLEY

instancy NOUN
urgency
• *He begged me for a [drink] with such instancy ... that at last I handed him [brandy].*—KIDNAPPED, ROBERT LOUIS STEVENSON

instantly ADVERB
urgently; insistently
• *[I] instantly invited myself to that meal.*—THE MOONSTONE, WILKIE COLLINS

instrument NOUN
1 a means of doing something; a tool
• *That he should live to be an instrument of mischief disturbs me.*—FRANKENSTEIN, MARY SHELLEY
2 a piano or similar musical instrument
• *I am going to open the instrument, Eliza.*—PRIDE AND PREJUDICE, JANE AUSTEN

insupportable ADJECTIVE
intolerable; impossible to bear
• *The monster says his creator 'formed me and sent me forth to this insupportable misery'.*—FRANKENSTEIN, MARY SHELLEY

integument NOUN
a tough outer skin or casing
• *The Martian has a 'grey-brown, shiny, leathery integument'.*—THE WAR OF THE WORLDS, H. G. WELLS

intelligence NOUN
information
• *To Mr Darcy it was welcome intelligence.*—PRIDE AND PREJUDICE, JANE AUSTEN

interchange *to* invective

interchange *VERB*
to exchange words or looks
• *I don't know the gentlemen here. I have scarcely interchanged a syllable with one of them.*—JANE EYRE, CHARLOTTE BRONTË

interchange *NOUN*
an exchange of words or looks
• *This interchange of Christian name was effected.* —*meaning that they told each other their names.* —A TALE OF TWO CITIES, CHARLES DICKENS

intercourse *NOUN*
conversation or dealings with another person or with other people; communication
• *[Scrooge] had no further intercourse with Spirits.* —A CHRISTMAS CAROL, CHARLES DICKENS

interdict *NOUN*
an order forbidding something
• *Catherine learnt ... that her secret visits were to end. In vain she wept and writhed against the interdict.* —WUTHERING HEIGHTS, EMILY BRONTË

interdict *VERB*
to forbid something
• *On a confession of that nature, politeness would interdict comment.*—VILLETTE, CHARLOTTE BRONTË
➤ **interdicted** *ADJECTIVE* forbidden • *The dry-room was 'interdicted to the ... uninitiated'.*—THE BLACK TULIP, ALEXANDRE DUMAS

interest *NOUN*
a group of people sharing a particular interest or benefit
• *the landed interest*—SILAS MARNER, GEORGE ELIOT

interlocutor *NOUN*
a person involved in a conversation with someone
• *I was in mortal terror of my interlocutor.*—GREAT EXPECTATIONS, CHARLES DICKENS
➤ **interlocutress / interlocutrice** *NOUN* a female interlocutor • *Mr Rochester asks Mrs Fairfax 'to serve [Adèle] as auditress and interlocutrice'.*—JANE EYRE, CHARLOTTE BRONTË

interpose *VERB*
1 to intervene; to interrupt
• *Mrs Reed interposed, telling me to sit down.* —JANE EYRE, CHARLOTTE BRONTË
• *'How can I?' I interposed , as Herbert paused.* —GREAT EXPECTATIONS, CHARLES DICKENS
2 to put something between people or things
• *He stepped back a pace or two ... to interpose some wider space between them.*—DOMBEY AND SON, CHARLES DICKENS

interposition *NOUN*
intervention
• *I was released at last, not by my own efforts, but by Sir Percival's interposition.*—THE WOMAN IN WHITE, WILKIE COLLINS

interregnum *NOUN*
an interval, in particular a period between one person being in authority and the next
• *The feudal chieftains [had] taken advantage of the ... long interregnum.*—RIP VAN WINKLE, WASHINGTON IRVING

interview *NOUN*
a face-to-face meeting for conversation
• *Sarah did not object to William's occasional presence in their Sunday interviews.*—SILAS MARNER, GEORGE ELIOT
USAGE In modern English, you might expect an *interview* to be conducted by an employer, the police, or a reporter, rather than taking place between friends or acquaintances.

intimacy *NOUN*
friendship; closeness
• *I am astonished at his intimacy with Mr Bingley!* —PRIDE AND PREJUDICE, JANE AUSTEN

intimate *ADJECTIVE*
(said about friends or acquaintances) close
• *Herbert was my intimate companion and friend.* —GREAT EXPECTATIONS, CHARLES DICKENS
➤ **intimate** *NOUN* a person's close friend or acquaintance • *the young man's intimates in the regiment*—PRIDE AND PREJUDICE, JANE AUSTEN

intimate *VERB*
1 to let something be known by stating it plainly
• *I have intimated my view of the case.*—JANE EYRE, CHARLOTTE BRONTË
2 to suggest or hint at something
• *But ... my present sensations strongly intimated that the fiend would follow me.*—FRANKENSTEIN, MARY SHELLEY

intimation *NOUN*
1 a piece of information or news; an announcement
• *Hannah entered with the intimation that 'a poor lad was come ... to fetch Mr Rivers'.*—JANE EYRE, CHARLOTTE BRONTË
2 a sign or suggestion of something
• *There was scarcely an intimation of movement from the pit.*—THE WAR OF THE WORLDS, H. G. WELLS

invective *NOUN*
a critical or abusive comment; criticism or verbal abuse
• *Mrs Bennet ... received them ... with tears and ... invectives against the villanous conduct of Wickham.* —PRIDE AND PREJUDICE, JANE AUSTEN

Inverness cape *to* isinglass

Inverness cape NOUN
a coat or cloak with a removable cape

invest VERB
1 to make someone seem to have a particular quality
• Lucetta's new situation with *'servants, house, and fine clothing ... invested [her] with a startling novelty in [Henchard's] eyes'.*—THE MAYOR OF CASTERBRIDGE, THOMAS HARDY
2 to dress someone in something
• *The long nun proved [to be] a long bolster dressed in a long black stole, and artfully invested with a white veil.*—VILLETTE, CHARLOTTE BRONTË

inveterate ADJECTIVE
1 habitual; unlikely to change
• *an inveterate drunkard*—BLEAK HOUSE, CHARLES DICKENS
2 bitter; full of hatred
• *I felt inveterate against him.*—GREAT EXPECTATIONS, CHARLES DICKENS

inwrought ADJECTIVE
interwoven; intertwined
• *some curls ... inwrought with a few hairs like silver wires*—WESSEX TALES, THOMAS HARDY

ire NOUN
anger
• *I felt pain, and then I felt ire.*—JANE EYRE, CHARLOTTE BRONTË
➤ **ireful** ADJECTIVE angry • *an ireful glance*—JACK AND JILL, LOUISA M. ALCOTT

irid NOUN
an iris (of someone's eye)
• *In Jane's portrait of Mr Rochester, she draws 'the eyelashes ... long and sombre; the irids lustrous and large'.*—JANE EYRE, CHARLOTTE BRONTË

irksome ADJECTIVE
annoying; tiresome
• *Company was irksome to me.*—FRANKENSTEIN, MARY SHELLEY

iron-bound ADJECTIVE
1 strict; inflexible
• *Mrs Pipchin's middle-aged niece ... [possessed] a gaunt and iron-bound aspect.*—DOMBEY AND SON, CHARLES DICKENS
2 rocky; surrounded by rocks
• *Mrs Sparsit's eyes warn people off 'like a couple of lighthouses on an iron-bound coast'.*—HARD TIMES, CHARLES DICKENS

ironclad NOUN
a type of warship protected by metal armour, used in the 19th century
• *About a couple of miles out lay an ironclad, very low in the water.*—THE WAR OF THE WORLDS, H. G. WELLS

irradiate VERB
to shine on something; to light something up
• *[She had] a quiet oval face ... irradiated by a pair of very gentle eyes.*—HARD TIMES, CHARLES DICKENS
➤ **irradiation** NOUN • *The ecstasy of faith ... set upon her face a glowing irradiation.*—TESS OF THE D'URBERVILLES, THOMAS HARDY

inexpressible ADJECTIVE
too strong to be expressed in words
• *I experienced an inexpressible sadness.*—JANE EYRE, CHARLOTTE BRONTË
➤ **inexpressibly** ADVERB • *The recollection of what I then said ... is ... inexpressibly painful to me.*—PRIDE AND PREJUDICE, JANE AUSTEN

irruption NOUN
a sudden or violent entrance; an invasion
• *A large group of people 'made a disorderly irruption into Mr Bounderby's dining-room'.*—HARD TIMES, CHARLES DICKENS

isinglass (say **igh-zing-glaass**) NOUN
1 a firm, semi-transparent kind of gelatin extracted from fish
• *A whale's body is covered in 'an infinitely thin, transparent substance, somewhat resembling the thinnest shreds of isinglass'.*—MOBY DICK, HERMAN MELVILLE
2 thin transparent sheets of mica, a mineral substance
• *[The stove], through the isinglass of its door, seemed to glare ... like a red-eyed demon.*—THE SNOW-IMAGE, NATHANIEL HAWTHORNE

Jj

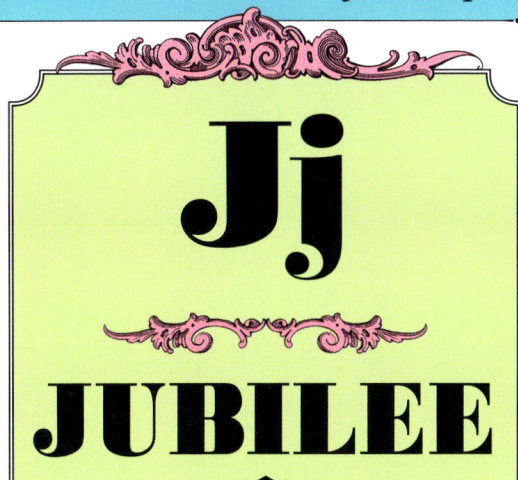

JUBILEE

On Sunday 20th June, **1897**, **Queen Victoria** celebrated her **Diamond Jubilee**, marking the 60th anniversary of her accession to the throne. Celebrations took place across the British Empire, which by then spread over more than a quarter of the world's population. An estimated million people lined the streets of London to cheer the Queen as she rode in an open carriage at the head of a royal procession of 50,000 troops.

jackanapes (say jak-uh-nayps) NOUN
1 a cheeky or self-important person
• Henchard ridicules a new machine that *'was brought here … on the recommendation of a jumped-up jackanapes of a fellow'.*—THE MAYOR OF CASTERBRIDGE, THOMAS HARDY
2 a pet monkey
• *I could see him climbing like a jackanapes.*—KIDNAPPED, ROBERT LOUIS STEVENSON

jack-towel NOUN
a long towel with its ends joined, hung on a roller
• *[His closet] had an unusually large jack-towel on a roller inside the door.*—GREAT EXPECTATIONS, CHARLES DICKENS

jargon NOUN
language or a mixture of languages that was meaningless or full of mistakes
• Mr Paul attempts to speak English *'in a jargon the most execrable that ever was heard'.*—VILLETTE, CHARLOTTE BRONTË

jessamine NOUN
jasmine
• The garden has *'roses, lavender, sage, balm (for tea), rosemary, pinks and wallflowers, onions and jessamine'.*—MARY BARTON, ELIZABETH GASKELL

jetty ADJECTIVE
shiny black
• *jetty hair*—JANE EYRE, CHARLOTTE BRONTË

jiggered ADJECTIVE
➤ **I'll be jiggered / I'm jiggered**: used for expressing surprise or for emphasizing a statement
• *'Well, then … I'm jiggered if I don't see you home!'*—meaning 'I will see you home.'—GREAT EXPECTATIONS, CHARLES DICKENS

jilt NOUN
a person who rejected a boyfriend or girlfriend unfairly after encouraging them
• *'She said she did love me then.' 'Confound it … Is she a jilt?'*—THE MILL ON THE FLOSS, GEORGE ELIOT

jingo NOUN
➤ **by jingo / jingoes / jings / by the living jingo**: an expression of surprise or emphasis
• *Hey, by jingo, there's the young Squire leading off now.*—SILAS MARNER, GEORGE ELIOT
• *I'll foller him; I will, by jingoes!*—THE ADVENTURES OF TOM SAWYER, MARK TWAIN

jocose ADJECTIVE
joking; light-hearted
• *He was jocose with Tom at table, and corrected his provincialisms … in the most playful manner.*—THE MILL ON THE FLOSS, GEORGE ELIOT
➤ **jocosely** ADVERB • *The prisoner winked at my friend jocosely.*—A STUDY IN SCARLET, ARTHUR CONAN DOYLE
🏛 Latin *jocos*, meaning 'joke, wordplay'
RELATED WORD The word *joke* probably comes from the same root.

jolly-boat NOUN
a small boat carried on a larger ship
• *It was decided that Hunter and I should go ashore with the jolly-boat.*—TREASURE ISLAND, ROBERT LOUIS STEVENSON

jorum NOUN
a large bowl for drinks; the drink that it contained
• *Miss Skiffins brewed … a jorum of tea.*—GREAT EXPECTATIONS, CHARLES DICKENS

joseph NOUN
a woman's riding cloak
• Nancy is *'attired in a drab joseph and a drab beaver-bonnet'.*—SILAS MARNER, GEORGE ELIOT

journeyman to justly

journeyman NOUN
a skilled craftsman or worker who was employed, often on a short-term basis, rather than being an apprentice or master
• *Joe kept a journeyman at weekly wages whose name was Orlick.*—GREAT EXPECTATIONS, CHARLES DICKENS

Jove NOUN
The roman god Jupiter
➢ **by Jove:** an expression of surprise or emphasis
• *'By Jove! this won't do,' cried Tom.*—MANSFIELD PARK, JANE AUSTEN

Juggernaut NOUN
1 a huge, powerful, unstoppable vehicle or force
• *That human Juggernaut trod the child down and passed on regardless of her screams.*—THE STRANGE CASE OF DR JEKYLL AND MR HYDE, ROBERT LOUIS STEVENSON
2 Jagannath or Jagannatha, a name for a form of the god Vishnu in Hinduism, Buddhism, and Jainism
USAGE 19th century Western writers often used *Juggernaut* when referring to a festival in Puri, eastern India, in which Jaganath's image is pulled through the streets on a very heavy chariot. European travellers reported that worshippers would deliberately throw themselves under its wheels.

Juno NOUN
in Roman mythology, the most important goddess, Jupiter's wife
• *Troy describes Bathsheba as 'this haughty goddess, dashing piece of womanhood, Juno-wife of mine'.*—FAR FROM THE MADDING CROWD, THOMAS HARDY

justice NOUN
a magistrate or judge
• *It was to be hoped Mr Godfrey would not ... prevent the justice from drawing up a warrant.*—SILAS MARNER, GEORGE ELIOT

justly ADVERB
exactly; precisely
• *I've laid something up though I can't justly put my hand on it.*—SILAS MARNER, GEORGE ELIOT

102

Kk

KIPLING

Born in Bombay, India in **1837**, **Rudyard Kipling** was a popular Victorian writer. Many of his poems (such as *Mandalay*) and stories celebrated the British Empire, but have also been criticized for promoting a view of British superiority. One of Kipling's most famous works is *The Jungle Book*, a collection of animal stories for children that was first published in 1894. He also wrote the popular autobiographical story *Kim* about a white boy growing up in India.

keel NOUN
a red substance used for marking animals or yarn; the mark made
• a sheep ... marked, with his owner's keel—MOONFLEET, J. MEADE FALKNER

keen ADJECTIVE
1 intense or acute; strongly felt
• Silas turned a look of keen reproach on him.—SILAS MARNER, GEORGE ELIOT
2 sensitive; aware
• The keenest reasoner may occasionally be deceived.—THE SIGN OF FOUR, ARTHUR CONAN DOYLE
➤ **keenly** ADVERB • How often and how keenly I have thought of this I will not say.—A CHRISTMAS CAROL, CHARLES DICKENS
• These angry symptoms were keenly observed by Maggie.—THE MILL ON THE FLOSS, GEORGE ELIOT
➤ **keenness** NOUN • the first keenness of suffering—THE MOONSTONE, WILKIE COLLINS
• 'Well, then,' said Bob, whose keenness saw at once what was implied.—THE MILL ON THE FLOSS, GEORGE ELIOT

ken NOUN
someone's mind, knowledge, or sight; awareness
• One of these thoughts sailed into Henchard's ken.—THE MAYOR OF CASTERBRIDGE, THOMAS HARDY
• Mr Hyde had disappeared out of the ken of the police as though he had never existed.—THE STRANGE CASE OF DR JEKYLL AND MR HYDE, ROBERT LOUIS STEVENSON

ken VERB
to know something or someone
• Why ... how else would I ken?—KIDNAPPED, ROBERT LOUIS STEVENSON

kex NOUN
a dried plant stem, especially from a large wild plant such as cow parsley
• Crick would be thirsty—'as dry as a kex'.—TESS OF THE D'URBERVILLES, THOMAS HARDY

key NOUN
the tone or pitch of someone's voice
• One [voice] was my Jonathan's, raised in a high key of passion.—DRACULA, BRAM STOKER

key-note NOUN
1 the first and main note in a musical key
2 the main tone or theme
• The mighty shout of joy which greeted Elizabeth's entry into London, was the key-note of fifty glorious years.—WESTWARD HO!, CHARLES KINGSLEY

khitmutgar (also **khidmutgar**) NOUN
in India, a male servant who served at the table

kid gloves NOUN
gloves made from soft leather, typically from the skin of a young goat
USAGE In modern English, you would expect the term *kid gloves* only to be used figuratively, with reference to handling someone or something very gently.

kindle VERB
1 to get a fire going; to set light to something
• A fire had been lately kindled in the damp old-fashioned grate.—GREAT EXPECTATIONS, CHARLES DICKENS
2 to arouse, fill with, or show a strong feeling
• The latter part of his tale had kindled anew in me the anger that had died away.—FRANKENSTEIN, MARY SHELLEY
• I saw his face all kindled.—JANE EYRE, CHARLOTTE BRONTË
• Meg's mild eyes kindled with anger.—LITTLE WOMEN, LOUISA M. ALCOTT

kit NOUN
1 a small violin
• [He] sometimes played the kit, dancing ... , while he set a pupil right.—BLEAK HOUSE, CHARLES DICKENS

knacker to knell

2 a kitten or other young animal
• *The unhappy kits were rescued.*—EIGHT COUSINS, LOUISA M. ALCOTT
3 a group or number of people or things
• *I'll show a better gentleman than the whole kit on you put together!*—GREAT EXPECTATIONS, CHARLES DICKENS

knacker NOUN
a person whose job was to buy and slaughter unwanted horses for their hides and meat
• *My plan is to work [the horses] as long as they'll go, and then sell 'em for what they'll fetch, at the knacker's.*—BLACK BEAUTY, ANNA SEWELL

knave NOUN
a dishonest man
• *the knaves he lived amongst*—JANE EYRE, CHARLOTTE BRONTË

knavery NOUN
wicked or dishonest behaviour
• *Monks dies in prison after 'a long confinement for some fresh act of fraud and knavery'.*—OLIVER TWIST, CHARLES DICKENS

knavish ADJECTIVE
wicked; dishonest
• *that knavish trick*—LORNA DOONE, R. D. BLACKMORE

knell NOUN
the sound of a bell, typically rung to mark a death or funeral
• *A knell from the church bell broke harshly on these youthful thoughts.*—OLIVER TWIST, CHARLES DICKENS

lackaday to languish

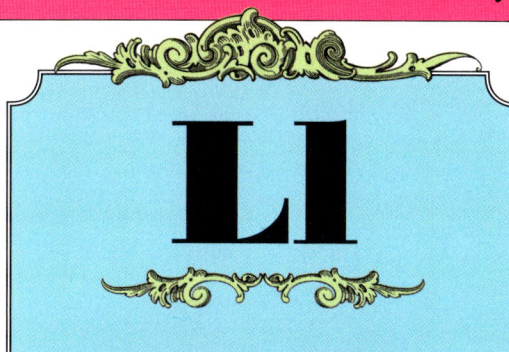

Ll

LIBRARIES

Circulating libraries such as those run by W.H. Smith and Son allowed 19th-century readers to borrow books for a fee. In **1852** the first public library was opened in Salford, and it allowed the reading public to borrow books for free. Public libraries spread as rising literacy rates in the second half of the century brought a greater demand for novels, especially amongst women. The arrival of gas and electric lighting in people's homes also made it easier to read after dark.

lackaday ADJECTIVE
without enthusiasm or interest; lackadaisical
• *I have been living on in a ... lackaday way.*—TESS OF THE D'URBERVILLES, THOMAS HARDY

lade VERB
to load goods onto a ship or vehicle
• *When a ship had been laden with [the gold] ... they crossed the seas.*—THE BLUE FAIRY BOOK, ANDREW LANG
➤ **lading** NOUN • *She was still superintending the lading of the cart.*—SHIRLEY, CHARLOTTE BRONTË

lady-clock NOUN
a ladybird

lam VERB
to hit or beat someone
• *But I bet you I'll lam Sid for that.*—THE ADVENTURES OF TOM SAWYER, MARK TWAIN

lambent ADJECTIVE
shining; bright
• *gleaming like lambent fire*—SUNK AT SEA, R. M. BALLANTYNE

lamentable ADJECTIVE
showing sadness; mournful
• *this lamentable cry*—THE POMEGRANATE SEEDS, NATHANIEL HAWTHORNE
RELATED WORD *lament* and *lamentation* meaning 'expression of grief or regret'; *lament* meaning 'to express grief or regret'

lameter (say **lay-mit-uhr**) NOUN
a person who could not walk; a lame person
• *But ... you have ... friends who will ... not suffer you to devote yourself to a blind lameter like me?*—JANE EYRE, CHARLOTTE BRONTË

lamplighter NOUN
a person whose job was to light streetlights
• *Then came the lamplighter, and two lengthening lines of light all down ... the street.*—HARD TIMES, CHARLES DICKENS

landau (say **lan-daw**) NOUN
a carriage with four wheels, a front cover that could be removed, and a back cover that could be raised or lowered
• *Up the lane came a neat little landau.*—THE ADVENTURES OF SHERLOCK HOLMES, ARTHUR CONAN DOYLE

lander NOUN
a person who brought cargo ashore
• *old lander Jordan's gang*—MOONFLEET, J. MEADE FALKNER

landsman NOUN
a person who was not used to the sea or to being on a ship
• *the sickness of an unused landsman on the sea*—KIDNAPPED, ROBERT LOUIS STEVENSON

languid ADJECTIVE
1 weary or dull; lacking energy or enthusiasm
• *I felt languid and unable to reflect on all that had passed.*—FRANKENSTEIN, MARY SHELLEY
2 unhurried; slow-moving; leisurely
• *In appearance he was ... thin ... and large-eyed, with languid and yet courtly manners.*—THE MEMOIRS OF SHERLOCK HOLMES, ARTHUR CONAN DOYLE
➤ **languidly** ADVERB • *He raised his eyes languidly.*—THE SIGN OF FOUR, ARTHUR CONAN DOYLE

languish VERB
1 to deliberately look or sound full of concern or affection
• *He was ... ready to sigh and languish ponderously ... on the smallest provocation.*—THE WOMAN IN WHITE, WILKIE COLLINS
2 to yearn for someone or something
• *The church, far from 'languishing for the company of other churches', is surrounded by them.*—DOMBEY AND SON, CHARLES DICKENS

languor to lay

3 to become less significant; to fade away
• *The robbery at the Bank had not languished.* —HARD TIMES, CHARLES DICKENS

languor NOUN
weariness, depression, or lack of energy
• *I nearly sank to the ground through languor and extreme weakness.* —FRANKENSTEIN, MARY SHELLEY

lanthorn NOUN
an old spelling of lantern
• *Bob was not long after her ... with the lanthorn in his hand.* —THE MILL ON THE FLOSS, GEORGE ELIOT

lappet NOUN
a loose part of a garment, for example a long hanging part on a hat or an overlapping lapel on a coat
• *[He put] on a rabbit-skin cap with hanging lappets which covered the ears.* —THE SIGN OF FOUR, ARTHUR CONAN DOYLE

lapse NOUN
an interval; the passage of time
• *Silas's body is 'much enfeebled by the lapse of the sixteen years'.* —SILAS MARNER, GEORGE ELIOT

lapse VERB
(said about time) to pass; elapse
• *Captain Cuttle decided not to go ... until ... some little time should have lapsed.* —DOMBEY AND SON, CHARLES DICKENS

larboard NOUN
the port side of a ship
• *I looked to starboard, and ... then to larboard.* —MOONFLEET, J. MEADE FALKNER

larry NOUN
excitement; a confused state
• *Oh, please, ma'am, 'tis this larry about Mr Henchard.* —THE MAYOR OF CASTERBRIDGE, THOMAS HARDY

lascar NOUN
an Indian sailor
🏛 Portuguese *lascari*; Urdu and Persian *laškarī*, meaning 'soldier'

lassitude NOUN
physical or mental tiredness; lack of energy
• *It was a day of lassitude ... hot and close.* —WAR OF THE WORLDS, H. G. WELLS

late ADJECTIVE
1 no longer alive
• *His father ... the late Mr Darcy, was one of the best men that ever breathed.* —PRIDE AND PREJUDICE, JANE AUSTEN

2 recent
• *I was seriously affected ... by late events.* —DAVID COPPERFIELD, CHARLES DICKENS
➤ **of late years:** in recent years; recently • *Of late years he had had doubts.* —SILAS MARNER, GEORGE ELIOT

late ADVERB
➤ **late of:** previously, but no longer, living or working in the place mentioned • *'Mr Henry Wood, late of India, I believe,' said Holmes, affably.* —THE MEMOIRS OF SHERLOCK HOLMES, SIR ARTHUR CONAN DOYLE

late NOUN
➤ **of late:** recently • *He has been very silent and doleful of late.* —HARD TIMES, CHARLES DICKENS NOUN

lath-and-plaster NOUN
a building material for walls, made from thin strips of wood coated with plaster
• *He knocked a hole ... in the lath-and-plaster ceiling.* —THE SIGN OF FOUR, ARTHUR CONAN DOYLE

laudanum (say law-duh-nuhm, lod-uhn-uhm) NOUN
a strong medicine containing alcohol and opium, used as a painkiller and sedative
• *if Molly should ... take a drop too much laudanum ... and make a widower of you* —SILAS MARNER, GEORGE ELIOT

lawn NOUN
fine linen or cotton material
• *young ladies clad in lawn and muslin* —THE ADVENTURES OF TOM SAWYER, MARK TWAIN
➤ **lawny** ADJECTIVE • *[clouds] of the most diaphanous and lawny texture* —THE STRANGE CASE OF DR JEKYLL AND MR HYDE, ROBERT LOUIS STEVENSON

lay NOUN
1 an occupation or business
• *What's your lay?* —THE ADVENTURES OF HUCKLEBERRY FINN, MARK TWAIN
2 a song
• *The poets ... were called 'Minstrels', and their poems 'Lays'.* —IVANHOE, WALTER SCOTT

lay VERB
to present information; to make an accusation
• *Come, come, Master Marner ... if you've got any information to lay, speak it out sensible.* —SILAS MARNER, GEORGE ELIOT
➤ **lay by:**
1 to stop work; to retire • *But you're getting rather past such close work, Marner: it's time you laid by and had some rest.* —SILAS MARNER, GEORGE ELIOT
2 to set aside money or goods • *Mr Bennet had very often wished ... that ... he had laid by an annual sum, for the better provision of his children, and of his wife, if she survived him.* —PRIDE AND PREJUDICE, JANE AUSTEN
• *And she is laying by: she goes every quarter to the bank at Millcote.* —JANE EYRE, CHARLOTTE BRONTË

lea to liberty

lea NOUN
a meadow; an open grassy area
• *the sombre woodland, the clear and sunny lea*—JANE EYRE, CHARLOTTE BRONTË

lead VERB
➢ **lead away:** to persuade someone to do something bad; to lead someone astray • *But I have no confidence in you, Maggie. You would be led away to do anything.*—THE MILL ON THE FLOSS, GEORGE ELIOT

leaden ADJECTIVE
made of lead
• *the narrow leaden roof* —THE WOMAN IN WHITE, WILKIE COLLINS

leal ADJECTIVE
loyal
• *Mr Toots, like the leal and trusty soul he was*—DOMBEY AND SON, CHARLES DICKENS

leastwise ADVERB
at least
• *'Tisn't a city, the place I mean; leastwise 'twaddn' when I was there.*—TESS OF THE D'URBERVILLES, THOMAS HARDY

leathern ADJECTIVE
leather
• *leathern bags*—SILAS MARNER, GEORGE ELIOT

leave NOUN
permission
• *And so you did give him leave to sell the horse, eh?*—SILAS MARNER, GEORGE ELIOT
➢ **by your leave:** with your permission • *I will explain my business, by your leave.*—GREAT EXPECTATIONS, CHARLES DICKENS
➢ **take leave of:** to say goodbye to someone and go away • *Elizabeth took leave of the whole party in the liveliest spirits.*—PRIDE AND PREJUDICE, JANE AUSTEN
➢ **take leave to:** to venture or presume to do something • *'Tell your sovereign master, Sir,' said Edith, 'that I will take leave to speak to him on this subject by-and-bye.'*—DOMBEY AND SON, CHARLES DICKENS

legatee NOUN
a person receiving a legacy
• *his intention to adopt me and make me his legatee*—JANE EYRE, CHARLOTTE BRONTË

leg-iron NOUN
a metal band or chain put around a prisoner's ankle
• *a convict's leg-iron which had been filed asunder*—GREAT EXPECTATIONS, CHARLES DICKENS

leman (say lem-uhn, lee-muhn) NOUN
a person's sweetheart or lover
• *Thy leman is lost, and thou shalt be lost with her.*—THE FISHERMAN AND HIS SOUL, OSCAR WILDE

lens NOUN
a magnifying glass
• *He whipped out his lens and a tape measure.*—THE SIGN OF FOUR, SHERLOCK HOLMES

letterpress NOUN
the text of a book, as opposed to the illustrations
• *The letterpress ... I cared little for ... and yet there were certain ... pages that ... I could not pass.*—JANE EYRE, CHARLOTTE BRONTË
🏛 Only the text was produced by pressing letters onto the page.

letters NOUN
➢ **a man of letters:** a writer; a learned or educated man • *But not being a man o' letters, I can't read writing.*—THE MAYOR OF CASTERBRIDGE, THOMAS HARDY

leviathan (say li-vy-uh-thuhn) NOUN
a sea monster; a whale
• *a stranded leviathan*—DOMBEY AND SON, CHARLES DICKENS

liberal ADJECTIVE
generous
• *There can scarcely be a doubt that her father is ... a gentleman of fortune.—Her allowance is very liberal.* EMMA, JANE AUSTEN
➣ **liberally** ADVERB generously; a lot • *I was liberally paid.*—GREAT EXPECTATIONS, CHARLES DICKENS

liberty NOUN
freedom
• *I was beginning to feel my liberty of action somewhat curtailed.*—DREAM DAYS, KENNETH GRAHAME
➢ **at liberty:**
1 free • *Another effort set me at liberty, and I stood erect before him.*—JANE EYRE, CHARLOTTE BRONTË
2 not busy • *Mr Rochester was now at liberty.*—JANE EYRE, CHARLOTTE BRONTË
➢ **at liberty to:** allowed or able to do something
• *I am not at liberty to say how I know it.*—THE WOMAN IN WHITE, WILKIE COLLINS
➢ **take the liberty of:** to do something without asking for permission first • *And now let me take the liberty of asking you a question.*—GREAT EXPECTATIONS, CHARLES DICKENS
➢ **take liberties:** to behave in a disrespectful way
• *I ... asked ... how he could allow such a wretch to take such liberties with himself and his household.*—THE MEMOIRS OF SHERLOCK HOLMES, ARTHUR CONAN DOYLE

library NOUN
a room in a house where books were kept
• *Their father then went to the library to write, and the girls walked into the breakfast-room.*—PRIDE AND PREJUDICE, JANE AUSTEN
➤ **circulating library:** a small library from which members could borrow books for a small fee • *Mr Collins is shocked to see that 'every thing announced [the book] to be from a circulating library'.*—PRIDE AND PREJUDICE, JANE AUSTEN

Penny dreadful

Costing just a penny for a single weekly issue, the 'penny dreadful' or 'penny blood' was an eight-page booklet containing sensational stories of highwaymen, pirates, and notorious criminals. Sometimes based on true crimes, this cheap fiction became extremely popular amongst working-class readers in the first half of the 19th century. *The String of Pearls* told the fictional story of a murderous London barber named Sweeney Todd. From the 1860s, penny dreadfuls were aimed at children and were blamed for leading young readers into a life of crime. Rival publications such as *The Boy's Own Paper*, which was first published in 1879, were launched to provide more wholesome stories.

---

licence (also **license**) NOUN
1 freedom; permission to do something
• *[They] were allowed almost unlimited license.*—JANE EYRE, CHARLOTTE BRONTË
2 bad or immoral behaviour
• *that disgraceful license by which that age was stained*—IVANHOE, WALTER SCOTT

lief (say leef)
➤ **as lief:** just as happily • *I'd as lief not invite sister Deane.*—THE MILL ON THE FLOSS, GEORGE ELIOT

liege (say leej) ADJECTIVE
loyal; bound in service
• *liege subjects*—THE MAYOR OF CASTERBRIDGE, THOMAS HARDY

life-interest NOUN
a right that ended with a person's life rather than being passed on to their children
• *the property in which she had a life-interest*—THE WOMAN IN WHITE, WILKIE COLLINS

light VERB
➤ **light on / upon:**
1 to descend or settle somewhere • *Being far away, as he told Scrooge, from any shore, they lighted on a ship.*—A CHRISTMAS CAROL, CHARLES DICKENS
2 to arrive at a place or to meet someone by chance; to come upon someone or something • *She knew that she would light upon a … cottage of some sort from time to time.*—WESSEX TALES, THOMAS HARDY

lighter NOUN
a barge or small boat used for transferring goods to and from ships in a harbour
➤ **lighterman** NOUN a man whose job was to operate a lighter • *sailors and lightermen*—THE WAR OF THE WORLDS, H. G. WELLS

lightly ADVERB
without thought or difficulty; carelessly
• *[They] had lightly put their limbs in fetters from which no struggle could loose them.*—SILAS MARNER, GEORGE ELIOT

lights NOUN
1 a person's character and abilities
• *'He acted according to his lights,' said Holmes.*—THE SIGN OF FOUR, SIR ARTHUR CONAN DOYLE
2 animals' lungs used as food, usually for cats and dogs
• *The butcher says he would 'keep [Solomon] in liver and lights for nothing'.*—SILAS MARNER, GEORGE ELIOT
➤ **scare the lights** (or **liver and lights**) **out of:** to frighten someone a lot • *It most scared the livers and lights out of me.*—THE ADVENTURES OF HUCKLEBERRY FINN, MARK TWAIN

lightsome ADJECTIVE
1 carefree; light-hearted
• *Lorna speaks in a 'lightsome manner'.*—LORNA DOONE, R. D. BLACKMORE
2 graceful; light-footed
• *her … lightsome step*—SHIRLEY, CHARLOTTE BRONTË

likeness NOUN
1 a person who looked like someone else
• *I never met your likeness.*—JANE EYRE, CHARLOTTE BRONTË
2 a portrait. To 'take someone's likeness' was to make a portrait of them.
• *Did you ever have your likeness taken?*—EMMA, JANE AUSTEN

limb NOUN
a rascal or scoundrel
• *'Now listen, you young limb,' whispered Sikes.*—OLIVER TWIST, CHARLES DICKENS

lime NOUN
1 limestone, or the substance produced by heating limestone in a kiln
- *The lime was burning with a sluggish stifling smell.* —GREAT EXPECTATIONS, CHARLES DICKENS

2 used for talking about various substances containing calcium
- *a hen's egg, laid without enough of lime, and looking only a poor jelly*—LORNA DOONE, R. D. BLACKMORE

3 a sticky substance used for catching small birds

lime VERB
to catch birds with lime; also used figuratively
- *Abraham ... seemed to have been limed and caught by the ensnaring inn.*—TESS OF THE D'URBERVILLES, THOMAS HARDY

limekiln NOUN
a chamber or building in which limestone was heated in order to process it

limpid ADJECTIVE
clear; transparent
- *the limpid waters of the lowland brook*—THE MERRY ADVENTURES OF ROBIN HOOD, HOWARD PYLE

line NOUN
1 a rope, cord, or string
- *'I opened the staircase window and ... nearly beheaded myself, for the lines had rotted away, and it came down like the guillotine.'*—the cords holding up the sliding sash window.—GREAT EXPECTATIONS, CHARLES DICKENS

2 a short letter
- *For a long time I have thought that each post would bring this line.*—FRANKENSTEIN, MARY SHELLEY

lineament (say lin-i-uh-muhnt) NOUN
a feature in someone's face
- *I saw ... tenderness and passion in every lineament.* —JANE EYRE, CHARLOTTE BRONTË

link NOUN
a torch made with fibres soaked in pitch and burnt
- *Meanwhile the fog and darkness thickened so, that people ran about with flaring links, proffering their services to go before horses in carriages, and conduct them on their way.*—A CHRISTMAS CAROL, CHARLES DICKENS

linnet NOUN
a bird of the finch family
- *It seemed as if a linnet had hopped to my foot and proposed to bear me on its tiny wing.*—JANE EYRE, CHARLOTTE BRONTË

list (also 'list) VERB
to enlist or join up as a soldier or sailor
- *I had 'listed under another name, and I went abroad.* —BLEAK HOUSE, CHARLES DICKENS

list NOUN
a fabric border or strip; the material from which this was made
- *I watched her glide along the gallery, her quiet tread muffled in a list slipper.*—JANE EYRE, CHARLOTTE BRONTË
➢ **the lists:** the enclosed area where a tournament took place • *Then ... he started blindly across the lists towards the gate.*—MEN OF IRON, HOWARD PYLE

literally ADVERB
not metaphorically or in an exaggerated way, but truly; really
- *a part of town where there was literally nothing to be seen but lamps*—THE STRANGE CASE OF DR JEKYLL AND MR HYDE, ROBERT LOUIS STEVENSON

lithodome NOUN
a creature with a shell like a mussel

livelong ADJECTIVE
the whole of a period of time
- *The livelong day he sat in his loom.*—SILAS MARNER, GEORGE ELIOT

livery NOUN
1 a uniform
- *the livery of the servant*—PRIDE AND PREJUDICE, JANE AUSTEN

2 livery stable
a stable keeping horses for hire, or for their owners
- *the master of some livery stables*—BLACK BEAUTY, ANNA SEWELL

3 Livery
members of a *livery company*, a trade association whose members wore ceremonial uniforms and supported good causes
- *the corporation, aldermen, and livery*—A CHRISTMAS CAROL, CHARLES DICKENS

livid ADJECTIVE
1 deathly pale
- *[The face] was of a livid chalky white.*—THE MEMOIRS OF SHERLOCK HOLMES, ARTHUR CONAN DOYLE

2 very flushed; red
- *His face was livid ... He was heaving and panting.* —THE RED BADGE OF COURAGE, STEPHEN CRANE

3 purplish, bluish, or greyish
- *a crop of livid fungi*—A STUDY IN SCARLET & OTHER SHERLOCK HOLMES ADVENTURES, ARTHUR CONAN DOYLE

living NOUN
a position held by a priest, providing income and / or a home
- *I was brought up for the church, and I should ... have been in possession of a most valuable living.*—PRIDE AND PREJUDICE, JANE AUSTEN

loafer to lot

loafer NOUN
a person loitering on the street; a homeless person
• *I went in the shape of a loafer.*—THE ADVENTURES OF SHERLOCK HOLMES, ARTHUR CONAN DOYLE

loath (say loth) ADJECTIVE
➤ **nothing loth**: very willing to do something
• *Then she began to drag him, in her childish eagerness, towards the door; and he, nothing loath to go, accompanied her.*—A CHRISTMAS CAROL, CHARLES DICKENS

locomotive ADJECTIVE
mobile; moving around
• *He ... followed his locomotive nephew with his eyes.*—DOMBEY AND SON, CHARLES DICKENS
➤ **locomotively** ADVERB • *He always slouched, locomotively.*—GREAT EXPECTATIONS, CHARLES DICKENS

loft NOUN
a balcony or upper floor in a building
• *As there was a loft above, I called, 'Is there any one here?'*—GREAT EXPECTATIONS, CHARLES DICKENS

lofty ADJECTIVE
1 high or tall
• *The rooms were lofty and handsome.*—PRIDE AND PREJUDICE, JANE AUSTEN
2 haughty
• *a lofty contempt*—THE MOONSTONE, WILKIE COLLINS
3 of high social standing
• *the bright bar or kitchen ... where the less lofty customers of the house were in the habit of assembling*—SILAS MARNER, GEORGE ELIOT

loiter VERB
to walk idly somewhere; to dawdle
• *We loitered down to the Temple stairs.*—GREAT EXPECTATIONS, CHARLES DICKENS

lone ADJECTIVE
lonely; remote
• *'But you'll never be lone again, father,' said Eppie, tenderly.*—SILAS MARNER, GEORGE ELIOT
• *lone public-houses*—GREAT EXPECTATIONS, CHARLES DICKENS

long-clothes NOUN
a long garment worn by a small baby
• *[The girl] carried in her arms ... an infant in long clothes.*—TESS OF THE D'URBERVILLES, THOMAS HARDY

long-headed ADJECTIVE
sensible; showing good judgment
• *The workhouse board (i.e. the people in charge) are 'long-headed men'.*—OLIVER TWIST, CHARLES DICKENS

long-winded ADJECTIVE
able to continue for a long time without being short of breath

loo NOUN
a card game in which players paid a fine, also called a 'loo', for losing a trick or for breaking a rule
• *On entering the drawing-room she found the whole party at loo.*—PRIDE AND PREJUDICE, JANE AUSTEN

look VERB
➤ **look forward to**: to anticipate or think about a future event (not necessarily with pleasure)
• *We looked forward to his arrival with some curiosity.*—BLEAK HOUSE, CHARLES DICKENS
• *I shall get older and helplesser ... and when I look for'ard to that, I like to think as you'd have somebody else besides me—somebody young and strong.*—SILAS MARNER, GEORGE ELIOT

lop VERB
1 to hang down
• *The sheep have spiral horns 'lopping gracefully on each side of their cheeks'.*—FAR FROM THE MADDING CROWD, THOMAS HARDY
2 to move around drooping or slouching
• *She 'lopped round, as if she'd lost every friend she had'.*—UNCLE TOM'S CABIN, HARRIET BEECHER STOWE

loquacious ADJECTIVE
talkative
• *For the next half-hour, he was quite loquacious.*—DAVID COPPERFIELD, CHARLES DICKENS
➤ **loquacity** NOUN talkativeness; fluent or uninterrupted speech • *Uncle Glegg stood open-mouthed with astonishment at this unembarrassed loquacity.*—FAR FROM THE MADDING CROWD, THOMAS HARDY

lor (also **lordy**, **lors**) EXCLAMATION
used for showing emphasis or surprise
• *Lor, you'll be so smart.*—DOMBEY AND SON, CHARLES DICKENS

lordling NOUN
a minor lord
• *this kind little lordling*—LITTLE LORD FAUNTLEROY, FRANCES HODGSON BURNETT

lore NOUN
a set of rules of facts; instruction or knowledge
• *[St John] pondered a mystic lore of his own: that of some Eastern tongue.*—JANE EYRE, CHARLOTTE BRONTË

lot NOUN
a person's fate, condition, or situation in life
• *I was moved with a sense of grief at his lot.*—WUTHERING HEIGHTS, EMILY BRONTË
➤ **the common lot**: everyone's fate • *Your destiny can be no exception to the common lot.*—SHIRLEY, CHARLOTTE BRONTË
➤ **fall to someone's lot**: to be someone's fate
• *Miss Bingley says she would not like to write so many letters. Mr Darcy replies, 'It is fortunate, then,*

lottery tickets *to* lymphatic

that they fall to my lot instead of yours'.—PRIDE AND PREJUDICE, JANE AUSTEN

lottery tickets (also **lottery**) NOUN
a game using two packs of cards, in which players won a prize if their card matched a card from the other pack
• Mrs Philips protested that they would have a nice comfortable noisy game of lottery tickets, and a little bit of hot supper afterwards.—PRIDE AND PREJUDICE, JANE AUSTEN

lounger NOUN
an idle person
• Among the loungers ... happened to be Trabb's boy.—GREAT EXPECTATIONS, CHARLES DICKENS

love NOUN
➢ **make love to:** to declare to someone your love for them; to flirt with someone or try to win their affection • a certain man, who made love to Miss Havisham—GREAT EXPECTATIONS, CHARLES DICKENS
• He simpers, and smirks, and makes love to us all.—PRIDE AND PREJUDICE, JANE AUSTEN

love-lock NOUN
a curl of hair
• that small boy with the mop of yellow love-locks—LITTLE LORD FAUNTLEROY, FRANCES HODGSON BURNETT

lovemaking NOUN
courtship; declarations of love
• You shall hear all I say to her. It will help you in your love-making when I am gone.—FAR FROM THE MADDING CROWD, THOMAS HARDY
USAGE In modern English, you would not expect *lovemaking* to refer to speech.

lozenge NOUN
1 a diamond shape
• Diamond's name came from a white lozenge on his forehead.—AT THE BACK OF THE NORTH WIND, GEORGE MACDONALD
2 a stone slab
• five little stone lozenges ... beside [his parents'] grave—GREAT EXPECTATIONS, CHARLES DICKENS
➢ **lozenged** ADJECTIVE diamond-shaped • the lozenged panes of a very small latticed window—JANE EYRE, CHARLOTTE BRONTË

lubber NOUN
a clumsy, stupid, or lazy person; a sailor unused to the sea
• shirking lubbers—TREASURE ISLAND, ROBERT LOUIS STEVENSON

lucent (say loo-suhnt) ADJECTIVE
shining; giving off light

lucid (say loo-sid) ADJECTIVE
bright; shining
• a pale face ... with two great lucid eyes—AT THE BACK OF THE NORTH WIND, GEORGE MACDONALD

lucubrations NOUN
the activity of writing or studying; a piece of writing
• [Elizabeth-Jane] appeared, surprised in the midst of her lucubrations.—THE MAYOR OF CASTERBRIDGE, THOMAS HARDY

lumber NOUN
unwanted items; junk
• There is more litter and lumber in it than of old.—BLEAK HOUSE, CHARLES DICKENS

luminary NOUN
1 the moon, sun, or other source of light
• the great luminary ... dipping close to the sea—CHASING THE SUN, R. M. BALLANTYNE
2 an important person in a particular field; a leading light

lustre NOUN
soft brightness; a sheen
• [Mary's] face lacked expression, her eye lustre.—JANE EYRE, CHARLOTTE BRONTË

lustreless ADJECTIVE
dull; not shiny
• a lustreless eye—DAVID COPPERFIELD, CHARLES DICKENS

lustrous ADJECTIVE
shiny or glowing
• Even now ... his lustrous eyes dwell on me with all their melancholy sweetness.—FRANKENSTEIN, MARY SHELLEY

luxuriant ADJECTIVE
growing thickly or abundantly
• The pines are not tall or luxuriant.—FRANKENSTEIN, MARY SHELLEY
➢ **luxuriance** NOUN abundance; thick growth
• For a time, however, the red weed grew with astonishing vigour and luxuriance.—THE WAR OF THE WORLDS, H. G. WELLS

lying-in NOUN
childbirth; time spent by a woman away from other people before and after childbirth
• She was preparing for her ninth lying-in.—MANSFIELD PARK, JANE AUSTEN

lymphatic ADJECTIVE
sluggish; pale and flabby
• I am unable to say whether she was of an usually lymphatic temperament.—THE HAUNTED HOUSE, CHARLES DICKENS

Mm

MORSE CODE

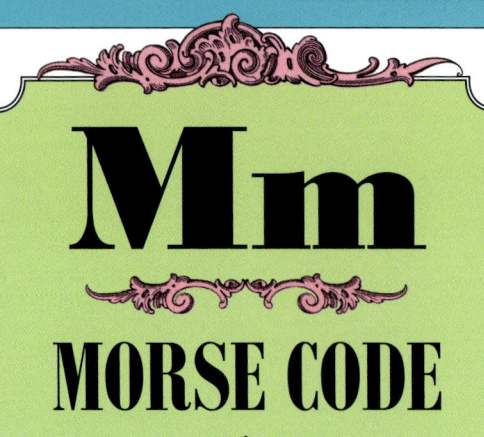

Samuel Morse developed **Morse code** in the **1830s** as a way of almost instantly transmitting information via electric telegraph. In Morse code, each letter of the English alphabet is represented by a sequence of short and long electrical signals, known as **dots** and **dashes**. When in 1910 the murderer Dr Crippen fled London to escape his pursuers, police were waiting for him on his arrival in New York thanks to the morse code message they had received.

machinations NOUN
schemes; plotting
• *Have my murderous machinations deprived you also, my dearest Henry, of life?*—FRANKENSTEIN, MARY SHELLEY

magnanimous ADJECTIVE
very good; generous or forgiving
• *Well, … it's all over now, I hope, and it will be magnanimous in you if you'll forgive me.*—GREAT EXPECTATIONS, CHARLES DICKENS
➤ **magnanimous** ADVERB
• *Jack, however, magnanimously forgave his foe.* —WESTWARD HO!, CHARLES KINGSLEY
➤ **magnanimity** NOUN extreme goodness; generosity or forgiveness
• *I should have appealed to your nobleness and magnanimity.*—JANE EYRE, CHARLOTTE BRONTË

maid NOUN
1 a female servant
• *Let me call your maid.*—PRIDE AND PREJUDICE, JANE AUSTEN
2 a girl or young woman
• *A headstrong maid, that's what she is.*—FAR FROM THE MADDING CROWD, THOMAS HARDY

COMPOUND WORDS There were many different roles for female servants. Here are some compound nouns containing the word 'maid'.
• *Accordingly, when she retired at night, she asked the chambermaid.*—PRIDE AND PREJUDICE, JANE AUSTEN
• *Bessie went into the housemaid's apartment, which was near.*—JANE EYRE, CHARLOTTE BRONTË
• *Meanwhile … the kitchen-maid toasted bread, and boiled eggs.*—MARY BARTON, ELIZABETH GASKELL
• *We dined very well, and were waited on by a maid-servant whom I had never seen.*—GREAT EXPECTATIONS, CHARLES DICKENS
• *The little parlour-maid came out.* DAVID COPPERFIELD —CHARLES DICKENS

main ADVERB
extremely
• *The man … was main angry, sir, and he threw it back to me like so much dirt.*—THE STRANGE CASE OF DR JEKYLL AND MR HYDE, ROBERT LOUIS STEVENSON

maintain VERB
to support someone financially
• *I am sure I do not know who is to maintain you when your father is dead.*—PRIDE AND PREJUDICE, JANE AUSTEN

majestic ADJECTIVE
1 like a queen or king; regal
• *Mrs Crupp … thanked me with a majestic curtsey.*— DAVID COPPERFIELD, CHARLES DICKENS
2 very large, powerful, beautiful, or important
• *The river in Oxford 'reflects its majestic assemblage of towers, and spires, and domes'.*—FRANKENSTEIN, MARY SHELLEY

majesty NOUN
great size, power, beauty, or importance
• *the beauty and majesty of Nature*—RIP VAN WINKLE, WASHINGTON IRVING

majority NOUN
adulthood; the age of legal responsibility
• *Herbert himself had come of age … . As he had nothing else than his majority to come into, the event did not make a profound sensation.*—GREAT EXPECTATIONS, CHARLES DICKENS

make VERB
➤ **make it up**: to decide to do something
• *He and Miss Georgiana made it up to run away.* —JANE EYRE, CHARLOTTE BRONTË
➤ **make up to**:
1 to approach someone or something
• *Dick Jackson [was] making up to the servants' hall-door.*—MANSFIELD PARK, JANE AUSTEN
2 to try to win someone's favour
• *He called me Mr Pip, and began rather to make up to me.*—GREAT EXPECTATIONS, CHARLES DICKENS

malady to mantle

malady NOUN
an illness or disease; an ailment
• *Your master ... is plainly seized with one of those maladies that both torture and deform the sufferer.*—THE STRANGE CASE OF DR JEKYLL AND MR HYDE, ROBERT LOUIS STEVENSON

malefactor NOUN
a criminal; a wrongdoer
• *The other prisoners are 'malefactors, but not incapable of kindness'.*—GREAT EXPECTATIONS, CHARLES DICKENS

malevolent ADJECTIVE
wishing harm to others
• *Captain Tilney must have heard some malevolent misrepresentation of her.*—NORTHANGER ABBEY, JANE AUSTEN
➤ **malevolence** NOUN a desire to harm others
• *It was a bearded, hairy face, with wild cruel eyes and an expression of concentrated malevolence.*—THE SIGN OF FOUR, ARTHUR CONAN DOYLE

malignant ADJECTIVE
1 evil
• *But ... the fallen angel becomes a malignant devil.*—FRANKENSTEIN, MARY SHELLEY
2 dangerous; poisonous
• *But the general aspect of the swamp was malignant.*—FAR FROM THE MADDING CROWD, THOMAS HARDY
3 extremely unpleasant
• *There was such a malignant enjoyment in her utterance of the last words.*—GREAT EXPECTATIONS, CHARLES DICKENS
➤ **malignantly** ADVERB • *Mrs Mann ... [looked] malignantly at Dick.*—OLIVER TWIST, CHARLES DICKENS
RELATED WORD malign meaning 'evil' and 'say bad things about someone'
USAGE In modern English, you might expect a tumour to be *malignant*, rather than a person or their behaviour.

malignity NOUN
evil; danger; extreme unpleasantness
• *No guilt, no mischief, no malignity, no misery, can be found comparable to mine.*—FRANKENSTEIN, MARY SHELLEY

malison (say **mal-i-suhn, mal-iz-uhn**) NOUN
a curse
• *For taking the cake, the young man has 'his mother's malison'.*—THE BLUE FAIRY BOOK, ANDREW LANG

malmsey (say **maam-zi**) NOUN
a type of strong, sweet wine
• *his cup of malmsey*—WESTWARD HO!, CHARLES KINGSLEY

maltster NOUN
a person who made malt, used to make beer
• *The old maltster ... when the malting season ... had passed, made himself useful upon ... the bordering farmsteads.*—FAR FROM THE MADDING CROWD, THOMAS HARDY

man-at-arms NOUN
a soldier
• *a group of mail-clad men-at-arms*—OTTO OF THE SILVER HAND, HOWARD PYLE

manciple NOUN
a man in charge of buying food and other provisions, for example for a monastery

manhood NOUN
1 male adulthood
• *Boyhood was past and manhood had begun.*—JO'S BOYS, LOUISA MAY ALCOTT
2 masculinity; masculine qualities
• *He so far forgot his manhood as to cry.*—DOMBEY AND SON, CHARLES DICKENS

manifold ADJECTIVE
of many kinds; very varied
• *In spite of your manifold attractions, it is by no means certain that another offer of marriage may ever be made you.*—PRIDE AND PREJUDICE, JANE AUSTEN

manor NOUN
1 a large country house with a large area of land around it
• *I possess an old house, Ferndean Manor.*—JANE EYRE, CHARLOTTE BRONTË
2 a large area, traditionally belonging to a member of the nobility. Some of the land and some of its buildings were farmed and lived in by tenants.
• *Lord Hilton, the lord of the manor*—THE WAR OF THE WORLDS, H. G. WELLS

mantel-shelf NOUN
a shelf above a fireplace; a mantelpiece
• *He ... stood at the side of the fire, with his heavy brown hand on the mantel-shelf.*—GREAT EXPECTATIONS, CHARLES DICKENS

mantle NOUN
1 a cloak or shawl
• *I ... drew my grey mantle close about me.*—JANE EYRE, CHARLOTTE BRONTË
2 a covering
• *The climbing roses are 'like a sort of hazy mantle spreading over everything'.*—THE SECRET GARDEN, FRANCES HODGSON BURNETT
USAGE This word was often used figuratively to refer to something offering secrecy or protection.
• *'But for me, in my impenetrable mantle, the safety was complete.'*—the 'mantle' is the fact that

mantle to material

Dr Jekyll transforms himself into a different person.—*THE STRANGE CASE OF DR JEKYLL AND MR HYDE*, ROBERT LOUIS STEVENSON

mantle VERB
to appear on something; to cover or fill something
• 'I will not retire,' cried Kate, with flashing eyes and the red blood mantling in her cheeks.—*NICHOLAS NICKLEBY*, CHARLES DICKENS

manufactory NOUN
a factory
• a large building, formerly used as a manufactory of some kind—*OLIVER TWIST*, CHARLES DICKENS

mare's nest NOUN
a fantasy, misconception, or confusion
• We shall ... leave this fellow Jones to exult over any mare's-nest which he may choose to construct.—*THE SIGN OF FOUR*, ARTHUR CONAN DOYLE

marine store NOUN
goods and supplies needed on board a ship
• the marine-store shop in the back street—*GREAT EXPECTATIONS*, CHARLES DICKENS

market-woman NOUN
a woman who ran a market stall

marplot NOUN
someone causing things to go wrong; a spoilsport or mischief-maker
• I'm sorry to be such a marplot.—*ROSE IN BLOOM*, LOUISA M. ALCOTT

marry EXCLAMATION
used showing emphasis or surprise
• Marry, good souls, let us proceed gently.—*THE PRINCE AND THE PAUPER*, MARK TWAIN

marshal NOUN
a high-ranking official in public office
• The summons was ... read ... by the city marshal himself.—*THE PRINCESS AND CURDIE*, GEORGE MACDONALD

massy ADJECTIVE
solid or heavy; large
• massy walls of grey stone—*NORTHANGER ABBEY*, JANE AUSTEN

mast NOUN
acorns, chestnuts, beech nuts, etc., especially when fallen to the forest floor
• a herd of half-wild swine that fed on the mast in the wood—*JANE EYRE*, CHARLOTTE BRONTË

master NOUN
1 a man seen as the head of a household; a man who had staff working for him; a woman's husband
• 'O, sir,' cried Poole, 'do you think I do not know my master after twenty years?'—*THE STRANGE CASE OF DR JEKYLL AND MR HYDE*, ROBERT LOUIS STEVENSON
• 'Do you mean your husband?' said I. 'Yes, miss, my master.'—*BLEAK HOUSE*, CHARLES DICKENS
2 a man in charge of people or things; a man with a great deal of power or authority
• No more than two months ago, I was not only my own master, but everybody else's.—*OLIVER TWIST*, CHARLES DICKENS
3 a male teacher
• 'He speaks as a pupil to his master,' said I.—*THE SIGN OF FOUR*, ARTHUR CONAN DOYLE
4 a man who was a skilled worker or craftsman and who worked for himself. A master would often have an apprentice.
• Miss Havisham asks Pip about Joe: 'Meaning the master you were to be apprenticed to?'—*GREAT EXPECTATIONS*, CHARLES DICKENS
5 Master
a title for a boy or man
• 'Aye, Master Marner, what do you want wi' me?' said Jem.—*SILAS MARNER*, GEORGE ELIOT

master VERB
to overcome, overpower, or control someone or something
• Oh, I have no respect for myself when I think of that act!—an agony of inward contempt masters me.—*JANE EYRE*, CHARLOTTE BRONTË

matchless ADJECTIVE
better than anyone or anything else
• [Her hair] fell, in its matchless beauty, over her back and shoulders.—*THE WOMAN IN WHITE*, WILKIE COLLINS

matchlock NOUN
a type of early gun
• The sleepy guards ... were lounging on their matchlocks.—*MOONFLEET*, J. MEADE FALKNER

material ADJECTIVE
1 important or relevant
• I had heard of some discoveries ... the knowledge of which was material to my success.—*FRANKENSTEIN*, MARY SHELLEY
2 substantial; great
• Kitty, to her very material advantage, spent the chief of her time with her two elder sisters.—*PRIDE AND PREJUDICE*, JANE AUSTEN
3 relating to physical, rather than spiritual or emotional, things
• What could be more hopelessly prosaic and material?—*THE SIGN OF FOUR*, ARTHUR CONAN DOYLE
➤ **materially** ADVERB greatly; significantly • You are materially changed since we talked on this subject before.—*EMMA*, JANE AUSTEN

material NOUN
military equipment or supplies
• Never before ... had there been such a vast or rapid concentration of military material.—*THE WAR OF THE WORLDS*, H. G. WELLS

matins *to* meed

matins *NOUN*
1 a morning church service; morning prayers
• *Father ... we have prayed at matins.*—NICHOLAS NICKLEBY, CHARLES DICKENS
2 morning birdsong
• *the skylark saying his matins high up in the air*—THE WATER BABIES, CHARLES KINGSLEY

matron *NOUN*
1 a respectable older woman
• *Scrooge ... saw her, now a comely matron, sitting opposite her daughter.*—A CHRISTMAS CAROL, CHARLES DICKENS
2 a woman whose job was to look after the people in a school or workhouse
• *Mrs Corney, the matron of the workhouse*—OLIVER TWIST, CHARLES DICKENS
➤ **matronly** *ADJECTIVE* looking or sounding like an older woman • *I saw a woman attired like a well-dressed servant, matronly, yet still young.*—JANE EYRE, CHARLOTTE BRONTË

mature *ADJECTIVE*
carefully considered; thoughtful
• *On mature deliberation, it was decided that the whole family should go.*—UNCLE TOM'S CABIN, HARRIET BEECHER STOWE

mature *VERB*
to develop or perfect a plan
• *[The Captain] had matured this notable scheme.*—DOMBEY AND SON, CHARLES DICKENS

mawkin (also **malkin**) *NOUN*
a scarecrow; a grotesque puppet
• *But as for being ugly, look at me ... Anybody 'ud say you wanted to make a mawkin of me.*—SILAS MARNER, GEORGE ELIOT

Maxim *NOUN*
a type of large machine gun
• *Maxims have been absolutely useless against their armour.*—THE WAR OF THE WORLDS, H. G. WELLS

maxim *NOUN*
a short saying; a general rule or truth
• *I had fifty minds to buy it myself, for it is one of my maxims always to buy a good horse when I meet with one.*—NORTHANGER ABBEY, JANE AUSTEN

mayhap *ADVERB*
perhaps
• *I think, mayhap, a little of it does me more good than so much at once.*—SILAS MARNER, GEORGE ELIOT

mazed *ADJECTIVE*
1 confused; dazed
• *I know nothing—I'm ... mazed.*—SILAS MARNER, GEORGE ELIOT

2 insane
• *Come home, and let me know whether I am sane or mazed.*—WESTWARD HO!, CHARLES KINGSLEY

mead *NOUN*
a meadow
• *the arrival of the cows from the meads*—TESS OF THE D'URBERVILLES, THOMAS HARDY

mean *ADJECTIVE*
poor in quality or appearance
• *But now crime has degraded me beneath the meanest animal.*—FRANKENSTEIN, MARY SHELLEY
➤ **meanly** *ADVERB* • *Yet she was meanly dressed.*—FRANKENSTEIN, MARY SHELLEY
➤ **meanness** *NOUN* • *Undoubtedly, ... there is meanness in all the arts which ladies sometimes condescend to employ for captivation.*—PRIDE AND PREJUDICE, JANE AUSTEN

measure *VERB*
1 to assess someone's character or qualities
• *He had not measured this wife with whom he had lived so long.*—SILAS MARNER, GEORGE ELIOT
2 to travel the distance mentioned
• *I walked fast, but not far: ere I had measured a quarter of a mile, I heard the tramp of hoofs.*—JANE EYRE, CHARLOTTE BRONTË

measureless *ADJECTIVE*
infinite; without limit
• *a long, low cry of measureless despair*—FAR FROM THE MADDING CROWD, THOMAS HARDY

meditate *VERB*
to consider a course of action
• *By the bye, Charles, are you really serious in meditating a dance at Netherfield?*—PRIDE AND PREJUDICE, JANE AUSTEN
➤ **meditation** *NOUN* • *I told him, after a little meditation over the fire, that I would like to ask him a question.*—GREAT EXPECTATIONS, CHARLES DICKENS

meditated *ADJECTIVE*
planned or thought about
• *Not a syllable had ever reached her of Miss Darcy's meditated elopement.*—PRIDE AND PREJUDICE, JANE AUSTEN

medley *ADJECTIVE*
containing different types of people or things; motley
• *that medley race of vagabonds*—DOMBEY AND SON, CHARLES DICKENS

meed *NOUN*
a reward; praise or honour
• *If I do anything worthy of praise, she gives me my meed liberally.*—JANE EYRE, CHARLOTTE BRONTË

meet ADJECTIVE
proper; suitable
• *This is not a meet place for Christians to tarry in.* —THE LAST OF THE MOHICANS, JAMES FENIMORE COOPER

memorialize VERB
to create a memorial to someone; to commemorate something
• *He is memorializing the Lord Chancellor, or the Lord Somebody or other.*—DAVID COPPERFIELD, CHARLES DICKENS

mend VERB
1 to change or improve something; to put something right
• *It is one of those affairs that cannot be mended by talking.*—THE STRANGE CASE OF DR JEKYLL AND MR HYDE, ROBERT LOUIS STEVENSON
2 to add fuel to a fire
• *I ... mended the fire in the room where we had been.* —GREAT EXPECTATIONS, CHARLES DICKENS
➢ **mend your pace:** to go faster; to change your speed • *He mended his pace with suitable haste.* —THE RED BADGE OF COURAGE, STEPHEN CRANE

USAGE In modern English, you might expect objects to be *mended*, rather abstract things.

menial ADJECTIVE
to do with housework and similar tasks; domestic
• *[The child] shall aid the mistress in ... menial offices connected with her ... house.*—JANE EYRE, CHARLOTTE BRONTË

menial NOUN
a servant
• *the lowest menials of the palace*—THE PRINCESS AND CURDIE, GEORGE MACDONALD

mercantile ADJECTIVE
to do with trade; commercial
• *There were mercantile families in the district boasting twice the income.*—SHIRLEY, CHARLOTTE BRONTË
🏛 Italian *mercante*, meaning 'merchant'

mercer NOUN
a trader in silks and other fabrics; the owner of a haberdashery shop
• *silks and satins at the mercers*—OTTO OF THE SILVER HAND, HOWARD PYLE

merchant NOUN
1 a trader
• *the merchants; who hurried up and down, and chinked the money in their pockets*—A CHRISTMAS CAROL, CHARLES DICKENS
2 (also **merchantman**)
a ship carrying goods to be traded
• *This letter will reach England by a merchantman now on its homeward voyage.*—FRANKENSTEIN, MARY SHELLEY

merino NOUN
soft woollen cloth, originally made with wool from a type of sheep called *merino*
• *a black merino cloak*—JANE EYRE, CHARLOTTE BRONTË

mercy EXCLAMATION
used for expressing surprise or fear
• *Scrooge fell upon his knees, and clasped his hands before his face. 'Mercy!' he said. 'Dreadful apparition, why do you trouble me?'*—A CHRISTMAS CAROL, CHARLES DICKENS

meritorious ADJECTIVE
deserving praise
• *It was very meritorious and highly praiseworthy in Mrs Kenwigs to do as she had done.'*—NICHOLAS NICKLEBY, CHARLES DICKENS

meretricious (say merr-i-trish-uhss) ADJECTIVE
1 showy
• *a startling, though possibly a meretricious, effect* —THE RETURN OF SHERLOCK HOLMES, ARTHUR CONAN DOYLE
2 gaudy and inappropriate; like a prostitute
• *her ... painted and meretricious face*—VILLETTE, CHARLOTTE BRONTË

mesmeric ADJECTIVE
to do with hypnosis
• *Their boy is unquestionably a sensitive subject to the mesmeric influence.*—THE MOONSTONE, WILKIE COLLINS

mesmerism NOUN
hypnosis
• *[He] is dying to try his quack remedies (mesmerism included) on my patient.*—THE WOMAN IN WHITE, WILKIE COLLINS

mesmerize VERB
to hypnotize someone
• *[The boy] has no doubt reflected what was already in the mind of the person mesmerising him.*—THE MOONSTONE, WILKIE COLLINS

mess NOUN
1 mushy food
• *a mess of cold porridge*—JANE EYRE, CHARLOTTE BRONTË
2 a place for soldiers to live and eat
• *She ... could remember ... the regard which his social powers had gained him in the mess.*—PRIDE AND PREJUDICE, JANE AUSTEN

messmate NOUN
a companion in the army or navy, especially someone who shared a person's meals or living quarters
• *He drew some cognac from the cask into a tin cannikin. 'Will you taste, messmate?'*—TREASURE ISLAND, ROBERT LOUIS STEVENSON

mete to minute-gun

mete (say meet) VERB
to give someone a portion of something
• Chance has meted you a measure of happiness.
—JANE EYRE, CHARLOTTE BRONTË

metempsychosis NOUN
the passing of the soul from one person or animal to another; re-incarnation
• Many of their works, also, undergo a kind of metempsychosis, and spring up under new forms.
—RIP VAN WINKLE, WASHINGTON IRVING

metheglin (say muh-**theg**-lin, **meth**-uh-glin) NOUN
a type of alcoholic drink made with honey

mettlesome ADJECTIVE
lively; high-spirited
• The mettlesome creature bounded from the earth with a sudden spring, that threw his master sprawling.—UNCLE TOM'S CABIN, HARRIET BEECHER STOWE

midmost ADJECTIVE
right in the middle
• the very midmost spot of the whole world—THE DRAGON'S TEETH, NATHANIEL HAWTHORNE

mien (say meen) NOUN
a person's manner and expression
• Two young ladies appeared before me; one ... with a sallow face and severe mien.—JANE EYRE, CHARLOTTE BRONTË

milliner NOUN
a person who made or sold women's hats
• Martha ... was a poor apprentice at a milliner's.
—A CHRISTMAS CAROL, CHARLES DICKENS

millrace NOUN
the fast-flowing stream of water driving a water mill
• [The river] runs like a mill-race, and I could feel no bottom.—KING SOLOMON'S MINES, H. RIDER HAGGARD

mince VERB
to express disapproval or bad news in a gentle or roundabout way; to hold back when speaking
• I didn't mince the matter with him.—HARD TIMES, CHARLES DICKENS

mincemeat NOUN
a mixture of currants, raisins, spices, etc. In the 19th century, it was still common for the mixture to contain minced meat.
• He was gobbling mincemeat, meatbone, bread, cheese, and pork pie.—GREAT EXPECTATIONS, CHARLES DICKENS
➤ **mince-pie** NOUN • There ... was a great piece of Cold Boiled, and there were mince-pies, and plenty of beer.—A CHRISTMAS CAROL, CHARLES DICKENS

mind NOUN
➤ **make up your mind:**
1 to accept an idea or fact; to be reconciled to something • You'll make up your mind to't a bit better when you've seen iverything; you'll get used to't.
—THE MILL ON THE FLOSS, GEORGE ELIOT
2 to expect something • Miss Bertram had made up her mind to something different, and was a little disappointed.—MANSFIELD PARK, JANE AUSTEN

minim NOUN
a very small measure of liquid equal to approximately 0.06 ml; a tiny drop
• He ... measured out a few minims of the red tincture and added one of the powders.—THE STRANGE CASE OF DR JEKYLL AND MR HYDE, ROBERT LOUIS STEVENSON

ministration NOUN
attention to someone's needs; care given to someone
• The effect, either of her ministrations or of her mere presence, was a rapid recovery.—THE MAYOR OF CASTERBRIDGE, THOMAS HARDY

ministry NOUN
care and attention; ministrations
• Jane's soft ministry will be a perpetual joy.—JANE EYRE, CHARLOTTE BRONTË

minority NOUN
childhood or youth; the period when someone was legally not an adult
• [He] was to inherit the money ... on the stipulation that in his minority he should never have stained his name.—OLIVER TWIST, CHARLES DICKENS
RELATED WORD minor meaning a person under the age of legal responsibility

minute ADJECTIVE
very precise or detailed; particular
• I should not have understood ... this book had not Felix, in reading it, given very minute explanations.
—FRANKENSTEIN, MARY SHELLEY
➤ **minutely** ADVERB precisely; in detail • I enquired more minutely concerning my father.—FRANKENSTEIN, MARY SHELLEY
➤ **minuteness** NOUN precision; detail • Here ... every view was pointed out with a minuteness which left beauty entirely behind.—PRIDE AND PREJUDICE, JANE AUSTEN

minute-gun NOUN
a gun firing repeatedly, once a minute
• [My aunt] ejaculated at intervals, 'Mercy on us!' letting those exclamations off like minute guns.—DAVID COPPERFIELD, CHARLES DICKENS

117

mire to mode

mire NOUN
mud; a muddy or boggy place
• *The ground was covered, nearly ankle-deep, with filth and mire.*—OLIVER TWIST, CHARLES DICKENS

mischief NOUN
harm; a bad thing
• *I thought some mischief had happened.*—SILAS MARNER, GEORGE ELIOT

mischievous ADJECTIVE
harmful; causing trouble
• *He ... knew her state and how mischievous a shock would be.*—DRACULA, BRAM STOKER
➤ **mischievously** ADVERB • *[Elizabeth] fancied that praise ... from her might be mischievously construed.*—PRIDE AND PREJUDICE, JANE AUSTEN

misconstruction NOUN
misinterpretation; misunderstanding
• *I reminded her that she would be exposing herself to the most odious misconstruction of her motives.*—THE MOONSTONE, WILKIE COLLINS
RELATED WORD misconstrue meaning 'to understand or interpret something wrongly'

misdoubt VERB
1 to have doubts about something
• *I entirely misdoubted my own ability to influence it.*—SHIRLEY, CHARLOTTE BRONTË
2 to fear something
• *The prisoner misdoubted him to be an apparition of his own imagining.*—A TALE OF TWO CITIES, CHARLES DICKENS
➤ **I misdoubt me: I suspect** • *I misdoubt me that I disobey my God in obeying him!*—MOBY DICK, HERMAN MELVILLE

misgive VERB
to make someone afraid that something bad would happen; to cause someone fear or distress
• *And when he heard this, his heart misgave him.*—MARY BARTON, ELIZABETH GASKELL
• *Poor Harry Jekyll ... my mind misgives me he is in deep waters!*—THE STRANGE CASE OF DR JEKYLL AND MR HYDE, ROBERT LOUIS STEVENSON

missal NOUN
a Catholic prayer book
• *Van Helsing opened his missal and began to read.*—DRACULA, BRAM STOKER

missent ADJECTIVE
sent to the wrong place; directed wrongly
• *[Elizabeth] received two letters from [Jane] at once, on one of which was marked that it had been missent elsewhere.*—PRIDE AND PREJUDICE, JANE AUSTEN

mistress NOUN
1 a woman who ran a household; a woman who had staff working for her; a man's wife
• *May I speak to your mistresses?*—JANE EYRE, CHARLOTTE BRONTË
• *He's in the dining-room, sir, along with mistress.*—A CHRISTMAS CAROL, CHARLES DICKENS
2 a woman in charge of people or things
• *I told you I am independent, sir, as well as rich: I am my own mistress.*—JANE EYRE, CHARLOTTE BRONTË
3 a female teacher
• *I am going to try to get the place of mistress in the new school.*—GREAT EXPECTATIONS, CHARLES DICKENS
4 a woman loved by a man; the object of his affections
• *[My friend] heard that his former mistress was married.*—FRANKENSTEIN, MARY SHELLEY
5 a man's lover
• *If I lived with you as you desire, I should then be your mistress.*—JANE EYRE, CHARLOTTE BRONTË
6 **Mistress**
a title for a woman or girl; Mrs or Miss
• *Mistress Fry*—LORNA DOONE, R. D. BLACKMORE
• *Mistress Alice, his daughter*—THE HOUSE OF THE SEVEN GABLES, NATHANIEL HAWTHORNE

mistrust VERB
to suspect something
• *I mistrusted a design to entrap me.*—GREAT EXPECTATIONS, CHARLES DICKENS
USAGE In modern English, you would usually *mistrust* a person, rather than a plan or trick.

mither (also **moither**) (say my-thuhr, moy-thuhr) VERB
to bother, confuse, or exhaust someone
• *You'll happen be a bit moithered with [the child] while it's so little.*—SILAS MARNER, GEORGE ELIOT

mitten NOUN
➤ **get the mitten: to be rejected or jilted** • *He's got the mitten again, and it's turned his head.*—JOHN CHARRINGTON'S WEDDING, EDITH NESBIT

mockery NOUN
a totally useless or inappropriate action; a futile thing
• *All joy was but a mockery which insulted my desolate state.*—FRANKENSTEIN, MARY SHELLEY

mode NOUN
1 a way or means of doing something
• *But he wanted to show ... that he was grateful, and the only mode that occurred to him was to offer Aaron a bit more cake.*—SILAS MARNER, GEORGE ELIOT
2 a fashion; a fashionable item of clothing
• *She did not choose to adopt English fashions ... she adhered to her old Belgian modes.*—SHIRLEY, CHARLOTTE BRONTË

moiety to mote

moiety NOUN
one of two parts; a portion
• *Tom divided the cake and Becky ate with good appetite, while Tom nibbled at his moiety.*—THE ADVENTURES OF TOM SAWYER, MARK TWAIN

molest VERB
to upset or harass someone
• *I was well received by my fellow-pupils; treated as an equal by those of my own age, and not molested by any.*—JANE EYRE, CHARLOTTE BRONTË
➤ **molestation** NOUN • *But we held our own without any appearance of molestation.*—GREAT EXPECTATIONS, CHARLES DICKENS

moment NOUN
importance
• *My revenge is of no moment to you.*—FRANKENSTEIN, MARY SHELLEY

momently ADVERB
1 by the moment; continually
• *During all that time ... her face grew momently darker, more dissatisfied.*—JANE EYRE, CHARLOTTE BRONTË
2 for a moment; briefly
• *The news had to be told [to him] twice ... and even then he dwelt on it but momently.*—VILLETTE, CHARLOTTE BRONTË

Money

In the 19th century in Britain, money was made up of pounds (£), shillings (s), and pence (d).

one pound = 20 shillings
one crown = 5 shillings
half a crown = 2 shillings and 6 pence
a florin = 2 shillings
one shilling = 12 pence
one groat* = 4 pence
one penny = 2 half penny
half penny = 2 farthings
one guinea = 1 pound and 1 shilling

*this word usually referred to a much older coin, or just to a very small amount of money

To rent a terraced house might cost £100 a year, to buy a man's suit might cost £2.10s, a ticket to the music hall might be sixpence, and a meal three pence, and a beer or a coffee might cost a penny.

monomania NOUN
an obsession with one particular topic or thing
• *I call it quite my monomania, it is such a subject of mine.*—DAVID COPPERFIELD, CHARLES DICKENS

monstrous ADJECTIVE
1 to do with a monster; like a monster
• *the monstrous image*—FRANKENSTEIN, MARY SHELLEY
2 extremely large
• *his monstrous shirt collar*—A CHRISTMAS CAROL, CHARLES DICKENS
3 dreadful or shocking
• *Pip describes his lie as 'a monstrous invention'.*—GREAT EXPECTATIONS, CHARLES DICKENS
4 utterly immoral or evil
• *The pleasures which I made haste to seek in my disguise ... soon began to turn toward the monstrous.*—THE STRANGE CASE OF DR JEKYLL AND MR HYDE, ROBERT LOUIS STEVENSON

moreen NOUN
a type of heavy fabric used for curtains and furniture
• *the red moreen curtain*—JANE EYRE, CHARLOTTE BRONTË

morocco NOUN
soft leather, typically from goatskin, used for example, for book covers and shoes
• *a morocco pocket-book*—JANE EYRE, CHARLOTTE BRONTË

morrow NOUN
the following day
• *[Mr Collins] was to begin his journey too early on the morrow to see any of the family.*—PRIDE AND PREJUDICE, JANE AUSTEN

mort NOUN
a large number or amount of something
• *I've put the question to myself a mort o' times.*—DAVID COPPERFIELD, CHARLES DICKENS

mortification NOUN
1 shame; embarrassment
• *I was filled with the bitterest sensations of despondence and mortification.*—FRANKENSTEIN, MARY SHELLEY
2 death of body tissue; gangrene
• *Mortification set in, and they had to amputate him.*—THE ADVENTURES OF HUCKLEBERRY FINN, MARK TWAIN

mortify VERB
1 to humiliate someone
• *I could easily forgive his pride, if he had not mortified mine.*—PRIDE AND PREJUDICE, JANE AUSTEN
2 to subdue or control someone or something
• *It is one thing to mortify curiosity, another to conquer it.*—THE STRANGE CASE OF DR JEKYLL AND MR HYDE, ROBERT LOUIS STEVENSON

mote NOUN
a speck
• *the falling motes of dust*—DOMBEY AND SON, CHARLES DICKENS

motive to myrmidon

motive ADJECTIVE
producing or causing movement
• *So still he remained that he could be imagined to have left in him no motive power whatever.*—FAR FROM THE MADDING CROWD, THOMAS HARDY

mountebank NOUN
a travelling salesman and / or entertainer
• *a mountebank … swallowing a sword-blade*—DAVID COPPERFIELD, CHARLES DICKENS

mountebank ADJECTIVE
using tricks or cunning; typical of a mountebank
• *mountebank bravado*—THE WOMAN IN WHITE, WILKIE COLLINS

mourner NOUN
a person attending a funeral, either as a friend or relative of the dead person, or because they were hired to attend
• *But … she was … inclined to shake her head and sigh … like a funereal mourner who is not a relation.*—SILAS MARNER, GEORGE ELIOT

mow VERB
to cut grass or another crop with a curved tool called a scythe
• *The under gardener, mowing, saw Tom, and threw down his scythe.*—THE WATER BABIES, CHARLES KINGSLEY

muff NOUN
a tube-shaped hand warmer, typically made of fur
• *I jumped up, took my muff and umbrella, and hastened into the inn-passage.*—JANE EYRE, CHARLOTTE BRONTË

muffin NOUN
a small, round, flat bread roll for toasting; an English muffin
• *The subject was revived … over the tea and muffins.* —THE MILL ON THE FLOSS, GEORGE ELIOT

mullion NOUN
an upright bar between window panes
➤ **mullioned** ADJECTIVE • *mullioned and latticed windows*—JANE EYRE, CHARLOTTE BRONTË

multiplicity NOUN
a great variety or large number of things
• *A strange multiplicity of sensations seized me.* —FRANKENSTEIN, MARY SHELLEY

mummery NOUN
1 ridiculous ceremony or costumes
• *When … Trabb and his men … had crammed their mummery into bags, and were gone too, the house felt wholesomer.*—GREAT EXPECTATIONS, CHARLES DICKENS

2 **mummers' play**
a traditional play performed by actors called 'mummers' who wore masks or other disguises
• *Christmas mummeries*—RIP VAN WINKLE, WASHINGTON IRVING

mun VERB
must
• *Poor folk mun get on as they can.*—JANE EYRE, CHARLOTTE BRONTË

murmur (also **murmur against**) VERB
to complain or speak badly about someone
• *Nancy talks about her husband but says, 'But I won't murmur.'*—SILAS MARNER, GEORGE ELIOT
• *But the rest … began murmuring against the captain.*—WESTWARD HO!, CHARLES KINGSLEY

murrey ADJECTIVE & NOUN
blood-red or purple-red
• *They were dressed in striped hose … and doublets of murrey and blue cloth.*—THE PRINCE AND THE PAUPER, MARK TWAIN

mushed ADJECTIVE
crumpled or crushed; looking wretched
• *Master Marner … you're a young man … for all you look so mushed.*—SILAS MARNER, GEORGE ELIOT

musket NOUN
a long-barrelled gun used by a soldier
• *I had … learned to handle my musket.*—THE SIGN OF FOUR, ARTHUR CONAN DOYLE

musketry NOUN
the sound or use of muskets
• *a volley of musketry*—SHIRLEY, CHARLOTTE BRONTË
• *One evening … it was raining so heavily that ivy and laurel resounded like distant musketry.*—THE MAYOR OF CASTERBRIDGE, THOMAS HARDY

muslin NOUN
thin cotton cloth
• *her white muslin dress and blue sash*—JANE EYRE, CHARLOTTE BRONTË

mute NOUN
a funeral attendant; a professional mourner
• *two mutes in very stiff neckcloths … with a hearse drawn by four black steeds*—OLIVER TWIST, CHARLES DICKENS

myrmidon NOUN
someone working for another person, typically carrying out their orders without question
• *Pip wonders whether 'myrmidons of Justice … would be lying in ambush behind the gate'.* —GREAT EXPECTATIONS, CHARLES DICKENS

name to naughty

Nn

NEWSPAPERS

In the first half of the century, the price of **newspapers** was kept high by taxes on advertising, paper, and even newspapers themselves. Critics called this a 'tax on knowledge' and over time these taxes were abolished. This lead to a rise in the number of newspapers and their readership in the **1850s**. The spread of railways meant that daily papers could be delivered across the country. *The Times*, which had been read only in London, became a national newspaper.

name NOUN
➤ **give someone a good / bad name:** to say good / bad things about someone • *There is not one of his tenants or servants but what will give him a good name.*—meaning they all say good things about him.—PRIDE AND PREJUDICE, JANE AUSTEN

nameless ADJECTIVE
1 extreme; indescribable
• *I dreamed it would be nameless bliss.*—JANE EYRE, CHARLOTTE BRONTË
• *a nameless, horrible dread*—HARD TIMES, CHARLES DICKENS
2 not famous or distinguished; obscure
• *nameless men*—IVANHOE, WALTER SCOTT
3 born to parents who were not married to each other; illegitimate
• *a nameless child*—TESS OF THE D'URBERVILLES, THOMAS HARDY

napoleon NOUN
1 a gold coin worth 20 French francs
• *We ... borrowed ... 30,000 napoleons from the Bank of France.*—THE ADVENTURES OF SHERLOCK HOLMES, ARTHUR CONAN DOYLE
2 an ambitious or ruthless person who is at the top of their field
• *Moriarty ... is the napoleon of crime.*—THE MEMOIRS OF SHERLOCK HOLMES, ARTHUR CONAN DOYLE

nash ADJECTIVE (See **nesh**)

natal ADJECTIVE
to do with birth or with a particular person's birth
• *Saint Godrick ... whose natal day this is*—THE MERRY ADVENTURES OF ROBIN HOOD, HOWARD PYLE

native ADJECTIVE
inborn; natural, rather than learnt
• *Well, for cool native impudence and pure innate pride, you haven't your equal.*—JANE EYRE, CHARLOTTE BRONTË

natty ADJECTIVE
neat and tidy; smart or fashionable
• *What a figure, so trim and natty!*—VILLETTE, CHARLOTTE BRONTË
➤ **nattiness** NOUN • *Everything belonging to Miss Nancy was of delicate purity and nattiness.*—SILAS MARNER, GEORGE ELIOT

natural ADJECTIVE
1 (said about a person's child) born outside of marriage
• *Then, lowering her voice a little, she said to Elinor, 'She is his natural daughter.'*—SENSE AND SENSIBILITY, JANE AUSTEN
2 to do with being a blood relation
• *She is my own child—her mother was my wife. I've a natural claim on her that must stand before every other.*—SILAS MARNER, GEORGE ELIOT
3 innate or inborn
• *Bingley has great natural modesty.*—PRIDE AND PREJUDICE, JANE AUSTEN

natural philosophy NOUN
branches of science dealing with the physical world, for example, physics, chemistry, biology, and geology; the natural sciences
• *a man of great research in natural philosophy*—FRANKENSTEIN, MARY SHELLEY

nature NOUN
a particular type of person
• *A new species would bless me as its creator and source; many happy and excellent natures would owe their being to me.*—FRANKENSTEIN, MARY SHELLEY

naughty ADJECTIVE
wicked
• *a naughty child addicted to falsehood and deceit*—JANE EYRE, CHARLOTTE BRONTË

necessitous *to* niche

necessitous ADJECTIVE
needy; poor
• They were, in fact, a necessitous family.
—NORTHANGER ABBEY, JANE AUSTEN

neckcloth NOUN
a man's scarf, worn instead of a tie; a cravat
• The rector wears an *'ample, many-creased white neckcloth'*.—SILAS MARNER, GEORGE ELIOT

negative VERB
to say 'no' to something
• Mr Eshton ... seemed to propose that I should be asked to join them; but Lady Ingram instantly negatived the notion.—JANE EYRE, CHARLOTTE BRONTË

negative NOUN
an answer meaning 'no'
• His daughter's request ... received at first an absolute negative.—PRIDE AND PREJUDICE, JANE AUSTEN

negus (say **nee-guhss**) NOUN
an alcoholic hot drink, usually containing port or sherry
• There ... was cake, and there was negus, and ... a great piece of Cold Roast.—A CHRISTMAS CAROL, CHARLES DICKENS

Capital letters

Cold Roast (in the quotation at *negus*) is an example of capitalization where it would not occur in modern English.

Capital letters were often used to indicate importance or to show that something was called a particular thing.
• *In comparison with [this] young man I am a **Angel**.*
—GREAT EXPECTATIONS, CHARLES DICKENS

Of course, capital letters often alert you to the fact that the word is a proper noun representing a particular person, place, or institution.
• *Charles, when you build your house, I wish it may be half as delightful as **Pemberley**.*—PRIDE AND PREJUDICE, JANE AUSTEN

Some proper nouns refer to well-known people of the time, or to characters or places from myths or religious stories. Even if you are not familiar with the person or place mentioned, you can often work out what kind of person or thing is being referred to.
• *[She] was over-anxious to please, and bustled about like a true **Martha**, cumbered with many cares.*
—LITTLE MEN, LOUIS M. ALCOTT

---

neophyte (say **nee-uh-fyt, nee-oh-fyt**) NOUN
1 a novice monk or priest; a new convert to a religion
• He ... put his hands behind him, after the approved fashion of a neophyte who is examined in his catechism.—THE MOONSTONE, WILKIE COLLINS
2 someone who was new to something; a novice
• You have no right to preach to me, you neophyte, that ... are absolutely unacquainted with [life's] mysteries.—JANE EYRE, CHARLOTTE BRONTË

nervous ADJECTIVE
suffering from, or related to, a disorder of the nerves
• When she was discontented, she fancied herself nervous.—PRIDE AND PREJUDICE, JANE AUSTEN
• a nervous fever which confined me for several months
—FRANKENSTEIN, MARY SHELLEY

nesh (also **nash**) ADJECTIVE
feeble; weak
• I knew blind folks must not be nesh about using their tongues.—MARY BARTON, ELIZABETH GASKELL
• They're nash things, them lop-eared rabbits.—THE MILL ON THE FLOSS, GEORGE ELIOT

net VERB
to make a mesh or net by securing threads, ropes, etc.; to make things using this technique
• I was shown into a ... drawing-room, and there sat Agnes, netting a purse.—DAVID COPPERFIELD, CHARLES DICKENS

next PREPOSITION
beside; next to
• 'You see this goes first, next the skin,' proceeded Dolly, taking up the little shirt, and putting it on.
—SILAS MARNER, GEORGE ELIOT

nice ADJECTIVE
1 precise; exact
• I ... ascertained from the clerk with the nicest precision ... the earliest moment at which the coach could be expected.—GREAT EXPECTATIONS, CHARLES DICKENS
2 particular; strict or fussy; paying attention to detail
• I concealed my feelings by an appearance of hilarity that brought ... joy to ... my father, but hardly deceived the ever-watchful and nicer eye of Elizabeth.
—FRANKENSTEIN, MARY SHELLEY
▶ **nicely** ADVERB in an exact way • a nicely calculated distance—THE STRANGE CASE OF DR JEKYLL AND MR HYDE, ROBERT LOUIS STEVENSON

niche NOUN
a recess or alcove in a wall or rock face
• Mary ... remained fixed like a statue in its niche.
—JANE EYRE, CHARLOTTE BRONTË

nick to notable

nick *NOUN*
a gap or indentation in a surface
• *And then ... we shall be ... where there's the nick in the road for the water to run.*—SILAS MARNER, GEORGE ELIOT

nightcap *NOUN*
a cap worn in bed
• *[Scrooge] put on his dressing-gown and slippers, and his nightcap; and sat down before the fire to take his gruel.*—A CHRISTMAS CAROL, CHARLES DICKENS

noddy *NOUN*
a foolish person
• *To think that I should be such a noddy!*—NICHOLAS NICKLEBY, CHARLES DICKENS

nodus *NOUN*
a tricky problem
• *Tom's despair ... did not constitute a nodus worthy of interference.*—THE MILL ON THE FLOSS, GEORGE ELIOT

noggin *NOUN*
a small amount of drink, usually alcoholic
• *a noggin o' rum*—TESS OF THE D'URBERVILLES, THOMAS HARDY

nohow *ADJECTIVE*
not well; out of sorts
• *Maggie's eyes 'made him feel nohow'.*—THE MILL ON THE FLOSS, GEORGE ELIOT

noise *NOUN*
a comment or reaction; conversation, argument, or fuss
• *'This will make a deal of noise,' he said.*—THE STRANGE CASE OF DR JEKYLL AND MR HYDE, ROBERT LOUIS STEVENSON

noisome *ADJECTIVE*
1 smelling very bad
• *His ... father and ... sister lay in a noisome dungeon.*—FRANKENSTEIN, MARY SHELLEY
2 extremely unpleasant
• *that noisome den*—THE WAR OF THE WORLDS, H. G. WELLS

nominally *ADVERB*
1 supposedly; in theory
• *Mr Collins was in the library 'nominally engaged with one of the ... folios ... but really talking to Mr Bennet'.*—PRIDE AND PREJUDICE, JANE AUSTEN
2 in name
• *You shall be Mrs Rochester—both virtually and nominally.*—JANE EYRE, CHARLOTTE BRONTË
USAGE *Nominally* is often contrasted with *virtually* (meaning 'in effect' or 'in practice'.) • *His income, though nominally a large one, was virtually, for a man in his position, next to nothing.*—THE WOMAN IN WHITE, WILKIE COLLINS

nonce *NOUN*
➤ **for the nonce:** for the time being; temporarily
• *They sheared in the great barn, called for the nonce the Shearing-barn.*—FAR FROM THE MADDING CROWD, THOMAS HARDY

noodle *NOUN*
a foolish or silly person
• *I'd be a match for all noodles and all rogues.*—GREAT EXPECTATIONS, CHARLES DICKENS

noonday *NOUN*
midday; the middle of the day
• *Stockdale ... remained as broadly awake as at noonday.*—WESSEX TALES, THOMAS HARDY

nooning *NOUN*
the time around midday; a lunch break

nor *CONJUNCTION & PREPOSITION*
1 than
• *You can't do better nor keep quiet, dear boy.*—GREAT EXPECTATIONS, CHARLES DICKENS
• *It seemed more like a wedding nor a funeral.*—MARY BARTON, ELIZABETH GASKELL
2 and not
• *[He] quitted his country, nor returned until he heard that his former mistress was married.*—FRANKENSTEIN, MARY SHELLEY
• *Whitcross is no town, nor even a hamlet.*—JANE EYRE, CHARLOTTE BRONTË

nosegay *NOUN*
a bunch of scented flowers
• *On the other seat was a large nosegay of choice flowers.*—RUPERT OF HENTZAU, ANTHONY HOPE
• *The smell of sweet herbs and ... the neighbouring meadows ... made the whole air a great nosegay.*—BLEAK HOUSE, CHARLES DICKENS

not *ADVERB*
➤ **not but what / not but that:** nevertheless; however • *Her thoughts ran on Jem's manner and words; not but what she had known the tale they told for many a day.*—MARY BARTON, ELIZABETH GASKELL
• *Not but that I shall be down again by the end of a fortnight.*—NORTHANGER ABBEY, JANE AUSTEN

notable *ADJECTIVE*
1 prominent or noticeable; significant
• *London was startled by a [violent] crime ... rendered all the more notable by the high position of the victim.*—THE STRANGE CASE OF DR JEKYLL AND MR HYDE, ROBERT LOUIS STEVENSON
2 excellent
• *a notable example*—NICHOLAS NICKLEBY, CHARLES DICKENS
3 very competent and hard-working, especially in household matters

123

• *The place ... had that look of order and neatness which bespeaks ... a notable English housewife.* —RIP VAN WINKLE, WASHINGTON IRVING

notable NOUN
an important or famous person
• *Uncle Winthrop had to go to a dinner among some notables.* —A LITTLE GIRL IN OLD BOSTON, AMANDA MINNIE DOUGLAS

notice NOUN
attention; being noticed
• *The little one [was] accustomed to be left to itself for long hours without notice from its mother.* —SILAS MARNER, GEORGE ELIOT

notice VERB
1 to mention something
• *Excuse my noticing it, but I am sorry to see you not looking so well as you were when we last met.* —THE WOMAN IN WHITE, WILKIE COLLINS
2 to acknowledge someone; to treat someone as being worthy of attention
• *Yes, Miss Bennet ... do not expect to be noticed by his family or friends.* —PRIDE AND PREJUDICE, JANE AUSTEN

notion NOUN
1 an idea
• *'Had you any notion that it was so late?' he asked.* —WESSEX TALES, THOMAS HARDY
2 an intention
• *I had no notion of going back.* —DAVID COPPERFIELD, CHARLES DICKENS

novelty NOUN
newness; something new, unusual, or original
• *There was something strange in my sensations, something indescribably new and, from its very novelty, incredibly sweet.* —THE STRANGE CASE OF DR JEKYLL AND MR HYDE, ROBERT LOUIS STEVENSON
• *This was a new scene to us ... the majestic oaks ... and the herds of stately deer were all novelties to us.* —FRANKENSTEIN, MARY SHELLEY

noways ADVERB
not in any way
• *If you was noways unwilling, I'd talk to Mr Macey about it this very day.* —SILAS MARNER, GEORGE ELIOT

nowhither ADVERB
to nowhere
• *a lone wind that seemed to come from nowhere and to go nowhither* —THE PRINCESS AND CURDIE, GEORGE MACDONALD

numbskull (also numskull) NOUN
a foolish person
• *That fellow is ... the most ... pig-headed numskull, ever.* —BLEAK HOUSE, CHARLES DICKENS

nurse NOUN (also nursemaid)
a woman or girl whose job was to look after young children
• *Is that your mistress, nurse?* —JANE EYRE, CHARLOTTE BRONTË
➢ **monthly nurse:** a nurse who looked after a woman in the month after childbirth • *She was the person always first thought of in Raveloe when there was illness or death in a family ... or there was a sudden disappointment in a monthly nurse.* —SILAS MARNER, GEORGE ELIOT
➢ **wet nurse:** a woman whose job was to breastfeed someone else's baby • *You wasn't to go and worrit the wet nurse.* —DOMBEY AND SON, CHARLES DICKENS

nursery NOUN
a room or rooms in a house where young children were looked after, especially by a nursemaid
• *Adèle left me to go and play in the nursery.* —JANE EYRE, CHARLOTTE BRONTË

nutting NOUN
the activity of gathering nuts
• *The Raveloe boys ... would often leave off their nutting ... to peep in at the window.* —SILAS MARNER, GEORGE ELIOT

Oo

ORPHANS

In the 19th century, children who had lost both their parents, been abandoned by their families, or been forced out of their homes due to poverty or overcrowding were classed as **orphans**. **Orphanages** and **workhouses** took in such children, but many children ended up living homeless on the streets to escape the cruelty they found in these institutions. Orphans were found in the fiction of this period, with characters including Oliver Twist and Jane Eyre.

oakum NOUN
fibres obtained by picking old rope to pieces, a job done by people in workhouses and prisons. Oakum was used as a sealant, for example, in wooden ships.
• *So you'll begin to pick oakum to-morrow morning at six o'clock.*—OLIVER TWIST, CHARLES DICKENS

oaten ADJECTIVE
made of oats
• *a thin oaten cake*—JANE EYRE, CHARLOTTE BRONTË

oath NOUN
a swear word
• *Godfrey ... seized him by the arm, saying, with an oath—'I tell you, I have no money.'*—SILAS MARNER, GEORGE ELIOT

obeisance NOUN
a respectful bow or curtsy
• *Mr Collins [was] in waiting near the lodges, to make them his parting obeisance.*—PRIDE AND PREJUDICE, JANE AUSTEN

object NOUN
1 the subject or target of a feeling, conversation, action, thought, etc.
• *I was a more legitimate object of suspicion than any one else.*—GREAT EXPECTATION, CHARLES DICKENS
• *I am sure she could not have bestowed her kindness on a more grateful object.*—PRIDE AND PREJUDICE, JANE AUSTEN
2 a purpose; an objective
• *He struck twice or thrice upon the door—evidently with no other object than to make a noise there.*—A TALE OF TWO CITIES, CHARLES DICKENS
• *I have come ... with the one object of seeing you and asking your advice.*—THE ADVENTURE OF THE SPECKLED BAND, ARTHUR CONAN DOYLE
➢ **no object / not an object**: not a factor; not important • *Time is no object here. We never know what o'clock it is, and we never care.*—BLEAK HOUSE, CHARLES DICKENS

objectless ADJECTIVE
without purpose; not directed at anything in particular
• *Jane is 'lingering here at the sign-post ... objectless and lost'.*—JANE EYRE, CHARLOTTE BRONTË
• *My whole frame thrilled with objectless and unintelligible fear.*—DAVID COPPERFIELD, CHARLES DICKENS

oblivious ADJECTIVE
1 not knowing or remembering something
• *I ... sat staring at her, quite oblivious ... of the laws of politeness.*—DAVID COPPERFIELD, CHARLES DICKENS
2 drunken; in a state of unconsciousness
• *He ... closed the door upon the men in their deep and oblivious sleep.*—FAR FROM THE MADDING CROWD, THOMAS HARDY
3 forgotten or unknown; obscure
• *a life which ... is more oblivious than death*—MOBY DICK, HERMAN MELVILLE

obsequies NOUN
funeral rites
• *the obsequies of his late ... Majesty*—THE PRINCE AND THE PAUPER, MARK TWAIN

observance NOUN
1 observation; watching something
• *his close observance of the game*—OLIVER TWIST, CHARLES DICKENS
2 a show of respect or other custom
• *Mr Collins made his declaration ... with all the observances, which he supposed a regular part of the business.*—PRIDE AND PREJUDICE, JANE AUSTEN

obtrude VERB
1 to suddenly impose or force something on someone
• *It was to take her at a disadvantage to obtrude love upon her at such a time.*—THE SIGN OF FOUR, ARTHUR CONAN DOYLE
2 to suddenly appear or become very noticeable
• *[Elizabeth] had not got beyond [these] words ... when some unlucky recollections obtruded.*—PRIDE AND PREJUDICE, JANE AUSTEN

obtrusive ADJECTIVE
very noticeable
• [My] slate somehow happened to slip from my hand, and [fell] with an obtrusive crash.—JANE EYRE, CHARLOTTE BRONTË

obviate VERB
to avoid or get round a problem
• The man who fetches our letters every morning ... shall bring [yours] to you. That will obviate all difficulties.—EMMA, JANE AUSTEN

occasion NOUN
1 a reason or cause
• There was no occasion to detain her longer; she had done her part.—MARY BARTON, ELIZABETH GASKELL
2 the opportunity to do something
• [Bingley] afterwards took occasion to ask her ... whether all her sisters were at Longbourn.—PRIDE AND PREJUDICE, JANE AUSTEN

occasion VERB
to cause something
• I am sorry to have occasioned pain to anyone.—PRIDE AND PREJUDICE, JANE AUSTEN

occult ADJECTIVE
secret or obscure
• He looked as if he suspected me of some occult medical design on Miss Verinder!—THE MOONSTONE, WILKIE COLLINS

occupation NOUN
an activity or task; something done to pass the time
• I had prepared an occupation for him.—JANE EYRE, CHARLOTTE BRONTË

oculist NOUN
an eye doctor
• He had the advice of an eminent oculist; and he eventually recovered the sight of ... one eye.—JANE EYRE, CHARLOTTE BRONTË

odious ADJECTIVE
extremely unpleasant; detestable
• such an odious, stingy, hard, unfeeling man as Mr Scrooge—A CHRISTMAS CAROL, CHARLES DICKENS

odorous ADJECTIVE
with a strong smell, often a sweet or pleasant one
• an odorous breakfast of toast and ale—SILAS MARNER, GEORGE ELIOT

odour NOUN
a smell, often a sweet or pleasant one
• a subtle and aromatic odor—THE SIGN OF FOUR, ARTHUR CONAN DOYLE
USAGE In modern English, you would expect an odour to be a bad smell, rather than to come from a flower, delicious food, etc.

offal NOUN
waste; rubbish
• [They] were picking their way on foot through the black mud and offal of [the] streets.—A TALE OF TWO CITIES, CHARLES DICKENS

office NOUN
1 a service or duty; a task
• I cleared their path from the snow and performed those offices that I had seen done by Felix.—FRANKENSTEIN, MARY SHELLEY
• Silas's promise to help Sally is an 'office of charity'.—SILAS MARNER, GEORGE ELIOT
2 a position of responsibility or authority; a public role
• the office of parish-clerk—SILAS MARNER, GEORGE ELIOT
3 offices the parts of a house or property (for example, the kitchens and stables) where work was done by servants
• I went in by the court-yard and the offices.—THE WOMAN IN WHITE, WILKIE COLLINS

oleograph NOUN
a print textured to look like an oil painting

omnibus NOUN
a bus
• Cabs and carriages, carts and omnibuses were all trying to get over the bridge together.—BLACK BEAUTY, ANNA SEWELL

only PREPOSITION & ADVERB
except for; apart from
• The hall was not dark, nor yet was it lit, only by the high-hung bronze lamp.—JANE EYRE, CHARLOTTE BRONTË

onset NOUN
an attack
• The old man made a stab at me ... but the vicious onset failed.—LORNA DOONE, R. D. BLACKMORE

operate VERB
to work or be active; to have an effect
• His fear of her has always operated ... when they were together.—PRIDE AND PREJUDICE, JANE AUSTEN
USAGE In modern English, you might only expect a machine or device to operate, rather than a feeling or quality.

operation NOUN
an activity or procedure; work
• The task of persuading Silas to invest his money is described as 'the operation on [his] mind'.—SILAS MARNER, GEORGE ELIOT

opinion NOUN
➤ **have no opinion of:** to have no respect for someone; to think badly of someone • She is a selfish, hypocritical woman, and I have no opinion of her.—PRIDE AND PREJUDICE, JANE AUSTEN

opportune ADJECTIVE
convenient; well timed
• *But they were both happily relieved by the opportune appearance of Mike.*—GREAT EXPECTATIONS, CHARLES DICKENS

oppose VERB
to stand or place something in front of someone or something
• *The challengers ... opposed themselves individually to the knights.*—IVANHOE, SIR WALTER SCOTT
➤ **opposing** ADJECTIVE opposite; facing • *the opposing sides of the glen* —SHIRLEY, CHARLOTTE BRONTË

opposition NOUN
1 conflict or argument; resistance
• *Let there be no opposition, and no discussion about it.*—JANE EYRE, CHARLOTTE BRONTË
• *She married me in opposition to her father's wish.* —DAVID COPPERFIELD, CHARLES DICKENS
2 a contrast or difference
• *Between him and Darcy there was a very steady friendship, in spite of a great opposition of character.* —PRIDE AND PREJUDICE, JANE AUSTEN
3 a position opposite, in particular the position of a planet appearing to be 180 degrees from the sun
• *Venus and Mars were in alignment with the sun; that is to say, Mars was in opposition from the point of view of an observer on Venus.*—THE WAR OF THE WORLDS, H. G. WELLS

opprobrium NOUN
criticism; disgrace
• *Maggie thinks running away is 'the only way of escaping opprobrium'.*—THE MILL ON THE FLOSS, GEORGE ELIOT
➤ **opprobrious** ADJECTIVE critical; scornful
• *He called the woman 'an opprobrious name'* —a rude name.—MARY BARTON, ELIZABETH GASKELL

optic NOUN
an eye
• *Miss Fanshawe's ... optics ... were upon us.*—VILLETTE, CHARLOTTE BRONTË

oracle NOUN
1 a message or prophecy from God or the gods
• *Never did his manner become so impressive ... as when he delivered the oracles of God.*—JANE EYRE, CHARLOTTE BRONTË
2 a person or book giving a message from God or the gods, or giving other mysterious or wise words
• *She had no idea ... but there was ... a Catalogue of Prices, and by this oracle Biddy arranged all the shop transactions.*—GREAT EXPECTATIONS, CHARLES DICKENS
🏛 In Greek mythology, this word referred to a person receiving a message from the gods, and to the place where this was said to happen.

oracular ADJECTIVE
1 speaking with the authority of a god or of a very wise person
• *'Yes, ma'am,' returned Bitzer, with a demonstration of great respect for Mrs Sparsit's oracular authority.* —HARD TIMES, CHARLES DICKENS
2 mysterious; unclear
• *[His] oracular words ... seemed almost to make the Captain giddy.*—DOMBEY AND SON, CHARLES DICKENS

orders NOUN
➤ **take orders:** to become a priest • *I understand that he intends to take orders.*—SENSE AND SENSIBILITY, JANE AUSTEN

ordnance NOUN
weapons; military equipment
• *The piece of ordnance ... was mounted in a separate fortress.*—GREAT EXPECTATIONS, CHARLES DICKENS

organ NOUN
a particular type of idea or emotion, or the part of the brain thought to be its source
• *Really your organs of wonder and credulity are easily excited.*—JANE EYRE, CHARLOTTE BRONTË

organism NOUN
a being
• *He had a 'look with his eye' which fell unpleasantly on Mr Snell's sensitive organism.*—SILAS MARNER, GEORGE ELIOT

orientalist NOUN
an expert in the languages, history, and cultures of the countries of the Middle East or Far East
• *The Persian, Arabic, and Sanskrit languages engaged his attention, and I ... [also found] consolation in the works of the orientalists.*—FRANKENSTEIN, MARY SHELLEY

orison NOUN
a prayer

orlop NOUN
the lowest deck of a ship

orts NOUN
scraps; leftovers
• *Their feasting caused a multiplication of orts, which were the heirlooms of the poor.*—SILAS MARNER, GEORGE ELIOT

osier NOUN
a willow tree
• *baskets of plaited osier*—THE FISHERMAN AND HIS SOUL, OSCAR WILDE

ostler (also hostler) NOUN
a man who looked after the horses of guests at an inn
- *The ostler at a roadside public-house was holding a pail of water to refresh my horses.*—WUTHERING HEIGHTS, EMILY BRONTË

out ADVERB
When a wealthy young woman *came out*, she was formally presented in public for the first time, typically at a ball. She was then *out*, i.e. part of the wealthy social scene and available for marriage.
- *Are any of your younger sisters out, Miss Bennet?*—PRIDE AND PREJUDICE, JANE AUSTEN

outlandish ADJECTIVE
foreign
- *He has an outlandish accent.*—SHIRLEY, CHARLOTTE BRONTË

outlive VERB
to live through something; to survive something
- *I can't outlive the disgrace.*—THE MAYOR OF CASTERBRIDGE, THOMAS HARDY

out-of-door relief (also out-relief) NOUN
assistance given to poor people who did not live in the workhouse
- *According to Mr Bumble, if the poor are given what they do not want, they stop asking; he calls this the 'great principle of out-of-door relief'.*—OLIVER TWIST, CHARLES DICKENS

outwork NOUN
an outer section of a fort or castle; a fortification
- *Little Aaron has 'made an outwork of his mother's chair'—he is hiding behind it.*—SILAS MARNER, GEORGE ELIOT

overlook VERB
1 to supervise people or activities
- *Sir ... do what you are told ... without any person being present to overlook you.*—THE MOONSTONE, WILKIE COLLINS
- *Besides, he intended to overlook the whole business of land and mill pretty closely.*—THE MILL ON THE FLOSS, GEORGE ELIOT

2 to look down on something; to see something
- *The murder had been overlooked.*—THE STRANGE CASE OF DR JEKYLL AND MR HYDE, ROBERT LOUIS STEVENSON

overlooker NOUN
a supervisor
- *I don't pretend to know the names of the men I employ; that I leave to the overlooker.*—MARY BARTON, ELIZABETH GASKELL

overmaster VERB
to overpower someone or something
- *an overmastering weakness and weariness*—KIDNAPPED, ROBERT LOUIS STEVENSON

overset VERB
1 to overturn something; to knock something over
- *[Cleopatra] made a dab at the Major with her fan, but overset Mr Dombey's breakfast cup instead.*—DOMBEY AND SON, CHARLES DICKENS

2 to overwhelm or upset someone
- *Elizabeth says they 'have been overset already' by soldiers and dances.*—PRIDE AND PREJUDICE, JANE AUSTEN

overthrow VERB
1 to put an end to something; to cause something to go wrong
- *I always delight in overthrowing those kind of schemes.*—PRIDE AND PREJUDICE, JANE AUSTEN

2 to knock someone over
- *He had been overthrown into gutters.*—DOMBEY AND SON, CHARLES DICKENS

overthrow NOUN
the end or destruction of something
- *an overthrow of all order and neatness*—PERSUASION, JANE AUSTEN

overtop VERB
to be larger, higher, better, or more important than something else
- *The comical side of the affair so completely overtopped every other consideration that we both burst out into a roar of laughter.*—THE ADVENTURES OF SHERLOCK HOLMES, ARTHUR CONAN DOYLE

overture (also overtures) NOUN
an approach to someone with an offer or suggestion
- *I flatter myself that my present overtures of good-will are highly commendable.*—PRIDE AND PREJUDICE, JANE AUSTEN

own VERB
1 to acknowledge or admit something
- *'She seems a very pleasant young woman.' ... 'Oh! dear, yes; but you must own she is very plain.'*—PRIDE AND PREJUDICE, JANE AUSTEN

2 to acknowledge someone as a child or relation
- *Perhaps [the child] would be just as happy in life without being owned by its father.*—SILAS MARNER, GEORGE ELIOT

CONTENTS

130 CHILDHOOD

132 WORKING LIFE

134 RICH AND POOR

136 AT HOME

138 FASHION

140 SPORT AND ENTERTAINMENT

142 TRANSPORT

144 SCIENCE

146 CRIME

148 DEATH AND DISEASE

150 POLITICS

152 WAR AND EMPIRE

CHILDHOOD

The life of a poor child in the 1800s was a harsh one. Children as young as four years old worked for 12-hour shifts in factories and mills, down mines, and on the streets as road sweepers and chimney sweeps. It was a dangerous, terrifying, and unhealthy life. The Factory Acts of 1833 put a stop to much of the child labour.

A census from the 1800s shows children aged 11 and 12 years old doing the following jobs:

- soap maker
- street seller selling matches or ribbons
- general or house servant
- errand boy or girl
- railway message boy
- apprentice carpenter
- boiler cleaner on tug boat
- shop boy
- druggist (chemist) assistant
- milk boy
- apprentice chair maker
- sawyer (someone who sawed wood)
- wheelwright
- apprentice dressmaker
- pushing coal trucks in the mines
- cleaning streets of horse dung

Children working in mills were tasked with unskilled but often dangerous jobs. They had to clean the machines by crawling underneath and wiping fluff off the wheels and spindles while the machinery moved. This was called *fettling*. They had to repair broken threads on the spinning machines, which was called *piecing*.

In wealthier families, boys were sent away to fee-paying boarding schools whilst girls were usually taught at home by governesses. But even these children could face cruel punishments such as beatings or being made to wear a dunce's cap. It was only in 1870 that laws made it compulsory for every child between the ages of five and ten to attend school.

◀ This 1840 illustration shows Michael Armstrong, who was adopted by a mill owner, embracing his brother who worked in rags in the mill. From The Life and Adventures of Michael Armstrong by Frances Trollope who campaigned against child labour

▶ Games such as this early version of pinball would only be played by rich people.

◀ Everyday toys might be a doll or a hoop and a stick. Marbles, catch, and hopscotch were also popular games played by children at the time.

▼ This early photograph shows children at a ragged school in London. The schools were still helping destitute children into the 1900s.

Rich children learned their alphabet with ABC books in their playroom or nursery with a governess.

When they were able to read, they could enjoy books such as:
- *Treasure Island* by Robert Louis Stevenson
- *Black Beauty* by Anna Sewell
- *Alice's Adventures in Wonderland* by Lewis Carroll.

Ragged schools provided destitute and orphaned children with a basic education in the mid-1800s. They were set up by charitable organizations to enable all children to learn how to read and write. The schools also tried to instil a sense of morality to try to improve children's chances of avoiding a life of crime.

If destitute children aged between 7 and 14 years old committed an offence, they might be sent to an *industrial school* rather than prison. Here they might learn a trade or domestic skills.

Older teenagers who had been in trouble with the police might attend a *reformatory school*. These were strict and discipline was harsh in an attempt to turn them away from crime.

While richer children played with toy soldiers and tea sets, poorer children often only had homemade dolls or balls made out of bundles of rags. Candles provided the only light in the home once it was dark, so children mainly played outside during daylight hours. Electric lights only appeared in wealthier homes from the late 19th century.

▲ A tricycle horse with wooden wheels shows the craftsmanship that went into wealthy children's toys.

WORKING LIFE

In the early 19th century, Great Britain became known as the 'workshop of the world' and the Industrial Revolution transformed the jobs that people did both in the towns and countryside. On farms, men, women, and children had traditionally done back-breaking work such as spreading manure and harvesting crops by hand or using horses. However, in the second half of the century, new agricultural machines could carry out these tasks so many farm workers were no longer needed. They were forced to move away from the countryside to the towns in search of work.

Working life in the 1800s was based around the main industries of textiles, coal, iron, steel, and farming. Many entrepreneurial businesses also started up and family firms employed increasing numbers of people.

There was a huge demand for coal to fuel the factories and also to be exported around the world. Deep mines and pits were opened across Britain, especially in South Wales.

Some professions in the 1800s were:
- truss-hook maker
- shoemaker
- journeyman
- weaver
- bookseller
- spring maker
- basket maker
- milliner
- draper
- pewterer

▲ A painting showing a ploughman having his plough pulled by a woman and child in the 1800s. By the end of the century, farmers used machinery for ploughing, reaping, and milking.

The mass production of cotton and textiles, steel-making, ship-building, and other industries created new jobs for people. But these factory jobs were dangerous ones with horrendous working conditions which often led to injury, illness, and even death. Workers fought for shorter hours, higher wages, and better safety, but until 1871, they were banned from joining trade unions—the organizations which could help them understand their rights at work.

In the latter part of the century, many men worked in the steel industry—building ships, bridges, buildings, railways, tools, and machinery.

In the 1840s and '50s, the fifth largest industry in America was whaling. The oil from whale blubber was used to make candles and, with the increase in industrialization, to lubricate machinery. Whalebone was also used for women's corsets. Engraved and decorated whale teeth were known as *scrimshaw*.

▶ This advertisement is for Victorian gardening tools. The lawnmower was invented in 1830 by Edward Beard Budding who took inspiration for the cutting blade from a machine in a local cloth mill. In the mid-1800s, with the removal of taxes on glass, glasshouses could be afforded by the rising middle classes. The glazier's knife would have been useful in the glasshouse.

▲ Victorian streets were busy with costermongers, who called out for people to buy fruit and vegetables from their stalls which were often pulled by a donkey.

▼ An apothecary would prepare and sell drugs. This is a satirical scene showing an apothecary dispensing medicines made from poison mixed by his 'assistant'.

Few women worked in professions such as medicine, law, and banking until later in the century. Elizabeth Garrett Anderson obtained her medical licence in 1865. Educated women were often restricted to roles such as governesses, which involved teaching wealthy children in their homes. Many working-class women worked in wealthy homes in domestic service.

Rich or poor, the lives of women in the 1800s were restricted to the home, with little, if any education, and few opportunities other than marriage. The writing of women authors such as Brontë and Austen reflected this. As the century wore on, women began their fight for more equality in society.

Many women worked in a domestic service setting—either as housekeepers, maids, or servants. Some worked in the cloth and clothing factories, particularly in those areas such as Lancashire and Yorkshire where the woollen and cotton factories were centred. They might be employed as seamstresses, in laundries, or as cleaners, or shop workers.

Lace-making, glove-making, and hosiery were among the textile industries which often employed more women than men.

▶ This is a Christmas card depicting medication that would help with digestion over the festive period.

133

RICH AND POOR

The rich and the poor led very different lives. Aristocratic families, wealthy merchants, and industrialists owned land, lived in grand country mansions, and made money from the farms, mines, and quarries that made up their estates. The poor worked on the land, for long hours and low wages, and lived in overcrowded and unsanitary conditions. sometimes sharing a single-room house with pigs and cows.

A new class, the middle class, emerged between the working class and the upper class. This was made up of bankers, factory managers, and teachers etc. who earned good salaries. With this wealth came a desire from some people to help those living in extreme poverty. Charitable works, ragged schools, and workhouses were examples of this.

Whether rich or poor, women had a lot of babies as there was no contraception. Queen Victoria had nine children and Charles Dickens had ten. Many women died in childbirth and many children died young from disease.

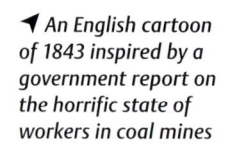

◀ An English cartoon of 1843 inspired by a government report on the horrific state of workers in coal mines

◀ A destitute mother begs for herself and her baby and child.

▶ Dinnertime at a Marylebone workhouse in London around 1900. A report of 1867 said that 'about 11,000 men, women and children obtained relief here in the last six months'.

As the Industrial Revolution drove people to towns and cities in search of work, poor families crowded together in slums. Living conditions were desperate with open sewers spreading disease. In London in the hot summer of 1858, a foul smell hanging over the city for months was named the Great Stink. Workhouses provided shelter and work for the destitute, but some turned to crime to survive. The issue of poverty became a matter of national debate, with many saying that the poor did not deserve help. Others set up charities to give aid to poor people and in 1870 the philanthropist Thomas Barnardo founded his first children's home to look after homeless orphans living on the streets.

▶ This is a late Victorian advertisement for a toilet for the rich. Once running water was installed in houses, Victorian toilets and baths were often made from porcelain and mahogany and ornately decorated.

◀ Two well-dressed girls meet an impoverished child.

A saying, 'the poor are always with us', was often used by people to remind them to be charitable to those less fortunate than they were. Others, such as Samuel Smiles who wrote a bestselling book called *Self-Help: with Illustrations of Character, Conduct and Perseverance*, believed that people could improve their fortunes through hard work. The symbol of the hardworking bee and beehive, often engraved on buildings in cities such as Manchester, was a sign of this. In the late 1800s George Cadbury built housing specially for workers at his chocolate factory to 'alleviate the evils of modern, more cramped living conditions'.

In 1851, Henry Mayhew (one of the founders of *Punch* magazine) published an important record of society in his book called *London Labour and the London Poor*.

Disease was rife and affected both rich and poor. The sewer system only came to London because of the Great Stink. It was thought that disease was spread by *miasma* or smell, so it was important to get rid of the smell. Bazalgette's sewers opened in 1866. For poor people, the toilet or privy was used by the whole street. It was usually a bench over a hole. At first, even wealthy households did not have running water and so did not have a flushing toilet.

Even in a large house, there was only one sink and it would be in the scullery for washing clothes and dishes. For poor people living in cramped houses, water would be fetched from a pump on the street. Baths would be taken by heating water from the street tap over the kitchen fire to fill a bathtub. All the family would bathe in the same water.

AT HOME

A home could be a grand country mansion with land and servants or a rented room in a crowded, unsanitary tenement block. In towns and cities, industrialists built houses for their workers. Middle-class professionals moved into the growing suburbs and used the expanding rail network to commute to work.

In the house:
- house steward
- butler
- housekeeper
- cook
- lady's maid
- valet
- first footman
- second footman
- head nurse
- chamber maids
- parlour maids
- house maid
- nurse
- under cook
- kitchen maid
- scullery maid
- laundry maid
- page

In the grounds:
- head groom
- groom
- stable boy
- head gardener
- game keeper
- ground keeper

A country estate, owned by a titled gentleman or a wealthy businessman, might employ thirty or forty men, women, and children.

A wealthy town house might employ up to twenty staff.

Even middle-class households employed a daily girl or a charwoman. A general maid, often aged 13 or 14 years old, might live in a small room in the house, usually at the top of the house.

In a country house, a wealthy family would employ a large staff. The house was split between the grand rooms upstairs which were used by the family, and the rooms 'below stairs' where the servants worked. The first house to be lit by electric lights was Cragside in Northumberland in 1880.

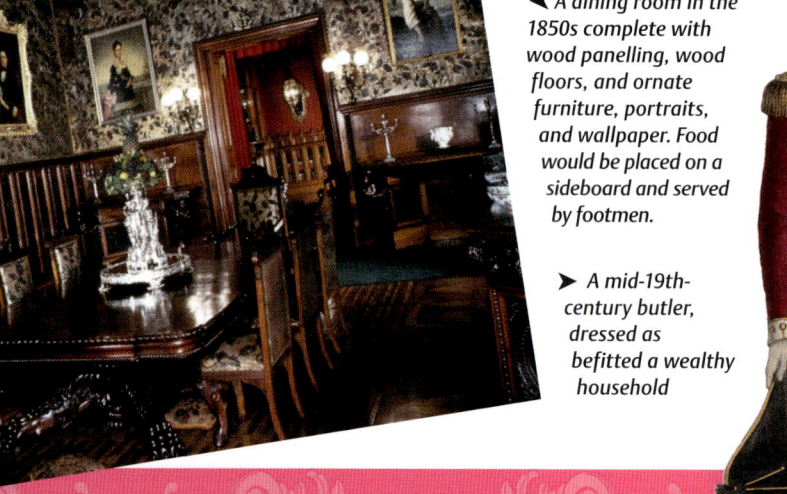

◀ A dining room in the 1850s complete with wood panelling, wood floors, and ornate furniture, portraits, and wallpaper. Food would be placed on a sideboard and served by footmen.

▶ A mid-19th-century butler, dressed as befitted a wealthy household

▶ Mrs Beeton's cookery and household management books were originally published in a magazine and, with a growing wealthy middle class, became the absolute guide for any home.

▼ Cookery books and improved kitchen equipment turned food into an industry. Jelly moulds, pie dishes, cutters, and graters could be used to make desserts and pies look decorative as well as taste delicious.

Every room served a different purpose. Family life revolved around the drawing room, which was often furnished with a piano for after-dinner entertainment. To help them to run their homes, housewives referred to etiquette guides such as *Mrs Beeton's Book of Household Management* (first published in 1861). Labour-saving inventions such as the gas cooker (1850s) and the carpet sweeper (1876) found their way into Victorian homes. However, dangers lurked there too with arsenic-rich wallpaper and lead-painted toys poisoning unwitting families.

▶ The carpet sweeper was used from the late 1800s. In America, Melville Bissell patented his invention in 1876 and in the UK, the Ewbank became a popular brand of carpet sweeper. Both of these brands remained familiar household names for many years.

With the invention of ice houses to keep food frozen, the Victorians enjoyed eating ice cream and sorbet between meat and fish courses.

Menus were seasonal and usually stayed the same every day of the week, with just the vegetables changing.

Meals were breakfast, luncheon, afternoon tea, dinner, and supper. With the change in working routines, the evening meal moved from between 5 and 6pm to around 8 or 9pm. Afternoon tea was introduced as people felt they needed a light meal in the late afternoon before dinner.

After the first commercial canning factory was founded in the UK in 1813, food could be stored and transported without spoiling. By the end of the 19th century, condensed milk, baked beans, meat, fruit, and vegetables were canned and transported around the world.

The food that people ate depended on their social standing:

• In the workhouse people were fed bread, potatoes, *parings* (peelings), and *gruel* (a thin watery soup).

• People who were not earning would eat bread, *dripping* (animal fat), and vegetables, and drink tea.

• If you were earning a wage, you could afford to eat bacon and sausage twice a week along with cheese, vegetables, and bread.

• Farmers ate well with bacon, cheese, sausage, and vegetables more than once a week.

• Very wealthy families served banquets which, in the early 1800s, could be two huge courses of up to twenty dishes for a special occasion.

FASHION

Women's and men's fashions changed significantly between 1800 and 1900. At the beginning of the century, the dominant style for women was to wear a long, loose-fitting dress with a high waistline. But as the century wore on, dresses became fuller with enormous hooped crinoline skirts. Modesty and etiquette dictated clothing styles—even a glimpse of a lady's ankle would be frowned upon. At the beginning of the century, upper-class men wore top hats whilst the working man wore a bowler hat. By the end of the century men wore a range of different hats for casual wear and sporting activities.

From padded *bustles* tied round the waist to *crinolinettes* with steel hoops sewn into a petticoat, women tried to give themselves a rounded shape.

Gigot sleeves were voluminous at the upper arm, narrowing to a tight forearm or wrist. Sleeves and bodices were often separate items. Lace *engageantes* were flouncy sleeves which could be pulled on up to the elbow underneath a dress's sleeves.

A *pelerine* was a narrow strip of fabric or fur with pointed ends which was worn like a cape. Later, it became part of a dress to hide where the sleeves were tied to the separate bodice.

European terms such as *basque, bolero, corsage, galoon, ruche, pagoda, revers,* and *Swiss waists* gave fashion an exclusive aura.

A *basque* was a close-fitting bodice which extended to the waist or just below.

A *galloon* was a narrow ornamental strip of braid or lace which trimmed clothing or upholstery.

A *corsage* was the upper part of a woman's dress.

A *bolero* was a short open jacket.

Pagoda sleeves were wide and flounced to create the impression of delicate wrists and hands.

◀ Shoes and boots for Victorian men and women in 1880. Length, buttoning, contrasting top sections, and the shape of the toe all changed through the period.

▲ A mantle, or sleeveless cloak, with chiffon ruffles and passementerie or decorative tassels and braid trimming, was popular in the later years of the 19th century.

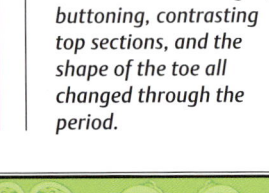

138

For men, knee breeches were increasingly replaced by long trousers in the early years of the 1800s, whilst the fashionable top hat became easier to pack with the invention of the first collapsible top hat. For the upper-class man, frock coats, waistcoats, and stiff-collared shirts were worn during the day and black tail-coats and trousers in the evening.

◀ Gold braid frogging decorates this military uniform from 1849.

▼ Corsets and stays were laced tightly and stiffened by strips of whalebone.

A *Swiss waist* was a boned garment worn under the bust on the outside of a dress or ball gown. It was also called a *postilion*, *corselet*, or *corselet belt*.

The *revers* was the part of clothing, often the lapels, which was turned back to reveal a brightly-coloured silk lining.

Coats and outer wear

A *pelisse* was a loose coat with a high waist for women. A *paletôt* matched the wearer's crinoline or bustle and later referred to a coat generally. A *redingote* was a long richly decorated velvet or wool overcoat; a *sacque* was a version of the men's loose-fitting coat called a sack coat. Women's clothes did not feature pockets and before handbags became popular, women might carry a drawstring *reticule*, often tied to a belt.

Men wore *spats* (short for *spatterdashes*) or cloth gaiters over their boots to cover the ankle. In the 1870s wealthy men might wear a *Norfolk jacket* with *knickerbockers* for shooting, fishing, or walking.

Jeans became a common clothing choice for working men and women in the US in the late 1800s, when Levi Strauss patented his design for denim trousers reinforced with rivets to make the jeans more hard-wearing.

Underwear

Small clothes in the Victorian era might refer to underwear or to men's *breeches*. Breeches were often made from silk. Men and women wore *drawers*. Women's drawers were made of two separate legs joined at the waist. Women's clothes used whale bone to add structure. In corsets, they would be laced and tightened to create a tiny, neat waist. The *nonchalante* was an elasticized corset.

Hose was the name for legwear, often worn in layers, made from silk or wool.

▶ The wealthier traveller's bag was lined in silk and fitted with compartments for brushes and silver-topped lotion bottles.

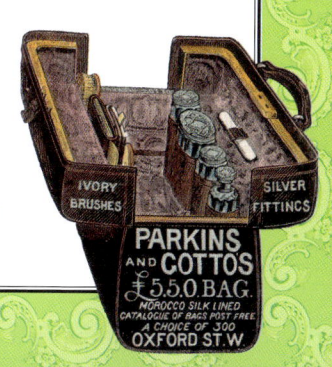

SPORT AND ENTERTAINMENT

As the Industrial Revolution changed people's working lives, it altered the way they spent their free time too. The 1850 Factory Act introduced the five-and-a-half-day working week and, with their free Saturday afternoons, men went in their thousands to support their local football team. The Football Association was founded in 1863 and, in 1872, the first recognized international football match was played between England and Scotland. Rugby Football Union split away from football in 1871. In cricket, Australia's famous defeat of England in 1882 led to the establishment of the Ashes Test cricket series.

In the US, a PE teacher invented the sport of basketball in 1891, whilst volleyball was invented in 1895 as a sport that young athletes could play indoors.

◀ Victorian sportsmen dressed for lacrosse, hockey, running, and horse racing.

▼ This is a Daguerreotype camera from 1839. Before this, having a portrait painted was the only way to preserve what someone looked like. Daguerreotypes were taken on silver so they were also costly, but this was the start of the popularity and affordability of photography.

In the absence of television, radio, or computers, popular pastimes were sketching, painting, and reading, along with the following activities:

• *Bagatelle* was a game in which small balls were hit and allowed to roll down a sloping board on which there were numbered holes with different scores and pins acting as obstructions.

• *Battledore and shuttlecock* was a forerunner of badminton.

• *Cycling* was enjoyed by both men and women. It required particular clothing, especially for women who started to wear *bloomers* instead of long skirts and dresses.

◀ Bearded ladies such as Mademoiselle Lefort, depicted in 1818, were popular exhibits at freak shows.

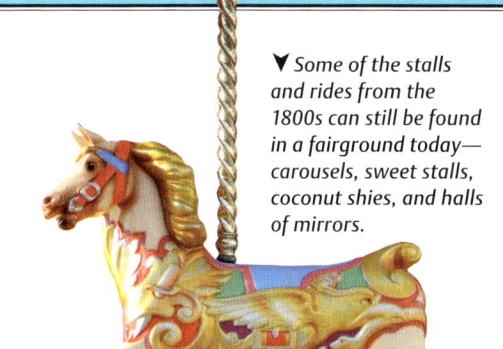

▼ Some of the stalls and rides from the 1800s can still be found in a fairground today—carousels, sweet stalls, coconut shies, and halls of mirrors.

Fun fairs which combined acrobats, prize-fighters, 'freak shows', and menageries of wild animals were popular in the first half of the century, whilst the later years of the century saw the introduction of steam-powered 'gallopers', carousels, and other fairground rides. In the evenings, wealthy audiences flocked to the theatre to see plays by writers such as Oscar Wilde and George Bernard Shaw, or Gilbert and Sullivan's comic operas. For the working classes, the entertainment of choice was going to the pub or to the music hall, where performers included singers, comedians, magicians, and all-round entertainers.

Victorian entertainment also took a supernatural turn with spiritualists who claimed to be able to contact the dead and mesmerists with strange hypnotic powers. Filmmakers such as the Lumière brothers in France produced the first moving pictures or movies, whilst the invention of the gramophone allowed people to listen to recordings of musical performances in the comfort of their own homes.

- **Swimming**—Victorians enjoyed swimming in the sea. They wore modest and often impractical and uncomfortable swimming suits, which they changed into in huts on the sea edge.

- *The piers, promenades, botanical gardens* and *entertainment halls* of many of today's seaside towns in England date from the 1800s.

- **Card games** included Whist, Old Maid, Bread and Honey, and Snap.

- **Singing** around the household piano was also popular.

In music and the arts, many great and famous names were born or worked during the 19th century. Only a few names from the many are given here:

- **In music,** Ludwig van Beethoven, Frederick Chopin, Franz Liszt, Giacomo Puccini, Robert Schumann, Pyotr Tchaikovsky

- **In literature,** Louisa May Alcott, Jane Austen, Charlotte Brontë, Lewis Carroll, Charles Dickens, George Eliot, Elizabeth Gaskell, Leo Tolstoy, Mark Twain

- **In poetry,** Elizabeth Barrett Browning, William Blake, Robert Browning, Lord Byron, Samuel Taylor Coleridge, John Keats, Percy Bysshe Shelley, William Wordsworth, William Butler Yeats

◀ The cover of a programme for the Empire theatre, London. The bill featured comedians including Dan Leno and 'Cleopatra, A Grand Ballet Divertissement'.

▼ A Victorian greetings card with a playing card design, from around 1880

TRANSPORT

At the beginning of the 1800s, a journey across town or further afield was a slow, uncomfortable undertaking with horse-drawn carriages navigating potholed roads which turned into muddy quagmires whenever it rained. But by 1899, a driver in a motor car could complete the same journey with ease, travelling in comfort along smooth roads.

In the 19th century, horse-drawn carriages were used to travel across cities and for longer journeys across counties. However, not everyone wanted to travel in a common hackney carriage (probably named after Hackney in East London where the horses would graze on pasture); some people preferred to use their own privately-owned coach and horses.

▼ A stagecoach passes a stopping place where the passengers exchange greetings with a couple of gentlemen.

Some types of coaches were:
curricle: two wheels, drawn by two horses, driven by its owner, smart and sporty

fiacre: four wheels, drawn by one horse, usually with a folding roof, carrying two passengers and available for hire

gig: two wheels, drawn by one horse, relatively cheap to buy and driven by its owner, easy to overturn

hackney: four wheels, drawn by two horses, carrying six passengers and available for hire

landau: four wheels, enclosed carriage with a removable front cover and a back cover that could be raised and lowered

post-chaise: two or four horses, which would be changed for fresh ones at each stage of the journey, also used for carrying mail

stage coach: four wheels, drawn by four or six horses, up to eight passengers inside, with two cheaper seats attached to the back and any number on the roof holding on to the handrail

The 19th century was also the age of the train. In 1804, Richard Trevithick ran the first steam locomotive along a railway track at the Penydarren iron works in Merthyr Tydfil and soon railway lines were built across Great Britain, connecting Manchester and Liverpool in 1830, and London and Bristol in 1844.

▼ The 'iron horse' was the name given to the steam locomotive —from Stevenson's 'Rocket' in 1829 to the 'North Star' which worked on the Great Western Railway from 1836-70 to the engines of the late 1890s.

▲ James Sadler in his hot-air balloon in 1810. Sadler was an early balloonist in England. He undertook several ascents with varying success and was well known in his lifetime.

Coaches travelled on rutted roads at about four miles per hour until carriageways improved in the early 1800s. Thomas Telford built a number of roads in 1803 and John McAdam developed a way of layering large and small stones to create a hard surface. This design was the forerunner of *tarmacadam* or *tarmac*. It is still in use today.

In 1885, a German named Karl Benz put a new invention—the internal combustion engine—on a three-wheeled vehicle he had made in Mannheim, Germany. This is known as the first motorcar. Soon lots of companies started making cars and they became more popular.

Trains, with chilling and cooling devices, enabled fresh milk and food to be transported from the countryside to the urban areas. International trade and shipping meant that preserved food and dry goods such as tea and grain from China and America were soon to become commonplace.

▼ Early bicycles were made from a simple wooden frame with a front wheel that could be steered.

The world's first underground railway system, the London Underground, was opened in 1863 and carried 30,000 passengers on its opening day. In the US, the first transcontinental railroad was built in the 1860s, heralding the end of the Pony Express which had used relay teams of riders and horses to deliver mail quickly between the east and west coasts. By the end of the century, a network of railway lines criss-crossed the world, transforming the speed with which people and goods could be transported.

SCIENCE

Huge leaps in scientific knowledge were made in the 19th century. From Charles Darwin's theory of evolution to the discovery of X-rays by the German physicist Wilhelm Röntgen, scientific achievements transformed people's lives and changed the way they looked at the world. The invention of the electric telegraph meant that people could communicate information almost instantly across vast distances. Alexander Graham Bell's telephone enabled people in different places to speak to each other directly in person. In offices and homes, the invention of the electric light bulb meant people could work and entertain late into the night, and electric street lighting illuminated great cities such as Paris and New York.

▶ Wilhelm Röntgen's X-ray of his wife's hand showing her bones and her wedding ring

The 1800s was a period of great scientific change, in particular in the fields of light, heat, electricity, and magnetism. There was a fascination with life and nature: how was life created? Could the power of nature be harnessed? What exactly did death mean and what happened to people's spirits after they died?

In medicine, hospitals began to be used to study and research disease. Medical students could dissect a patient's corpse to find out causes

▲ One of the first football matches to use electric lights to illuminate the pitch at Kennington Oval in London. The lights caused shifting shadows which made it confusing for the players and it was reported to be unsatisfactory.

▶ Thomas Edison produced the first successful electric light bulb in 1879. These incandescent lights, with different forms of carbon filaments, were featured in the magazine Les Nouvelles Conquêtes de la Science (The New Conquests of Science).

◀ *This poster illustrates a lady using the newly-invented telephone whilst at the theatre. It was a novelty and a distraction from the acting, sets, and stage effects of the play.*

In 1800, the Italian scientist Alessandro Volta introduced the first battery.

In the early part of the century, the British chemist Humphrey Davy began working in what became known as the field of *electrochemistry*. He isolated substances such as *potassium*, *calcium*, and *magnesium*, and also discovered *iodine*. His other work led to the creation of the *Davy lamp* which helped reduce the number of mine explosions caused by the gas methane which was found deep in the pits.

Davy's assistant, Michael Faraday, went on to discover the principle behind the electric transformer and generator. The terms he used such as *electrode*, *cathode*, and *ion* are still used today when talking about generating electricity.

and effects of different illnesses. It was mainly the bodies of criminals that were dissected but, as fewer criminals faced the death penalty, bodies were in short supply. *Cadavers* became valuable and *body snatchers* dug up graves to sell the dead to doctors for medical research.

Laboratories were set up, often in universities, where chemists and physicists could experiment in order to understand *anatomy*. Improvements to scientific instruments, such as the *microscope* and *thermometer*, enabled scientists to piece together how the body worked.

Certain poisons were believed to have healing effects and they were taken for a range of medical ailments. However, the Pharmacy Act of 1868 regulated the selling of poisons such as *strychnine* and *potassium cyanide*. *Opium* and forms of it such as *laudanum* were in common use until they too were eventually regulated.

In the field of biology, the French scientist Louis Pasteur's discovery that microscopic organisms caused disease led to the development of treatments and vaccines. The use of aspirin as a treatment for pain relief was pioneered by a German chemist named Felix Hoffman and this wonder drug was patented in 1899. In physics, James Clerk Maxwell's theory of electromagnetic radiation and Joseph Thomson's discovery of the electron in 1897 gave the world the first understanding of the subatomic world of particles and waves that underpinned the universe.

◀ *Innovations in optical theory by Ernst Abbe, a German physicist, led to improved microscopes during the 1800s.*

145

CRIME

As the population in towns and cities grew, so did public fears about crime. The *Illustrated Police News* and other newspapers were filled with lurid reports of robberies and murders. In 1888 the violent crimes carried out in London's East End by a serial killer nicknamed 'Jack the Ripper' held the world spellbound.

▶ The weekly newspaper *The Illustrated Police News* was published from the mid-19th century. The public had an appetite for gruesome crime stories.

One report in *The Illustrated Police News* in 1897 tells the tale of Mr J. Mitchell who was walking down the Mile End Road in London and was garrotted from behind and had his trousers ripped off his body!

One of the most common items stolen was the silk handkerchief, which would often be put up for sale by being hung on a pole.

The introduction of police officers patrolling the streets led to a general decline in crime through the 19th century. The phrase 'recommended to mercy on account of their youth' was the phrase used in court to let juveniles off the death penalty.

Baby farming was the taking of unwanted babies in return for payment. One notorious person who took in babies and then murdered them was Margaret Waters, who lived in Brixton, London and who was executed in 1870.

A *flash house* was a pub where stolen goods were fenced or sold.

Garrotting was the seizing of a person from behind in a stranglehold in order for a companion to steal money and possessions.

The *jug* was an informal word for prison.

Police forces were established to combat crime. The Metropolitan Police Act of 1829 brought a full-time police force to the streets of London, and ten years later every county in Britain could establish its own constabulary. Police officers in uniform had truncheons and rattles to raise the alarm, and in 1842, the first plainclothes detectives were introduced to investigate serious crimes.

146

THE "ANTI-PICKPOCKET" PURSE
FOR NOTES AND GOLD.
Absolutely safe. Easily accessible to the wearer without removal.
Buttons on the two Brace Buttons.

Worn inside the waistband of Trousers. A pickpocket cannot tell whether you wear it or not; and even if he knew you would feel the slightest attempt to touch it. (See Cassell's Magazine, Sept. 1889.)
In Solid Leather, post-free, **1s. 1d.**, fr

▲ A purse like this might protect a person from being a victim of crime while queuing for an omnibus or when in a crowd.

▶ This is the prison record for Emma Wilks, who was arrested in 1872 for stealing a neckcloth or cravat (an early version of a tie).

Newgate prison was the main convict prison in London. In 1836, in *Sketches by Boz*, Charles Dickens describes the separate pew in the prison chapel that was allocated to prisoners facing execution that week.

The *hulks* (referred to in *Great Expectations*) were the old ships, docked in Woolwich or on the south coast, which held prisoners in disease-ridden conditions.

The punishments criminals faced were harsh. At the beginning of the 1800s, minor offenders such as pickpockets could be sentenced to death, but by 1861 the death penalty was reserved for more serious crimes such as treason and murder. Until the 1850s, convicted criminals could be transported to British colonies such as Australia where they would be forced to carry out hard labour.

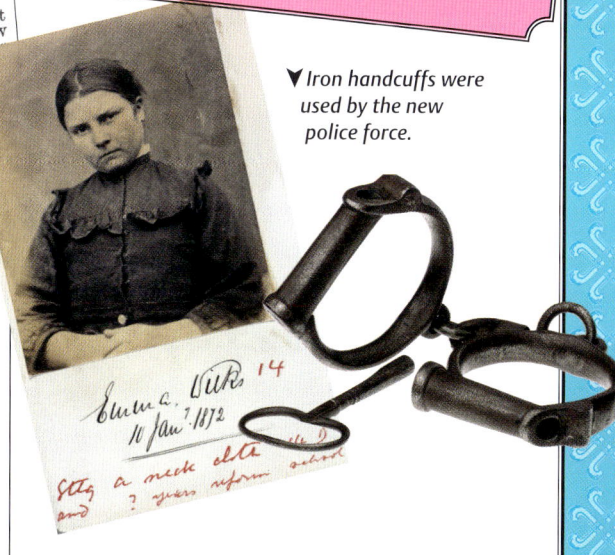

▼ Iron handcuffs were used by the new police force.

Transportation was the process of sending convicted criminals to Australia. There they were put to work building roads and bridges, labouring in quarries, and helping farmers on the land. The journey there took six months in degrading conditions in ships. Both men and women were transported either for a set number of years or for life. The policy ended in 1857 and many people remained in Australia.

Elizabeth Fry campaigned for the improvement of the squalid conditions suffered by women and children in prison. Her work in Newgate Prison, and then across Britain, changed the way prisoners were treated and influenced modern thinking.

◀ Victorian policemen in south-east London

DEATH AND DISEASE

Whilst Queen Victoria lived to be eighty-one, the average life expectancy for lower-class Victorians stretched only into their forties by the end of the century. With overcrowded houses and poor sanitation, towns and cities were breeding grounds for deadly diseases such as smallpox, typhus, and cholera. Child mortality was high, with fifteen out of one hundred babies born in the 1890s dying before their first birthday.

Death was part of life for Victorians. They had large families but, with diphtheria and cholera and other diseases affecting life expectancy, many did not survive beyond five years old.

Common infectious diseases in the 1800s:
- pneumonia
- tuberculosis
- cholera
- typhoid

To remember their dead, it was not unusual for photographs to be taken with the dead family member. These were called *memento mori*. Children might be propped up, babies held in a mother's arms, and teenagers positioned languishing against pillows. Because taking a photograph took a long time, the dead person was often in sharper focus than the living because they had remained perfectly still. These photographs were often printed with a card and sent to family members as part of the funeral process.

There were strict expectations of how long people should be in mourning depending on their relationship:
- husband or wife: 2 years
- parents: 1 year
- children: 1 year
- grandparents and siblings: 6 months
- aunts and uncles: 2 months
- great uncles and aunts: 6 weeks
- first cousins: 1 month

The mourning period started as *deep mourning* which dictated the mourner wear all black. This was seen to be an outward sign of inner sorrow. Women wore dresses made from a fabric called *bombazine* and trimmed with *crape*, a scratchy silk with a hard crimped appearance. They often wore brooches and rings with jet (a black gemstone) in them and locks of the dead person's hair part of them too. A bonnet made of crape with a veil would be worn. After three months, the veil could be moved to the back of the bonnet but would be worn for a full year.

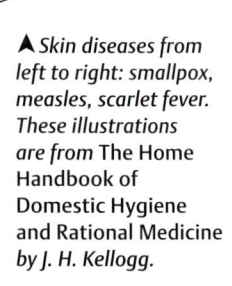

▲ Skin diseases from left to right: smallpox, measles, scarlet fever. These illustrations are from The Home Handbook of Domestic Hygiene and Rational Medicine by J. H. Kellogg.

▶ Bacillus of tuberculosis, discovered by Koch, 1884. Koch also invented ways of using dyes to stain specific microbes so that they would stand out from the other germs under the microscope.

Some medical conditions were self-inflicted, with the tight corsets worn by women blamed for an epidemic of fainting fits. Police constables even carried smelling salts to revive any swooning women they encountered on their duties. 'Quacks' sold bogus medical treatments which claimed to offer miracle cures. The American Clark Stanley marketed snake oil as a treatment for sprains, swellings, toothache, and even frostbite. Some 19th-century medicines had dangerous side effects, with now-illegal drugs such as cocaine used to treat a sore throat!

Men wore a black suit, black gloves and black necktie, and some wore black studs in their collars and cuffs.

After the deep mourning period, the colours of clothing could lighten to grey and mauve and this was called *half mourning*. People mourning children's deaths wore white.

Once the mourning period was over, the clothes were all disposed of. It was bad luck to have them in the house. This meant that for the next death in the family, new clothes had to be purchased and supplying mourning clothes became a thriving business.

Funerals were an expensive business with carriages and funeral *mutes* (or professional mourners) being hired for processions. Mutes wore black sashes and carried a staff, called a *wand*, draped in cloth.

In the fight against disease, the British parliament passed the Anatomy Act in 1832 which permitted the bodies of hanged criminals and people who had died in the workhouse to be used for medical research. In the second half of the century, improvements in hygiene and sanitation, as well as advances in medical science such as the invention of chloroform as an anaesthetic in 1847 and Joseph Lister's antiseptic spray in 1867, led to an increase in life expectancy.

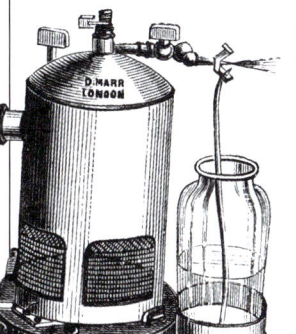

▲ A spirit seance held by a medium during the early years of spiritualism. Seances were also known as 'table tapping'.

◄ An engraving of a device for spraying antiseptic during surgery. This was devised by the surgeon Joseph Lister.

People suffering from mental illness had been diagnosed as being insane and put in *sanatoriums* and asylums. In 1845, a law was introduced which marked a change in attitude. The law changed the status of mentally ill people to 'patients', not lunatics, and set up a system to improve the places where patients were housed. Holloway Sanatorium in Surrey was opened in 1885 and was called 'a hospital for the insane of the middle-class'. It was also believed that women were more likely to suffer from madness than men and that they were *hysterical*.

In the 1830s and 1840s, there was a belief that invisible flows of *animal magnetism* could heal ailments. The practice of *mesmerism* saw *mesmerists* put people in a trance and then pass magnetism into their bodies. It was discredited by experts, although many, including Charles Dickens, believed in it.

POLITICS

In the early years of the 19th century, the two main political parties in Great Britain were the Whigs and Tories. By the end of the 1800s these had evolved into the Liberal Party and the Conservative Party.

However, the only people who could vote before 1832 were wealthy men who owned land. The political system was easy to rig, with *rotten boroughs* where people could easily be bribed to vote a certain way. The French Revolution of 1789 had created waves of unease through Europe. The year 1848 saw revolutions across Europe and in Britain, the mood of the people was for democracy. The century saw protests and marches which forced the government to change the laws and give working men and then women the right to vote.

◄ A picket protests on behalf of suffragettes. Pickets (people protesting outside a place) were also called picketers. This woman is demanding that suffragettes be treated as political prisoners, not as criminals.

► The Houses of Parliament in 1890

The *Suffragists*, and later the *Suffragettes*, campaigned for women's rights, particularly *suffrage*, or the right to vote. This involved picketing, hunger strikes, marching, and disruption so that they gained as much publicity for their cause as possible.

The *Chartists* campaigned to bring in the *People's Charter*, which would give working men the right to vote and an election every year. They also wanted to be able to stand for Parliament and become an MP with a salary.

In 1801 the *Act of Union* made Ireland part of the United Kingdom. However, throughout the 1800s, rebels tried to destabilize and end British rule in Ireland and gain *Home Rule* instead.

Jeremy Bentham founded the dominant philosophy in Britain, *Utilitarianism*. It influenced thinking about how society might be organized.

Karl Marx, founder of *Marxism*, and other socialists believed that the only way to improve the lives of poor people was through violent revolution.

Although the Reform Act of 1832 expanded the rights of the working classes, employers resisted making improvements in working conditions and giving better pay. Although by law workers were not allowed to strike in the early 1800s, unrest grew. Dock workers, engineers, miners, agricultural labourers and other skilled men organized themselves into national and regional trade unions.

- In 1834, six labourers who formed a union were arrested and transported to Australia. They were known as the *Tolpuddle Martyrs*. Their harsh and unfair transportation put men off joining a union.
- mid-1800s: powerful trades unions were set up
- 1868: the *Trades Union Congress* (TUC) was founded in Manchester
- 1871: unions were made legal by Gladstone's Liberal Party
- 1874: around a million workers were members of a union
- 1888: female match workers at *Bryant and May* went on strike
- 1900: the TUC and other socialist organizations formed the Labour Representation Committee, which later became the Labour Party

By 1833, Britain had made the slave trade illegal and abolished slavery throughout its colonies. While the British profited from the ownership of millions of slaves and built much of the nation's wealth on its profits, British *abolitionists* initiated the end to slavery. At first they targeted the buying, selling, and transportation of slaves and then later, the ownership of slaves. It was 1865 before the US followed suit.

In Great Britain, reformers such as Thomas Clarkson, Elizabeth Heyrick, and William Wilberforce campaigned for the end of slavery. The Abolition of Slavery Act was passed in 1833, which outlawed slavery throughout the British Empire. In the US, the American Civil War was fought over slavery with President Abraham Lincoln leading the Union states to victory against the Confederate states who wished to continue the practice. Following the end of the civil war in 1865, the 13th Amendment to the US Constitution outlawing slavery was signed into law.

◀ Abraham Lincoln was US President from 1861 until 1865, when he was assassinated. During his term, the Southern states, the Confederates, wanted to leave the Union and the American Civil War broke out. Lincoln did not believe in secession (leaving the Union) and managed to keep the country intact and lay the path to emancipate, or free, slaves.

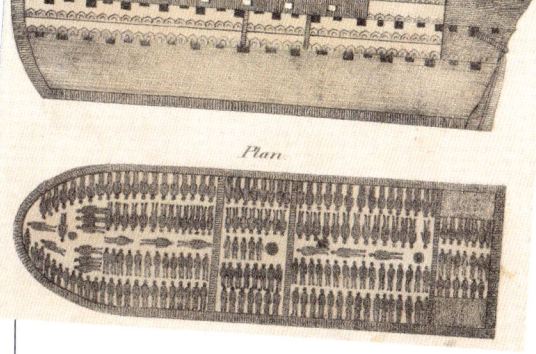

◀ In 1872 the British Prime Minister William Gladstone introduced voting by secret ballot. Stepping into a polling booth to cast your vote meant that no-one could see your choice and was designed to stop people being bribed and intimidated into voting a certain way.

▲ Men, women and children were taken from Africa to the West Indies and America to be sold. They were stowed in ships in filthy, cruel, and inhumane conditions so that traders could get as much money from each trip as they could.

WAR AND EMPIRE

Great Britain spent the 1800s building a vast empire which stretched across the globe. In 1815, British colonies already included Canada and Australia and, after defeating Napoleon's navy at Trafalgar in 1805 and then finally his army at Waterloo in 1815 Britain was firmly on course to become a global superpower. In 1876, the British government took control of India and also joined Germany, France, and Belgium in the 'Scramble for Africa', by invading and colonizing this vast continent and ruling over its inhabitants. British armies fought many wars overseas including the Crimean War, the Boer Wars, and also the Anglo-Burmese Wars.

Britain lost the American colonies after the *American War of Independence* (1775 to 1783) but it still governed Australia, India, New Zealand, large areas of Canada, and some parts of South America and Africa.

In 1858, the British government took direct control of India and in the late 1800s, joined Germany, France, and Belgium in what became known as the 'Scramble for Africa'.

By 1900, large parts of Africa were under British control. The British Empire was now the largest in the world.

Britain wanted wealth from trade—from importing cotton, tea, and rubber, and exporting machinery, tools, and engineering parts.

In 1882 the British controlled the Suez Canal, an important trade route linking the Mediterranean Sea, through Egypt, to the Red Sea and the Indian Ocean. This meant British ships no longer had to sail around the African continent to get to India and the Far East; it was a much shorter and easier route.

The 19th century was full of conflict, and much of it involved British armed forces as Britain depended on its empire for its trade and wealth.

◀ *The British Victoria Cross, with a crimson ribbon. Medals issued to the British Navy changed from blue ribbons in 1918 to crimson when the RAF, which used blue ones, was created.*

Here are some of the wars the British were involved with.

Napoleonic Wars
Napoleon Bonaparte's French empire fought several wars from 1803 to 1815. These were grouped under the name the *Napoleonic Wars*.

Britain was joined by a number of different allies in Europe against France and was finally victorious at the Battle of Waterloo (in modern-day Belgium), led by the Duke of Wellington.

Crimean War
Britain joined with the French and Turkish armies to stop Russia expanding into the region called the Crimea.

The nurse Florence Nightingale is remembered for her work in the Crimean War from 1854 to 1856 because many soldiers died as much from poor medical care as from war wounds. The appalling conditions meant that one in six soldiers died of disease rather than wounds. She was known as 'the lady with the lamp' and she was the founder of modern nursing.

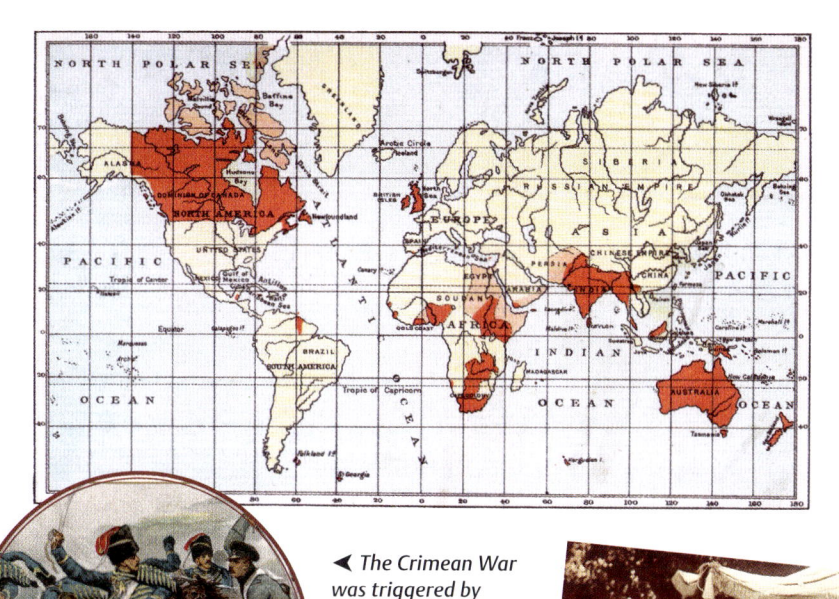

◀ This 1880 map shows the extent of the British Empire, depicted here in red.

▼ Queen Victoria, ruler of the British Empire, at work in her garden tent at Windsor in Berkshire, with an Indian servant

◀ The Crimean War was triggered by Russian expansion into Turkish territory in the area called the Crimea. This painting depicts the Battle of Inkerman in 1854.

Indian Rebellion

In 1857, the Indian Army mutinied against the British East India Company's rule and took the cities of Delhi and Lucknow.

The rebellion was brutal and violent on both sides and continued until 1858.

After gaining control of India, the British government then imposed direct rule. From 1877, Queen Victoria used the title Empress of India.

Boer Wars

There were two wars in southern Africa in the 1800s as the *Boers* (the Dutch and Afrikaans name for farmers) wanted independence from the British. Garrisons at Ladysmith, Mafeking, and Kimberley were besieged by the Boers. The siege of Mafeking lasted 217 days and the garrison commander, Robert Baden-Powell, became a British hero. He went on to found the Scouting movement.

The Empire provided Great Britain with a wealth of resources that fuelled the Industrial Revolution. Raw materials such as rubber and cotton were imported from foreign territories to make goods in British factories which could then be sold at a profit to these same colonial countries. This meant that the colonies stayed poor while Britain became rich. Any protests against British rule, such as the Indian Rebellion of 1857, were harshly dealt with.

Pp

PENNY BLACK

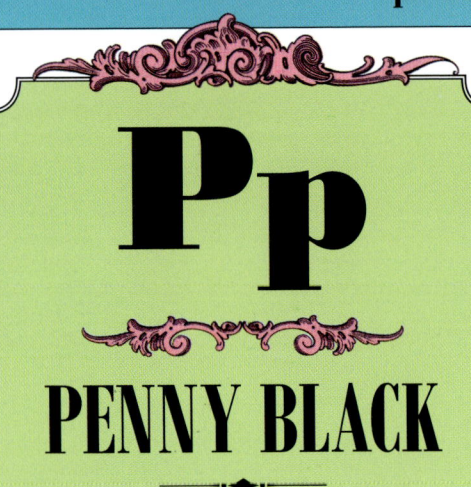

The **Penny Black** was the world's first postage stamp with a sticky back. Before **1840**, postage was charged by the distance a letter was sent and the number of sheets it contained, and it was paid by the person receiving the letter. To simplify this, the British government introduced the Penny Black, a pre-paid postage stamp bearing a picture of Queen Victoria that could be used to send letters any distance for the price of one penny.

pacific ADJECTIVE
peaceful; wanting agreement rather than conflict
• *I rang at the gate, and was admitted in a most pacific manner.*—GREAT EXPECTATIONS, CHARLES DICKENS

pack-horse NOUN
a horse for carrying loads
• *The adventurers would bring back with them pack-horses laden with bales of goods.*—OTTO OF THE SILVER HAND, HOWARD PYLE

packman NOUN
a travelling salesman; a pedlar
• *We don't want anything. I don't deal wi' packmen.*—THE MILL ON THE FLOSS, GEORGE ELIOT

pageant NOUN
a very striking scene; a spectacle
• *The Christmas trade is 'a glorious pageant'.*—A CHRISTMAS CAROL, CHARLES DICKENS

palanquin NOUN
a large box with a bed or cushions inside and long poles, used, especially in the past in India and the East, for carrying someone
• *A kind of shabby palanquin is borne towards them.*—BLEAK HOUSE, CHARLES DICKENS

pale (also **paling**) NOUN
a stake in a fence
• *She was quite glad to find herself at the gate in the pales opposite the Parsonage.*—PRIDE AND PREJUDICE, JANE AUSTEN
• *a row of wooden palings*—WESSEX TALES, THOMAS HARDY

paletôt (say **pal-uh-toh**) NOUN
1 a loose coat or cloak
2 a woman's fitted jacket

palfrey NOUN
a horse for riding, in particular one that could be ridden by a woman
• *a milk-white palfrey*—THE MERRY ADVENTURES OF ROBIN HOOD, HOWARD PYLE

palimpsest NOUN
a document on which the original writing was erased and then covered with later writing
• *It will be harder to read now than that palimpsest.*—THE RETURN OF SHERLOCK HOLMES, ARTHUR CONAN DOYLE

palisade NOUN
a spiked fence
• *a long terrace walk, backed by iron palisades*—MANSFIELD PARK, JANE AUSTEN

pall (say **pawl**) NOUN
1 a piece of cloth used as a covering, especially over a coffin
• *a black velvet gown, that looks as if it had been made out of a pall*—DAVID COPPERFIELD, CHARLES DICKENS
2 a covering or cloud of something; darkness
• *the great black velvet pall outside my little window*—GREAT EXPECTATIONS, CHARLES DICKENS

pall VERB
to become less enjoyable or appealing
• *But ... after a time the silence palled upon me.*—MOONFLEET, J. MEADE FALKNER

palmer NOUN
a pilgrim
• *wandering palmers ... muttering prayers*—IVANHOE, WALTER SCOTT

palpitate VERB
to tremble; (of a heart) to beat fast
• *'I do so palpitate,' observed Miss Squeers.*—NICHOLAS NICKLEBY, CHARLES DICKENS

palpitation NOUN
a rapid heart beat, typically caused by a strong emotion or by illness
• *Sometimes my pulse beat so quickly ... that I felt the palpitation of every artery.*—FRANKENSTEIN, MARY SHELLEY
USAGE Having *palpitations* and fainting were not seen as unusual.

palsy to part

• *I assure you, excepting those little nervous head-aches and palpitations which I am never entirely free from anywhere, I am quite well.* EMMA—JANE AUSTEN
• *'Just give me your hand,' he said: 'it will not do to risk a fainting fit.'* JANE EYRE—CHARLOTTE BRONTË

palsy (say **pawl-zi, pol-zi**) NOUN
paralysis or uncontrollable shaking
• *I think it's a stroke o' the palsy. Any rate she has lost the use of one side.*—MARY BARTON, ELIZABETH GASKELL
➤ **palsied** ADJECTIVE • *two palsied women, who shook and tottered as they walked*—OLIVER TWIST, CHARLES DICKENS

palter VERB
1 to deliberately speak or act in a way that was not clear or did not show your feelings
• *She was embarrassed ... and as if fearful of betraying her secret, she paltered with him at the last moment.*—TESS OF THE D'URBERVILLES, THOMAS HARDY
2 to do a deal with someone, especially a dishonourable deal
• *Nancy 'had dared to palter with strangers'.*—OLIVER TWIST, CHARLES DICKENS

panegyric NOUN
a speech or piece of writing praising someone or something
• *a panegyric upon modern chemistry*—FRANKENSTEIN, MARY SHELLEY

pannikin NOUN
a small metal cup
• *He gave me some brandy and water in a tin pannikin.*—KIDNAPPED, ROBERT LOUIS STEVENSON

pant VERB
to yearn or long to do something
• *I longed to be his; I panted to return.*—JANE EYRE, CHARLOTTE BRONTË

paragon NOUN
someone or something that was perfect
• *My young lady was ... no paragon of patience.*—WUTHERING HEIGHTS, EMILY BRONTË

parcel NOUN
a group or set of people or things
• *a parcel of heavy-headed fellows*—DAVID COPPERFIELD, CHARLES DICKENS
• *He's a likely young parcel of bones.*—GREAT EXPECTATIONS, CHARLES DICKENS

parish-clerk NOUN
an official who keeps church or parish records

park NOUN
the grounds of a country house
• *'You have a very small park here,' returned Lady Catherine after a short silence.*—PRIDE AND PREJUDICE, JANE AUSTEN

parley NOUN
discussion
• *They went in, without further parley.*—NICHOLAS NICKLEBY, CHARLES DICKENS
🏛 French *parler* meaning 'speech' or 'to speak'

parlour NOUN
1 a sitting or dining room; a room where guests were received
• *But ... the best parlor seemed to be in use.*—GREAT EXPECTATIONS, CHARLES DICKENS
2 a meeting room; a room in which conversation was possible, for example, in an inn
• *He ... turned into the bright bar ... on the right hand ... the parlour on the left being reserved for the more select society.*—SILAS MARNER, GEORGE ELIOT

parlous ADJECTIVE
dangerous; precarious
• *Thou art in a parlous state, Angel Clare.*—TESS OF THE D'URBERVILLES, THOMAS HARDY

parlous ADVERB
extremely; excessively
• *There is Walter Blunt; he is parlous strong.*—MEN OF IRON, HOWARD PYLE

paroxysm NOUN
a sudden strong attack or outburst
• *paroxysms of anguish and despair*—FRANKENSTEIN, MARY SHELLEY

parson NOUN
a clergyman; a vicar
• *Reader, I married him. A quiet wedding we had: he and I, the parson and clerk, were alone present.*—JANE EYRE, CHARLOTTE BRONTË

parsonage NOUN
a parson's house

parsonic ADJECTIVE
like a parson or vicar
• *His manners, I think, [are] priggish and parsonic?*—JANE EYRE, CHARLOTTE BRONTË

part NOUN
an ability or good deed
• *men of parts and of power*—MARY BARTON, ELIZABETH GASKELL
• *a friendly part*—BLEAK HOUSE, CHARLES DICKENS
➤ **take someone's part / take part with someone:** to take someone's side; to stand up for someone
• *Most of the men said he was a fool, but two or three took his part.*—BLACK BEAUTY, ANNA SEWELL
• *Nobody is on my side, nobody takes part with me.*—PRIDE AND PREJUDICE, JANE AUSTEN

155

parterre to patron

parterre NOUN
a flat area of decorative flower beds in a garden
• Jane prefers to wear black and grey but Mr Rochester *'would yet see me glittering like a parterre'.*—JANE EYRE, CHARLOTTE BRONTË

particular NOUN
a detail
• [Elizabeth] was referred for the truth of every particular to Colonel Fitzwilliam.—PRIDE AND PREJUDICE, JANE AUSTEN

partie carree (also **partie carrée**)
(say par-tee karr-ay) NOUN
a group of four people, especially two women and two men
• The partie carrée took their seats—the bride and bridegroom and Mr and Mrs Crick.—TESS OF THE D'URBERVILLES, THOMAS HARDY

partly ADVERB
almost
• I reckon the weaving makes you handier ... you're partly as handy as a woman, for weaving comes next to spinning.—SILAS MARNER, GEORGE ELIOT

party NOUN
1 a group of people
• He ... advanced towards the party, and spoke to Elizabeth.—PRIDE AND PREJUDICE, JANE AUSTEN
2 a game, or the people playing it
• The whist party soon afterwards breaking up, the players gathered round the other table.—PRIDE AND PREJUDICE, JANE AUSTEN
3 a trip taken by a group of people
• Their parties abroad were less varied than before.—PRIDE AND PREJUDICE, JANE AUSTEN
4 a person
• There was the old party ... a-waitin' in the 'ouse.—DRACULA, BRAM STOKER
5 one of the people involved in an agreement or dispute
• I began to cherish hopes ... that one or both parties had changed their minds.—JANE EYRE, CHARLOTTE BRONTË
6 a contributing part of something
• [Scrooge] tried to say they were fine children, but the words choked themselves, rather than be parties to a lie of such enormous magnitude.—A CHRISTMAS CAROL, CHARLES DICKENS

parure (say puh-roor) NOUN
a matching set of jewellery
• Look at this parure ... The brooch, the ear-rings, the bracelets.—VILLETTE, CHARLOTTE BRONTË

pass VERB
to be done or said
• Elizabeth ... was ... attending to what passed between Darcy and his companion.—PRIDE AND PREJUDICE, JANE AUSTEN

pass NOUN
a situation or state of affairs
• I am come to a strange pass: I have heavy troubles.—JANE EYRE, CHARLOTTE BRONTË

passenger NOUN
a passer-by or traveller; a pedestrian
• *the busy thoroughfares of a city, where shadowy passengers passed and repassed*—A CHRISTMAS CAROL, CHARLES DICKENS
USAGE In modern English, you would expect a *passenger* to be in a vehicle, not on foot.

pasteboard NOUN
1 thin board, for example, for book covers
• *a pasteboard placard*—DAVID COPPERFIELD, CHARLES DICKENS
2 card; a card
USAGE This word was often used for suggesting that a thing was worthless or not real.
• Sir Mulberry throws Nicholas's card at the man, telling him to *'put that piece of pasteboard in the fire'.*—NICHOLAS NICKLEBY, CHARLES DICKENS,

pate NOUN
someone's head or hair
• Laurie ... did honor to the coming guest by brushing his curly pate.—LITTLE MEN, LOUISA MAY ALCOTT

patent ADJECTIVE
obvious
• The next day, came the news that ... the guilt of Hyde was patent to the world.—THE STRANGE CASE OF DR JEKYLL AND MR HYDE, ROBERT LOUIS STEVENSON

patent NOUN
an official document, licence, or stamp; a mark or sign of something
• Mr Rochester says that nature *'has stamped her patent of nobility'* on Jane's brow.—JANE EYRE, CHARLOTTE BRONTË

pathetic ADJECTIVE
sad; emotional; moving
• The separation between her and her family was rather noisy than pathetic.—PRIDE AND PREJUDICE, JANE AUSTEN
➤ **pathetically** ADVERB with emotion • *I wrote it as fervently and pathetically as I could.*—GREAT EXPECTATIONS, CHARLES DICKENS

patron NOUN
1 a person offering financial or other support
• Pip has *'a mysterious patron'.*—GREAT EXPECTATIONS, CHARLES DICKENS
2 a wealthy person with the right to offer a position to a priest
• The noble patron of his living esteemed him highly.—SHIRLEY, CHARLOTTE BRONTË

patronage to penitential

➤ **patroness** NOUN a female patron • *the very noble lady whom I have the honour of calling patroness* —PRIDE AND PREJUDICE, JANE AUSTEN

patronage NOUN
1 the support of a patron
• *the patronage of the Right Honourable Lady Catherine de Bourgh*—PRIDE AND PREJUDICE, JANE AUSTEN
2 a patronizing or condescending tone
• *Pip asks Joe 'with a modest patronage' how to spell Joe's surname.*—GREAT EXPECTATIONS, CHARLES DICKENS

patten NOUN
a clog, thick-soled shoe, or overshoe. Some pattens consisted of a wooden sole on a metal frame, with a leather strap to hold them in place.
• *a pair of pattens*—GREAT EXPECTATIONS, CHARLES DICKENS
• *the ceaseless clink of pattens*—PERSUASION, JANE AUSTEN

pauper NOUN
a person who received aid from public charity or under the Poor Law
• *a room where some of the female paupers were usually employed in washing the parish linen*—OLIVER TWIST, CHARLES DICKENS
• *a pauper's grave*—JANE EYRE, CHARLOTTE BRONTË

pavement NOUN
a paved or other hard surface
• *The dull, rumbling sound of wheels was heard on the pavement in the yard.*—SHIRLEY, CHARLOTTE BRONTË

pea-coat (also **pea-jacket**) NOUN
a short double-breasted woollen coat
• *We had our pea-coats with us, and I took a bag.* —GREAT EXPECTATIONS, CHARLES DICKENS

peart (say pee-uht) ADJECTIVE
lively; cheerful
• *Aint she a peart young un?*—UNCLE TOM'S CABIN, HARRIET BEECHER STOWE

peculiar ADJECTIVE
particular; special
• *Silas has reared Eppie with 'tender and peculiar love'.*—SILAS MARNER, GEORGE ELIOT
➤ **peculiarly** ADVERB • *Felix seemed peculiarly happy.*—FRANKENSTEIN, MARY SHELLEY

pecuniary ADJECTIVE
relating to money; financial
• *It depended entirely on his pecuniary position, of which I knew nothing.*—THE MOONSTONE, WILKIE COLLINS

pedlar NOUN
a travelling salesman
• *the visits of the pedlar or the knife-grinder* —SILAS MARNER, GEORGE ELIOT

pelisse NOUN
a woman's full-length coat with armholes or sleeves
• *[Bessie] helped me on with my pelisse and bonnet.* —JANE EYRE, CHARLOTTE BRONTË

pellucid (say pell-you-sid) ADJECTIVE
clear; translucent
• *The water in the fountain, pellucid as crystal, was alive with … gold and silver fishes.*—UNCLE TOM'S CABIN, HARRIET BEECHER STOWE

pence-table NOUN
a list for converting a number of pence into shillings or pounds
• *Mr Pumblechook then put me through my pence-table from 'twelve pence make one shilling,' up to 'forty pence make three and fourpence'.*—GREAT EXPECTATIONS, CHARLES DICKENS

pencil-head NOUN
a sketch of someone's head done in pencil
• *some sketches, including a pencil-head of a pretty little cherub-like girl*—JANE EYRE, CHARLOTTE BRONTË

pendent ADJECTIVE
hanging
• *a bronze lamp pendent from the ceiling*—JANE EYRE, CHARLOTTE BRONTË

penetralium (PLURAL **penetralia**)
the innermost part; a secret place
• *I had no desire to aggravate his impatience previous to inspecting the penetralium.*—WUTHERING HEIGHTS, EMILY BRONTË
• *In these penetralia were chairs and a table, which, on candles being lighted, made quite a cozy and luxurious show.*—FAR FROM THE MADDING CROWD, THOMAS HARDY

penetration NOUN
insight; awareness; perception
• *Young ladies have great penetration in such matters as these.*—PRIDE AND PREJUDICE, JANE AUSTEN

penitential ADJECTIVE
feeling or showing penitence (regret for something you have done wrong)
• *fasts, and vigils, and other penitential performances* —GREAT EXPECTATIONS, CHARLES DICKENS

penny-a-liner *to* personate

penny-a-liner NOUN
a writer of low-quality journalism
• *Penny-a-liners abuse the Times, because they have not wit enough to get on its staff.*—WATER BABIES, CHARLES KINGSLEY

pent ADJECTIVE
1 pent-up; not expressed
• *But this time his feelings were all pent in his heart.*—JANE EYRE, CHARLOTTE BRONTË
2 penned in; shut in
• *a tumultuous stream of dirty, hurrying people, pent in between the villas*—THE WAR OF THE WORLDS, H. G. WELLS
3 making you feel confined; oppressive
• *the pent air of the hiding-place*—THE LAST OF THE MOHICANS, JAMES FENIMORE COOPER

penury NOUN
great poverty
• *The thought of their coming ... and dragging him back to penury and degradation and the slums, made him shudder.*—THE PRINCE AND THE PAUPER, MARK TWAIN

peradventure ADVERB
perhaps
• *Peradventure I have been unwise.*—THE PRINCE AND THE PAUPER, MARK TWAIN

perchance ADVERB
perhaps
• *Your cousin Edmund moves slowly; detained, perchance, by parish duties.*—MANSFIELD PARK, JANE AUSTEN

percussion-cap NOUN
a small metal case of gunpowder, used in a gun; a paper version of this, used in a toy gun
• *a small box of percussion-caps*—THE MILL ON THE FLOSS, GEORGE ELIOT

per diem ADVERB
for each day
• *Unless he had another basin of gruel per diem, he was afraid he might some night happen to eat the boy who slept next him.*—OLIVER TWIST, CHARLES DICKENS

peregrination NOUN
a pilgrimage or journey; travel
• *Your peregrinations in this metropolis have not as yet been extensive.*—DAVID COPPERFIELD, CHARLES DICKENS

peremptory ADJECTIVE
authoritative; requiring obedience
• *I had no right to refuse compliance with such a peremptory command.*—DAVID COPPERFIELD, CHARLES DICKENS

perfidy NOUN
treachery; disloyalty
• *a forsaken lady ... bewailing the perfidy of her lover*—JANE EYRE, CHARLOTTE BRONTË

➤ **perfidious** ADJECTIVE treacherous; disloyal
• *'You perfidious goblin,' said the lady in the chair.*—DOMBEY AND SON, CHARLES DICKENS

perforce ADVERB
out of necessity; unavoidably
• *He stood in my way, so that I had perforce to tap his shoulder.*—THE ISLAND OF DR MOREAU, H. G. WELLS

Peri (also **peri**) NOUN
a beautiful or graceful person; a fairy or angel
• *What did St John Rivers think of this earthly angel? He had already withdrawn his eye from the Peri.*—JANE EYRE, CHARLOTTE BRONTË
USAGE In Persian mythology, a *peri* was a winged supernatural being sometimes depicted as an evil spirit and sometimes as beautiful and benevolent. Western writers often used the word to refer to a kind of exotic angel or a fairy.

periwig NOUN
a wig, especially of the style worn in the 17th and 18th centuries
• *a little man in a periwig*—MOONFLEET, J. MEADE FALKNER

perplex VERB
to complicate something
• *He ... seemed to think it might perplex the thread of his narrative.*—GREAT EXPECTATIONS, CHARLES DICKENS
USAGE In modern English, you might only expect to *perplex* a person, rather than a matter, story, etc.

person NOUN
someone's body as opposed to their inner self; someone's physical appearance
• *Mr Wickham was ... far beyond them all in person, countenance, air, and walk.*—PRIDE AND PREJUDICE, JANE AUSTEN
➤ **in the person of:** in the form of • *Passepartout is very pleased with the companion that he has 'in the person of the delightful Fix'.*—AROUND THE WORLD IN EIGHTY DAYS, JULES VERNE
➤ **in your own person:**
1 yourself; used for emphasis • *I became, in my own person ... solely occupied by one thought.*—THE STRANGE CASE OF DR JEKYLL AND MR HYDE, ROBERT LOUIS STEVENSON
2 yourself; without anyone else • *Bathsheba's decision to be a farmer in her own person*—FAR FROM THE MADDING CROWD, THOMAS HARDY

personate VERB
to act the part of someone; to impersonate someone
• *Nicholas personated a vast variety of characters with undiminished success.*—NICHOLAS NICKLEBY, CHARLES DICKENS
• *Do you think they'll love a King who was too drunk to be crowned, and sent a servant to personate him?*—THE PRISONER OF ZENDA, ANTHONY HOPE

persuaded to phantasm

➤ **personation** NOUN • *his personation of the chief character*—FAR FROM THE MADDING CROWD, THOMAS HARDY

persuaded ADJECTIVE
believing something; convinced
• *My aunt [was] firmly persuaded that every house in London was going to be burnt down.*—DAVID COPPERFIELD, CHARLES DICKENS
➤ **persuasion** NOUN a belief • *He could not expel from his mind the persuasion that he should see Marianne no more.*—SENSE AND SENSIBILITY, JANE AUSTEN

pertinacious ADJECTIVE
stubborn; persistent
• *his pertinacious assertion of what was evidently an untruth*—WUTHERING HEIGHTS, EMILY BRONTË
➤ **pertinaciously** ADVERB • *Why do you remain pertinaciously perched on my knee, when I have given you notice to quit?*—JANE EYRE, CHARLOTTE BRONTË
➤ **pertinacity** NOUN • *The pertinacity with which I continually recurred to the same subject persuaded him.*—FRANKENSTEIN, MARY SHELLEY

peremptory ADJECTIVE
authoritative; requiring obedience
• *I had no right to refuse compliance with such a peremptory command.*—DAVID COPPERFIELD, CHARLES DICKENS

peruse VERB
to read or examine something
• *She broke the seal and perused the document.*—JANE EYRE, CHARLOTTE BRONTË
➤ **perusal** NOUN • *Nicholas returned to the perusal of the book he had been reading.*—NICHOLAS NICKLEBY, CHARLES DICKENS

pestiferous ADJECTIVE
full of disease; dangerous or harmful
• *a hemmed-in churchyard, pestiferous and obscene, whence malignant diseases are communicated*—BLEAK HOUSE, CHARLES DICKENS

pestilence NOUN
1 a deadly disease affecting a lot of people; plague
• *That forest-dell, where Lowood lay, was the cradle of fog and fog-bred pestilence.*—JANE EYRE, CHARLOTTE BRONTË
2 evil; a cause of trouble
• *moral pestilence*—DOMBEY AND SON, CHARLES DICKENS

pestilent (also **pestilential**) ADJECTIVE
1 deadly; poisonous; morally or physically dangerous
• *pestilential gas*—BLEAK HOUSE, CHARLES DICKENS
• *Here is a fellow who [is] infected by the most pestilent and blasphemous code of devilry that ever was known.*—A TALE OF TWO CITIES, CHARLES DICKENS

2 troublesome; annoying
• *Pestilent moods had come, and teased away his quiet.*—FAR FROM THE MADDING CROWD, THOMAS HARDY

petrifaction NOUN
1 a state of being petrified
• *[He] paused on the threshold in a state of petrifaction.*—SHIRLEY, CHARLOTTE BRONTË
2 a thing formed of or turned into stone
• *that dull petrifaction of a hearth*—A CHRISTMAS CAROL, CHARLES DICKENS

petrify VERB
1 to make someone unable to move because of fear, shock, or another strong emotion
• *I stood petrified and staring.*—THE WAR OF THE WORLDS, H. G. WELLS
2 to turn something into stone
• *[He] has discovered … a means of petrifying the body after death.*—THE WOMAN IN WHITE, WILKIE COLLINS

petticoat NOUN
an undergarment worn under a dress or skirt; an underskirt
• *I hope you saw her petticoat, six inches deep in mud, I am absolutely certain.*—PRIDE AND PREJUDICE, JANE AUSTEN

pettish ADJECTIVE
bad-tempered or sulky; childish
• *her pettish wilful manner*—DAVID COPPERFIELD, CHARLES DICKENS
➤ **pettishly** ADVERB • *'You're very hard-hearted, Nancy,' said Godfrey, pettishly.*—SILAS MARNER, GEORGE ELIOT
➤ **pettishness** NOUN • *Surely not! why, she is too old for such pettishness.*—JANE EYRE, CHARLOTTE BRONTË

pettitoe NOUN
a pig's trotter as a food
• *a present of pigs' pettitoes*—SILAS MARNER, GEORGE ELIOT

pew-opener NOUN
someone who showed people to their seats in a church; an usher
• *The pew-opener [arranged] us, like a drill-sergeant, before the altar rails.*—DAVID COPPERFIELD, CHARLES DICKENS

phaeton NOUN
an open four-wheeled carriage
• *A low phaeton, with a nice little pair of ponies, would be the very thing.*—PRIDE AND PREJUDICE, JANE AUSTEN

phantasm NOUN
1 an apparition; a ghost or phantom
• *Whenever I dozed I dreamt of horrible phantasms.*—THE WAR OF THE WORLDS, H. G. WELLS

philippic to piquancy

2 an illusion; a poor imitation of a feeling or idea
• *But now ... the evening had no phantasm of delight to still the poor soul's craving.*—SILAS MARNER, GEORGE ELIOT

philippic NOUN
a bitter verbal attack
• *He would have delivered [a] philippic on the extraordinary habits of his niece.*—SHIRLEY, CHARLOTTE BRONTË
🏛 From speeches delivered by the Ancient Greek orator Demosthenes condemning Philip II of Macedon

philosopher NOUN
a thinker; a wise or learned person
• *He grew calm, as a philosopher should under the heaviest trials.*—THE MORTAL IMMORTAL, MARY SHELLEY

philter (also philtre) NOUN
a magic potion, especially a love potion
• *Can't you give me a charm, or a philter, or something of that sort, to make me a handsome man?*—JANE EYRE, CHARLOTTE BRONTË

phlegmatic ADJECTIVE
unemotional; unexcitable
• *She said 'Good morning, Miss,' in her usual phlegmatic and brief manner.*—JANE EYRE, CHARLOTTE BRONTË
🏛 From *phlegm*, one of the four humours.
USAGE The four humours were *blood, phlegm, choler* or *yellow bile*, and *melancholy* or *black bile*.

phrenology NOUN
the study of the mind, especially with reference to the shape of the skull
➤ **phrenological** ADJECTIVE • *His mind is unimpaired. ... In respect of ... phrenological attributes, it is no worse off than it used to be.*—BLEAK HOUSE, CHARLES DICKENS
➤ **phrenologically** ADVERB • *The pie crust is 'like a disappointing head, phrenologically speaking: full of lumps and bumps, with nothing particular underneath'.*—DAVID COPPERFIELD, CHARLES DICKENS

phthisis (say ty-siss, thy-siss, fthy-siss) NOUN
a disease causing wasting, especially tuberculosis
• *... that dungeon ... smelling of damp and mould, rank with phthisis and catarrh*—VILLETTE, CHARLOTTE BRONTË

phylactery NOUN
a small box containing Hebrew texts, attached to a strap wound around the head or arm during prayer by observant Jewish men
• *Miss Scatcherd writes 'Slattern' on a piece of card and ties it 'like a phylactery round Helen's ... forehead'.*—JANE EYRE

physic NOUN
medicine
• *When Doctor Kimble gave physic, it was natural that it should have an effect.*—SILAS MARNER, GEORGE ELIOT

physic VERB
to give someone medicine
• *I ... recommend ... do not spoil them, and do not physic them.*—EMMA, JANE AUSTEN

pieman NOUN
a man whose job was to sell pies in the street

pile NOUN
a pile of wood etc. for burning a corpse; a pyre
• *my funeral pile*—FRANKENSTEIN, MARY SHELLEY

pillion NOUN
a cushion attached to the back of a horse's saddle, for a second rider
• *Nancy is 'seated on the pillion behind her ... father'.*—SILAS MARNER, GEORGE ELIOT

pilot-boat NOUN
a small boat used by a pilot (an expert who guided a ship into or out of a harbour) to get to and from ships
• *The pilot-boat had struggled home against the wind.*—MARY BARTON, ELIZABETH GASKELL

pinion VERB
to hold or tie someone's arms or legs so they could not move
• *But the relentless Ghost pinioned him in both his arms, and forced him to observe what happened next.*—A CHRISTMAS CAROL, CHARLES DICKENS

pinion NOUN
a bird's wing, especially its outer part
• *She plucked the feathers from a pinion of some rare and beautiful bird.*—DOMBEY AND SON, CHARLES DICKENS

pink NOUN
➤ **the pink of:** the epitome or best example of something • *At one time I thought she was a story-teller, and at another time that she was the pink of truth.*—BLEAK HOUSE, CHARLES DICKENS

pinnace (say pin-iss) NOUN
a small sailing boat that was carried on a larger ship
• *The pinnace was lifted from the bridge, pulled from its socket, and let down into the sea.*—20,000 LEAGUES UNDER THE SEA, JULES VERNE

piquancy NOUN
an exciting or pleasantly stimulating quality
• *Maggie's confession of poverty '[gave] greater piquancy to her beauty in Stephen's eyes'.*—THE MILL ON THE FLOSS, GEORGE ELIOT

pique to plaster

pique VERB
to provoke or irritate someone; to arouse an emotion
• *[His] reply ... piqued my curiosity more than ever.*—JANE EYRE, CHARLOTTE BRONTË
➤ **pique yourself:** to pride yourself on something
• *Lady Middleton piqued herself upon the elegance of her table.*—SENSE AND SENSIBILITY, JANE AUSTEN
➤ **piqued** ADJECTIVE • *I was a little surprised—perhaps a little piqued also—by these last words.*—THE WOMAN IN WHITE, WILKIE COLLINS

pique NOUN
irritation; wounded pride
• *'Oh no, not at all,' said Lucy, with a little air of pique.*—THE MILL ON THE FLOSS, GEORGE ELIOT

piquet (also **picquet**) (say **pee-kay**) NOUN
a card game for two players
• *Mr Hurst and Mr Bingley were at piquet, and Mrs Hurst was observing their game.*—PRIDE AND PREJUDICE, JANE AUSTEN

pis aller (say **pee-zal-ay**) NOUN
a last resort
• *And what are letters? Only a sort of pis aller.*—SHIRLEY, CHARLOTTE BRONTË

pish EXCLAMATION
an exclamation of impatience, annoyance, or disgust
• *Pish! I can't stand here chattering.*—WESTWARD HO!, CHARLES KINGSLEY

pish VERB
to exclaim in impatience, annoyance, or disgust
• *He fretted, pished, and pshawed.*—JANE EYRE, CHARLOTTE BRONTË

pitch NOUN
a dark substance like tar, used for waterproofing, or for burning on torches
• *thick smoke from the pitch torches*—MOONFLEET, J. MEADE FALKNER

pitch VERB
to cover a surface with pitch
• *He had been pitching the canoe.*—HILDEGARDE'S NEIGHBORS, LAURA E. RICHARDS
➤ **pitch it in red-hot:** to speak or act with a lot of force • *We told the man we could and would ... make his name stink from one end of London to the other. ... [We] were pitching it in red hot.*—THE STRANGE CASE OF DR JEKYLL AND MR HYDE, ROBERT LOUIS STEVENSON
➤ **pitch into someone:** to attack someone verbally or physically • *Village boys could not go stalking about the country ... pitching into the studious youth of England.*—GREAT EXPECTATIONS, CHARLES DICKENS

pitcher NOUN
a large jug
• *This morning we were obliged to dispense with ... washing; the water in the pitchers was frozen.*—JANE EYRE, CHARLOTTE BRONTË

pitchy ADJECTIVE
1 completely dark; pitch black
• *a pitchy darkness*—FRANKENSTEIN, MARY SHELLEY
2 containing pitch
• *Our lights warmed the air about us with their pitchy blaze.*—GREAT EXPECTATIONS, CHARLES DICKENS

pith NOUN
1 strength; toughness
• *his look of native pith and genuine power*—JANE EYRE, CHARLOTTE BRONTË
2 the central or most essential part
• *That was the pith of the information with which Holmes left the office.*—THE RETURN OF SHERLOCK HOLMES, ARTHUR CONAN DOYLE
USAGE This word was often used in the phrase 'the pith and marrow', also meaning 'the central or most essential part'. Both *pith* and *marrow* could refer to the inner part of the spine.
• *He composed himself for more serious business, and entered upon the pith and marrow of his negotiation.*—NICHOLAS NICKLEBY—CHARLES DICKENS

placable ADJECTIVE
calm and not angry
• *I drew Joe away, and he immediately became placable.*—GREAT EXPECTATIONS, CHARLES DICKENS
➤ **placably** ADVERB **calmly** • *'Aye, aye,' said Dunstan, very placably, 'you do me justice, I see.'*—SILAS MARNER, GEORGE ELIOT

plaint NOUN
a sad cry; a complaint
• *That involuntary plaint of hers, 'Oh, I must go,' had remained with him as the sign that she was undergoing some inward conflict.*—THE MILL ON THE FLOSS, GEORGE ELIOT

plain work NOUN
ordinary needlework or sewing, as opposed to embroidery
• *She procured plain work ... and by various means contrived to earn a pittance.*—FRANKENSTEIN, MARY SHELLEY
➤ **plain-workwoman** NOUN • *I asked her 'if there were any dressmaker or plain-workwoman in the village?'*—JANE EYRE, CHARLOTTE BRONTË

plaster NOUN
a bandage or dressing spread with a medicinal substance (also called a 'plaster')
• *Then she took some butter ... on a knife and spread it on the loaf, in an apothecary kind of way, as if she*

were making a plaster.—GREAT EXPECTATIONS, CHARLES DICKENS

plate NOUN
1 crockery and cutlery made from gold or silver
• In the dining-room, the sideboard flashed resplendent with plate.—JANE EYRE, CHARLOTTE BRONTË
2 crockery and cutlery plated with silver or gold, or made of other materials

pledge NOUN
1 a promise
• I readily gave the pledge required.—TREASURE ISLAND, ROBERT LOUIS STEVENSON
2 an item left as security against a loan
• [Your brother] could not have redeemed the pledge.—THE SIGN OF FOUR, ARTHUR CONAN DOYLE
3 a sign or token
• No fear of death will darken St John's last hour … . His own words are a pledge of this.—JANE EYRE, CHARLOTTE BRONTË
4 a toast drunk to someone
• Robin held his cup aloft. … 'Tarry in your drinking till I give you a pledge. Here is to good King Richard … ' Then all drank the King's health.—THE MERRY ADVENTURES OF ROBIN HOOD, HOWARD PYLE

pledge VERB
1 to commit someone to do something
• We are persuaded that he has pledged himself to assist Mr Wickham with money.—PRIDE AND PREJUDICE, JANE AUSTEN
2 to promise something; to give your word
• She has consented: she has pledged her word.—JANE EYRE, CHARLOTTE BRONTË
3 to drink a toast to someone
• Sitting in this amicable posture, they had pledged each other.—DOMBEY AND SON, CHARLES DICKENS
➢ **be pledged to:** to be promised in marriage to someone • I was always to remember that I was pledged to him.—THE ADVENTURES OF SHERLOCK HOLMES, ARTHUR CONAN DOYLE

plenteous ADJECTIVE
plentiful; abundant
• I had known what it was … to long for a plenteous meal and a good fire, and to be unable to get either.—JANE EYRE, CHARLOTTE BRONTË

pliant ADJECTIVE
co-operative; easily persuaded
• Her rigidity unbent; she grew smiling and pliant.—SHIRLEY, CHARLOTTE BRONTË
➢ **pliancy** NOUN • Elizabeth has 'more quickness of observation and less pliancy of temper than her sister'.—PRIDE AND PREJUDICE, JANE AUSTEN

plight VERB
to promise; to swear
• I have plighted my word to another maiden.—THE GREEN FAIRY BOOK, ANDREW LANG
USAGE Plight was often used in the phrase 'plight your troth', meaning to promise to be true to someone as part of a marriage ceremony.
• So … they plight their troth to one another, and are married.—DOMBEY AND SON, CHARLES DICKENS

ploughboy NOUN
a boy who led animals pulling a plough; a farm boy
• Edgar refers contemptuously to Heathcliff as 'What! the gipsy—the ploughboy?'—WUTHERING HEIGHTS, EMILY BRONTË

plumbless ADJECTIVE
extremely deep; hard to reach the bottom of
• the plumbless depths of the past—HARD TIMES, CHARLES DICKENS

plum-cake NOUN
a cake containing dried fruits; fruitcake
• … another dozen of mince-pies for the dinner, and a large plum-cake for the children.—A CHRISTMAS DINNER, CHARLES DICKENS

plume NOUN
a large feather or set of feathers, for example worn on a hat or by a horse as decoration
• Fluttering veils and waving plumes filled the vehicles.—JANE EYRE, CHARLOTTE BRONTË

plume VERB
➢ **plume yourself on something:** to pride yourself on something; to feel self-satisfied about something • They plume them-selves on their gentility there, I can tell you.—DAVID COPPERFIELD, CHARLES DICKENS

plump VERB
to fall, drop, or dive suddenly or heavily
• I plumped right down from the bough, and bruised my shins.—THE MILL ON THE FLOSS, GEORGE ELIOT

plump NOUN
a sudden or heavy fall
• 'Straight!' said Stryver, with a plump of his fist on the desk.—A TALE OF TWO CITIES, CHARLES DICKENS

plump ADVERB
with a sudden or heavy fall
• I took a shot at him and brought him down plump.—OUR MUTUAL FRIEND, CHARLES DICKENS

pocket-pistol NOUN
1 a small pistol that could be carried in a pocket
2 a hip flask
• a draught of brandy from his pocket-pistol—SILAS MARNER, GEORGE ELIOT

point *to* portend

point NOUN
➢ **in point of:** in terms of; regarding • *I consider the clerical office as equal in point of dignity with the highest rank in the kingdom.*—PRIDE AND PREJUDICE, JANE AUSTEN
➢ **in point of fact:** in fact • *In spite of his ... baldness, he gave the impression of youth. In point of fact he had just turned his thirtieth year.*—THE SIGN OF FOUR, ARTHUR CONAN DOYLE

poise VERB
to hold something steady, or hold it ready in position
• *I saw him lift and poise the book ... to hurl it.*—JANE EYRE, CHARLOTTE BRONTË

police-court NOUN
a lower court where charges brought by police could be tried; a magistrates' court
• *A series of disgraceful brawls took place, two of which ended in the police-court.*—THE ADVENTURES OF SHERLOCK HOLMES, ARTHUR CONAN DOYLE

policy NOUN
prudence; deliberate caution
• *Henchard's failure to act is either 'from policy or want of nerve'.*—THE MAYOR OF CASTERBRIDGE, THOMAS HARDY

politic ADJECTIVE
sensible in the circumstances
• *I was ready to sink from fatigue and hunger, but being surrounded by a crowd, I thought it politic to rouse all my strength.*—FRANKENSTEIN, MARY SHELLEY

polity NOUN
civilization; society
• *a ... polity of multifarious ... independent [citizens]*—THE STRANGE CASE OF DR JEKYLL AND MR HYDE, ROBERT LOUIS STEVENSON

pollard NOUN
a tree that had its top removed, resulting in dense new growth
• *I saw ... a pollard willow ... rising up still and straight.*—JANE EYRE, CHARLOTTE BRONTË

poltroon NOUN
a coward; a worthless person
• *What a miserable little poltroon had fear ... made of me in those days!*—JANE EYRE, CHARLOTTE BRONTË

pomp (also **pomps**) NOUN
ostentatiousness; vain display
• *He certainly conceived a liking for Peepy and would take the child out walking with great pomp.*—BLEAK HOUSE, CHARLES DICKENS
• *Her thoughts dwelt ... on the circumstances of ease, and the pomps and vanities awaiting her.*—MARY BARTON, ELIZABETH GASKELL
➢ **pompous** ADJECTIVE • *the pompous sumptuousness of the room*—MARY BARTON, ELIZABETH GASKELL
➢ **pomposity** NOUN • *the ... futile pomposity of a would-be aristocrat*—SHIRLEY, CHARLOTTE BRONTË

poniard NOUN
a small, thin dagger
• *a lady's knife ... as sharp-pointed as a poniard*—SHIRLEY, CHARLOTTE BRONTË

pony-chaise (also **pony-carriage**) NOUN
a small carriage drawn by a pony
• *the little pony-chaise in which they had been driving*—THE WAR OF THE WORLDS, H. G. WELLS

pooh EXCLAMATION
an exclamation of impatience or contempt
• *'Pooh, pooh! Don't you talk nonsense, my good fellow,' said Mr Bounderby.*—HARD TIMES, CHARLES DICKENS

pool NOUN
a game of cards; the people playing it
• *She had ... sent for him ... to make up her pool of quadrille.*—PRIDE AND PREJUDICE, JANE AUSTEN

poorhouse NOUN
a workhouse

poor-spirited ADJECTIVE
cowardly
• *He had never been one of those poor-spirited sneaks who would refuse to give a helping hand to a fellow-traveller.*—THE MILL ON THE FLOSS, GEORGE ELIOT

popery NOUN
an insulting word for Roman Catholicism or Roman Catholic beliefs or practices
• *The more I saw of Popery the closer I clung to Protestantism.*—VILLETTE, CHARLOTTE BRONTË

porringer NOUN
a small bowl, usually with a handle
• *Of this [gruel] each boy had one porringer, and no more.*—OLIVER TWIST, CHARLES DICKENS

port NOUN
a person's posture
• *His ... port was still erect.*—JANE EYRE, CHARLOTTE BRONTË

portend VERB
to mean something; to signify something
• *What do these sounds portend?*—FRANKENSTEIN, MARY SHELLEY

portent NOUN
an omen; a sign of things to come
• [I] was, in spite of myself, thrown back on ... doubts and portents, and dark conjectures.—JANE EYRE, CHARLOTTE BRONTË

portentous ADJECTIVE
important or meaningful, or trying to seem important
• 'I wish to make mention of no names,' said Mr Kenwigs, with a portentous look.—NICHOLAS NICKLEBY, CHARLES DICKENS
➤ **portentously** ADVERB • He received us ... portentously arrayed in his best black suit. —THE MOONSTONE, WILKIE COLLINS

porter NOUN
a type of dark brown beer similar to stout
• Mrs Poole asks for 'my pint of porter and bit of pudding on a tray'.—JANE EYRE, CHARLOTTE BRONTË
➤ **porter-pot** NOUN a metal or glass mug for drinking porter

portico NOUN
a porch
• I ... found a small man crouching against the pillars of the portico.—THE STRANGE CASE OF DR JEKYLL AND MR HYDE, ROBERT LOUIS STEVENSON

portion NOUN
1 the money or property received by a husband from his wife's family when they married; a dowry
• Your portion is unhappily so small that it will in all likelihood undo the effects of your loveliness and amiable qualifications.—PRIDE AND PREJUDICE, JANE AUSTEN
2 a person's fate or destiny
• If I have no ties and no affections, hatred and vice must be my portion.—FRANKENSTEIN, MARY SHELLEY
➤ **portionless** ADJECTIVE without a dowry; poor
• a friendless, portionless, girl—OLIVER TWIST, CHARLES DICKENS

portmanteau (say port-man-toh) NOUN
a travelling bag
• a man in dirty black, with a thick stick ... and a small portmanteau—THE WAR OF THE WORLDS, H. G. WELLS

portress NOUN
a female porter or doorkeeper
• Rosine, the portress, will not be very slow in answering your ring.—VILLETTE, CHARLOTTE BRONTË

possess VERB
1 to have a quality or thing
• I still possessed my senses, though just now I could not speak.—JANE EYRE, CHARLOTTE BRONTË
2 to control or dominate someone's thoughts or actions
• At this dismal time we were evidently all possessed by the idea that we were followed.—GREAT EXPECTATIONS, CHARLES DICKENS
➤ **be possessed of something:** to have something • men ... [who] are certainly possessed of dauntless courage—FRANKENSTEIN, MARY SHELLEY
➤ **possess yourself of something:** to take something • [The room] contained a bookcase: I soon possessed myself of a volume.—JANE EYRE, CHARLOTTE BRONTË

possession NOUN
1 the state of having something
• It is a truth universally acknowledged, that a single man in possession of a good fortune, must be in want of a wife.—PRIDE AND PREJUDICE, JANE AUSTEN
2 ownership or control
• Three things struggled for possession of my mind. —THE WAR OF THE WORLDS, H. G. WELLS
➤ **take possession of something:**
1 to take something • I at last reached the larder; there I took possession of a cold chicken, a roll of bread ... a plate or two and a knife and fork.—JANE EYRE, CHARLOTTE BRONTË
2 to control or dominate someone's thoughts or actions • This idea taking full possession of his mind, he got up softly, and shuffled ... to the door. —A CHRISTMAS CAROL, CHARLES DICKENS

posset NOUN
a hot drink containing milk and alcohol, taken as a cold remedy or to help you sleep
• That cold is hanging about you yet ... you must let me make a posset for you.—THE DISTRACTED PREACHER, THOMAS HARDY

post ADVERB
➤ **travel / go post:** to travel using the public carriage that was also used for carrying mail
• I cannot bear the idea of two young women travelling post by themselves. It is highly improper.—PRIDE AND PREJUDICE, JANE AUSTEN

post-chaise (also **post-coach**) NOUN
a horse-drawn carriage for passengers and mail
• Finding that the afternoon coach was gone ... he resolved to follow in a post-chaise.—GREAT EXPECTATIONS, CHARLES DICKENS

postern NOUN
a back or side entrance, especially to a castle or other large building
• I passed through the postern and crossed the drawbridge.—GREAT EXPECTATIONS, CHARLES DICKENS

post-horse *to* precipitance

post-horse NOUN
a horse kept at an inn to be used by travellers or by riders carrying mail
• *Their first pause was at the Crown Inn ... where a couple of pair of post-horses were kept.*—EMMA, JANE AUSTEN

posting-house (also **post-house**) NOUN
an inn by the side of a road, where horses were kept to be used by travellers or riders carrying mail
• *A porter guided them to the nearest inn and posting-house.*—THE MILL ON THE FLOSS, GEORGE ELIOT

post-road NOUN
a road on which mail was carried, with inns or stops for post-horses

pother NOUN
fuss; commotion
• *The disturbed chickens 'took flight with much pother and cackling'.*—THE MILL ON THE FLOSS, GEORGE ELIOT

pot-house NOUN
an alehouse; a pub
• *Bauer, the rascal, drunk in some pot-house*—RUPERT OF HENTZAU, ANTHONY HOPE

potman NOUN
a man who served drinks in a pub; a barman
• *The potman ... was just unlocking the doors of the public-house by Horsell Bridge.*—THE WAR OF THE WORLDS, H. G. WELLS

pottage NOUN
a soup or stew
• *herrings and pottage and bread*—THE BLUE FAIRY BOOK, ANDREW LANG

pottle NOUN
1 a half-gallon measure or container for liquids
• *The landlord came and brought a pottle of wine.*—THE MERRY ADVENTURES OF ROBIN HOOD, HOWARD PYLE
2 a cone-shaped punnet
• *He had ... a pottle of strawberries in one hand.*—GREAT EXPECTATIONS, CHARLES DICKENS

pounce NOUN
fine powder used for stopping ink from spreading

powdered ADJECTIVE
used for describing a wig or hairstyle dusted with pale powder, popular in the 18th century
• *an old gentleman with a powdered head*—DOMBEY AND SON, CHARLES DICKENS
USAGE In the 19th century, a *powdered* wig or hair would only be worn by someone old-fashioned, by a judge or barrister, or as part of a uniform.
• *mighty Justices (one with a powdered head)*—GREAT EXPECTATIONS, CHARLES DICKENS

powder-horn NOUN
a container for gunpowder made of an animal's horn
• *The next thing I laid hold of was a brace of pistols, and as I already had a powder-horn and bullets, I felt myself well supplied with arms.*—TREASURE ISLAND, ROBERT LOUIS STEVENSON

power NOUN
1 an ability
• *A man without high birth or money is 'doomed to waste his powers for the profits of the chosen few!'*—FRANKENSTEIN, MARY SHELLEY
2 a large amount; a lot
• *when I'm sorry for folks, and feel as I can't do a power to help 'em*—SILAS MARNER, GEORGE ELIOT

power-loom NOUN
a weaving machine powered by water or steam, which became common in the 19th century

prate VERB
to talk too much or foolishly
• *'Oh! prate away,' said she, 'your son will never be anything to boast of.'*—THE GREEN FAIRY BOOK, ANDREW LANG

pray ADVERB
please; used when making a polite request or asking a sarcastic question
• *'Pray come in,' said Mr Pocket, Junior.*—GREAT EXPECTATIONS, CHARLES DICKENS
• *Go on: what fault do you find with me, pray?*—JANE EYRE, CHARLOTTE BRONTË

pre-Adamite ADJECTIVE
ancient; extremely old
• *Detached broken fossils of pre-adamite whales ... have ... been found.*—MOBY DICK, HERMAN MELVILLE

prebend NOUN
the income or position of a canon (a member of the clergy on the staff of a cathedral)
• *He thought religion was a very excellent thing ... and deaneries and prebends useful institutions.*—THE MILL ON THE FLOSS, GEORGE ELIOT
➤ **prebendary** NOUN a canon • *a prebendary of Verona*—BLEAK HOUSE, CHARLES DICKENS

precept NOUN
a rule about how to behave or what to think; a principle
• *[The Spirit] left his blessing, and taught Scrooge his precepts.*—A CHRISTMAS CAROL, CHARLES DICKENS

precipitance (also **precipitancy** or **precipitation**) NOUN
haste; speed of action
• *His father and mother had written a rather sad letter, deploring his precipitancy in rushing into marriage.*—TESS OF THE D'URBERVILLES, THOMAS HARDY

precipitate to presently

• *I did not act, however, with undue precipitation.*
—A STUDY IN SCARLET, ARTHUR CONAN DOYLE

precipitate ADJECTIVE
1 hasty; sudden
• *I am cautious of appearing forward and precipitate.*
—PRIDE AND PREJUDICE, JANE AUSTEN
2 very steep
• *The cutting was extremely deep, and unusually precipitate.*—THE SIGNAL-MAN, CHARLES DICKENS
➤ **precipitation** NOUN haste • *I would have seized him, but he eluded me and quitted the house with precipitation.*—FRANKENSTEIN, MARY SHELLEY

prefer VERB
1 to promote someone to a position
• *Mr Collins praises Lady Catherine de Bourgh, who 'has preferred me to the valuable rectory of this parish'.*
—PRIDE AND PREJUDICE, JANE AUSTEN
2 to put something forward for consideration
• *[Adèle] can prefer the claim of old acquaintance.*
—JANE EYRE, CHARLOTTE BRONTË
USAGE This meaning is still used in the phrase 'prefer charges' meaning 'to charge someone (with an offence)'.

prefigure VERB
to imagine something before it happened
• *Henchard bent and kissed her cheek. The moment and the act he had prefigured for weeks with a thrill of pleasure.*—THE MAYOR OF CASTERBRIDGE, THOMAS HARDY

pregnant ADJECTIVE
full of something, especially of meaning or significance
• *The fact seemed to me curious and pregnant.*
—VILLETTE, CHARLOTTE BRONTË
• *Exhibiting a face pregnant with intention, he entered the snowy field.*—FAR FROM THE MADDING CROWD, THOMAS HARDY
➤ **pregnancy** NOUN meaningfulness; significance
• *Godfrey, unqualified by experience to discern the pregnancy of Marner's simple words, felt rather angry again.*—SILAS MARNER, GEORGE ELIOT

premise VERB
to state something as an introduction or premise (a statement from which other arguments follow)
• *I will tell you, reader, what [my pictures] are: and first, I must premise that they are nothing wonderful.*—JANE EYRE, CHARLOTTE BRONTË

premonitory ADJECTIVE
warning that something bad is about to happen
• *Tess, without any premonitory symptoms, burst out crying.*—TESS OF THE D'URBERVILLES, THOMAS HARDY

prentice NOUN
an apprentice
• *Your young fellow—the 'prentice, there—what's his name?*—SILAS MARNER, GEORGE ELIOT

prentice VERB
to take someone on as an apprentice
• *The kind and blessed gentleman … Oliver … are a going to 'prentice' you.*—OLIVER TWIST, CHARLES DICKENS

prepense ADJECTIVE
in law, deliberate or premeditated
• *It is unclear whether the dog acted out of 'ignorance of his own duty, or malice prepense'.*—IVANHOE, WALTER SCOTT

prepossessed ADJECTIVE
biased; having made a judgement in advance
• *Those to whom she endeavoured to give pleasure were prepossessed in her favour.*—PRIDE AND PREJUDICE, JANE AUSTEN

prepossessing ADJECTIVE
attractive; appealing
• *Her manners were by no means so elegant as her sister's, but they were much more prepossessing.*
—SENSE AND SENSIBILITY, JANE AUSTEN

prepossession NOUN
a preconceived opinion, especially a favourable one; a liking for someone or something
• *We all conceived a prepossession in his favour.*
—BLEAK HOUSE, CHARLES DICKENS

prescriptive ADJECTIVE
based on tradition or custom
• *the prescriptive respectability of [such] a family*—SILAS MARNER, GEORGE ELIOT

present ADJECTIVE
immediate
• *Is there nothing you could take to give you present relief? A glass of wine; shall I get you one?*—PRIDE AND PREJUDICE, JANE AUSTEN

presentiment NOUN
a premonition; a feeling about the future
• *I had a presentiment that I should never be there again.*—GREAT EXPECTATIONS, CHARLES DICKENS

presently ADVERB
soon afterwards; then
• *'See, daddy, I can carry this quite well,' she said, going along … for a few steps, but presently letting it fall.*—SILAS MARNER, GEORGE ELIOT

presentment to proctor

presentment NOUN
a representation; an image
• Her childish recollection of that terrible old woman was [a] grotesque and exaggerated ... presentment of the truth.—DOMBEY AND SON, CHARLES DICKENS

preservative NOUN
a protection from something
• Charlotte considers marriage the *'pleasantest preservative from want'*.—PRIDE AND PREJUDICE, JANE AUSTEN

preserve VERB
1 to keep someone or something safe
• Mrs Allen congratulated herself ... on having preserved her gown from injury.—NORTHANGER ABBEY, JANE AUSTEN
2 to keep something the same; to retain something
• 'What?' said Estella, preserving her attitude of indifference.—GREAT EXPECTATIONS, CHARLES DICKENS

preside VERB
to be in charge of something
• Agnes made the tea, and presided over it.—DAVID COPPERFIELD, CHARLES DICKENS

presuming ADJECTIVE
too bold; presumptuous
• Pray forgive me, if I have been very presuming.
—PRIDE AND PREJUDICE, JANE AUSTEN

pretend VERB
1 to claim to do something
• Though we have seen him once or twice at my uncle's, it is rather too much to pretend to know him very well.—SENSE AND SENSIBILITY, JANE AUSTEN
2 to aspire, try, or presume to do something
• I cannot pretend to describe what I then felt.
—FRANKENSTEIN, MARY SHELLEY
➤ **pretend to something:** to claim to have something • I do not pretend to Emma's genius for foretelling and guessing.—EMMA, JANE AUSTEN
➤ **pretend to someone:** to aspire to marry someone; to try to win someone's affections • I am not such a fool as to pretend to 'ee now I am poor.—FAR FROM THE MADDING CROWD, THOMAS HARDY

pretension NOUN
a claim
• I make no pretension to be better than my fellows.
—SHIRLEY, CHARLOTTE BRONTË

preternatural ADJECTIVE
beyond what is normal; unnatural
• I only know that the day seemed to me of a preternatural length.—JANE EYRE, CHARLOTTE BRONTË
➤ **preternaturally** ADVERB • In that darkling calm my senses seemed preternaturally sharpened.—THE TIME MACHINE, H. G. WELLS

pretty ADJECTIVE
good; fine; polite
• The older man bowed ... with a very pretty manner of politeness.—THE STRANGE CASE OF DR JEKYLL AND MR HYDE, ROBERT LOUIS STEVENSON
➤ **prettily** ADVERB • She then thanked me very prettily for my advice.—THE MOONSTONE, WILKIE COLLINS

prevalent ADJECTIVE
powerful; predominant
Miss Crawford hopes there is nothing seriously wrong with Tom, but *'the report is so prevalent that I confess I cannot help trembling'*.—MANSFIELD PARK, JANE AUSTEN

prevision NOUN
a premonition or prediction of a future event
• Mr Utterson has *'a strong, superstitious prevision of success'*.—THE STRANGE CASE OF DR JEKYLL AND MR HYDE, ROBERT LOUIS STEVENSON

pride NOUN
the best condition or prime of something
• He was in the full bloom and pride of beadlehood.
—OLIVER TWIST, CHARLES DICKENS

prison VERB
to imprison; to capture
• I arrested his wandering hand, and prisoned it in both mine.—JANE EYRE, CHARLOTTE BRONTË
• At first I thought ... that my being prisoned in the darkness was but the horror of a nightmare.
—MOONFLEET, J. MEADE FALKNER

privateer NOUN
an armed ship that was privately owned but authorized by the government to capture enemy merchant ships
• [The ship] was too small for a privateer, too large for a fishing-smack.—MOONFLEET, J. MEADE FALKNER
➤ **privateersman** NOUN a commander or crew member of a privateer • He was usually addressed as Captain ... and had been a pilot, or a skipper, or a privateersman.—DOMBEY AND SON, CHARLES DICKENS

privily ADVERB
privately; secretly
• She was labouring under the effects of a final taste of gin-and-water which had been privily administered ... by the worthy old ladies.—OLIVER TWIST, CHARLES DICKENS

proctor NOUN
a solicitor who could work in certain courts, particularly ecclesiastical (church) courts
• 'What is a proctor, Steerforth?' said I. 'Why, he is a sort of monkish attorney,' replied Steerforth.—DAVID COPPERFIELD, CHARLES DICKENS

procure to prognostic

procure VERB
to obtain something or cause something to happen
• *I made some discoveries ... which procured me great esteem and admiration at the university.* —FRANKENSTEIN, MARY SHELLEY

prodigality NOUN
generosity; abundance
• *The rich furnishings and ornaments were 'quite ... perplexing from the prodigality with which they were scattered around'.* —NICHOLAS NICKLEBY, CHARLES DICKENS

prodigy NOUN
1 a very good or extreme example of something
• *[He] ... publicly heralded the new actor as a prodigy of genius and learning.* —NICHOLAS NICKLEBY, CHARLES DICKENS
2 an unusual or unnatural thing
• *I had sprung to my feet and leaped back against the wall, my arms raised to shield me from that prodigy.* —THE STRANGE CASE OF DR JEKYLL AND MR HYDE, ROBERT LOUIS STEVENSON
USAGE In modern English, you might expect a *prodigy* to be a child, rather than an adult or an event.

profane ADJECTIVE
1 not sacred or religious
• *Quoting Homer, Mr Glennie apologizes 'for presuming to refer to profane authors after citing Holy Scripture'.* —MOONFLEET, J. MEADE FALKNER
2 disrespectful of something important or sacred
• *When Graham says his mother's brooch is not genuine she responds, 'Profane boy! you know that it is a stone of value'.* —VILLETTE, CHARLOTTE BRONTË

profane VERB
to disrespect something important or sacred
• *Catherine hates Hareton reading from her precious books, saying, 'I hate to have them debased and profaned in his mouth!'* —WUTHERING HEIGHTS, EMILY BRONTË

profess VERB
to declare or claim something
• *He professed himself extremely anxious about her fair friend.* —EMMA, JANE AUSTEN
• *Mr Rochester professed to be puzzled.* —JANE EYRE, CHARLOTTE BRONTË

profession NOUN
a declaration
• *The communication excited many professions of concern.* —PRIDE AND PREJUDICE, JANE AUSTEN

Nouns

The word *profession* now usually refers to a job, but here it is used meaning that someone professes, or declares, something.
• *Elizabeth ... was welcomed by her two friends with many professions of pleasure.* —PRIDE AND PREJUDICE, JANE AUSTEN

The use of abstract nouns to represent ideas, actions, and thoughts is very common in 19th-century writing. These nouns may have the same meaning as in modern English, but they may also have a meaning which is linked with another word in the same family.

For example, you might expect the word *activity* to mean 'a thing you do'. However, in this example it is used meaning that someone is active.
• *With great activity, considering his bulk, he sprang up the steps.* —THE SIGN OF FOUR, ARTHUR CONAN DOYLE

In this example, the word *execution* is related to the verb 'execute', in the sense of 'carry out' a plan.
• *Such was my purpose. ... I went down to the old place to put it in execution.* —GREAT EXPECTATIONS, CHARLES DICKENS

In some cases, the meaning of the noun is obvious, but the way that it is used differs from modern English.
• *I thought it my duty to give the speediest intelligence of this to my cousin.* —PRIDE AND PREJUDICE, JANE AUSTEN

profligate ADJECTIVE
1 wicked; immoral
• *It was a profligate haunt of the worst repute.* —NICHOLAS NICKLEBY, CHARLES DICKENS
2 wasteful; extravagant
USAGE In this quotation, these meanings are combined.
• *Elizabeth says about Wickham, 'We both know that he has been profligate in every sense of the word.'* PRIDE AND PREJUDICE—JANE AUSTEN,

profligate NOUN
a wicked or wasteful person
• *Sir Mulberry's world was peopled with profligates.* —NICHOLAS NICKLEBY, CHARLES DICKENS

prognostic (also **prognostication**) NOUN
a prediction or prophecy
• *Mrs Bennet, hoping Jane will be kept at the Bingleys' house by bad weather, sees her off 'with many cheerful prognostics of a bad day'.* —PRIDE AND PREJUDICE, JANE AUSTEN

➤ **prognosticate** VERB to predict or foretell something • *Is this to prognosticate peace?* —FRANKENSTEIN, MARY SHELLEY

progress NOUN
➢ **in the progress of something**: as something continued; in the course of something • *Of course, St John Rivers' name came in frequently in the progress of my tale.*—JANE EYRE, CHARLOTTE BRONTË

prolix ADJECTIVE
dull and lengthy; too wordy
• *prolix conversations about nothing*—GREAT EXPECTATIONS, CHARLES DICKENS

promiscuous ADJECTIVE
random; haphazard
• *He went on contentedly enough, picking up a promiscuous education chiefly from things that were not intended as education at all.*—THE MILL ON THE FLOSS, GEORGE ELIOT
USAGE In modern English, you might expect *promiscuous* to be used in the context of sexual behaviour.

promise NOUN
an indication that something was likely, especially something good
• *I thought of the promise of virtues which he had displayed on the opening of his existence.*—FRANKENSTEIN, MARY SHELLEY

promise VERB
to make something seem likely, especially something good
• *She grew, and promised to be very beautiful.* —GREAT EXPECTATIONS, CHARLES DICKENS

promptitude NOUN
promptness; lack of delay
• *The doctor arrived with unhoped-for promptitude.* —THE MAYOR OF CASTERBRIDGE, THOMAS HARDY

pronounce VERB
to declare or announce something
• *The gentlemen pronounced him to be a fine figure of a man.*—PRIDE AND PREJUDICE, JANE AUSTEN
• *No voice pronounced these words in Scrooge's ears, and yet he heard them.*—A CHRISTMAS CAROL, CHARLES DICKENS

proof ADJECTIVE
able to withstand or resist something
• *I looked about me, noticing how ... the house ... would not be proof against the weather much longer.*—GREAT EXPECTATIONS, CHARLES DICKENS
• *[Wickham] was not likely to be proof against the temptation.*—PRIDE AND PREJUDICE, JANE AUSTEN

USAGE In modern English, you might expect *proof* as an adjective to be used in combination with nouns rather than on its own, to make words such as *windproof* or *childproof*.

propagate VERB
to spread something
• *the doctrines which he had made it his life's mission and desire to propagate*—TESS OF THE D'URBERVILLES, THOMAS HARDY

proper ADJECTIVE
socially appropriate; suitable
• *She could not help asking him ... whether he would think it proper to join in the evening's amusement.* —PRIDE AND PREJUDICE, JANE AUSTEN
• *She will make him a very proper wife.*—PRIDE AND PREJUDICE, JANE AUSTEN

propitiate VERB
to placate someone; to win someone's favour
• *She could have thought of nothing more likely to propitiate her brother than this praise of Maggie.* —THE MILL ON THE FLOSS, GEORGE ELIOT

propitious ADJECTIVE
favourable
• *Her answer ... was not propitious, at least not to Elizabeth's wishes.*—PRIDE AND PREJUDICE, JANE AUSTEN

propound VERB
to put forward a question, an idea, etc.
• *Again Mr Rochester propounded his query.* —JANE EYRE, CHARLOTTE BRONTË

proscenium NOUN
the part of a theatre stage in front of the curtain
• *The manager's voice recalled him ... to the opposite side of the proscenium.*—NICHOLAS NICKLEBY, CHARLES DICKENS

proscribe VERB
to outlaw someone
• *a proscribed fugitive, with a price upon his head* —HARD TIMES, CHARLES DICKENS

prose VERB
to talk a lot in a tedious way
• *I went on prose, prose, prosing for a length of time.*—BLEAK HOUSE, CHARLES DICKENS
➤ **prosing** ADJECTIVE • *Miss Bates! so silly—so satisfied—so smiling—so prosing.*—EMMA, JANE AUSTEN

prospect NOUN
the view from a place
• *You have a sweet room here, Mr Bingley, and a charming prospect over that gravel walk.*—PRIDE AND PREJUDICE, JANE AUSTEN

prosper to puissant

prosper VERB
to be successful or healthy; to do well
- *His suit had prospered, and his marriage had been considered as a settled and certain thing.* —THE MOONSTONE, WILKIE COLLINS

prosperous ADJECTIVE
successful; fortunate; thriving
- *Everybody around her was gay and busy, prosperous and important.* —MANSFIELD PARK, JANE AUSTEN

prostrate ADJECTIVE
lying face down; collapsed
- *He made an effort to stand upright; but, shuddering from head to foot, fell prostrate on the ground.* —OLIVER TWIST, CHARLES DICKENS

prostrate VERB
to knock someone down; to cause someone to collapse
- *This was a blow: but I did not let it prostrate me.* —JANE EYRE, CHARLOTTE BRONTË

prostration NOUN
1 the state of being very weak or overwhelmed by something
- *the prostration of thought under an overpowering passion* —SILAS MARNER, GEORGE ELIOT
2 physical or emotional collapse; extreme exhaustion
- *More of that horrible pain in the early morning; followed, this time, by complete prostration.* —THE MOONSTONE, WILKIE COLLINS

prosy ADJECTIVE
1 dull; tedious
- *Would his uncle give him a place in the bank? It would be very dull, prosy work, he thought.* —THE MILL ON THE FLOSS, GEORGE ELIOT
2 long-winded; talking a lot
- *You will be pleased with my mother—SHE IS A LITTLE VAIN AND PROSY ABOUT ME, but that you can forgive her.* —DAVID COPPERFIELD, CHARLES DICKENS

protest VERB
to declare or say something
- *He protested that except Lady Catherine and her daughter, he had never seen a more elegant woman.* —PRIDE AND PREJUDICE, JANE AUSTEN
➤ **protestation** NOUN • *Many protestations of friendship … were exchanged.* —NICHOLAS NICKLEBY, CHARLES DICKENS

provender NOUN
food, especially animal food
- *[He] smelt of lamp-oil, straw, orange-peel, horses' provender, and sawdust.* —HARD TIMES, CHARLES DICKENS

provide VERB
➤ **provide for someone:** to ensure that a person has enough money or material things • *I must be provided for by a wealthy marriage.* —JANE EYRE, CHARLOTTE BRONTË
- *It's my duty … to own Eppie as my child, and provide for her.* —SILAS MARNER, GEORGE ELIOT
➤ **provision** NOUN a means of providing for someone • *[Marriage] was the only honourable provision for well-educated young women of small fortune.* —PRIDE AND PREJUDICE, JANE AUSTEN

prurient ADJECTIVE
excessively curious, especially about other people's private lives
- *Eustace is questioned and discovered to be in love by 'prurient Campian'.* —WESTWARD HO!, CHARLES KINGSLEY
➤ **prurience** NOUN • *the idiotic rivalries of society, the prurience* —JANE EYRE, CHARLOTTE BRONTË

pshaw (say pshaw, shaw) EXCLAMATION
an exclamation of impatience, contempt, or disgust
- *Pshaw! it's time you'd done with fooleries.* —SILAS MARNER, GEORGE ELIOT

pshaw VERB
to exclaim in impatience, contempt, or disgust
- *Cedric tushed and pshawed more than once at the message.* —IVANHOE, WALTER SCOTT

publish VERB
to make something known; to publicize something
- *Far from desiring to publish the connection, he became as anxious to conceal it as myself.* —JANE EYRE, CHARLOTTE BRONTË

pudden NOUN
pudding
- *I know what the pudden's to be,—apricot roll-up!* —THE MILL ON THE FLOSS, GEORGE ELIOT

puff VERB
to try to sell or talk up something or someone
- *There never was a man who stood by a friend more staunchly than the Major, when in puffing him, he puffed himself.* —DOMBEY AND SON, CHARLES DICKENS

pugilistic (say pyoo-jil-ist-ik) ADJECTIVE
involving boxing or punching
- *a pugilistic contest across the table* —NICHOLAS NICKLEBY, CHARLES DICKENS
🏛 Latin *pugil* meaning 'boxer'

puissant (say pyoo-iss-uhnt, pwee-suhnt) ADJECTIVE
powerful
- *a noble and puissant nation* —RIP VAN WINKLE, WASHINGTON IRVING
🏛 French *puissant*, meaning 'powerful'

pulled down to putrescent

pulled down *ADJECTIVE*
ill or exhausted
• *You look a good deal pulled down, though you're not an old man, are you?*—SILAS MARNER, GEORGE ELIOT

puncheon *NOUN*
a large barrel or cask
• *a puncheon of water*—TREASURE ISLAND, ROBERT LOUIS STEVENSON

punctual *ADJECTIVE*
strictly observed; precise or meticulous
• *Eliza was gone to ... church—for ... no weather ever prevented the punctual discharge of ... her devotional duties.*—JANE EYRE, CHARLOTTE BRONTË
➤ **punctually** *ADVERB* precisely; without missing anything out • *[Mr Collins] punctually repeated all his wife's offers of refreshment.*—PRIDE AND PREJUDICE, JANE AUSTEN

purblind *ADJECTIVE*
1 unable to see well; partly blind
• *Had I stayed there very long, I should have become purblind.*—BLACK BEAUTY, ANNA SEWELL
2 not understanding well; slow
• *I began, in a purblind groping way, to read, write, and cipher.*—GREAT EXPECTATIONS, CHARLES DICKENS

purl *VERB*
to flow and swirl, making a babbling sound
• *They were never out of the sound of some purling weir.*—TESS OF THE D'URBERVILLES, THOMAS HARDY
➤ **purl** *NOUN* • *the purl of water falling into a pool*—FAR FROM THE MADDING CROWD, THOMAS HARDY

purlieu (say **purl-yoo**) *NOUN*
an area near or around a place
• *farmers who lived in an eastern purlieu called Durnover*—THE MAYOR OF CASTERBRIDGE, THOMAS HARDY

pursuant *ADJECTIVE*
following
• *Bob ... was looking at her with the pursuant gaze of an ... animal.*—THE MILL ON THE FLOSS, GEORGE ELIOT
➤ **pursuant to:** in accordance with; following
• *And pursuant to this idea of a holiday, he insisted upon playing cards after we had eaten.*—THE WAR OF THE WORLDS, H. G. WELLS

pursy *ADJECTIVE*
1 out of breath
• *Sleary [was] rendered more pursy than ever, by so much talking.*—HARD TIMES, CHARLES DICKENS
2 fat
• *a short pursy man*—RIP VAN WINKLE, WASHINGTON IRVING

purveyor *NOUN*
a supplier or provider of something, especially food
• *Tess is described as 'supervisor, purveyor, nurse, surgeon, and friend' to the chickens.*—TESS OF THE D'URBERVILLES, THOMAS HARDY

put *VERB*
➤ **put a horse to (something):** to harness a horse to a carriage, etc. • *Our horses were put to with great speed.*—BLEAK HOUSE, CHARLES DICKENS
• *[He] went down into the yard to get out his horse and put him to the cab.*—AT THE BACK OF THE NORTH WIND, GEORGE MACDONALD
➤ **putting-to** *NOUN* • *the putting-to of the horses*—GREAT EXPECTATIONS, CHARLES DICKENS

putrefactive *ADJECTIVE*
causing or relating to rotting or decay
• *The Martians do not bury their dead, showing 'an entire ignorance of the putrefactive process'.*—THE WAR OF THE WORLDS, H. G. WELLS

putrefy *VERB*
to rot; to decompose
• *The kennel was stagnant and filthy. The ... rats lay putrefying in its rottenness.*—OLIVER TWIST, CHARLES DICKENS

putrescent *ADJECTIVE*
rotting; decomposing
• *[I] saw ... a dog with a piece of putrescent red meat in his jaws.*—THE WAR OF THE WORLDS, H. G. WELLS

Qq

QUEEN VICTORIA

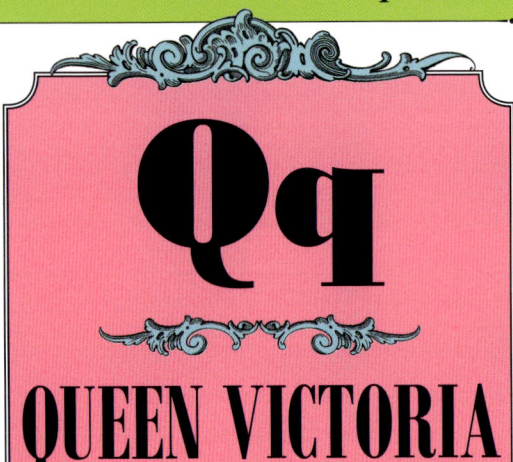

Queen Victoria was eighteen years old when she became queen in **1837**. Victoria and her husband Albert had nine children. After his death from typhoid aged 42, Victoria remained in mourning until her death aged eighty-one in **1901**. Her reign saw the rise of Great Britain as a global power, and in 1877 she was named Empress of India. It was also a period of great industrial and social change.

quadrille NOUN
1 a card game for four players, using forty cards
• [They] sat down to quadrille.—PRIDE AND PREJUDICE, JANE AUSTEN
2 a square dance, typically for four couples
• I opened [the ball] by dancing a quadrille with Flavia.
—THE PRISONER OF ZENDA, ANTHONY HOPE

quaff VERB
to drink
• On such occasions he would … quaff a cup of wine.
—IVANHOE, WALTER SCOTT

quag NOUN
a muddy place; a mess
• You can see what a quag 'twould get me out of.
—THE MAYOR OF CASTERBRIDGE, THOMAS HARDY

quail VERB
1 to feel or show fear
• Mr Utterson had already quailed at the name of Hyde.
—THE STRANGE CASE OF DR JEKYLL AND MR HYDE, ROBERT LOUIS STEVENSON
2 to give in to someone or something; to falter or yield
• [His] eye never quailed under the penetrating look it encountered.—THE LAST OF THE MOHICANS, JAMES FENIMORE COOPER

quail NOUN
a short-tailed game bird
• They will be a tender morsel for you, as fat as young quails.—THE BLUE FAIRY BOOK, ANDREW LANG

quaint ADJECTIVE
strange; curious
• Utterson says the fact that the two handwriting samples are similar is 'rather quaint'.—THE STRANGE CASE OF DR JEKYLL AND MR HYDE, ROBERT LOUIS STEVENSON

qualification NOUN
a skill or quality making someone suitable for something
• I shall speak in the highest terms of your modesty, economy, and other amiable qualifications. PRIDE AND PREJUDICE, JANE AUSTEN

quality NOUN
1 high social status
• [He] seemed to be a person of quality.—THE BLUE FAIRY BOOK, ANDREW LANG
2 people with high social status
• It was 'baker's bread'—what the quality eat.
—THE ADVENTURES OF HUCKLEBERRY FINN, MARK TWAIN
3 a profession, capacity, or role; status
• He does not wish to 'renounce the quality of doctor'.
—SILAS MARNER, GEORGE ELIOT

qualm NOUN
1 a sudden feeling of nausea or weakness
• The doctor seemed seized with a qualm of faintness.
—THE STRANGE CASE OF DR JEKYLL AND MR HYDE, ROBERT LOUIS STEVENSON
2 a sudden occurrence of an emotion
• He now felt a strangely distressing qualm from a new thought.—FAR FROM THE MADDING CROWD, THOMAS HARDY

quantum NOUN
an amount needed or allowed
• [He] swallowed his quantum of tea.—SHIRLEY, CHARLOTTE BRONTË

quarter NOUN
1 an area
• The whole quarter reeked with crime, with filth and misery.—A CHRISTMAS CAROL, CHARLES DICKENS
• What made him seek this quarter of the house?
—JANE EYRE, CHARLOTTE BRONTË
2 a person or group
• Already … spectators … were seated … and great was the admiration and satisfaction in that quarter.
—SILAS MARNER, GEORGE ELIOT
3 the direction of one of the compass points
• The wind blew from the quarter where the day would soon appear.—HARD TIMES, CHARLES DICKENS

4 a measure for grain, equal to 64 gallons (approximately 291 litres)
• The price paid for the corn was *'higher by many shillings a quarter'*.—THE MAYOR OF CASTERBRIDGE, THOMAS HARDY
5 one of the sides at the rear end of a boat
• *[The ship was] nearly hull down on our starboard quarter.*—THE MEMOIRS OF SHERLOCK HOLMES, ARTHUR CONAN DOYLE

quarter VERB
1 to accommodate people, typically soldiers, in a place
• *a young officer whose regiment had been recently quartered in the neighborhood*—RIP VAN WINKLE, WASHINGTON IRVING
2 to move in a slanting direction
• *He swam quartering upstream.*—THE ADVENTURES OF TOM SAWYER, MARK TWAIN

quartern loaf NOUN
a loaf of bread weighing about four pounds (just under 2 kg)
• *Why here's one man that ... has a quartern loaf and a good pound of cheese.*—OLIVER TWIST, CHARLES DICKENS

quarter-staff NOUN
a thick pole used as a weapon; fighting with thick poles
• *You can be Friar Tuck ... and lam me with a quarter-staff.*—THE ADVENTURES OF TOM SAWYER, MARK TWAIN

quean NOUN
a prostitute; used as a term of abuse for a woman or girl
• *a vile, flirting quean as thou art*—MARY BARTON, ELIZABETH GASKELL

queer ADJECTIVE
strange
• *But a queer thing happened a year since.*—JANE EYRE, CHARLOTTE BRONTË
➢ **Queer Street**: trouble; a difficult situation
• *No, sir ... the more it looks like Queer Street, the less I ask.*—THE STRANGE CASE OF DR JEKYLL AND MR HYDE, ROBERT LOUIS STEVENSON
• *It's lucky for you, my man, that nothing is missing, or you would find yourself in Queer Street.*—THE RETURN OF SHERLOCK HOLMES, Arthur Conan Doyle

quench VERB
to silence someone
• *Jo quenched [Amy] by slamming down the window.*—LITTLE WOMEN, LOUISA M. ALCOTT

querulous ADJECTIVE
complaining; whining
• *Mr Jaggers was querulous and angry with me.*—GREAT EXPECTATIONS, CHARLES DICKENS

➤ **querulously** ADVERB • *'Why need you go?' said she querulously, at length.*—MARY BARTON, ELIZABETH GASKELL

quick ADJECTIVE
able to notice, think, or learn quickly; intelligent
• *He has all the ... power of quick intuition.*—THE SIGN OF FOUR, ARTHUR CONAN DOYLE
➤ **quickness** NOUN • *Lizzy has something more of quickness than her sisters.*—PRIDE AND PREJUDICE, JANE AUSTEN

quick NOUN
➢ **to the quick**: to the core; very intensely or to the greatest possible extent • *The insult to her stung him to the quick.*—TESS OF THE D'URBERVILLES, THOMAS HARDY

quickset NOUN
a hedge; trees such as hawthorn used for hedging
• *[A] field-labourer ... glanced through the quickset.*—THE MAYOR OF CASTERBRIDGE, THOMAS HARDY

quiescence (say kwee-ess-uhnss, kwy-ess-uhnss) NOUN
quiet inactivity or quiet obedience
• *Heathcliff threatens to 'knock [Edgar Linton] down, and ... insure his quiescence'.*—WUTHERING HEIGHTS, EMILY BRONTË
➤ **quiescent** ADJECTIVE quiet, inactive, or obedient
• *Mrs Reed cannot understand 'how for nine years [Jane] could be patient and quiescent ... and in the tenth break out all fire and violence'.*—JANE EYRE, CHARLOTTE BRONTË

quiet ADJECTIVE
gentle; unhurried or calm
• *Stephen ... stalked along at a quieter pace.*—THE MILL ON THE FLOSS, GEORGE ELIOT

quietus NOUN
1 death
• *I nearly got my quietus.*—KITTY'S CLASS DAY AND OTHER STORIES, LOUISA M. ALCOTT
2 something bringing a situation or feeling to an end
• *Her advice 'proved a quietus for many'.*—A GARLAND FOR GIRLS, LOUISA M. ALCOTT

quite ADVERB
just; merely
• *My father was an officer in an Indian regiment who sent me home when I was quite a child.*—THE SIGN OF FOUR, ARTHUR CONAN DOYLE

quittance to quoth

quittance NOUN
1 departure or release; instruction or permission to leave or to end something
- *She could not ... resist a notice of quittance.*
—*VILLETTE*, CHARLOTTE BRONTË

2 a receipt
- *Whether 'twas a forged quittance ... we knew not.*
—*MOONFLEET*, J. MEADE FALKNER

quiz NOUN
an odd or ridiculous person or thing; a joke
- *Young ladies have a remarkable way of letting you know that they think you a 'quiz' without actually saying the words.*—*JANE EYRE*, CHARLOTTE BRONTË

quiz VERB
1 to mock or tease someone
- *Louisa and I used to quiz our governess too; but she was such a good creature, she would bear anything.*
—*JANE EYRE*, CHARLOTTE BRONTË

2 to question someone or something
- *That night he looked as if he would like the fun of quizzing her figures and pretending to be horrified at her extravagance.*—*LITTLE MEN*, LOUISA M. ALCOTT

quizzical ADJECTIVE
1 odd; ridiculous
- *You needn't think it an unmanly or quizzical thing to be particular about your nightcap.*—*NICHOLAS NICKLEBY*, CHARLES DICKENS

2 playful; mocking or witty
- *Mrs Merryweather had a quizzical reply on the tip of her tongue, but glancing at Roger's face, thought better of it.*—*HILDEGARDE'S NEIGHBORS*, LAURA E. RICHARDS

3 questioning but also amused
- *'Where did you learn all this sort of thing?' he asked with a quizzical look.*—*LITTLE MEN*, LOUISA M. ALCOTT

quizzing-glass NOUN
an eye piece; a monocle
- *He carried a jaunty sort of a stick ... and a quizzing-glass hung outside his coat.*—*DAVID COPPERFIELD*, CHARLES DICKENS

quoth VERB
said
- *'I believe, sir,' quoth Mrs Sparsit, 'you wished to see me.'*—*HARD TIMES*, CHARLES DICKENS

Rr

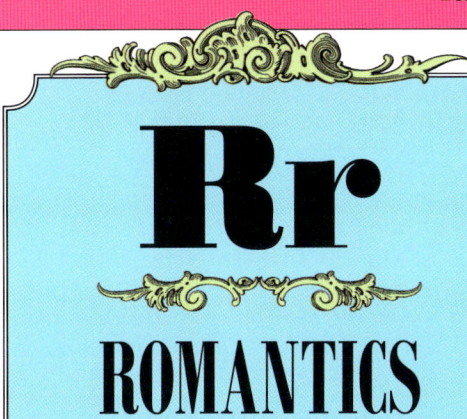

ROMANTICS

The poets **Percy Bysshe Shelley, Robert Burns, William Blake, William Wordsworth, Samuel Taylor Coleridge,** and **John Keats** became known as the **Romantic poets.** Their poetry was about the importance of emotion over cold reason and celebrated the natural world and the imagination. Other Romantic poets such as **Lord Byron** supported the revolutionary movements that were sweeping through Europe.

rack VERB
to torment someone
- *A change had come over me. It was … the horror of being Hyde that racked me.*—THE STRANGE CASE OF DR JEKYLL AND MR HYDE, ROBERT LOUIS STEVENSON

rage NOUN
a passion or strong desire for something
- *her rage for admiration*—PRIDE AND PREJUDICE, JANE AUSTEN

ragged school NOUN
a free school for children of the poor
- *This was the Class I saw at the Ragged School. They could not be trusted with books; they could only be instructed orally.*—RAGGED SCHOOLS, CHARLES DICKENS

rag-shop NOUN
a shop selling second-hand things, especially clothes

raiment NOUN
clothes; clothing
- *this stout lady in a quaint black dress, who looks young enough to wear much smarter raiment*—SHIRLEY, CHARLOTTE BRONTË

rajah (also **raja**) NOUN
an Indian king or prince
- *His mother had got an emerald … that was taken out of the footstool of a Rajah.*—DOMBEY AND SON, CHARLES DICKENS

rampion NOUN
a type of plant
- *Gathering a handful of rampion leaves, he returned with them to his wife.*—THE RED FAIRY BOOK, ANDREW LANG

randy NOUN
a noisy celebration; merry-making
- *a rattling good randy wi' fiddles and bass-viols*—TESS OF THE D'URBERVILLES, THOMAS HARDY

rank NOUN
1 a person's position in society
- *Lady Catherine will not think the worse of you for being simply dressed. She likes to have the distinction of rank preserved.*—PRIDE AND PREJUDICE, JANE AUSTEN

2 a high position in society
- *an accomplished lady of rank*—JANE EYRE, CHARLOTTE BRONTË

rank ADJECTIVE
growing thickly or abundantly; overgrown
- *rank tufted grass*—SILAS MARNER, GEORGE ELIOT

rapine NOUN
the violent taking of things belonging to other people
- *There was a past time when 'war and rapine dwelt in place of peace and justice'.*—OTTO OF THE SILVER HAND, HOWARD PYLE

rascality NOUN
bad or dishonourable behaviour
- *Tom has often heard his father talk about 'the lawyer's rascality'.*—THE MILL ON THE FLOSS, GEORGE ELIOT

rate VERB
to scold; to speak angrily to someone
- *Berry … cried for six weeks (being soundly rated by her good aunt all the time).*—DOMBEY AND SON, CHARLES DICKENS

RELATED WORD The word *berate* has the same meaning and is still current.

rathe (say **raydh**) ADJECTIVE
prompt; early
- *Come rathe or come late it don't much matter.*—WESSEX TALES, THOMAS HARDY

rave to reclaim

rave VERB
to speak in an uncontrolled way, because of being mentally ill or disturbed
• *The form of the monster ... was forever before my eyes, and I raved incessantly concerning him.* —FRANKENSTEIN, MARY SHELLEY

ravel NOUN
a knot, cluster, or tangle
• *the ravel of traffic* —GREAT EXPECTATIONS, CHARLES DICKENS

ravel VERB
to entangle or muddle something
• *Before she had finished ... she had disentangled her ravelled ideas.* —MARY BARTON, ELIZABETH GASKELL

ravish VERB
1 to delight someone; to please someone very much
• *I had been pleased with Robin's playing, Alan's ravished me.* —KIDNAPPED, ROBERT LOUIS STEVENSON
2 to take by force; to snatch away
• *Soon the bolt will fall which must ravish from you your happiness forever.* —FRANKENSTEIN, MARY SHELLEY

ready ADJECTIVE
quick; prompt
• *No scheme could have been more agreeable to Elizabeth, and her acceptance of the invitation was most ready and grateful.* —PRIDE AND PREJUDICE, JANE AUSTEN
➤ **readiness** NOUN • *Mrs Nickleby assented with equal readiness.* —NICHOLAS NICKLEBY, CHARLES DICKENS
USAGE In modern English, you might expect a person to be *ready*, rather than their reply or reaction.

realize VERB
1 to make something happen; to make something real
• *I had imagined something which I was quite powerless to realise.* —JANE EYRE, CHARLOTTE BRONTË
2 to think of something as real; to fully understand something
• *I can hardly realise my own happiness.* —THE WOMAN IN WHITE, WILKIE COLLINS
➤ **realization** NOUN • *I thought I ... beheld a form, which announced the realisation of my dream.* —JANE EYRE, CHARLOTTE BRONTË

recall VERB
to make someone turn their attention back to something
• *I was obliged to recall him to a theme which was of necessity one of close and anxious interest to me.* —JANE EYRE, CHARLOTTE BRONTË

➤ **recall someone to himself / herself:**
to get someone's attention or make someone fully conscious
• *Just then the whistle blew, and the train moved off. This recalled him to himself.* —DRACULA, BRAM STOKER
USAGE Robert Louis Stevenson uses this phrase to talk about Dr Jekyll changing back to his normal self.
• *It took on this occasion a double dose to recall me to myself.* —THE STRANGE CASE OF DR JEKYLL AND MR HYDE, ROBERT LOUIS STEVENSON

recede VERB
to go back on a promise or agreement; to abandon an idea
• *Lady Catherine warns Lizzie, 'Do not deceive yourself into a belief that I will ever recede. I shall not go away, till you have given me the assurance I require'.* —PRIDE AND PREJUDICE, JANE AUSTEN
USAGE In modern English, you might expect hairlines or memories to *recede*, rather than people.

receipt NOUN
the act of receiving something
• *I really had not been myself since the receipt of the letter.* —GREAT EXPECTATIONS, CHARLES DICKENS

recherché ADJECTIVE
rare, exotic, or unusual
• *Ah, now, this really is something a little recherché.* —THE MEMOIRS OF SHERLOCK HOLMES, ARTHUR CONAN DOYLE

recital NOUN
a spoken account, especially a long one
• *She listened with parted lips and shining eyes to my recital of our adventures.* —THE SIGN OF FOUR, ARTHUR CONAN DOYLE
USAGE In modern English, you might expect a *recital* to involve a musical performance.

reck VERB
to pay attention to something; to take notice
• *Little recked he of thorns and briers that scratched his flesh.* —THE MERRY ADVENTURES OF ROBIN HOOD, HOWARD PYLE
USAGE The line *[He] recks not his own rede* from Shakespeare's Hamlet is often quoted, meaning 'he does not follow his own advice'.
• *She could show others the steep and thorny way, but 'reck'd not her own rede'.* —FAR FROM THE MADDING CROWD, THOMAS HARDY

reclaim VERB
to make someone reform their bad behaviour; to redeem someone
• *I thought your sister's influence might yet reclaim him.* —SENSE AND SENSIBILITY, JANE AUSTEN

USAGE In modern English, you might expect to *reclaim* a thing that belongs to you, rather than a person.

recluse ADJECTIVE
solitary; preferring to be alone
• *I was recluse, desolate, young, and ignorant.* —SHIRLEY, CHARLOTTE BRONTË

recollect VERB
➢ **recollect yourself:** to get your thoughts in order; to compose yourself or reflect
• *'But,' she continued, recollecting herself, '... it is not fair to condemn him.'*—PRIDE AND PREJUDICE, JANE AUSTEN

recollection NOUN
thought; reflection
• *This was a lucky recollection—it saved her from something like regret.*—PRIDE AND PREJUDICE, JANE AUSTEN

recreant (say rek-ree-uhnt) ADJECTIVE
cowardly
• *I ... summoned back my recreant courage, and looked under the seat.*—THE WOMAN IN WHITE, WILKIE COLLINS

recreant NOUN
a coward
• *[What] will you say of that working-man ... who, at such a time, turns a traitor and a craven and a recreant?*—HARD TIMES, CHARLES DICKENS

recrudescence NOUN
a recurrence; a revival or a repeat of something
• *Tess's action is 'the recrudescence of a trick' practised by her ancestors.*—TESS OF THE D'URBERVILLES, THOMAS HARDY

rectitude NOUN
moral correctness
• *The spirit of rectitude ... in Nancy's character, had made it a habit with her to scrutinize her past feelings and actions.*—SILAS MARNER, GEORGE ELIOT

recumbent ADJECTIVE
lying down
• *Here, recumbent on a small sofa ... was Mrs Micawber.* —DAVID COPPERFIELD, CHARLES DICKENS

recur VERB
1 to return to what you were saying, thinking, or doing
• *[Dolly] was not long before she recurred to the subject.*—SILAS MARNER, GEORGE ELIOT
• *I [was not] inclined to recur to these studies.* —FRANKENSTEIN, MARY SHELLEY

2 to occur to someone again; to come back to someone
• *I had half-forgotten my own wretched position: now it recurred to me.*—JANE EYRE, CHARLOTTE BRONTË

redcoat NOUN
a British soldier
• *About half a mile up the water was a camp of red-coats.*—KIDNAPPED, ROBERT LOUIS STEVENSON

redeem VERB
1 to save someone from something
• *Thus not the tenderness of friendship, nor the beauty of earth, nor of heaven, could redeem my soul from woe.*—FRANKENSTEIN, MARY SHELLEY
2 to compensate or make up for something
• *I resolved in my future conduct to redeem the past.*—THE STRANGE CASE OF DR JEKYLL AND MR HYDE, ROBERT LOUIS STEVENSON
3 to buy someone out of slavery or captivity
• *You shall be redeemed as soon as I can any way bring together means.*—UNCLE TOM'S CABIN, HARRIET BEECHER STOWE
4 to repay a debt; to recover goods left as a guarantee for a loan
• *He had redeemed his better coat from the pawn-shop before he left.*—MARY BARTON, ELIZABETH GASKELL
5 to fulfil a promise
• *I reminded Herbert of his promise to tell me about Miss Havisham. 'True,' he replied. 'I'll redeem it at once.'* —GREAT EXPECTATIONS, CHARLES DICKENS
➢ **redeeming** ADJECTIVE making up for something
• *His redeeming quality is a love of animals.*—DRACULA, BRAM STOKER

redemption NOUN
1 saving someone; being saved from something
• *It yet remained to be seen if I had lost my identity beyond redemption.*—THE STRANGE CASE OF DR JEKYLL AND MR HYDE, ROBERT LOUIS STEVENSON
2 the process of redeeming a debt, promise, or action
• *I would ... claim your hand, as in redemption of some old mute contract that had been sealed between us!*—OLIVER TWIST, CHARLES DICKENS
3 buying someone out of slavery or captivity
• *He inquires very anxiously ... when the money for his redemption is to be raised.*—UNCLE TOM'S CABIN, HARRIET BEECHER STOWE

red tape NOUN
red or pink material tape used to tie together official documents
• *a gentleman ... who was looking over some papers tied together with red tape*—DAVID COPPERFIELD, CHARLES DICKENS
USAGE This expression was also used figuratively in the 19th century, as it is today, to mean 'excessive paperwork or official rules'.

• There is so much red tape in these matters.
—THE RETURN OF SHERLOCK HOLMES, ARTHUR CONAN DOYLE
RELATED WORD red tapeworm meaning 'a person who likes paperwork and rules'

reek VERB
to give off steam or smoke
• a thick steam, perpetually rising from the reeking bodies of the cattle—OLIVER TWIST, CHARLES DICKENS

reek NOUN
clouds of steam or smoke
• [The star] shone intermittently through a driving reek of thunder-clouds.—THE STAR, H. G. WELLS

reel NOUN
a lively folk dance
• [Tess] could hear the fiddled notes of a reel.—TESS OF THE D'URBERVILLES, THOMAS HARDY

reel VERB
to stagger or lose your balance
• A cry followed; he reeled, staggered, clutched at the table and held on.—THE STRANGE CASE OF DR JEKYLL AND MR HYDE, ROBERT LOUIS STEVENSON

refer VERB
1 to think that something is caused by a particular thing
• I assume I may refer the project to her influence.—DAVID COPPERFIELD, CHARLES DICKENS
2 to direct or send someone to a person or place
• I must refer you to Mrs Clements, who knows more of the subject than I do.—THE WOMAN IN WHITE, WILKIE COLLINS

referable ADJECTIVE
➤ **referable to:** able to be explained by something
• Miss Tox has 'a blue nose and … frosty face, referable to her being very thinly clad'.—DOMBEY AND SON, CHARLES DICKENS

reference NOUN
1 consultation; seeking information
• A reference to the passenger list showed that Miss Fraser, of Adelaide … had made the voyage.—THE RETURN OF SHERLOCK HOLMES, ARTHUR CONAN DOYLE
2 referring or being referred to
• I may remark that when Mr Wopsle referred to me, he considered it a necessary part of such reference to rumple my hair and poke it into my eyes.—GREAT EXPECTATIONS, CHARLES DICKENS
➤ **bear reference to:** to indicate or refer to something • Everything is related in [these papers] which bears reference to my accursed origin.
—FRANKENSTEIN, MARY SHELLEY

reflection NOUN
1 thinking; a thought
• 'No,' said Catherine, after a few moments' reflection.—NORTHANGER ABBEY, JANE AUSTEN
• I had sufficient leisure for these and many other reflections during my journey.—FRANKENSTEIN, MARY SHELLEY
2 harm to someone's reputation; a criticism
• Emma could not like what bordered on a reflection on Mr Weston.—EMMA, JANE AUSTEN
USAGE In modern English, you might expect to find the second sense of the word only in the phrase 'no reflection on' someone.

reft VERB
torn or snatched (from the verb 'reave')
• leaves and flowers reft into fragments by her passionate hand—DOMBEY AND SON, CHARLES DICKENS
RELATED WORD Bereave meaning 'deprive of', and its past participle bereft

refulgent ADJECTIVE
shining brightly
• On a painted sign, 'in golden characters, these names shine refulgent, GILLS AND CUTTLE'.—DOMBEY AND SON, CHARLES DICKENS

regain VERB
to go back to a place
• I regained my couch, but never thought of sleep.
—JANE EYRE, CHARLOTTE BRONTË

regale VERB
to offer someone generous amounts of food or drink
• The five little boys were put to thaw by the fire, and regaled with sandwiches.—NICHOLAS NICKLEBY, CHARLES DICKENS

regard VERB
1 to pay attention to; to take notice of
• You can let her come and go without regarding me.
—DOMBEY AND SON, CHARLES DICKENS
2 to relate to; to concern
• One perplexity, however, arose … It regarded a supper-room.—EMMA, JANE AUSTEN

regard NOUN
1 admiration, affection, or respect
• I have an excessive regard for Miss Jane Bennet.
—PRIDE AND PREJUDICE, JANE AUSTEN
2 attention
• Do you pay no regard to the wishes of his friends?
—PRIDE AND PREJUDICE, JANE AUSTEN

regardless ADJECTIVE
indifferent; not showing any interest
• [She] kept her eyes on me in a cool, regardless manner, exceedingly embarrassing and disagreeable.
—WUTHERING HEIGHTS, EMILY BRONTË

regimentals *to* remembrancer

➤ **regardless of:** not aware of or caring about something • *the falling rain, of which, in his first surprise, he had been quite regardless*—NICHOLAS NICKLEBY, CHARLES DICKENS

➤ **regardlessness** NOUN indifference; carelessness
• *What stupid regardlessness now?*—JANE EYRE, CHARLOTTE BRONTË

regimentals NOUN
a military uniform
• *The young man wanted only regimentals to make him completely charming.*—PRIDE AND PREJUDICE, JANE AUSTEN

regulars NOUN
the regular army; the official army of a country
• *It is Mr Wickham's intention to go into the regulars.*—PRIDE AND PREJUDICE, JANE AUSTEN

reindue VERB (See **endue**)

relapse VERB
to return to a previous position; to settle or fall back
• *I relapsed into my chair.*—THE SIGN OF FOUR, ARTHUR CONAN DOYLE
USAGE In modern English, you might expect to *relapse* into a condition rather than a position or place.

relation NOUN
1 a relationship
• *Silas's relation to Eppie*—SILAS MARNER, GEORGE ELIOT
2 a spoken account of something
• *Mrs Rushworth began her relation.*—MANSFIELD PARK, JANE AUSTEN

reliance NOUN
1 trust; dependence
• *My son's tutor is a conscientious gentleman; and … I … have reliance on him.*—DAVID COPPERFIELD, CHARLES DICKENS
2 a person or thing that you depend on
• *his lonely daughter, bereft of her final hope and reliance*—A TALE OF TWO CITIES, CHARLES DICKENS

relic NOUN
an object surviving from an earlier time, especially an interesting or holy one
• *Miss Havisham had settled down … upon the floor, among the faded bridal relics.*—GREAT EXPECTATIONS, CHARLES DICKENS

relict NOUN
a widow
• *Forty years at least had elapsed since … the death of Mr Pipchin; but his relict still wore black bombazeen.*—DOMBEY AND SON, CHARLES DICKENS
RELATED WORD *Relict* and *relic* are both from the same Latin root.

relieve VERB
to give relief (charitable help) to someone
• *losses that would be felt only by the poorer sort, whom charity would relieve*—THE MILL ON THE FLOSS, GEORGE ELIOT

relieving officer NOUN
an official with the job of giving relief (charitable help) to the poor in a parish
• *A relieving officer is not used to being cut.*—meaning ignored or snubbed.—TALES OF MEAN STREETS, ARTHUR MORRISON

Religion and philosophy

Religion played a prominent part in many people's lives. However, Darwin's theory of evolution and other scientific advances changed people's understanding of the world. Darwin's theory seemed to go against religious teachings that God made the earth and all living things. Many saw it as a direct attack on their faith. Philosophical movements such as Romanticism in the early part of the century, Marxism, and Utilitarianism also dominated British society at the time.

---

relish NOUN
a delicious taste
• *[These] snacks had such a relish in the mouths of these young Toodles, that … they performed private dances of ecstasy among themselves.*—DOMBEY AND SON, CHARLES DICKENS

remark VERB
to notice something
• *Did you ever remark that door?*—THE STRANGE CASE OF DR JEKYLL AND MR HYDE, ROBERT LOUIS STEVENSON
🏛 French *remarquer* meaning 'to notice, to note'

remark NOUN
comment; notice
• *It is worthy of remark … that these people are … very proud.*—BLEAK HOUSE, CHARLES DICKENS

remembrance NOUN
(a) memory
• *There were four similar occasions, to the best of my remembrance.*—GREAT EXPECTATIONS, CHARLES DICKENS

remembrancer NOUN
a reminder; a memento
• *the divine ideas of liberty and self sacrifice of which these sights were the monuments and the remembrancers*—FRANKENSTEIN, MARY SHELLEY

remissness to repose

remissness NOUN
neglect of a duty; carelessness or forgetfulness
- *The general ... [was] offended every morning by Frederick's remissness in writing.*—NORTHANGER ABBEY, JANE AUSTEN

remittent ADJECTIVE
coming and going; fluctuating
- *[The dying woman] lay there almost unheeded: the very servants paid her but a remittent attention.*—JANE EYRE, CHARLOTTE BRONTË

remonstrance NOUN
an expression of disapproval; a protest
- *After some ineffectual remonstrance I kept away from him.*—THE WAR OF THE WORLDS, H. G. WELLS

remonstrate VERB
to protest; to express disapproval
- *'Don't be cheeky, Jack,' remonstrated the landlord.*—GREAT EXPECTATIONS, CHARLES DICKENS

remotely ADVERB
from or at a distance; indirectly
- *Farfrae asked ... questions in the comfortably indifferent tone of one whom the matter very remotely concerned.*—THE MAYOR OF CASTERBRIDGE, THOMAS HARDY

remove VERB
to move or go somewhere
- *She ... then left the sofa, removing to a seat by her sister.*—EMMA, JANE AUSTEN
- *When the ladies removed after dinner, Elizabeth ran up to her sister.*—PRIDE AND PREJUDICE, JANE AUSTEN
- ➤ **removal** NOUN • *Mrs Dashwood [remained] at the cottage, without attempting a removal to Delaford.*—SENSE AND SENSIBILITY, JANE AUSTEN

remunerate VERB
to pay or reward someone
- *I felt that no suit of clothes could possibly remunerate him for his pains.*—GREAT EXPECTATIONS, CHARLES DICKENS
- ➤ **remuneration** NOUN • *Mary was to work for two years without any remuneration.*—MARY BARTON, ELIZABETH GASKELL
- ➤ **remunerative** ADJECTIVE lucrative • *Much depends upon our being able to find remunerative investments for our funds.*—THE ADVENTURES OF SHERLOCK HOLMES, ARTHUR CONAN DOYLE

rencounter (also **rencontre**) NOUN
a chance meeting; an encounter
- *During this interval ... all my acquaintance with him was confined to an occasional rencontre in the hall.*—JANE EYRE, CHARLOTTE BRONTË
- 🏛 French *rencontre* meaning 'meeting'; *rencontrer* meaning 'to meet'

rend (past tense and past participle **rent**) VERB
to tear or pierce something
- *The night—its silence—its rest, was rent in twain by a savage ... sound that ran from end to end of Thornfield Hall.*—JANE EYRE, CHARLOTTE BRONTË

renovated ADJECTIVE
renewed; refreshed
- *Mary watched ... with a renovated keenness of perception.*—MARY BARTON, ELIZABETH GASKELL

repair VERB
to go somewhere
- *In Meryton they parted; the two youngest repaired to the lodgings of one of the officers' wives.*—PRIDE AND PREJUDICE, JANE AUSTEN

repass VERB
to pass again
- *Old Barley was growling and swearing when we repassed his door.*—GREAT EXPECTATIONS, CHARLES DICKENS

repast NOUN
a meal
- *The breakfast laid out was 'a substantial repast of coffee, eggs, and a cold ham'.*—TESS OF THE D'URBERVILLES, THOMAS HARDY

repetition NOUN
the reciting of poems or passages from memory; a recitation from memory
- *Prepare your lessons for repetition.*—SHIRLEY, CHARLOTTE BRONTË

repine VERB
to express or feel sadness or regret
- *Mrs Bennet still continued to wonder and repine at [Mr Bingley's] returning no more.*—PRIDE AND PREJUDICE, JANE AUSTEN
- ➤ **repining** NOUN • *Elizabeth is disappointed not to get a letter from Jane, 'but on the third [day], her repining was over'.*—PRIDE AND PREJUDICE, JANE AUSTEN

repose VERB
1 to rest; to sleep
- *Then the two invalids were ordered to repose.*—LITTLE WOMEN, LOUISA M. ALCOTT
2 to lie or rest somewhere
- *How charming she looked ... with her fair long curls reposing on her white shoulders.*—VILLETTE, CHARLOTTE BRONTË
3 to put your confidence or trust in someone
- *Mrs Poole [is] close and quiet; any one may repose confidence in her.*—JANE EYRE, CHARLOTTE BRONTË

repose NOUN
calm or tranquillity; rest
- *This idea pursued me and tormented me at every moment from which I might otherwise have snatched repose and peace.*—FRANKENSTEIN, MARY SHELLEY

represent to retard

➤ **reposeful** *ADJECTIVE* • Her mother's marriage had given Elizabeth a *'reposeful, easy, affluent life'.*
—THE MAYOR OF CASTERBRIDGE, THOMAS HARDY

represent *VERB*
1 to describe or say something
• *She represented to her sister as forcibly as possible what she felt on the subject.*—PRIDE AND PREJUDICE, JANE AUSTEN
2 to portray or depict something
• *These pictures were in water-colours. The first represented clouds ... over a swollen sea.*—JANE EYRE, CHARLOTTE BRONTË

representation *NOUN*
1 a description or opinion of someone or something
• *I know those who would be shocked by such a representation of Mr Elliot.*—PERSUASION, JANE AUSTEN
2 a picture or portrait
• *The drawing is 'a very faithful representation of Mr Rochester'.*—JANE EYRE, CHARLOTTE BRONTË

reprobate *VERB*
to disapprove of; to express disapproval of
• *I attach no importance to such an insolent observation as this on the part of a servant. I reprobated it at the time.*—THE WOMAN IN WHITE, WILKIE COLLINS
➤ **reprobation** *NOUN* • *Tom ... had always heard such people spoken of by his own friends with contempt and reprobation.*—THE MILL ON THE FLOSS, GEORGE ELIOT

reprobate *ADJECTIVE*
immoral; beyond salvation
• *The Church ... [watches] over its children to the last; never abandoning them until they are hopelessly reprobate.*—THE MILL ON THE FLOSS, GEORGE ELIOT

reprove *VERB*
to scold or criticize someone
• *No one had reproved John for wantonly striking me.*—JANE EYRE, CHARLOTTE BRONTË
➤ **reprovingly** *ADVERB* • *'Mama!' said Kate reprovingly. 'To think of such a thing!'*—NICHOLAS NICKLEBY, CHARLES DICKENS

repudiate *VERB*
to reject something or someone; to deny something
• *I ... should in my heart of hearts have repudiated the idea.*—GREAT EXPECTATIONS, CHARLES DICKENS

repugnance *NOUN*
dislike of something or someone
• *Their sense of his usefulness would have counteracted any repugnance or suspicion.*—SILAS MARNER, GEORGE ELIOT

repulse *VERB*
to reject someone; to turn someone away
• *'Why do you repulse me?' 'I don't repulse you. I like you to tell me you love me.'*—TESS OF THE D'URBERVILLES, THOMAS HARDY

repulse *NOUN*
a rejection
• *He hesitated and blushed, and positively trembled from fear of a repulse.*—VILLETTE, CHARLOTTE BRONTË

repulsive *ADJECTIVE*
unfriendly; unsympathetic
• *Mary was not so repulsive and unsisterly as Elizabeth.*—PERSUASION, JANE AUSTEN

requite *VERB*
to repay or return someone's actions or feelings
• *I had feelings of affection, and they were requited by detestation and scorn.*—FRANKENSTEIN, MARY SHELLEY

resent *VERB*
to express anger or disappointment
• *Miss Bingley warmly resented the indignity he had received.*—PRIDE AND PREJUDICE, JANE AUSTEN

reserve *NOUN*
1 lack of openness; unwillingness to show feelings or share information
• *His reserve springs from an aversion to showy displays of feeling.*—WUTHERING HEIGHTS, EMILY BRONTË
2 something not told to someone
• *Jane could have no reserves from Elizabeth.*—PRIDE AND PREJUDICE, JANE AUSTEN

resistless *ADJECTIVE*
impossible to resist
• *A resistless and almost frantic impulse urged me forward.*—FRANKENSTEIN, MARY SHELLEY

resort *NOUN*
a tendency to be visited; a place often visited
• *The Rainbow, in Marner's view, was a place of luxurious resort for rich and stout husbands.*—SILAS MARNER, GEORGE ELIOT
USAGE In modern English, you might expect a *resort* only to be a place where you go on holiday.

resort *VERB*
to go somewhere often
• *The Princess's Arms was also there, and much resorted to by splendid footmen.*—DOMBEY AND SON, CHARLES DICKENS

retard *VERB*
to delay someone or something
• *Out of the arched doorway in the tower came slowly, retarded by friendly greetings and questions, the richer parishioners.*—SILAS MARNER, GEORGE ELIOT

retardation to rheumatics

retardation NOUN
a slowing down; a delay
• There was concern about the planet Neptune and *'a suspected retardation in its velocity'.*—THE STAR, H. G. WELLS

reticule NOUN
a small, decorated drawstring bag
• She took from her reticule a morsel of sweet-cake. —SHIRLEY, CHARLOTTE BRONTË

retire VERB
1 to go somewhere, especially somewhere more private
• After tea, Mr Bennet retired to the library.—PRIDE AND PREJUDICE, JANE AUSTEN
2 to go to bed
• I retired for the night.—GREAT EXPECTATIONS, CHARLES DICKENS
3 to go back or backwards
• Oliver ... not knowing whether to advance or retire, stood looking on in silent amazement.—OLIVER TWIST, CHARLES DICKENS
🏛 French *retirer*, from *re-* 'back' + *tirer* 'draw'

retired ADJECTIVE
quiet, secluded
• Charmouth has a *'sweet, retired bay, backed by dark cliffs'.*—PERSUASION, JANE AUSTEN

retirement NOUN
1 a quiet or secluded place or situation; a state of being quiet and away from others
• I like Thornfield, its antiquity, its retirement, its old crow trees and thorn trees.—JANE EYRE, CHARLOTTE BRONTË
2 the action of going to bed or going somewhere more private
• I had, before my final retirement, a small interval alone.—THE TURN OF THE SCREW, HENRY JAMES

retort VERB
➢ **retort on someone / retort upon someone:** to use their own insult, accusation, or argument against someone • Lady Lucas felt *'triumph on being able to retort on Mrs Bennet the comfort of having a daughter well married'.*—PRIDE AND PREJUDICE, JANE AUSTEN

retort NOUN
a glass container with a long neck, used in a laboratory for distilling, etc.
• Broad, low tables were scattered about, which bristled with retorts, test-tubes, and little Bunsen lamps. —A STUDY IN SCARLET, ARTHUR CONAN DOYLE

retrieve VERB
to set something right; to make amends for something
• He is to have *'the opportunity of retrieving his former vices'.*—OLIVER TWIST, CHARLES DICKENS

➢ **retrieval** NOUN • *In Godfrey's case ... any retrieval of his error became more and more difficult.* —SILAS MARNER, GEORGE ELIOT

retrospect NOUN
a review of past events; the action of looking back
• Mr Deane ... [entered] with great readiness into a retrospect of his own career.—THE MILL ON THE FLOSS, GEORGE ELIOT

return VERB
to reply
• 'Why, of course, my dear boy,' returned Herbert, in a tone of surprise.—GREAT EXPECTATIONS, CHARLES DICKENS

return NOUN
thanks or acknowledgement for something someone has done
• And this is the return you make me for all the indulgences I've heaped on you?—THE MILL ON THE FLOSS, GEORGE ELIOT

review VERB
to think about something again
• I can scarcely bear to review the times to which I allude.—JANE EYRE, CHARLOTTE BRONTË

review NOUN
the act of thinking about something again
• Her astonishment, as she reflected on what had passed, was increased by every review of it.—PRIDE AND PREJUDICE, JANE AUSTEN

revolve VERB
to think about or consider something
• I have ... revolved the subject in my thoughts ever since you first mentioned your wish.—SHIRLEY, CHARLOTTE BRONTË

revulsion NOUN
a strong emotional reaction; a sudden change in someone's feelings
• We sat down together ... and the revulsion of feeling was so great that really I think we cried with joy.—KING SOLOMON'S MINES, H. RIDER HAGGARD

reynard (also **Reynard**) NOUN
a fox
• There would be no fun in fox-hunting, if Reynard yielded himself up without any effort to escape. —MARY BARTON, ELIZABETH GASKELL

rhapsody NOUN
an intense or poetic expression of feeling
• The rhapsody welled up within me ... and gushed out. —GREAT EXPECTATIONS, CHARLES DICKENS

rheumatics (also **rheumatize**) NOUN
rheumatism
• The Sergeant says he has *'a touch of the rheumatics in my back'.*—THE MOONSTONE, WILKIE COLLINS

ribald to rough

ribald *NOUN*
a vulgar, crude person
• *I hold him ... to be a ribald and an ignoramus.*
—WESTWARD HO!, CHARLES KINGSLEY

riband *NOUN*
a ribbon; a strip
• *Few people travelled this way ... and the long white riband of gravel that stretched before them was empty.*—WESSEX TALES, THOMAS HARDY

rick *NOUN*
a pile of hay, corn, etc. formed into a regular shape
• *wheat and barley ricks*—THE MAYOR OF CASTERBRIDGE, THOMAS HARDY
• *Pip is treated as if he has 'picked a pocket or fired a rick'*—*set fire to a rick.*—GREAT EXPECTATIONS, CHARLES DICKENS

rime *NOUN*
frost
• *A frosty rime was on his head, and on his eyebrows, and his wiry chin.*—A CHRISTMAS CAROL, CHARLES DICKENS

ring *VERB*
to put a ring through the nose of an animal
• *I know ... they'd make a fighting and a crying as if you was ringing the pigs.*—SILAS MARNER, GEORGE ELIOT

riot *NOUN*
uncontrolled or drunken behaviour
• *Assuredly ... there were some whom ... even riot could never drive into brutality.*—SILAS MARNER, GEORGE ELIOT

riot *VERB*
to behave or happen in an uncontrolled way
• *I had cast off all feeling ... to riot in the excess of my despair.*—FRANKENSTEIN, MARY SHELLEY

rive (say ryv) *VERB*
to tear; to split
• *He's ... riven up a whole row o' t' grandest currant-trees i' t' garden!*—WUTHERING HEIGHTS, EMILY BRONTË

Local accents

The quotation at *rive* shows how the character (Joseph) speaks.

Characters may speak in dialect or with a local accent. When their speech is written to reflect this, it can be easier to understand it by saying it aloud.
• *If Master Dowlas wants to know the **truh** on it ... let him go and stan' by himself—there's nobody **'ull** hinder him.*—SILAS MARNER, GEORGE ELIOT

The context of the sentence (or the wider context) can also help you to understand the vocabulary.

---

roasting-jack *NOUN*
a device with cog wheels and a handle for turning a spit (for roasting meat) over a fire

rockwork *NOUN*
a pile or group of rocks
• *I ... came to ... a rockwork that enabled me to get to the top [of the wall].*—THE WAR OF THE WORLDS, H. G. WELLS

Röntgen vibration (also **Röntgen ray**) *NOUN*
an X-ray
• *those Röntgen Rays there was so much talk about a year or so ago*—THE FIRST MEN IN THE MOON, H. G. WELLS
🏛 From the German physicist *Wilhelm Röntgen*, who discovered X-rays in 1895.

roof-tree *NOUN*
the top part of a roof, where the sloping sides met
• *From amid the branches there jutted out the grey gables and high roof-tree of a very old mansion.*—THE ADVENTURES OF SHERLOCK HOLMES, ARTHUR CONAN DOYLE
USAGE This word was also used figuratively to mean someone's home.
• *Dr and Mrs Blimber ... had been invited on a visit to the paternal roof-tree.*—DOMBEY AND SON, CHARLES DICKENS

rookery *NOUN*
a densely-populated slum
• *The whole rookery furnishes such a hateful and repulsive spectacle as can hardly be equalled.*—THE CONDITION OF THE WORKING CLASS IN ENGLAND, FRIEDRICH ENGELS

rooted *ADJECTIVE*
strongly-felt and unlikely to change; entrenched
• *He evidently has a rooted feeling on this point.*—BLEAK HOUSE, CHARLES DICKENS

rose (also **shoe rose**) *NOUN*
a rosette decorating the front of a shoe
• *He wore ... high-heeled shoes, with roses in them.*—RIP VAN WINKLE, WASHINGTON IRVING

rosery *NOUN*
a rose garden
• *Sergeant Cuff looked through the evergreen arch on our left, spied out our rosery, and walked straight in.*—THE MOONSTONE, WILKIE COLLINS

rough *NOUN*
a violent, noisy, or bad person
• *In Wellington Street my brother met a couple of sturdy roughs.*—THE WAR OF THE WORLDS, H. G. WELLS

round ADJECTIVE
1 large in amount
• *Now, Moses, this casket is worth a good round sum.*—UNDER THE WAVES, R. M. BALLANTYNE
2 rich and smooth-sounding
• *'Well, Sir,' said Doctor Parker Peps in a round, deep, sonorous voice.*—DOMBEY AND SON, CHARLES DICKENS

round NOUN
1 a rung of a ladder; a rung or level in a hierarchy
• *[The trees'] trunks were like the rounds of a ladder, by which we mounted.*—KIDNAPPED, ROBERT LOUIS STEVENSON
• *You'll prosper i' the world, my lad; you'll maybe see the day when Wakem and his son 'ull be a round or two below you.*—THE MILL ON THE FLOSS, GEORGE ELIOT
2 a thick round joint of beef cut from the leg
• *the rounds of beef and the barrels of ale*—SILAS MARNER, GEORGE ELIOT
3 a fight; a bout
• *There's my son Godfrey'll be wanting to have a round with you if you run off with Miss Nancy.*—SILAS MARNER, GEORGE ELIOT

round-house NOUN
a cabin or cabins at the back of a ship's upper deck, usually used by the ship's officers
• *The cabin-boy Ransome ... came in at times from the round-house, where he berthed and served.*—KIDNAPPED, ROBERT LOUIS STEVENSON

round-shot NOUN
metal balls fired from a cannon; a firing from a cannon
• *The pirate ship 'let fly with roundshot at close quarters'.*—DREAM DAYS, KENNETH GRAHAME

rowel NOUN
a spiked disc at the end of a spur
• *I had no spurs, neither was my horse one to need the rowel.*—LORNA DOONE, R. D. BLACKMORE

rubber NOUN
a game of cards, usually bridge
• *I dare say you will have no objection to join us in a rubber; shall you?*—MANSFIELD PARK, JANE AUSTEN

Rubicon NOUN
a point of no return
• *I began ... to feel that the Rubicon was passed.*—JANE EYRE, CHARLOTTE BRONTË
🏛 The Rubicon was a river which Julius Caesar crossed into Italy with his army, making war with the Roman Senate and Pompey inevitable.

rubicund ADJECTIVE
red-faced; red
• *He had a chubby, rubicund face.*—THE FIRST MEN IN THE MOON, H. G. WELLS

rude ADJECTIVE
1 roughly made; crude or unsophisticated
• *Close to the rude landing-stage was a small brick house.*—THE SIGN OF FOUR, ARTHUR CONAN DOYLE
2 ignorant; uneducated
• *The rude mind with difficulty associates the ideas of power and benignity.*—SILAS MARNER, GEORGE ELIOT
3 shockingly direct or sudden; abrupt
• *I should certainly have shocked Mr Fairlie by some of the hardest and rudest truths he has ever heard in his life.*—THE WOMAN IN WHITE, WILKIE COLLINS

ruin VERB
to destroy someone's good reputation
• *You heard him tell the Count that he believed his wife knew enough to ruin him?*—THE WOMAN IN WHITE, WILKIE COLLINS

ruin NOUN
the destruction of someone's good reputation
• *Loss of virtue in a female is irretrievable ... one false step involves her in endless ruin.*—PRIDE AND PREJUDICE, JANE AUSTEN

rum ADJECTIVE
strange; odd
• *'Lor, Noah!' said Charlotte, 'what a rum creature you are!'*—OLIVER TWIST, CHARLES DICKENS

rushlight NOUN
a candle made from the inside part of a rush dipped in tallow (animal fat)
• *The next day commenced as before, getting up and dressing by rushlight.*—JANE EYRE, CHARLOTTE BRONTË

ruth NOUN
pity; compassion
• *I came back to her now with no other emotion than a sort of ruth for her great sufferings.*—JANE EYRE, CHARLOTTE BRONTË

Ss

SLAVERY

The **slave trade** saw people from Africa captured and shipped to America and Britain to be forced to work as **slaves**. William Wilberforce campaigned for the abolition of the slave trade in Britain and, in **1807**, a law made it illegal to carry slaves on British ships. However it was only in **1833** that slaves were freed in British territories around the world. Slave owners received financial compensation from the government for the loss of their slaves.

sable ADJECTIVE
black
• *a team of four sable horses*—THE POMEGRANATE SEEDS, NATHANIEL HAWTHORNE

sacque NOUN
a loose-fitting back on a dress, coat, or jacket, with fabric falling from the shoulders
• *My silk sacque isn't a bit the fashion.*—LITTLE MEN, LOUISA M. ALCOTT

saddle-bow NOUN
a curved part that sticks up at the front or back of a saddle
• *This servant had ... a net of lemons (to brew punch with) hanging at the saddle-bow.*—KIDNAPPED, ROBERT LOUIS STEVENSON

sagacious ADJECTIVE
wise or shrewd; showing good mental abilities
• *a sagacious citizen and householder, bound to impart ... wisdom to an inexperienced youth*—DOMBEY AND SON, CHARLES DICKENS
➤ **sagaciously** ADVERB • *But if these suspicions were really his, he sagaciously refrained from verbally expressing them.*—MOBY DICK, HERMAN MELVILLE

sagacity NOUN
good mental abilities; wisdom or cleverness
• *Here ... was a problem which would tax his sagacity to the utmost.*—THE SIGN OF FOUR, ARTHUR CONAN DOYLE

salamander NOUN
a metal plate, heated and put over food to brown it
• *From the belief that the salamander, a type of lizard, could live in or be unharmed by fire.*

sally NOUN
1 a witty or lively remark
• *I heard ... how the father doted on the smiles of the infant, and the lively sallies of the older child.* —FRANKENSTEIN, MARY SHELLEY
2 an outing; an act of going out somewhere
• *Well ... there came a night when he made one of those drunken sallies from which he never came back.*—THE ADVENTURES OF SHERLOCK HOLMES, ARTHUR CONAN DOYLE

sally VERB
to set off somewhere, especially in a determined or daring way
• *Several clods of earth are thrown at Sid before Aunt Polly can 'collect her surprised faculties and sally to the rescue'.*—THE ADVENTURES OF TOM SAWYER, MARK TWAIN

saloon NOUN
1 a sitting or dining room
• *the saloon where they were all seated at dinner* —JANE EYRE, CHARLOTTE BRONTË
2 a public room or building
• *the great saloons of the British Museum*   RIP VAN WINKLE, WASHINGTON IRVING

salutary ADJECTIVE
good for the health
• *There was no time to be lost in getting Cleopatra to any place recommended as being salutary.* —DOMBEY AND SON, CHARLES DICKENS

sal-volatile NOUN
scented ammonium carbonate, used as smelling salts to revive someone after fainting, etc.
• *[She] had what they call an hysterical attack, took a dose of sal-volatile ... and was sent back to her bed.* —THE MOONSTONE, WILKIE COLLINS

same PRONOUN
➤ **the same:** the person or thing referred to
• *Miss Smith put into my hands a border of muslin ... with directions to hem the same.*—JANE EYRE, CHARLOTTE BRONTË

sanction VERB
to approve something; to permit something
• *Sarah could render no reason that would be sanctioned by the feeling of the community.* —SILAS MARNER, GEORGE ELIOT

sanction to scantling

sanction NOUN
permission; approval
• Mary's meetings with Mr Carson are *'unknown to her father, and certain, even did he know it, to fail of obtaining his sanction'*.—MARY BARTON, ELIZABETH GASKELL

sanguinary ADJECTIVE
bloody; bloodthirsty
• The Amphitheatre has sinister associations, partly because of *'the sanguinary nature of the games originally played therein'*.—THE MAYOR OF CASTERBRIDGE, THOMAS HARDY

sanguine ADJECTIVE
cheerful; optimistic
• *I know that had I been a sanguine, brilliant, careless ... romping child ... Mrs Reed would have endured my presence more complacently.*—JANE EYRE, CHARLOTTE BRONTË

sargasso NOUN
a kind of seaweed with air vessels like berries, usually floating in a mass
• *All around floated the sargasso beds, clogging her bows with their long snaky coils of weed.*—WESTWARD HO!, CHARLES KINGSLEY

sash NOUN
a window able to be slid up or down
• *[He] flew over to the window and threw up the sash.*—DRACULA, BRAM STOKER

sate VERB
1 sat
• *[Maggie's] mother sate crying at night.*—THE MILL ON THE FLOSS, GEORGE ELIOT
2 to satisfy someone's appetite, thirst, or desire

satirical ADJECTIVE
critical; sarcastic or mocking
• *He has a very satirical eye.*—PRIDE AND PREJUDICE, JANE AUSTEN

saturnine ADJECTIVE
looking gloomy and mysterious
• Heathcliff is described as *'grim and saturnine'*.—WUTHERING HEIGHTS, EMILY BRONTË

saucy NOUN
insolent; presumptuous; rude
• *Oh! how heartily did she grieve over ... every saucy speech she had ever directed towards him.*—PRIDE AND PREJUDICE, JANE AUSTEN

savage ADJECTIVE
1 wild; brutal
• *a savage laugh*—THE STRANGE CASE OF DR JEKYLL AND MR HYDE, ROBERT LOUIS STEVENSON
2 primitive; uncivilized
• *a savage inhabitant of some undiscovered island*—FRANKENSTEIN, MARY SHELLEY

savage NOUN
a primitive or uncivilized person
• *'A savage!' I exclaimed.*—THE SIGN OF FOUR, ARTHUR CONAN DOYLE

save PREPOSITION
except
• *I ... saw nothing on [the paper] save a few dingy stains of paint.*—JANE EYRE, CHARLOTTE BRONTË
• *[The house] was as dark as its neighbours, save for a single glimmer in the kitchen window.*—THE SIGN OF FOUR, ARTHUR CONAN DOYLE

savour NOUN
1 the taste or smell of something
• *The savour of the stew had floated from the cottage into the porch.*—THE MAYOR OF CASTERBRIDGE, THOMAS HARDY
2 enjoyment; delight
• *[They] would have ... found great savour in [the] marvellous anecdotes.*—SHIRLEY, CHARLOTTE BRONTË
3 a hint, trace, or impression of something
• *the savor of danger*—MEN OF IRON, HOWARD PYLE

savour VERB
to give the impression of something; to have a hint or trace of something
• *Take care, Lizzy; that speech savours strongly of disappointment.*—PRIDE AND PREJUDICE, JANE AUSTEN

savoury ADJECTIVE
1 appetizing; smelling or tasting good
• *Silas was thinking ... of his supper: ... it would be hot and savoury.*—SILAS MARNER, GEORGE ELIOT
2 reputable or acceptable; wholesome
• *Mr Cruncher's apartments were not in a savoury neighbourhood.*—A TALE OF TWO CITIES, CHARLES DICKENS

sawpit NOUN
a hole in the ground where wood was cut into planks by two men using a vertical saw
• *The snow makes it 'worse to walk than in a saw-pit newly used'.*—LORNA DOONE, R. D. BLACKMORE

scamp NOUN
a bad person; a rogue
• *Are you turning out a scamp? I tell you I won't have it.*—SILAS MARNER, GEORGE ELIOT

scantling NOUN
a small amount or number
• *Now last night, afore I went to bed, I only had a scantling o' cheese.*—THE MAYOR OF CASTERBRIDGE, THOMAS HARDY

scapegrace *to* scruple

scapegrace NOUN
a mischievous person; a rascal
• *Tom was a scapegrace, poor fellow, and always wanted help of one kind or another.*—MARY BARTON, ELIZABETH GASKELL

scaramouch (say **skarr-uh-mowch, skarr-uh-mooch**) NOUN
a boastful coward; a scoundrel
• *Stubb had exclaimed 'That's he! that's he!—the long-togged scaramouch ...!'*—MOBY DICK, HERMAN MELVILLE

scathe VERB
1 to burn or scorch something
• *The tree had been scathed by lightning.*—THE LEGEND OF SLEEPY HOLLOW, WASHINGTON IRVING
2 to injure or hurt someone
• *[He cast] a glance which scathed, or was intended to scathe, as it crossed me.*—VILLETTE, CHARLOTTE BRONTË

scathe (also **scath**) NOUN
injury; harm
• *I had ... come through these hardships and fearful perils without scath.*—KIDNAPPED, ROBERT LOUIS STEVENSON

scheme NOUN
a plan or idea
• *But you need not be a missionary. You might relinquish that scheme.*—JANE EYRE, CHARLOTTE BRONTË

schismatic (say **siz-mat-ik, skiz-mat-ik**) NOUN
a member of a group of believers who had separated from the mainstream Church
• *[These ideas] hardly survive except ... in the narrow communities of schismatics.*—THE MILL ON THE FLOSS, GEORGE ELIOT

scholar NOUN
a student
• *It is a village school: your scholars will be only poor girls.*—JANE EYRE, CHARLOTTE BRONTË

schooner NOUN
a sailing ship with two or more masts
• *The searchlight discovered some distance away a schooner with all sails set.*—DRACULA, BRAM STOKER

science NOUN
knowledge, study, or skill
• *You had not enough of the artist's skill and science.*—JANE EYRE, CHARLOTTE BRONTË

scion (say **sy-uhn**) NOUN
a descendant
• *the last scion of Saxon royalty*—IVANHOE, WALTER SCOTT

scold NOUN
a woman using bad or angry language
• *Who are you, I should like to know, that you dare to call me a scold?*—THE GREEN FAIRY BOOK, ANDREW LANG

sconce NOUN
1 a wall bracket for holding a candle
• *She carried a ... candle ... which she had probably taken from one of the sconces in her own room.*—GREAT EXPECTATIONS, CHARLES DICKENS
2 a humorous word for someone's head
• *Blows, aimed at me, fell on other sconces.*—WUTHERING HEIGHTS, EMILY BRONTË

score NOUN
twenty
• *Mr Macey [was] now a very feeble old man of fourscore and six.*—SILAS MARNER, GEORGE ELIOT
➤ **a score of:** a great deal of; many • *Peggotty said she would walk a score of miles to see him.*—DAVID COPPERFIELD, CHARLES DICKENS
➤ **on the score of:** on account of; with regard to
• *Mrs Bennet should only hear of [their] departure ... , without being alarmed on the score of the gentleman's conduct.*—PRIDE AND PREJUDICE, JANE AUSTEN

scrag NOUN
a neck; a cheap cut of meat from an animal's neck
• *Jane, I have your little pearl necklace ... fastened round my ... scrag under my cravat.*—JANE EYRE, CHARLOTTE BRONTË

screen NOUN
1 a panel or hanging used for dividing a room or for shielding someone from something
• *In front of the two large fire-places stood great screens broidered with parrots and peacocks.*—THE BIRTHDAY OF THE INFANTA, OSCAR WILDE
2 a hand-held panel used for shielding your face from the heat of the fire in the grate, or carried as a fashion accessory
• *My Lady ... sits before the fire with her screen in her hand.*—BLEAK HOUSE, CHARLES DICKENS

screw NOUN
a person who was mean with money
• *a wicked old screw*—A CHRISTMAS CAROL, CHARLES DICKENS

scruple NOUN
1 a hesitation or doubt because you thought something might be morally wrong
• *After abusing you so abominably to your face, I could have no scruple in abusing you to all your relations.*—PRIDE AND PREJUDICE, JANE AUSTEN
2 a very small amount of something
• *Jekyll risks being killed 'by the least scruple of an overdose'.*—THE STRANGE CASE OF DR JEKYLL AND MR HYDE, ROBERT LOUIS STEVENSON

scruple to self-conquest

scruple VERB
to hesitate to do something because you thought it might be wrong
• *The young man ... did not scruple publicly to insult Mr Clare, without respect for his gray hairs.*—TESS OF THE D'URBERVILLES, THOMAS HARDY

scrupulous ADJECTIVE
wanting to do the right thing; hesitant or doubtful as a result
• *Mr Folair was ... a man who delighted in mischief, and was by no means scrupulous.*—NICHOLAS NICKLEBY, CHARLES DICKENS

scud NOUN
a cloud, gust of wind, or shower of rain moving quickly across a place
• *The scud had banked over the moon, and it was now quite dark.*—THE STRANGE CASE OF DR JEKYLL AND MR HYDE, ROBERT LOUIS STEVENSON

scullery NOUN
a small kitchen or room next to a kitchen, for washing dishes and other housework

scullion NOUN
a kitchen servant who did menial tasks
• *Instructions are to be given to all of the servants 'from the cook to the scullion'.*—THE MOONSTONE, WILKIE COLLINS

seal NOUN
an engraved object used for stamping a pattern into wax on a document
• *a steel watch-chain to which were attached some large gold seals*—NICHOLAS NICKLEBY, CHARLES DICKENS

season NOUN
a period of time
• *an untimely season, when he should have been asleep in bed*—JANE EYRE, CHARLOTTE BRONTË

seasonable ADJECTIVE
convenient, suitable, or well-timed
• *It is not a seasonable hour to intrude on Mr Oliver.*—JANE EYRE, CHARLOTTE BRONTË

secure ADJECTIVE
certain of something
• *Elizabeth says that 'those who never change their opinion' should be 'secure of judging properly at first'.*—PRIDE AND PREJUDICE, JANE AUSTEN
➤ **securely** ADVERB with certainty • *Maria could now speak so securely of her happiness.*—MANSFIELD PARK, JANE AUSTEN

secure VERB
1 to obtain or achieve something
• *No ... it is a long-cherished scheme, and the only one which can secure my great end.*—JANE EYRE, CHARLOTTE BRONTË
2 to protect or free someone from something
• *Charlotte's ... object was ... to secure [Elizabeth] from any return of Mr Collins's addresses, by engaging them towards herself.*—PRIDE AND PREJUDICE, JANE AUSTEN

security NOUN
1 confidence or certainty
• *He spoke of apprehension and anxiety, but his countenance expressed real security.*—PRIDE AND PREJUDICE, JANE AUSTEN
2 a guarantee or assurance
• *You ... must wait till to-morrow; to leave my tale half told, will ... be a sort of security that I shall appear at your breakfast table to finish it.*—JANE EYRE, CHARLOTTE BRONTË
3 protection or freedom from someone or something
• *Only Mr Tulkinghorn. Always at hand. Haunting every place. No relief or security from him for a moment.*—BLEAK HOUSE, CHARLES DICKENS
4 an investment in stocks, shares, or bonds
• *They appear to be lists of Stock Exchange securities.*—THE RETURN OF SHERLOCK HOLMES, ARTHUR CONAN DOYLE

sedan-chair NOUN
a seat for transporting a passenger, carried by people in front and behind holding horizontal poles
• *First marched two men, carrying an open sedan chair with a young girl in it.*—HEIDI, JOHANNA SPYRI

sedulously ADVERB
with great care; diligently
• *The clerk laid the two sheets of paper alongside and sedulously compared their contents.*—THE STRANGE CASE OF DR JEKYLL AND MR HYDE, ROBERT LOUIS STEVENSON

self-command NOUN
control over your emotions; self-control
• *This very pressure of emotion that she was in danger of finding too strong for her roused all her power of self-command.*—SILAS MARNER, GEORGE ELIOT

self-conquest NOUN
control over your own actions or emotions; self-control
• *For many moments he was mute, struggling for the self-conquest necessary to the uttering of the difficult words.*—SILAS MARNER, GEORGE ELIOT

self-conscious to sequestered

self-conscious ADJECTIVE
self-aware; acting deliberately
• Miss Ingram ... was ... remarkably self-conscious. ... [Her behaviour] might be clever, but it was decidedly not good-natured.—JANE EYRE, CHARLOTTE BRONTË

self-consequence NOUN
self-importance
• He entered the room with a look of self-consequence. —SENSE AND SENSIBILITY, JANE AUSTEN

self-forgetful ADJECTIVE
thinking of others rather than yourself
• But the good-natured self-forgetful cheeriness ... of Priscilla would soon have dissipated the ... suspicion. —SILAS MARNER, GEORGE ELIOT
➤ **self-forgetfulness** NOUN • It was like her self-forgetfulness to transfer the remark to my sister. —GREAT EXPECTATIONS, CHARLES DICKENS

sennight NOUN
a week
• 'How long have I been lying here?' said he. 'A sennight, my lord,' said Master Rudolph.—OTTO OF THE SILVER HAND, HOWARD PYLE

sensibility NOUN
1 sensitivity
• Elinor saw, with concern, the excess of her sister's sensibility.—SENSE AND SENSIBILITY, JANE AUSTEN
• the higher sensibility that accompanies higher culture —SILAS MARNER, GEORGE ELIOT
2 consciousness
• When Marner's sensibility returned, he ... closed his door, unaware of the chasm in his consciousness. —SILAS MARNER, GEORGE ELIOT

sensible ADJECTIVE
1 aware of something
• [Scrooge] became sensible of confused noises in the air.—A CHRISTMAS CAROL, CHARLES DICKENS
2 sensitive
• He had not been displeased with her thoughtfulness ... it was what every sensible woman would show.—TESS OF THE D'URBERVILLES, THOMAS HARDY
3 easily noticed or felt
• [Tom] felt a sensible relief from the cooling application to his wounds.—UNCLE TOM'S CABIN, HARRIET BEECHER STOWE

sensibly ADVERB
1 strongly; very noticeably
• It is a matter of great joy to me; and I feel the goodness of Colonel Brandon most sensibly.—SENSE AND SENSIBILITY, JANE AUSTEN
2 sensitively; perceptively
• [He] often talked so sensibly and feelingly about his faults.—BLEAK HOUSE, CHARLES DICKENS

Sentence structure

You may notice sentences which might be written differently in modern English, but which are not difficult to understand. Here are some examples.
• For a moment perhaps I stood there, breast-high in the almost boiling water ... **hopeless of** escape. —THE WAR OF THE WORLDS, H. G. WELLS
• Jane was already **so much** recovered **as to** intend leaving her room for a couple of hours that evening. —PRIDE AND PREJUDICE, JANE AUSTEN
• He had been in a rage with Dunstan, and had thought of nothing but a thorough **break-up** of their mutual understanding.—SILAS MARNER, GEORGE ELIOT

In some cases the different structures reflect dialect use.
• But ... there's reasons in things **as** nobody knows **on**. —SILAS MARNER, GEORGE ELIOT

Sometimes words are combined in a different order from modern English.
• I **doubted not** that I should ultimately succeed. —FRANKENSTEIN, MARY SHELLEY
• What good would it do if I bent, if I **uptore**, if I crushed her?—JANE EYRE, CHARLOTTE BRONTË

---

sententious ADJECTIVE
saying wise things, sometimes (but not necessarily) in a pompous way
• So wrote Master Frank, in a long sententious letter, full of Latin quotations.—WESTWARD HO!, CHARLES KINGSLEY
➤ **sententiously** ADVERB • 'To a great mind, nothing is little,' remarked Holmes, sententiously.—A STUDY IN SCARLET, ARTHUR CONAN DOYLE

sepulchre NOUN
a tomb
• The stone had shut Brunton into what had become his sepulchre.—THE MEMOIRS OF SHERLOCK HOLMES, ARTHUR CONAN DOYLE

sepulture NOUN
burial
• The old Roman burial ground is still used 'as a place of sepulture'.—THE MAYOR OF CASTERBRIDGE, THOMAS HARDY

sequestered ADJECTIVE
isolated; secluded
• There once lived, in a sequestered part of the county of Devonshire, one Mr Godfrey Nickleby.—NICHOLAS NICKLEBY, CHARLES DICKENS

sequestration to shikari

sequestration NOUN
1 the fact of staying or being kept away from other people; isolation
• He might ... write and inquire of Elizabeth; but his instinct for sequestration had made the course difficult.—THE MAYOR OF CASTERBRIDGE, THOMAS HARDY
2 legal confiscation
• the sequestration of emigrant property—A TALE OF TWO CITIES, CHARLES DICKENS

seraglio NOUN
a harem

sere ADJECTIVE
dry; withered
• The days shorten, the leaves grow sere.—VILLETTE, CHARLOTTE BRONTË
USAGE Forms of the phrase 'in the sere and yellow leaf' (a quotation from *Macbeth*) were sometimes used to mean that someone was old or near the end of their life.
• Well, if a man can stride four and a-half feet without the smallest effort, he can't be quite in the sere and yellow. A STUDY IN SCARLET—ARTHUR CONAN DOYLE,

serve VERB
1 to have a particular effect or function
• Everything which has occurred since then has served to confirm my original supposition.—A STUDY IN SCARLET, ARTHUR CONAN DOYLE
2 to be of use; to be good enough
• Our companions are excessively stupid. What shall we do to rouse them? Any nonsense will serve.—EMMA, JANE AUSTEN
3 to present itself
• From time to time, as occasion served, he bestowed a variety of earnest glances.—OLIVER TWIST, CHARLES DICKENS

servitor NOUN
1 an attendant to a person of high social rank
• The grand stone steps have 'troops of brilliantly costumed servitors flitting up and down'.—THE PRINCE AND THE PAUPER, MARK TWAIN
2 an Oxford University student who did menial tasks in exchange for financial help

set NOUN
the couples dancing in a group
• Elizabeth made no answer, and took her place in the set.—PRIDE AND PREJUDICE, JANE AUSTEN

set-down NOUN
a remark intended to make someone feel bad; a put-down
• I wish you had been there ... to have given him one of your set-downs.—PRIDE AND PREJUDICE, JANE AUSTEN

set-off NOUN
something that reduces a debt or cost; something that partly made up for something bad
• Mrs Nickleby wants 'to counterbalance Miss La Creevy, and be herself an effectual set-off and atonement'.—NICHOLAS NICKLEBY, CHARLES DICKENS

settle VERB
1 to give or leave money or property to someone legally
• His mother ... told him she would settle on him the Norfolk estate.—SENSE AND SENSIBILITY, JANE AUSTEN
2 to ensure a person's future well-being, for example, through marriage, education, or money
• I wish with all my heart she were well settled.—PRIDE AND PREJUDICE, JANE AUSTEN
3 to decide something
• It was settled that I should stay there all the rest of the day.—GREAT EXPECTATIONS, CHARLES DICKENS

settlement NOUN
a legal agreement to give or leave money or property to someone; the amount given or left
• the marriage settlement of his wife—THE WOMAN IN WHITE, WILKIE COLLINS

shade NOUN
1 a fault
• Implacable resentment is a shade in a character.—PRIDE AND PREJUDICE, JANE AUSTEN
2 a ghost or spirit
• You're particular, for a shade.—A CHRISTMAS CAROL, CHARLES DICKENS
➢ **a shade: a little** • They had been a shade better at dinner-time.—MARY BARTON, ELIZABETH GASKELL

sharper NOUN
a cheat at cards; a swindler
• He is beset by sharpers.—JANE EYRE, CHARLOTTE BRONTË

sharp-set ADJECTIVE
very hungry
• Now let us make the fire up and pluck the birds, for ... father and Egbert, if they return this evening, will be sharp-set.—THE DRAGON AND THE RAVEN, G. A. HENTY

shay-cart NOUN
a horse-drawn carriage; a chaise

shift VERB
➢ **shift for yourself:** to look after yourself; to manage without relying on others • No, no, let me shift for myself.—PRIDE AND PREJUDICE, JANE AUSTEN

shikari NOUN
in India, a big-game hunter
From Urdu / Hindi, originally from the Persian word *šikārī* meaning 'of hunting'

ship-breaker *to* shuck

ship-breaker NOUN
a worker or business that broke up old ships for scrap
• *ship-breakers' yards*—DAVID COPPERFIELD, CHARLES DICKENS

shipping-broker (also **ship-broker**) NOUN
a merchant who bought and sold ships, or arranged shipping insurance or other business to do with a ship

shipwright NOUN
a shipbuilder
• *The fleet's crews include 'shipwrights, masons, carpenters, smiths, and such like'*.—WESTWARD HO!, CHARLES KINGSLEY

shire NOUN
a county
• *From the well-known names of these towns I learn in what county I have lighted; a north-midland shire.*—JANE EYRE, CHARLOTTE BRONTË
USAGE Both Jane Austen and Charlotte Brontë use –shire in order to avoid saying which county was meant.
• *The officers of the —shire [regiment] were in general a very creditable, gentlemanlike set.*—PRIDE AND PREJUDICE, JANE AUSTEN

shirk VERB
to avoid work, duty, or something you should do
• *Most likely he supposed that I was inclined to shirk my promise.*—WUTHERING HEIGHTS, EMILY BRONTË
➤ **shirking** ADJECTIVE lazy; avoiding work
• *a shirking fellow of five-and-twenty*—THE UNCOMMERCIAL TRAVELLER, CHARLES DICKENS

shoal ADJECTIVE
shallow
• *The entrance to this northern anchorage was ... narrow and shoal.*—TREASURE ISLAND, ROBERT LOUIS STEVENSON

shoal-lighthouse NOUN
a lighthouse warning of shallow water over a sandbar, underwater ridge, etc.

shoeblack NOUN
someone, often a boy, whose job was to polish people's shoes

shoeing-stool NOUN
a low stool used when shoeing a horse

shoon NOUN
shoes
• *[Catherine] hates me, and does not think me fit to wipe her shoon!*—WUTHERING HEIGHTS, EMILY BRONTË

shopman NOUN
a shopkeeper or man who worked in a shop
• *Eight o'clock was striking ... and the apprentices and shopmen were slamming up the shutters.*—WESSEX TALES, THOMAS HARDY

short-winded ADJECTIVE
out of breath; easily getting short of breath
• *I am such a short-winded talker that I must think a bit.*—BLEAK HOUSE, CHARLES DICKENS

should VERB
would
• *I had a presentiment that I should never be there again.*—GREAT EXPECTATIONS, CHARLES DICKENS
• *I should have fallen into the hands of the [enemy] had it not been for [his] devotion and courage.*—A STUDY IN SCARLET, ARTHUR CONAN DOYLE

shove-groat NOUN
a game like shove-halfpenny, in which coins were slid across a board, using coins known as 'groats'
• *playing at shove-groat with Spanish doubloons*—WESTWARD HO!. CHARLES KINGSLEY

shovel-hat NOUN
a hat with a low, round top and the brim curling up at each side, worn in the past especially by clergymen
• *The rector's shovel-hat had passed the porch.*—SHIRLEY, CHARLOTTE BRONTË

shrewd ADJECTIVE
1 bitterly cold
• *It happened to be an iron-grey autumnal day, with a shrewd east wind blowing.*—DOMBEY AND SON, CHARLES DICKENS
2 (of a hit) hard; powerful
• *That was a shrewd blow he fetched thee on the crown.*—MEN OF IRON, HOWARD PYLE

shrift NOUN
absolution; forgiveness of sins
• *She whispered her avowal; her shrift was whispered back.*—VILLETTE, CHARLOTTE BRONTË
➤ **short shrift**: a short time between being condemned to death and being executed • *Alan says, 'If they got hands on me, it would be a short shrift and a lang tow for Alan!'*—meaning that he would quickly be hanged.—KIDNAPPED, ROBERT LOUIS STEVENSON

shuck NOUN
1 the outer husk of a corn cob
• *'A straw tick' (a mattress stuffed with straw) is said to be 'better than ... a shuck tick'*—a mattress stuffed with corn husks.—THE ADVENTURES OF HUCKLEBERRY FINN, MARK TWAIN

sibyl to slightingly

2 something worthless
- *I'm glad we found it out detective fashion; I wouldn't give shucks for any other way.*—THE ADVENTURES OF HUCKLEBERRY FINN, MARK TWAIN

sibyl NOUN
a woman who could foretell the future
- *She found herself in the presence of an old sibyl.*—IVANHOE, WALTER SCOTT

sicken VERB
1 to become ill; to get sicker
- *He nearly fainted at the breakfast-table when he opened [the letter], and from that day he sickened to his death.*—THE SIGN OF FOUR, ARTHUR CONAN DOYLE

2 to feel sick or faint
- *Mary sickened with terror.*—MARY BARTON, ELIZABETH GASKELL

3 to feel disgusted or horrified
- *I sickened as I read. 'Hateful day when I received life!' I exclaimed in agony.*—FRANKENSTEIN, MARY SHELLEY

silly ADJECTIVE
wretched; weak or pitiful
- *a silly, helpless creature*—NICHOLAS NICKLEBY, CHARLES DICKENS

since ADVERB
ago
- *He lost his elder brother a few years since.*—JANE EYRE, CHARLOTTE BRONTË

singular ADJECTIVE
1 remarkable; extremely good
- *a singular piece of good fortune*—THE SIGN OF FOUR, ARTHUR CONAN DOYLE

2 odd; strange
- *He is a singular character.*—BLEAK HOUSE, CHARLES DICKENS

sirocco (also **siroc**) NOUN
a hot dry wind from Africa

sit VERB
➢ **sit up:** to stay awake at night, especially to watch over a sick or dying person • *The neighbour who was sitting up with her mother came to the top of the stairs, and whispered that Mrs Durbeyfield was no better.*—TESS OF THE D'URBERVILLES, THOMAS HARDY

sitter NOUN
a passenger in a rowing boat
- *The boat that came ashore is 'a four-oared galley ... and two sitters'.*—GREAT EXPECTATIONS, CHARLES DICKENS

situation NOUN
1 a job
- *'Let me hear another sound from you,' said Scrooge, 'and you'll keep your Christmas by losing your situation!'*—A CHRISTMAS CAROL, CHARLES DICKENS

2 a person's social position
- *You and Mr Elton are by situation called together; you belong to one another by every circumstance of your respective homes.*—EMMA, JANE AUSTEN

3 a location or place; a person's residence
- *She was busily searching through the neighbourhood for a proper situation for her daughter.*—PRIDE AND PREJUDICE, JANE AUSTEN

sketch NOUN
1 a brief account or description
- *The village paper published biographical sketches of the boys.*—THE ADVENTURES OF TOM SAWYER, MARK TWAIN

2 a plan or outline; a general idea
- *Everything ... went on smoothly, and was finally settled according to Charlotte's first sketch.*—PRIDE AND PREJUDICE, JANE AUSTEN

sketch VERB
to give a brief account or description, without going into details
- *'We have had the pleasure ... ,' said Holmes, and in a few words he sketched out what had occurred.*—THE ADVENTURES OF SHERLOCK HOLMES, ARTHUR CONAN DOYLE

skiff NOUN
a small light boat for one person
- *Several small punts and skiffs were lying about in the water and on the edge of the wharf.*—THE SIGN OF FOUR, ARTHUR CONAN DOYLE

slattern NOUN
a dirty, untidy woman
- *Miss Scatcherd wrote in conspicuous characters on a piece of pasteboard the word 'Slattern,' and bound it ... round [her] forehead.*—JANE EYRE, CHARLOTTE BRONTË
➢ **slatternly** ADVERB • *a slatternly girl, in shoes down at heel, and ... stockings very much out of repair*—OLIVER TWIST, CHARLES DICKENS

sleuth-hound NOUN
1 a bloodhound (i.e. a dog with a keen sense of smell, used for tracking)
2 a detective
- *Holmes the sleuth-hound*—THE ADVENTURES OF SHERLOCK HOLMES, ARTHUR CONAN DOYLE

slightingly ADVERB
in an insulting way
- *If I were to hear anybody speak slightingly of you, I should fire up in a moment.*—NORTHANGER ABBEY, JANE AUSTEN

slip NOUN
a cutting taken from a plant
• *I can bring you slips of anything.*—SILAS MARNER, GEORGE ELIOT

slipshod ADJECTIVE
wearing slippers, or shoes that do not fit well
• *She hurried off, as fast as she could in her slipshod shoes.*—DOMBEY AND SON, CHARLES DICKENS
USAGE In modern English, you might expect someone's work to be described as *slipshod*, rather than their appearance or their shoes.

slop-basin (also **slop-bowl**) NOUN
a dish for the dregs of tea or coffee
• *She wants help with 'handing cups, circulating the muffins, [and] lifting the plate from the slop-basin'.*—SHIRLEY, CHARLOTTE BRONTË

slops (also **slop**) NOUN
1 mushy or liquid food, or drink, especially when unappealing or considered suitable for a weak or sick person
• *Have you given him any nourishment, Bedwin? Any slops, eh?*—OLIVER TWIST, CHARLES DICKENS
2 waste food or liquid
• *As they passed, women from their doors tossed household slops of every description into the gutter.*—MARY BARTON, ELIZABETH GASKELL
3 sailors' clothing and bedding
• *[Magwitch] was at present dressed in a seafaring slop suit.*—GREAT EXPECTATIONS, CHARLES DICKENS
4 second-hand or cheap ready-made clothing

slop-seller NOUN
a person selling second-hand or cheap ready-made clothing
• *Nicholas hurried into a slopseller's hard by, and bought Smike a great-coat.*—NICHOLAS NICKLEBY, CHARLES DICKENS
➤ **slop-shop** NOUN

slouch (also **slouch hat**) NOUN
a soft hat with a brim bending or hanging downwards
• *His hat was laying on the floor; an old black slouch with the top caved in.*—THE ADVENTURES OF HUCKLEBERRY FINN, MARK TWAIN

slouch VERB
to pull the brim of a hat down over your eyes or face
• *He had a large sou'wester hat on, slouched over his face.*—DAVID COPPERFIELD, CHARLES DICKENS

sluice-house NOUN
a building holding a sluice gate (for controlling a flow of water, in a mill etc.)
• *Pip is to come to 'the little sluice-house ... on the marshes'.*—GREAT EXPECTATIONS, CHARLES DICKENS

sluice-keeper NOUN
a person whose job is to look after a lock or other gate for controlling a flow of water; a lock-keeper

slumberous ADJECTIVE
sleepy
• *I stepped out of the door into the slumberous heat of the late afternoon.*—THE ISLAND OF DOCTOR MOREAU, H. G. WELLS
➤ **slumberously** ADVERB • *I ... found that I had slumberously got to the turnpike without having taken any account of the road.*—GREAT EXPECTATIONS, CHARLES DICKENS

smack NOUN
1 a sailing boat
• *a small fishing-smack*—THE MILL ON THE FLOSS, GEORGE ELIOT
2 a trace or suggestion of something
• *the smack of adventure*—MEN OF IRON, HOWARD PYLE

small-coal NOUN
coal dust or small pieces of coal

smart ADJECTIVE
1 firm, fierce, or quick
• *John Browdie set spurs to his horse, and went off at a smart canter.*—NICHOLAS NICKLEBY, CHARLES DICKENS
2 sudden and loud
• *the smart sound its teeth made when the jaws were brought together*—A CHRISTMAS CAROL, CHARLES DICKENS

smart NOUN
1 mental pain or suffering
• *a smart which nobody feels but yourself*—JANE EYRE, CHARLOTTE BRONTË
2 a stinging physical pain
• *The smart of her hand, and the ache of her heart, were forgotten.*—LITTLE WOMEN, LOUISA M. ALCOTT

smart VERB
1 to sting; to feel a stinging pain
• *the smarting wound of his knuckles*—LORNA DOONE, R.D. BLACKMORE
2 to feel upset or angry
• *Joe Flint [was] still smarting from the rebuke.*—JACK AND JILL, LOUISA M. ALCOTT

smarty NOUN
someone who wanted to be fashionable and neat
• *that Saint Louis smarty, that thinks he dresses so fine and is aristocracy!*—THE ADVENTURES OF TOM SAWYER, MARK TWAIN

smash to sojourn

smash NOUN
a state of failure or destruction
• You'll ... hand over the money? If you don't, ... everything 'ull go to smash.—SILAS MARNER, GEORGE ELIOT

smelling-bottle NOUN
a small bottle containing smelling salts, a strong-smelling substance to revive someone who felt faint or had a headache
• Marie ... began sobbing and using her smelling-bottle.—UNCLE TOM'S CABIN, HARRIET BEECHER STOWE

smit VERB
struck; smitten
• Gray .... [was] suddenly smit with the desire to rise.—TREASURE ISLAND, ROBERT LOUIS STEVENSON

smite (also **smote** or **smitten**) VERB
to hit, attack, or affect someone
• He smote her in the face, and she fled.—THE STRANGE CASE OF DR JEKYLL AND MR HYDE, ROBERT LOUIS STEVENSON
• I was in my own room as usual ... nothing had smitten me, or scathed me, or maimed me.—JANE EYRE, CHARLOTTE BRONTË
➤ **smiter** NOUN • I'll tell you ... what real love is. It is blind devotion ... giving up your whole heart and soul to the smiter. (The smiter here is the person affecting you, i.e. making you fall in love with them.)
—GREAT EXPECTATIONS, CHARLES DICKENS

smock-frock NOUN
a long shirt worn in the past over clothes by a farm worker
• The public house had benches 'on which were seated several rough men in smock-frocks, drinking and smoking'.—OLIVER TWIST, CHARLES DICKENS

snuff NOUN
powdered tobacco that was sniffed rather than smoked
• Mr Wititterly took a pinch of snuff from his box.
—NICHOLAS NICKLEBY, CHARLES DICKENS

snuffer NOUN
a conical device for extinguishing a candle
➤ **(a pair of) snuffers**: a device like a pair of scissors with a small box on the end, for trimming the wick of a candle and extinguishing it • He ... brought out his ... candlesticks and stood them in line with the snuffers ... ready to be extinguished.—GREAT EXPECTATIONS, CHARLES DICKENS

snuffy ADJECTIVE
disapproving; easily offended
• He was not going to be a snuffy schoolmaster.
—THE MILL ON THE FLOSS, GEORGE ELIOT

sober ADJECTIVE
1 serious; solemn
• a very kind but sober face—LITTLE WOMEN, LOUISA M. ALCOTT
2 not bright or showy
• He wore ... a neat suit of sober black.—THE MEMOIRS OF SHERLOCK HOLMES, ARTHUR CONAN DOYLE
➤ **soberly** ADVERB • Tom ... contemplated him soberly.—THE PRINCE AND THE PAUPER, MARK TWAIN

sober VERB
to make someone serious or calm
• Sun elated them; quiet rain sobered them.—THE MAYOR OF CASTERBRIDGE, THOMAS HARDY

society NOUN
1 company; being with other people
• Jane pictured to herself a happy evening in the society of her two friends.—PRIDE AND PREJUDICE, JANE AUSTEN
2 the organized community in which people lived or socialized
• He had a ... sufficient income ... and ... an excellent position in society.—THE WOMAN IN WHITE, WILKIE COLLINS
3 a particular community or set of people
• Mr Wickham began to speak on more general topics, Meryton, the neighbourhood, the society.—PRIDE AND PREJUDICE, JANE AUSTEN
4 the people with whom a person socialized
• Rushworth must and would improve in good society.—MANSFIELD PARK, JANE AUSTEN
5 an organized group or association
• the Teetotal Society—HARD TIMES, CHARLES DICKENS
• the London Geographical Society—MOBY DICK, HERMAN MELVILLE

sod NOUN
turf; grassy ground
• Here is the place—green sod and a gray marble headstone.—SHIRLEY, CHARLOTTE BRONTË

soever ADVERB
however much; to whatever extent—used for emphasis
• My pupils ... how deep soever the interest I might take in them, could not be my friends.—SHIRLEY, CHARLOTTE BRONTË

soft head NOUN
a foolish or silly person
• 'Spooney!' said the clerk ... 'Soft Head!'—GREAT EXPECTATIONS, CHARLES DICKENS

sojourn VERB
to visit or stay somewhere
• You shall sojourn at Paris, Rome, and Naples.—JANE EYRE, CHARLOTTE BRONTË

sojourn NOUN
a visit or stay
• He ... spoke of going home, a subject he has never mentioned ... during his sojourn here.—DRACULA, BRAM STOKER

sojourner NOUN
a traveller staying somewhere temporarily
• the unsettled habits of a temporary sojourner in the land—DAVID COPPERFIELD, CHARLES DICKENS

solicitous ADJECTIVE
showing care; concerned
• I dressed myself with care ... I was still by nature solicitous to be neat.—JANE EYRE, CHARLOTTE BRONTË

solicitude NOUN
care; concern
• Elizabeth began to like [the Bingley sisters], when she saw how much affection and solicitude they shewed for Jane.—PRIDE AND PREJUDICE, JANE AUSTEN

solus (say soh-luhss) ADJECTIVE
alone
• She closed the door, leaving me solus with Mr St John.—JANE EYRE, CHARLOTTE BRONTË

sop NOUN
bread soaked in water, gravy, milk, or other liquid
• Mr Bounderby claims he was born in a ditch 'As wet as a sop. A foot of water in it'.—HARD TIMES, CHARLES DICKENS

sophistry (say sof-ist-ri) (also sophism) NOUN
a reason or reasoning which is clever, but false or misleading
• Then ... we snatch at any sophistry that will nullify our long struggles.—THE MILL ON THE FLOSS, GEORGE ELIOT
• I had before been moved by the sophisms of the being I had created.—FRANKENSTEIN, MARY SHELLEY
➤ **sophistical / sophistic** ADJECTIVE false; misleading • If I lived with you as you desire, I should then be your mistress: to say otherwise is sophistical.—JANE EYRE, CHARLOTTE BRONTË

🏛 In Ancient Greece, a *sophist* was a paid teacher of philosophy. The word later came to mean 'someone who reasons cleverly but falsely'.

sort NOUN
way; manner
• Joe became able in some sort to appreciate the greater quiet of his life.—GREAT EXPECTATIONS, CHARLES DICKENS

sovereign ADJECTIVE
excellent; very effective
• Mrs Pocket ... [prescribed] Bed as a sovereign remedy for baby.—GREAT EXPECTATIONS, CHARLES DICKENS

Capital letters

The quotation at *sovereign* contains an example of a capital letter which would be not be used in modern English. It was not uncommon for capital letters to be used differently from nowadays, for example to indicate importance or to show that something was called a particular thing.
• The folks of the **Great House** were to spend the evening of this day at the **Cottage**.—PERSUASION, CHARLOTTE BRONTË

As in modern English, capital letters also show that a word is a proper noun, indicating a particular person, place, or institution. People and places may be from myths and stories with which people nowadays are less familiar; however, you can often work out what kind of person or place is being talked about.
• A sense of **Cain**-like desolation made my breast ache.—SHIRLEY, CHARLOTTE BRONTË

---

spake VERB
spoke
• They received it with deep brooding silence, but spake never a word.—MARY BARTON, ELIZABETH GASKELL

spar NOUN
1 a strong pole or beam, for example one used on a ship to support the sail
• The sea ... carried men, spars, casks, planks ... into the boiling surge.—DAVID COPPERFIELD, CHARLES DICKENS
2 a type of mineral or rock
• vases of fine purple spar—JANE EYRE, CHARLOTTE BRONTË
3 a rod used for fixing thatch in place
• Driving in spars at any point and on any system, inch by inch he covered more and more.—FAR FROM THE MADDING CROWD, THOMAS HARDY
4 a jab or thrust when practising boxing; a pretend punch
• Mr Feeder ... made a spar at Mr Toots, and tapped him skilfully with the back of his hand on the breastbone.—DOMBEY AND SON, CHARLES DICKENS

spare ADJECTIVE
thin; lean
• His spare but healthy person ... was in strong contrast ... with the Squire's.—SILAS MARNER, GEORGE ELIOT

speak VERB
1 to say; to express
- *I do not speak it to be thanked.*—PRIDE AND PREJUDICE, JANE AUSTEN
- *She spoke her comment very gravely and somewhat severely.*—DRACULA, BRAM STOKER

2 to address someone in a particular way
- *[Marner] was worth speaking fair, if it was only to keep him from doing you a mischief.*—SILAS MARNER, GEORGE ELIOT

3 to show or reveal something about someone
- *In her acquaintance with Mr Darcy, Elizabeth has never seen 'any thing that spoke him of irreligious or immoral habits'.*—PRIDE AND PREJUDICE, JANE AUSTEN

USAGE In modern English, you would *say something* or *make a comment*, not *speak something* or *speak a comment*.

special NOUN
a private train; a train provided for a particular occasion
- *Even if we did have a special, it would probably not arrive as soon as our regular train.*—DRACULA, BRAM STOKER

spectre NOUN
a ghost
- *I walked about the isle like a restless spectre.* —FRANKENSTEIN, MARY SHELLEY

spectroscope NOUN
a device for recording and analysing light waves
- *The spectroscope ... indicated a mass of flaming gas, chiefly hydrogen, moving with an enormous velocity towards this earth.*—THE WAR OF THE WORLDS, H. G. WELLS

spencer NOUN
a short, fitted jacket worn by women and children
- *I had got my bonnet and spencer on, just ready to come out.*—EMMA, JANE AUSTEN

spendthrift NOUN
a person spending money extravagantly and wastefully
- *Blackbeard was a spendthrift, squandering all he had.*—MOONFLEET, J. MEADE FALKNER

spike NOUN
a sharp point at the top of one of the posts in a gate or fence
- *[He] stood laughing at us over the spikes of the wicket.*—GREAT EXPECTATIONS, CHARLES DICKENS

spile NOUN
a wooden peg for sealing a barrel
- *I groped about the barrels till ... my hand struck on the spile of a keg.*—MOONFLEET, J. MEADE FALKNER

spirit NOUN
➢ **in spirits:** in a good mood; happy • *[Edward] was attentive, and kind; but still he was not in spirits.* —SENSE AND SENSIBILITY, JANE AUSTEN
in the mood to do something • *Emma was in spirits to persuade them away.*—EMMA, JANE AUSTEN

spirit-rapping NOUN
knocks on a table etc. during a seance, said to be made by spirits of the dead
- *the science of spirit-rapping*—THE WATER BABIES, CHARLES KINGSLEY

spirituous ADJECTIVE
containing spirits; alcoholic
- *Christmas puddings, brawn, and abundance of spirituous liquors*—SILAS MARNER, GEORGE ELIOT

spleen NOUN
bad temper; spite
- *Upon this poor being, all the spleen and ill-humour that could not be vented on Nicholas were ... bestowed.*—NICHOLAS NICKLEBY, CHARLES DICKENS

spoil NOUN
items stolen or taken
- *[They] sat grouped about their spoil.*—A CHRISTMAS CAROL, CHARLES DICKENS

spoony (also spooney) ADJECTIVE
sentimental; foolishly in love
- *And then ... blest if he didn't go an' marry a gal! Just went and got spoony an' hadn't any more sense left!* —LITTLE LORD FAUNTLEROY, FRANCES HODGSON BURNETT

spoony (also spooney) NOUN
1 someone foolishly in love
- *Mr Rochester spends all his money on the woman he was in love with, 'like any other spoony'.*—JANE EYRE, CHARLOTTE BRONTË

2 a foolish or silly person
- *What are you crying for, you little spooney?*—THE MILL ON THE FLOSS, GEORGE ELIOT

sport NOUN
fun
- *Let her come—it will be excellent sport!*—JANE EYRE, CHARLOTTE BRONTË
- *A young girl came running ... laughing, as if she ran from someone in sport.*—FRANKENSTEIN, MARY SHELLEY

sportive ADJECTIVE
playful
- *Georgiana is surprised at Elizabeth's 'lively, sportive manner of talking to her brother'.*—PRIDE AND PREJUDICE, JANE AUSTEN

sportsman to start

sportsman NOUN
a hunter; someone who shot game
• Out on the moor, Jane *'had a vague dread … that some sportsman or poacher might discover [her]'.*—JANE EYRE, CHARLOTTE BRONTË

spree NOUN
an outing for pleasure
• Merrylegs does not want to pull *'some cart with three or four great men in it going out for a Sunday spree'.*—BLACK BEAUTY, ANNA SEWELL

sprig NOUN
a small bunch of flowers or leaves sewn or printed on fabric as a decoration
• *Caroline, dear child, take your embroidery. You may get three sprigs done to-night.*—SHIRLEY, CHARLOTTE BRONTË

sprightly ADJECTIVE
lively
• *I was endeavouring … to acquire … a more attractive and sprightly manner.*—JANE EYRE, CHARLOTTE BRONTË

spurn VERB
to tread on something or kick it away
• *As she said the words, she threw the money down upon the ground, and spurned it with her foot.*—DOMBEY AND SON, CHARLES DICKENS

squab ADJECTIVE
round; plump
• The Norfolk Biffin apples are *'squab and swarthy'.*—A CHRISTMAS CAROL, CHARLES DICKENS

squab NOUN
1 a cushion
• *the squabs of chairs and sofas*—DOMBEY AND SON, CHARLES DICKENS
2 a young bird, especially a pigeon
• *a fat young squab*—ROSE IN BLOOM, LOUISA M. ALCOTT

squib NOUN
a small firework
• *I saw a blue flare … as if a man had lit a squib and flung it overboard.*—MOONFLEET, J. MEADE FALKNER

squire NOUN
a significant landowner in a local area
• *The greatest man in Raveloe was Squire Cass, who lived in the large red house with the handsome flight of stone steps in front.*—SILAS MARNER, GEORGE ELIOT

staddle NOUN
a framework or stone supporting a rick (a pile of hay, corn, etc.)
• *The corn stood on stone staddles.*—FAR FROM THE MADDING CROWD, THOMAS HARDY

stagger VERB
to cause someone to hesitate or be uncertain
• *Several strange facts combined against her, which might have staggered anyone who had not such proof of her innocence as I had.*—FRANKENSTEIN, MARY SHELLEY
USAGE In modern English, you would expect *stagger* or *staggered* to suggest that someone is extremely surprised, rather than hesitant or uncertain.

stairhead NOUN
the top of the stairs
• *Every time the bell rang out he came on the stairhead, with 'What is that, Mrs Hudson?'* —THE SIGN OF FOUR, ARTHUR CONAN DOYLE

stalk VERB
1 to stride or march somewhere
• *With that she stalked out, and made the door bang after her.*—DAVID COPPERFIELD, CHARLES DICKENS
2 to prowl around; to walk somewhere in a sinister or stealthy way
• *the dusky figures that were silently stalking to and fro*—THE LAST OF THE MOHICANS, JAMES FENIMORE COOPER

stamp NOUN
1 a type or kind of person or thing
• *books of a serious stamp*—PRIDE AND PREJUDICE, JANE AUSTEN
2 a particular quality; the impression given
• *The narrator's manner and tone had the stamp of truth.*—WESSEX TALES, THOMAS HARDY

stanch ADJECTIVE
firm, strong, and loyal; staunch
• *He was stanch and true.*—THE SIGN OF FOUR, ARTHUR CONAN DOYLE

stanch VERB
to staunch or stop a flow of blood
• *[She] had tried to stanch his wound.*—THE PRISONER OF ZENDA, ANTHONY HOPE

stand VERB
➢ **stand up**: to dance with someone; to take part in a dance • *In vain did she entreat him to stand up with somebody else.*—PRIDE AND PREJUDICE, JANE AUSTEN

standing NOUN
1 a person's reputation, status, or social position
• *a member of society of about my own standing*—GREAT EXPECTATIONS, CHARLES DICKENS
2 the length of time that something existed
• *May I ask if your engagement is of long standing?*—SENSE AND SENSIBILITY, JANE AUSTEN

start VERB
to suddenly move, jump, sit or stand
• *Awaking suddenly, he listened, started up, and sat listening.*—DOMBEY AND SON, CHARLES DICKENS

starve to stocking

starve VERB
to suffer or die because of extreme cold
- *I had starved with cold and hunger on that island.*
—KIDNAPPED, ROBERT LOUIS STEVENSON

USAGE In modern Standard English, you would expect someone to *starve* because of lack of food, not cold.

Old English *steorfan* meaning 'to die'

starveling ADJECTIVE
starved; extremely thin
- *There were a couple of starveling [dogs], with strings about their necks.*—THE PRINCE AND THE PAUPER, MARK TWAIN

station NOUN
1 a person's social position
- *Gentlemen in his station are not accustomed to marry their governesses.*—JANE EYRE, CHARLOTTE BRONTË
2 a person's position in a place
- *Mr Collins took his station between his cousin Elizabeth and Mrs Philips.*—PRIDE AND PREJUDICE, JANE AUSTEN

statuary NOUN
someone who carved gravestones or statues; a sculptor
- *[The] villagers collected round the grave, where the statuary's man was waiting for us.*—THE WOMAN IN WHITE, WILKIE COLLINS

stay EXCLAMATION
used meaning 'wait a moment' or 'hang on'
- *And stay, let somebody run to Winthrop's and fetch Dolly—she's the best woman to get.*—SILAS MARNER, GEORGE ELIOT

staylace NOUN
ribbon or cord for lacing a corset
- *I have taken to the sofa with my staylace cut, and have lain there hours insensible.*—GREAT EXPECTATIONS, CHARLES DICKENS

stays NOUN
a corset
- *Louis ... says she creaked when she curtseyed ... Was it her shoes, her stays, or her bones?*—THE WOMAN IN WHITE, WILKIE COLLINS

stead NOUN
➢ **in the stead of:** in the place of • *I had come in, in Mary's stead, with the tray.*—JANE EYRE, CHARLOTTE BRONTË
➢ **stand someone in good stead:** to be very useful to someone • *Jack's former training stood him in good stead.*—JACK AND JILL, LOUISA M. ALCOTT

steel NOUN
a metal rod used with a piece of rock (called a 'flint') to produce sparks for making a fire
- *a tinder-box, with a flint and steel*—SILAS MARNER, GEORGE ELIOT

stentorian (also **stentorious**) ADJECTIVE
loud; booming
- *A stentorian voice bellowed to the driver to stop.*
—OLIVER TWIST, CHARLES DICKENS

stern ADJECTIVE
➢ **the sterner sex:** men • *Mamma does not have 'the best opinion of the sterner sex'.*—SHIRLEY, CHARLOTTE BRONTË

stertorous ADJECTIVE
(of breathing) noisy and laboured
- *His voice was becoming fainter and his breath more stertorous.*—DRACULA, BRAM STOKER

stick VERB
to stab or pierce something; to jab something into something
- *He recorded his winnings by sticking his jackknife into the table.*—GREAT EXPECTATIONS, CHARLES DICKENS

still ADJECTIVE
calm; silent; inactive
- *The early morning was wonderfully still, and the sun ... was already warm. He did not remember hearing any birds that morning, [and] there was certainly no breeze stirring.*—THE WAR OF THE WORLDS, H. G. WELLS

still VERB
to make someone or something calm
- *Instead of trying to still his fears, he encouraged them.*—SILAS MARNER, GEORGE ELIOT

stilly ADJECTIVE
quiet and still
- *There falls a stilly pause, a wordless silence.*—VILLETTE, CHARLOTTE BRONTË

stilly ADVERB
quietly or not moving much
- *The three boats now stilly floated.*—MOBY DICK, HERMAN MELVILLE

stipend NOUN
a wage or allowance
- *You will receive a liberal stipend in return for the discharge of certain duties.*—DOMBEY AND SON, CHARLES DICKENS

stirring ADJECTIVE
active; involving a lot of movement or action
- *I thought of ... your life, sir—an existence more expansive and stirring than my own.*—JANE EYRE, CHARLOTTE BRONTË

stocking NOUN
a man's long sock
- *a small boy without shoes or stockings*—SILAS MARNER, GEORGE ELIOT

stomacher NOUN
a decorative triangular part of a woman's bodice, with the wide part across the chest and a point at the waist

storied ADJECTIVE
written about in stories; legendary
- *I saw myself and Coralie ... pacing the world together, o'er hill and plain, through storied cities.*—DREAM DAYS, KENNETH GRAHAME

strain NOUN
1 a tune; a piece of music
- *[Adèle] commenced singing a song from some opera. It was the strain of a forsaken lady.*—JANE EYRE, CHARLOTTE BRONTË

2 the tone of someone's speech or writing
- *'I don't know this man!' said Mr Jaggers, in the same devastating strain: 'What does this fellow want?'*—GREAT EXPECTATIONS, CHARLES DICKENS

straiten VERB
to narrow
- *I watch her winding her bright curls round her fingers, and straitening her waist.*—DAVID COPPERFIELD, CHARLES DICKENS

strait-waistcoat NOUN
1 a straitjacket
- *He had a momentary idea of knocking Scrooge down ... and calling ... for help and a strait-waistcoat.*—A CHRISTMAS CAROL, CHARLES DICKENS

2 something very restrictive
- *They both were still in that strait-waistcoat of poverty from which she had tried so many times to be delivered.*—THE MAYOR OF CASTERBRIDGE, THOMAS HARDY

strap NOUN
a strip of leather used for beating someone; the punishment of being beaten like this
- *I have sometimes seen the little children drop asleep ... If they are catched asleep they get the strap.*—TESTIMONY OF HANNAH GOODE, GATHERED BY FACTORY INQUIRY COMMISSION, 1833,

struggle VERB
to try very hard to do something or overcome something
- *I struggled to repress a sob.*—PRIDE AND PREJUDICE, JANE AUSTEN

studied ADJECTIVE
not natural; said or done with deliberate effort
- *[He spoke] with a studied calmness.*—DRACULA, BRAM STOKER

study VERB
1 to try to achieve something
- *He is an excellent young man ... but he does ... study for compliments rather more than I could endure.*—EMMA, JANE AUSTEN
- *I must study to regain my former self.*—DAVID COPPERFIELD, CHARLES DICKENS

2 to think carefully about something
- *Just let me study a moment.*—THE ADVENTURES OF TOM SAWYER, MARK TWAIN

3 to pay attention to the wants or needs of someone
- *From her infancy, she had been surrounded with servants, who lived only to study her caprices.*—UNCLE TOM'S CABIN, HARRIET BEECHER STOWE

study NOUN
an aim or intention
- *But it has been the study of my life to avoid those weaknesses.*—PRIDE AND PREJUDICE, JANE AUSTEN

stuff NOUN
material; fabric, especially woollen fabric
- *I repaired to my room, and ... replaced my black stuff dress by one of black silk.*—JANE EYRE, CHARLOTTE BRONTË
- *household stuffs and goods*—GREAT EXPECTATIONS, CHARLES DICKENS

stupidity NOUN
1 lack of interest, sensitivity, or feeling; apathy or numbness
- *She felt ... obliged to assume a disinclination for seeing [the house]. Mrs Gardiner abused her stupidity.*—PRIDE AND PREJUDICE, JANE AUSTEN

2 a state of being almost unconscious; stupor
- *I must have stared upon it for near half a minute, sunk as I was in the mere stupidity of wonder.*—THE STRANGE CASE OF DR JEKYLL AND MR HYDE, ROBERT LOUIS STEVENSON

subaltern NOUN
a second-in-command; a deputy
- *The subalterns receive orders from their chiefs; they are in a good state of discipline.*—SHIRLEY, CHARLOTTE BRONTË

subjoin VERB
to add something
- *'They are soldiers—cavalry soldiers,' she subjoined quickly.*—SHIRLEY, CHARLOTTE BRONTË

➤ **subjoined** ADJECTIVE added or attached to something • *I can vouch for the accuracy of the subjoined account.*—A STUDY IN SCARLET, ARTHUR CONAN DOYLE

sublime VERB
to raise to a higher spiritual or social level; to elevate
- *Henchard considers 'the possibility that Lucetta had been sublimed into a lady of means'.*—THE MAYOR OF CASTERBRIDGE, THOMAS HARDY

sublimity NOUN
an impressive, awe-inspiring quality
• *I had found sublimity and wonder in the dread heights and precipices, in the roaring torrents, and the wastes of ice and snow.*—DAVID COPPERFIELD, CHARLES DICKENS

subscribe VERB
to sign something
• *These poems, subscribed with a masculine pseudonym, had appeared in various obscure magazines.*—WESSEX TALES, THOMAS HARDY
➤ **subscribe to:** to agree to something; to accept something • *[The dog] subscribed to the offer of his little mistress cheerfully, and devoted himself to her service.*—DOMBEY AND SON, CHARLES DICKENS

subscription NOUN
a collection; a donation
• *After the children's parents died 'Some neighbours … came forward with a little subscription'.*—BLEAK HOUSE, CHARLES DICKENS

subsist VERB
to continue to exist
• *Elizabeth felt persuaded that no real confidence could ever subsist between them again.*—PRIDE AND PREJUDICE, JANE AUSTEN

substantial ADJECTIVE
1 having a real, physical existence rather than imaginary
• *I am substantial enough—touch me.*—JANE EYRE, CHARLOTTE BRONTË
2 socially important
• *Squire Cass and other substantial parishioners*—SILAS MARNER, GEORGE ELIOT
➤ **substantiality** NOUN • *If you … make me pull [your] hair … I think you will cease to entertain doubts of my substantiality.*—JANE EYRE, CHARLOTTE BRONTË

succedaneum (say suk-sid-ay-ni-uhm) NOUN
a substitute
• *[His trousers'] waistband was so very broad and high, that it became a succedaneum for a waistcoat.*—DOMBEY AND SON, CHARLES DICKENS

succeed (also **succeed to**) VERB
to follow after something
• *A great tumult succeeded.*—JANE EYRE, CHARLOTTE BRONTË
• *This solemn proceeding always took place … the day succeeding his return.*—NICHOLAS NICKLEBY, CHARLES DICKENS
• *The cold light of morning had succeeded to night.*—DOMBEY AND SON, CHARLES DICKENS

succour NOUN
comfort or help
• *She continued by the side of her sister … supplying every succour.*—SENSE AND SENSIBILITY, JANE AUSTEN

succour VERB
to give someone help or comfort
• *I supplicate you … to succour and release me.*—A TALE OF TWO CITIES, CHARLES DICKENS

suffer VERB
to allow someone to do something
• *I don't suffer it to be spoken of.*—GREAT EXPECTATIONS, CHARLES DICKENS

sufficiency NOUN
1 the fact that something is enough
• *Sir Thomas has said that £10 is enough and Mrs Norris is 'not at all inclined to question its sufficiency'.*—MANSFIELD PARK, JANE AUSTEN
2 arrogance; self-satisfaction
• *I [smiled] down upon him, from the heights of my sufficiency.*—KIDNAPPED, ROBERT LOUIS STEVENSON
➤ **a sufficiency of something:** enough of something; plenty of something • *Mr Stelling … [had] a conviction that a growing boy required a sufficiency of beef.*—THE MILL ON THE FLOSS, GEORGE ELIOT

sugar-loaf NOUN
a large lump of sugar moulded into a cone shape; something shaped like this
• *They began to see the peak of Jan Mayen's Land, standing-up like a white sugar-loaf, two miles above the clouds.*—WATER BABIES, CHARLES KINGSLEY

sugar-plum NOUN
a boiled sweet

suit NOUN
a man's attempt to win a woman's affection or get her to marry him
• *Mr Collins says to Mrs Bennet, 'If [Lizzy] actually persists in rejecting my suit, perhaps it were better not to force her into accepting me.'*—PRIDE AND PREJUDICE, JANE AUSTEN

sullen ADJECTIVE
1 bad-tempered; sulky
• *I was termed naughty and tiresome, sullen and sneaking.*—JANE EYRE, CHARLOTTE BRONTË
2 dark; gloomy
• *There was a sullen darkness in the sky.*—NICHOLAS NICKLEBY, CHARLES DICKENS

sup VERB
to eat supper
• *Mina had supper ready, and when we had supped she told me of Van Helsing's visit.*—DRACULA, BRAM STOKER

sup NOUN
a drink
- *It was as much as I could do to get a bite or a sup.* —GREAT EXPECTATIONS, CHARLES DICKENS

superadd VERB
to add something on top of something else
- *Having superadded many injunctions to be sure and not take cold, the old lady at length permitted him to depart.* —OLIVER TWIST, CHARLES DICKENS

superincumbent ADJECTIVE
lying on top of something
- *The waggon ... was a creaking erection that would scarcely bear the weight of the superincumbent load.* —TESS OF THE D'URBERVILLES, THOMAS HARDY

superintendence NOUN
supervision or management; care
- *Gabriel should undertake the superintendence of the Lower Farm.* —FAR FROM THE MADDING CROWD, THOMAS HARDY

superior ADJECTIVE
1 of a very high standard; excellent
- *Such very superior dancing is not often seen.* —PRIDE AND PREJUDICE, JANE AUSTEN

2 better than other people or things
- *He will marry a woman superior in person and understanding to half her sex.* —SENSE AND SENSIBILITY, JANE AUSTEN

3 of a higher rank or position
- *men like myself, who are low down and are not superior in circumstances* —DOMBEY AND SON, CHARLES DICKENS

4 showing a belief in your own superiority
- *But he looked at me in a superior manner.* —LORNA DOONE, R. D. BLACKMORE

➤ **superior to:** above something; not giving in to or influenced by something • *I should have been superior to circumstances ... but ... I had not the wisdom to remain cool.* —JANE EYRE, CHARLOTTE BRONTË

superior NOUN
a person of higher rank, position, or quality
- *a man who thought of superiors as remote existences with whom he had personally little more to do than with America or the stars* —SILAS MARNER, GEORGE ELIOT

superiority NOUN
1 the fact of being superior to other people or things
- *There was no superiority of manner, accomplishment, or understanding.* —PERSUASION, JANE AUSTEN

2 a feeling of being superior to other people
- *With her air of superiority, and power ... she seemed to regard Ada and me as little more than children.* —BLEAK HOUSE, CHARLES DICKENS

supernal ADJECTIVE
coming from the sky or heaven
- *supernal thunder* —THE MILL ON THE FLOSS, GEORGE ELIOT

superscription NOUN
something written on top or outside of a document
- *It was directed to Philip Pip, Esquire, and on the top of the superscription were the words, 'PLEASE READ THIS, HERE.'* —GREAT EXPECTATIONS, CHARLES DICKENS

support VERB
to endure or bear something
- *The human frame could no longer support the agonies that I endured.* —FRANKENSTEIN, MARY SHELLEY

supposititious ADJECTIVE
not genuine; not real
- *George Gradgrind, or Augustus Gradgrind, or John Gradgrind, or Joseph Gradgrind (all supposititious, non-existent persons)* —HARD TIMES, CHARLES DICKENS

supreme ADJECTIVE
1 the greatest or most extreme
- *She was looking at me then with a look of supreme aversion.* —GREAT EXPECTATIONS, CHARLES DICKENS

2 the most important or powerful
- *For the rest ... she reigned supreme over all the office furniture.* —HARD TIMES, CHARLES DICKENS

3 final (especially with reference to death)
- *I have only one thing ... which weighs upon my mind at this supreme moment.* —THE SIGN OF FOUR, ARTHUR CONAN DOYLE

sure ADJECTIVE
➤ **make sure:** to be or become convinced of something • *Upon the reading of this letter, I made sure my colleague was insane.* —THE STRANGE CASE OF DR JEKYLL AND MR HYDE, ROBERT LOUIS STEVENSON

surtout NOUN
a man's overcoat

🏛 French *sur* meaning 'over' + *tout* meaning 'everything'

survey VERB
to look at someone or something
- *She surveyed my whole person.* —JANE EYRE, CHARLOTTE BRONTË

USAGE In modern English, you might expect a house or area of land to be *surveyed*, not a person.

survey NOUN
a look at something
- *Lady Catherine opened the doors into the dining-parlour and drawing-room ... pronouncing them, after a short survey, to be decent looking rooms.* —PRIDE AND PREJUDICE, JANE AUSTEN

suspend to syndic

suspend VERB
to stop something temporarily
• *Her occupation, suspended by Mr Rochester's announcement, seemed now forgotten.*—JANE EYRE, CHARLOTTE BRONTË
➤ **suspension** NOUN • *Jealousy ... had returned, after a short suspension.*—PERSUASION, JANE AUSTEN

sustain VERB
to bear, withstand, or endure something
• *He sustained a great deal of fatigue with ease.*—A TALE OF TWO CITIES, CHARLES DICKENS

swab VERB
to mop or wipe something
• *Huck ... swabbed the beaded drops from his brow with his sleeve.*—THE ADVENTURES OF TOM SAWYER, MARK TWAIN

swab NOUN
a person deserving no respect
• *He broke in cursing the doctor ... 'Doctors is all swabs,' he said.*—TREASURE ISLAND, ROBERT LOUIS STEVENSON

sward NOUN
grass; a grassy area
• *Tom lay motionless upon the sward.*—TREASURE ISLAND, ROBERT LOUIS STEVENSON

swart ADJECTIVE
dark or blackened
• *Defarge ... [followed] the letters with his swart forefinger, deeply engrained with gunpowder.*—A TALE OF TWO CITIES, CHARLES DICKENS

swarthy ADJECTIVE
dark-skinned
• *[Orlick] was a broadshouldered loose-limbed swarthy fellow of great strength.*—GREAT EXPECTATIONS, CHARLES DICKENS

swell NOUN
a fashionable person of high social status
• *You are a swell about town, and you know me, and I know you.*—BLEAK HOUSE, CHARLES DICKENS

swoon VERB
to faint
• *I was collected, and in no danger of swooning.*—JANE EYRE, CHARLOTTE BRONTË

swoon NOUN
a faint
• *Scrooge held on tight to his chair, to save himself from falling in a swoon.*—A CHRISTMAS CAROL, CHARLES DICKENS

sylvan (also **silvan**) ADJECTIVE
relating to or taking place in a forest
• *'The darkness of natural as well as of sylvan dusk gathered over me.'*—meaning the darkness was caused by night falling as well as by shade from trees.
—JANE EYRE, CHARLOTTE BRONTË

sympathetic ADJECTIVE
1 kind; compassionate
• *Her ... expression was sweet and amiable, and her large blue eyes were singularly spiritual and sympathetic.*—THE SIGN OF FOUR, ARTHUR CONAN DOYLE
2 with mutual understanding or a feeling of connection
• *[This sound] made the young people look at each other with sympathetic impatience for the end of the meal.*—SILAS MARNER, GEORGE ELIOT

sympathy NOUN
1 a feeling of mutual understanding and support; a connection between people
• *I mean, that human affections and sympathies have a most powerful hold on you.*—JANE EYRE, CHARLOTTE BRONTË
2 kindness; compassion
• *Her sympathy was ours; her smile, her soft voice, the sweet glance of her celestial eyes, were ever there to bless and animate us.*—FRANKENSTEIN, MARY SHELLEY
3 a positive attitude towards something
• *I had no sympathy in their appearance, their expression: yet I could imagine that most observers would call them attractive.*—JANE EYRE, CHARLOTTE BRONTË

symptom NOUN
a sign of something; an indication
• *I can remember no symptom of affection on either side.*—PRIDE AND PREJUDICE, JANE AUSTEN

syncope (say **sin**-co-pee) NOUN
loss of consciousness due to low blood pressure; fainting
• *The light ... had struck me into syncope.*—JANE EYRE, CHARLOTTE BRONTË

syndic NOUN
a government official
• *My ancestors had been ... counsellors and syndics, and my father had filled several public situations.*—FRANKENSTEIN, MARY SHELLEY

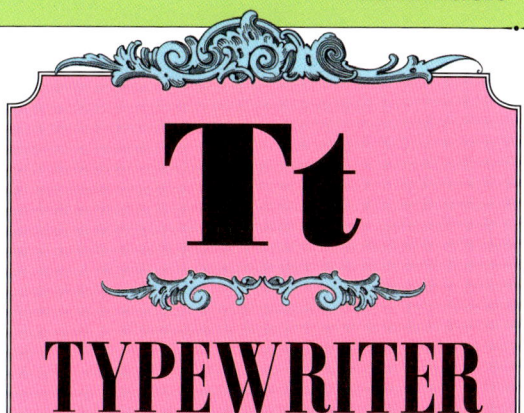

tabernacle to tale

Tt

TYPEWRITER

The first **modern typewriter** with a QWERTY keyboard layout was manufactured by the American firm **E. Remington and Sons** in **1873**. This invention revolutionized office life in the late 19th century, with tasks that had previously been carried out by male clerks now the responsibility of newly-recruited female typists. However male and female employees were kept strictly apart, with female typists even working behind screens to keep them out of sight.

tabernacle NOUN
1 a tent, especially one mentioned in the Bible that was a portable sanctuary or shrine
• *A bed ... hung with curtains of deep red damask, stood out like a tabernacle in the centre.*—JANE EYRE, CHARLOTTE BRONTË
2 the body as a dwelling place for the soul
• *Tess often has the feeling 'that in inhabiting the fleshly tabernacle with which Nature had endowed her she was somehow doing wrong'.*—TESS OF THE D'URBERVILLES, THOMAS HARDY

table NOUN
food and drink provided by someone
• *Kimble is 'a man of substance, able to keep an extravagant table'.*—SILAS MARNER, GEORGE ELIOT

table-beer NOUN
weak beer drunk with food
• *It was darkly rumoured that the butler ... had sometimes mingled porter with [Paul's] table-beer.*—DOMBEY AND SON, CHARLES DICKENS

tablet NOUN
a flat piece of stone or wood on which something was written
• *a name graven on a tablet*—JANE EYRE, CHARLOTTE BRONTË

tablette NOUN
a stiff sheet of paper, or several of these fixed together, used as a notebook
• *I made some entries in my tablettes this morning.*—THE WOMAN IN WHITE, WILKIE COLLINS

tag NOUN
➢ **tag, rag, and bobtail:** a rude expression referring to people of low social status • *I am a bit of dirty riff-raff, and a genuine scrap of tag, rag, and bobtail.*—HARD TIMES, CHARLES DICKENS

taint NOUN
a bad influence or quality making something less pure
• *They dwelled upon her matchless beauty ... without the taint of envy.*—THE LAST OF THE MOHICANS, JAMES FENIMORE COOPER
• *the faithful service of the heart ... so free from any mercenary taint*—A TALE OF TWO CITIES, CHARLES DICKENS

take VERB
to eat or drink something
• *[Scrooge] sat down before the fire to take his gruel.*—A CHRISTMAS CAROL, CHARLES DICKENS
➢ **take someone / something for something:** to think mistakenly that someone or something is a particular thing • *What will be his surprise ... when he knows who they are! He takes them now for people of fashion.*—PRIDE AND PREJUDICE, JANE AUSTEN
➢ **take someone up:**
1 to arrest someone • *I fully expected to find a Constable in the kitchen, waiting to take me up.*—GREAT EXPECTATIONS, CHARLES DICKENS
2 to contradict someone; to disagree with or criticize someone • *There is something truly forbidding in a child taking up her elders in that manner.*—JANE EYRE, CHARLOTTE BRONTË
➢ **take something up:** to pick something up
• *I motioned him to take up the letter.*—FRANKENSTEIN, MARY SHELLEY

taking ADJECTIVE
appealing; charming
• *Herbert Pocket had a frank and easy way with him that was very taking.*—GREAT EXPECTATIONS, CHARLES DICKENS

tale NOUN
the amount of something
• *a deficiency in the quality or the tale of the cloth he wove for them*—SILAS MARNER, GEORGE ELIOT

tallow to teetotum

tallow NOUN
a hard substance made from animal fat, used for making candles and soap
• He bore in his right hand a tallow candle stuck in the end of a cleft stick.—OLIVER TWIST, CHARLES DICKENS

tambour NOUN
a circular frame for holding cloth being embroidered
• I and my sister worked at tambour work.—BLEAK HOUSE, CHARLES DICKENS

tank NOUN
1 a small room, storage space, or cell
• the ... clerk in the tank—A CHRISTMAS CAROL, CHARLES DICKENS
2 a pool, lake, or reservoir
• They drank at the tanks and made the water all muddy.—THE JUNGLE BOOK, RUDYARD KIPLING

tanner NOUN
1 a person whose job was to tan hides to make leather
• It was discovered that the knacker and tanner would give only a very few shillings for [the horse's] carcase.—TESS OF THE D'URBERVILLES, THOMAS HARDY
2 a sixpence
• Three bob and a tanner for tickets.—THE SIGN OF FOUR, ARTHUR CONAN DOYLE

taper NOUN
a thin candle, or a wax-coated strip used for carrying a flame
• A small taper on the edge of the table shed a feeble light.—THE MEMOIRS OF SHERLOCK HOLMES, ARTHUR CONAN DOYLE

taproom NOUN
a room with a bar in a pub or hotel
• At the inn 'The girl had a little parlour to sit in, away from the noise of the taproom'.—THE WOMAN IN WHITE, WILKIE COLLINS

tarpaulin NOUN
a sailor
• this tarpaulin chap—DAVID COPPERFIELD, CHARLES DICKENS

tarry (say **tarr-i**) VERB
to wait around; to linger
• The Spirit did not tarry here.—A CHRISTMAS CAROL, CHARLES DICKENS

tarry (say **tar-ee**) ADJECTIVE
covered in or like tar
• Hanging to a bit of tarry string ... we found the key.—TREASURE ISLAND, ROBERT LOUIS STEVENSON

tar-water NOUN
cold water that had had tar or pine resin soaked in it, believed to work as a medicine

taste VERB
to enjoy or approve of something
• The Squire will be 'tasting a joke against [doctors] when he was in health, but ... eager for their aid when anything was the matter'.—SILAS MARNER, GEORGE ELIOT

tavern NOUN
a place where people could drink beer and other drinks, eat, and sometimes stay; an inn or pub
• Breakfast had been ordered at a pleasant little tavern.—GREAT EXPECTATIONS, CHARLES DICKENS

tax VERB
1 to say that someone did something; to accuse someone
• She taxed me with the offence at once.—SENSE AND SENSIBILITY, JANE AUSTEN
2 to put a strain or burden on a person or thing
• a clue which has taxed even his analytical genius—THE SIGN OF FOUR, ARTHUR CONAN DOYLE

tax NOUN
a burden or strain
• Mrs Philips's vulgarity was ... perhaps a greater tax on his forbearance.—PRIDE AND PREJUDICE, JANE AUSTEN

teaboard NOUN
a tray with things for serving tea
• Peggotty [came] in with the teaboard and candles.—DAVID COPPERFIELD, CHARLES DICKENS

tease (also **teaze**) VERB
to irritate or bother someone
• She was teazed by Mr Collins, who continued most perseveringly by her side.—PRIDE AND PREJUDICE, JANE AUSTEN

tea-things NOUN
a teapot, cups, and other things for serving tea
• She was presently surprised by the appearance of the servant with the tea-things.—SILAS MARNER, GEORGE ELIOT

teatime NOUN
the time in the afternoon when tea and perhaps cakes or bread and butter were served
• the precious morsel of brown bread distributed at tea-time—JANE EYRE, CHARLOTTE BRONTË

teetotum NOUN
a toy like a small spinning top with four sides, that could be used for gambling games
🏛 Originally *T totum*. The four sides had letters standing for Latin words, one being *T* for *totum*, or 'all', meaning that the player could take everything.

tell VERB
➣ **tell someone off:** to give someone a task; to assign someone • *A boat's-crew would be told off to cut the cables.*—DREAM DAYS, KENNETH GRAHAME
➣ **tell something off:** to count something off; to list something • *I saw the auctioneer's clerk walking on the casks and telling them off for the information of a catalogue-compiler.*—GREAT EXPECTATIONS, CHARLES DICKENS

temerarious ADJECTIVE
reckless, bold
• *To produce Tess ... as a d'Urberville and a lady, he had felt to be temerarious and risky.*—TESS OF THE D'URBERVILLES, THOMAS HARDY
RELATED WORD *temerity* meaning 'boldness, cheek' as in 'have the temerity to do something'

temper NOUN
someone's personality or temperament
• *Georgiana, who had a spoiled temper ... was universally indulged.*—JANE EYRE, CHARLOTTE BRONTË

tempest NOUN
a storm
• *I have seen this lake agitated by a tempest, when the wind tore up whirlwinds of water.*—FRANKENSTEIN, MARY SHELLEY
➤ **tempestuous** ADJECTIVE stormy • *Phileas Fogg gazed at the tempestuous sea.*—AROUND THE WORLD IN EIGHTY DAYS, JULES VERNE
➤ **tempestuously** ADVERB violently; because of or like a storm • *The rain beat strongly against the panes, the wind blew tempestuously.*—JANE EYRE, CHARLOTTE BRONTË
USAGE As in modern English, these words were also used figuratively to talk about a state of agitation or commotion.
• *These two base passions raged within him like a tempest.*—THE STRANGE CASE OF DR JEKYLL AND MR HYDE, ROBERT LOUIS STEVENSON
• *the storms of his tempestuous life*—THE RETURN OF SHERLOCK HOLMES, ARTHUR CONAN DOYLE

tenaculum (PLURAL tenacula) NOUN
a hook used in surgery
• *There was a board which was strewed with glittering instruments—forceps, tenacula, saws.*—ROUND THE RED LAMP, ARTHUR CONAN DOYLE

tenant VERB
to live somewhere; to inhabit something
• *[The cell] was most intolerably dirty; for ... it had been tenanted by six drunken people.*—OLIVER TWIST, CHARLES DICKENS
• *a large marble basin ... tenanted by goldfish*—JANE EYRE, CHARLOTTE BRONTË

tend VERB
1 to lead to or result in something
• *May I ask to what these questions tend?*—PRIDE AND PREJUDICE, JANE AUSTEN
2 to move towards a particular point or in a particular direction
• *immense processions, one ... tending westward ... the other ever tending eastward*—A TALE OF TWO CITIES, CHARLES DICKENS
3 to look after someone or something
• *Her father ... retired to his own rooms, where he was tended by servants.*—DOMBEY AND SON, CHARLES DICKENS

tenor NOUN
a manner of speaking or happening
• *the whole tenor of their conversation*—JANE EYRE, CHARLOTTE BRONTË
• *the quiet tenor of their usual employments*—PRIDE AND PREJUDICE, JANE AUSTEN

tenter NOUN
a frame on which cloth was stretched out after being made. Originally tenters were outdoors.
• *The cloth was torn from [the] tenters and left in shreds.*—SHIRLEY, CHARLOTTE BRONTË
USAGE The hooks on this frame were called tenterhooks, and we still use the phrase 'on tenterhooks' to describe a state of tension or suspense.

termination NOUN
an ending or result
• *[Lydia's] marriage would ... shortly give the proper termination to the elopement.*—PRIDE AND PREJUDICE, JANE AUSTEN

terrific ADJECTIVE
terrifying; terrible
• *I watched the tempest, so beautiful yet terrific.*—FRANKENSTEIN, MARY SHELLEY

tester NOUN
a canopy, for example over a bed

testify VERB
1 to express something
• *Mr George ... testified no great emotions of pleasure.*—BLEAK HOUSE, CHARLES DICKENS
2 to be evidence or proof of something
• *'Hold your tongue!' Poole said to her, with a ferocity of accent that testified to his own jangled nerves.*—THE STRANGE CASE OF DR JEKYLL AND MR HYDE, ROBERT LOUIS STEVENSON

that CONJUNCTION
1 in order that, so that
• *Go and buy it, and tell 'em to bring it here, that I may give them the directions where to take it.*—A CHRISTMAS CAROL, CHARLES DICKENS

thee to thitherward

2 used to express a wish
• *Oh, that some encouraging voice would answer in the affirmative!*—FRANKENSTEIN, MARY SHELLEY

thee PRONOUN
you
• *I knew I should find thee at last.*—MARY BARTON, ELIZABETH GASKELL

thence ADVERB
from there; from that place
• *Thence, he went straight to the inn which Mr Squeers frequented.*—NICHOLAS NICKLEBY, CHARLES DICKENS
USAGE 'From thence' means the same as *thence*.
• *From thence we proceeded to Oxford.*—FRANKENSTEIN, MARY SHELLEY

thenceforth ADVERB
from that time onwards
• *Evil thenceforth became my good.*—FRANKENSTEIN, MARY SHELLEY

thereabout (also **thereabouts**) ADVERB
1 around there; around that place
• *A few sheep grazed thereabout.*—THE MAYOR OF CASTERBRIDGE, THOMAS HARDY
2 around that number or amount
• *This is a boy ... of eighteen or nineteen, or thereabouts.*—NICHOLAS NICKLEBY, CHARLES DICKENS

thereat ADVERB
at that; at it
• *It was not the first time that a woman had hit off a grand idea and the men turned up their stupid noses thereat.*—THE WATER BABIES, CHARLES KINGSLEY

therefrom ADVERB
from there; from that place
• *I went therefrom to Norcombe.*—FAR FROM THE MADDING CROWD, THOMAS HARDY

therein ADVERB
1 in that place, document, or thing
• *Mr Squeers had taken lodgings therein.*—NICHOLAS NICKLEBY, CHARLES DICKENS
2 in that respect; in regard to that
• *He had some intention ... of studying the law, and ... one thousand pounds would be a very insufficient support therein.*—PRIDE AND PREJUDICE, JANE AUSTEN

thereof ADVERB
of that; of it
• *I undertook to ... fill up the office of parish-clerk ... and it's one of the rights thereof to sing in the choir.*—SILAS MARNER, GEORGE ELIOT

thereon (also **thereupon**) ADVERB
1 on there; on that thing or place
• *a scrap of paper with 'Mr Johnson' written thereon in pencil*—NICHOLAS NICKLEBY, CHARLES DICKENS

2 on that subject
• *Mrs Philips began to express her concern thereupon.*—PRIDE AND PREJUDICE, JANE AUSTEN
3 at that moment; immediately after that
• *Thereon he dashed out of the circle and dragged me into shelter.*—KING SOLOMON'S MINES, H. RIDER HAGGARD

thereto (also **thereunto**) ADVERB
to that; to it
• *[Tess] could not withstand his argument. But ... an answer thereto arose in Clare's own mind.*—TESS OF THE D'URBERVILLES, THOMAS HARDY
• *[They] delivered the masters' ultimatum, adding thereunto not one word of their own.*—MARY BARTON, ELIZABETH GASKELL

theretofore ADVERB
before that time
• *The authorities 'instead of compelling a man to support his family, as they had theretofore done, took his family away from him'.*—OLIVER TWIST, CHARLES DICKENS

therewith ADVERB
1 with that; with it
• *[She] got a fishing-line, and began amusing herself therewith.*—WESTWARD HO!, CHARLES KINGSLEY
2 at that point; with that
• *And therewith the little imp scurried off.*—MEN OF IRON, HOWARD PYLE

thew NOUN
muscular strength; a tendon or muscle as a sign of strength
• *She made no account whatever of his six feet, his manly thews and sinews.*—SHIRLEY, CHARLOTTE BRONTË

thine PRONOUN & DETERMINER (see the panel at **thou**)

thirtover ADJECTIVE
contrary; making things difficult
• *Dear, what a thirtover place this world is!*—FAR FROM THE MADDING CROWD, THOMAS HARDY

thither ADVERB
to or towards that place; there
• *On repairing thither, I found a man waiting for me.*—JANE EYRE, CHARLOTTE BRONTË

thitherward ADVERB
in that direction; towards there
• *I turned my ear thitherward to catch what they were saying.*—A TRADITION OF EIGHTEEN HUNDRED AND FOUR, THOMAS HARDY

thou *to* tithe

Thou, thee, thy, and thine

Thou and *thee* are second-person pronouns meaning 'you' when talking to a single person. *Thou* is a subject pronoun: 'thou wast' means 'you were'. *Thee* is an object pronoun: 'I love thee' means 'I love you'.
- *If **thou** wert a bit cleaner I'd put **thee** in my own bed.* —THE WATER BABIES, CHARLES KINGSLEY

Thy and *thine* are the related possessives: *thy* (or *thine* before a vowel sound) means 'your'; *thine* also means 'yours'.
- *I am **thy** creature.*—FRANKENSTEIN, MARY SHELLEY
- *I will do **thine** errand.*—IVANHOE, WALTER SCOTT
- *Half my kingdom is **thine** already, ... and the other half shall be **thine** after my death.*—THE RED FAIRY BOOK, ANDREW LANG

Originally *thou*, *thee*, *thy*, and *thine* were singular forms used in non-formal contexts and when addressing God, spirits, and people of lower status; 'you', 'your' and 'yours' were only used in the plural and to show respect.

By the 19th century, 'you,' 'your' and 'yours' had become widespread in all contexts and in both the singular and plural. However, *thou* and its related words were still much more widespread than they are today, especially in local dialects. They were also used in order to sound deliberately old-fashioned.

---

threap VERB
to argue
- *[The family] were so agreeable with each other—never fell out nor 'threaped'.*—JANE EYRE, CHARLOTTE BRONTË

threescore NOUN
sixty
- *There must have been threescore of us.*—LORNA DOONE, R. D. BLACKMORE

USAGE This word is often used with reference to the phrase 'threescore years and ten', which is a human lifespan according to the Bible.
- *wretched old sinner of more than threescore years and ten*—A TALE OF TWO CITIES, CHARLES DICKENS

throve VERB
thrived
- *Meanwhile, Oliver gradually throve and prospered under [their] united care.*—OLIVER TWIST, CHARLES DICKENS

thwart NOUN
a plank across a boat, for a rower to sit on
- *He laid himself down under the thwarts and waited.* —THE ADVENTURES OF TOM SAWYER, MARK TWAIN

thy DETERMINER (see the panel at **thou**)

ticklish ADJECTIVE
tricky; needing careful thought or handling
- *It was ... a ticklish decision that he had to make.* —THE STRANGE CASE OF DR JEKYLL AND MR HYDE, ROBERT LOUIS STEVENSON

USAGE In modern English, you might expect a person to be *ticklish*, not a problem or decision.

timbrel NOUN
a tambourine or similar instrument
- *And strike your loud timbrels for joy!*—IVANHOE, SIR WALTER SCOTT

tinder-box NOUN
a metal box containing things needed for lighting a fire
- *John resolves to 'get a candle and tinder-box, and return to the churchyard'.*—MOONFLEET, J. MEADE FALKNER

USAGE A *tinder-box* usually contained tinder (dry material that catches fire easily), a flint (a piece of rock), and a steel (a metal rod on which the flint could be struck to produce a spark).

tinkler NOUN
1 a travelling metalworker or gypsy
2 a small bell

tip VERB
a slang word meaning 'give' or 'let someone have'
- *Now, Aged Parent, tip us the paper.*—GREAT EXPECTATIONS, CHARLES DICKENS

tippet NOUN
a fur scarf or shawl
- *She wore a small sable tippet, which reached just to her shoulders.*—THE MILL ON THE FLOSS, GEORGE ELIOT

tithe NOUN
1 one tenth
- *At that time there were 'not a tithe or a twentieth part so many' steamships as now.*—GREAT EXPECTATIONS, CHARLES DICKENS
2 one-tenth of someone's earnings or produce, given to the church
- *The village of Raveloe 'held farms which ... paid highly-desirable tithes'.*—SILAS MARNER, GEORGE ELIOT

tittle to Tophet

tittle NOUN
a tiny bit
• The town goes about its business *'without caring a tittle for Farfrae's domestic plans'.*—THE MAYOR OF CASTERBRIDGE, THOMAS HARDY

toad-eater NOUN
someone who flattered and tried to please a more important or powerful person
• Nicholas does not want to be *'toad-eater to a mean and ignorant upstart'.*—NICHOLAS NICKLEBY, CHARLES DICKENS
🏛 A name for an assistant to a charlatan selling fake remedies. The assistant would eat a supposedly poisonous toad and then be 'cured' by the charlatan.
RELATED WORD The noun or verb *toady* is a shortened form of this word.

tobacco-stopper NOUN
a tool for pressing down tobacco in a pipe
• *a silver tobacco-stopper, in the form of a leg*—DAVID COPPERFIELD, CHARLES DICKENS

tocsin NOUN
a bell; the sound of bells as a signal or alarm
• *[He] sent word … that there might be need to ring the tocsin by-and-bye.*—A TALE OF TWO CITIES, CHARLES DICKENS

toilet (also **toilette**) NOUN
the process of washing, dressing, and getting ready
• *So making a hasty toilet, I went into the other room.*—DRACULA, BRAM STOKER
• *I continued my toilette rather noisily.*—WUTHERING HEIGHTS, EMILY BRONTË
🏛 French *toilette* meaning 'cloth, wrapper'; *toilet(te)* originally meant a cloth for wrapping clothes or covering a dressing table
RELATED WORD The word *toilet* only began to be used to mean 'lavatory' in the late 19th century in the US and in the early 20th century in Britain.

toilet-table NOUN
a table with a mirror and drawers, for keeping items used when getting ready; a dressing-table
• Fanny left *'her one ring, and another trinket or two on the toilet-table'.*—SHIRLEY, CHARLOTTE BRONTË

toils NOUN
a trap or net
• *I was like a wild beast that had broken the toils.*—FRANKENSTEIN, MARY SHELLEY

toilsome ADJECTIVE
hard and tiring
• Victor is *'wearied by a toilsome march'.*—FRANKENSTEIN, MARY SHELLEY

token NOUN
a sign; an indication
• *[Joe] secretly crossed his two forefingers, and exhibited them to me, as our token that Mrs Joe was in a cross temper.*—GREAT EXPECTATIONS, CHARLES DICKENS
➢ **in token:** as a sign or indication • *'I wish you all good-night, now,' said he, making a movement of the hand towards the door, in token that he was tired of our company.*—JANE EYRE, CHARLOTTE BRONTË

tolerable ADJECTIVE
to an acceptable extent or standard; fairly good
• *a tolerable cook*—THE MEMOIRS OF SHERLOCK HOLMES, ARTHUR CONAN DOYLE
USAGE In modern English, you might expect something *tolerable* to be unpleasant but bearable, rather than fairly good.

tolerably ADVERB
1 fairly; reasonably; moderately
• *Bingley and Jane meet tolerably often.*—PRIDE AND PREJUDICE, JANE AUSTEN
2 to an acceptable extent or standard
• *I dare say you can be made tolerably comfortable.*—THE MILL ON THE FLOSS, GEORGE ELIOT

Tophet (say **toh-fit**) NOUN
hell
• Every low-chimneyed house is *'as smoky as Tophet'.*—WESSEX TALES, THOMAS HARDY
🏛 From the Hebrew name of a place in Jerusalem where idols were said to be worshipped and child sacrifice by burning carried out

---

Capital letters

As in modern English, capital letters often show that a word is a proper noun, indicating a particular person, place, or institution. Even if you are not familiar with the character or place being talked about, you can often still work out the overall meaning of the sentence or passage: here, for instance, it is obvious that *Tophet* is a place with a lot of smoke.

Capital letters were sometimes used in places where they would not be used in modern English, for example to indicate importance or to show that something was called a particular thing.
• *If I had seen an **Ape** taking command of a **Man**, I should hardly have thought it a more degrading spectacle.*—DAVID COPPERFIELD, CHARLES DICKENS

top-sawyer to transport

top-sawyer NOUN
a superior person; the person in charge
• Fagin says of Dodger *'Wasn't he always the top-sawyer among you all!'*—OLIVER TWIST, CHARLES DICKENS
🏛 The *top-sawyer* was originally the person working at the top end of a vertical saw, as opposed to the person in the bottom of the saw pit.

torpid ADJECTIVE
inactive; moving or thinking slowly
• *Memory was not so utterly torpid in Silas that it could not be awakened by these words.*—SILAS MARNER, GEORGE ELIOT

town-pump NOUN
a place in a town where people went to get water pumped from a well
• *the gush of water into householders' buckets at the town-pump*—THE MAYOR OF CASTERBRIDGE, THOMAS HARDY

tow'rt PREPOSITION
towards
• *tow'rt daybreak*—SILAS MARNER, GEORGE ELIOT

trace NOUN
1 one of the straps attaching an animal to a vehicle, plough, etc.
• *It was a carriage, with a pole for a pair of horses, but only one was in the traces.*—THE WAR OF THE WORLDS, H. G. WELLS
2 a track or mark made by a person or thing
• *He winds [the watch] at night, and he leaves these traces of his unsteady hand.*—THE SIGN OF FOUR, ARTHUR CONAN DOYLE

trackless ADJECTIVE
1 with no paths or tracks on it
• *the stillness and the wide trackless snow*—SILAS MARNER, GEORGE ELIOT
2 leaving no track or trace
• *The winds and clouds are on their trackless flight.*—DOMBEY AND SON, CHARLES DICKENS

tract NOUN
1 an area of land
• *I had ... once more drawn near the tract of moorland.*—JANE EYRE, CHARLOTTE BRONTË
2 a leaflet containing a long essay, especially on a religious subject
• *The tract was one of a series addressed to young women on the sinfulness of dress.*—THE MOONSTONE, WILKIE COLLINS

tractable ADJECTIVE
easy to control or influence; not difficult in behaviour
• *I never heard any harm of her; and I dare say she is one of the most tractable creatures in the world.*—PRIDE AND PREJUDICE, JANE AUSTEN

➤ **tractability** NOUN • *[Tess said] 'Do what you like with me, mother.' Mrs Durbeyfield was only too delighted at this tractability.*—TESS OF THE D'URBERVILLES, THOMAS HARDY

traffic NOUN
business; trading or bargaining
• *She had a turn for traffic.*—JANE EYRE, CHARLOTTE BRONTË
USAGE In modern English, you might expect *traffic* to be trade in something illegal such as guns or drugs, rather than business in general.

train NOUN
1 a series or set of things
• *He was clearly a confirmed hypochondriac, and ... was pouring forth interminable trains of symptoms.*—THE SIGN OF FOUR, ARTHUR CONAN DOYLE
2 the course or direction of something
• *But why do I follow that train of ideas?*—JANE EYRE, CHARLOTTE BRONTË
3 a group of people surrounding an important person
• *It would have been such a fine thing ... if he had ridden with the good king's train.*—THE PRINCESS AND CURDIE, GEORGE MACDONALD
4 a steam train
• *Over the Maybury arch a train, a billowing tumult of white, firelit smoke, and a long caterpillar of lighted windows, went flying south.*—THE WAR OF THE WORLDS, H. G. WELLS
➤ **in the train of:** following; happening because of or after something • *The intelligence of his capture, coming in the train of many sorrows and disasters, proved fatal to his unhappy father.*—RIP VAN WINKLE, WASHINGTON IRVING

train oil NOUN
oil produced from sea creatures, especially from the blubber of a type of whale

transaction NOUN
dealings; interaction between people; an event or happening
• *I ... will simply relate the circumstances of the transaction.*—FRANKENSTEIN, MARY SHELLEY
USAGE In modern English, you might expect *transactions* to always be financial.

transmutation NOUN
a change into another state, form, or substance
• *the transmutation of metals*—A TALE OF TWO CITIES, CHARLES DICKENS

transport VERB
to send someone to a far-off country as a punishment
• *He ... knew of their being imprisoned, whipped, transported.*—GREAT EXPECTATIONS, CHARLES DICKENS

transport to trim

transport NOUN
1 a person sent to a far-off country as a punishment
• *This man was a returned transport.*—OLIVER TWIST, CHARLES DICKENS
2 a very strong feeling, typically of delight
• *He was checked in his transports by the churches ringing out the lustiest peals he had ever heard.*
—A CHRISTMAS CAROL, CHARLES DICKENS

travail NOUN
1 painful efforts or labours
• *What remains to you as the prize … of all the travail and pain you have endured?*—IVANHOE, WALTER SCOTT
2 the pains of childbirth; labour
• *What birth succeeded this travail?*—VILLETTE, CHARLOTTE BRONTË

travelling-dress NOUN
a dress or outfit designed for travelling
• *Estella is wearing 'her furred travelling-dress'.*
—GREAT EXPECTATIONS, CHARLES DICKENS

tremendous ADJECTIVE
awe-inspiring; terrifying
• *I perceived, as the shape came nearer (sight tremendous and abhorred!) that it was the wretch whom I had created.*—FRANKENSTEIN, MARY SHELLEY

tremulous ADJECTIVE
trembling
• *Caroline [began] in a low, rather tremulous voice, but [gained] courage as she proceeded.*—SHIRLEY, CHARLOTTE BRONTË
➤ **tremulously** ADVERB • *Maggie said tremulously, 'Let me go.'*—THE MILL ON THE FLOSS, GEORGE ELIOT

trenchant ADJECTIVE
sharp; cutting sharply
• *The trenchant blade [would have] shorn through his heart.*—DRACULA, BRAM STOKER

trepan VERB
1 to make a hole in someone's skull with a special saw, as a medical treatment
2 to trap someone; to kidnap someone
• *I was on my way to your house, when I was trepanned.*—KIDNAPPED, ROBERT LOUIS STEVENSON

trespass VERB
➤ **trespass on something**: to take advantage of something; to impose • *We must not think of moving her. We must trespass a little longer on your kindness.*
—PRIDE AND PREJUDICE, JANE AUSTEN
USAGE In modern English, you might expect someone to *trespass on* another person's land, rather than on their kindness or feelings.

trial NOUN
1 an attempt
• *But I have made the trial in homage to Christmas.*
—A CHRISTMAS CAROL, CHARLES DICKENS
2 a difficulty
• *'I'm so grieved to find you so deaf … ' 'Yes, dear, it's a trial.'*—MARY BARTON, ELIZABETH GASKELL

trifle VERB
1 to speak or act carelessly, and treat someone's feelings without respect
• *You are too generous to trifle with me. If your feelings are still what they were … tell me so at once.*—PRIDE AND PREJUDICE, JANE AUSTEN
2 to fiddle or play around with something
• *He had in his hand a heavy cane, with which he was trifling.*—THE STRANGE CASE OF DR JEKYLL AND MR HYDE, ROBERT LOUIS STEVENSON

trifle NOUN
1 a small amount
• *No beggars implored him to bestow a trifle.*
—A CHRISTMAS CAROL, CHARLES DICKENS
2 a small or unimportant thing
• *The fear of failure … harassed me worse than the physical hardships … though these were no trifles.*
—JANE EYRE, CHARLOTTE BRONTË
➤ **a trifle**: a little • *I'm … growing a trifle old.*
—GREAT EXPECTATIONS, CHARLES DICKENS

trifling ADJECTIVE
small or not serious; unimportant
• *My trifling occupations take up my time and amuse me.*—FRANKENSTEIN, MARY SHELLEY

trim VERB
1 to cut down the wick of a candle or oil lamp so it burnt well without smoking
• *The floor was swept and watered, the lamps were trimmed.*—A CHRISTMAS CAROL, CHARLES DICKENS
2 to decorate something
• *Mr Spenlow, in a black gown trimmed with white fur, came hurrying in.*—DAVID COPPERFIELD, CHARLES DICKENS

trim NOUN
1 a person's outfit
• *The old girl never appears in walking trim, in any season of the year, without a grey cloth cloak.*—BLEAK HOUSE, CHARLES DICKENS
2 the condition of someone or something
• *The kitchen was in perfect trim.*—JANE EYRE, CHARLOTTE BRONTË

trim ADJECTIVE
neat; in good order; attractive
• *The boat is 'as trim a little thing as any on the river'.*
—THE SIGN OF FOUR, ARTHUR CONAN DOYLE

trocar *to* tumbler

trocar NOUN
a surgical tool with a three-sided point at the end of a tube
French *trocart* or *trois-quarts*, from *trois* meaning 'three' + *carre* 'side, face'

troll VERB
to sing happily and loudly
• He saw a tinker coming, trolling a merry song.—THE MERRY ADVENTURES OF ROBIN HOOD, HOWARD PYLE

troublous ADJECTIVE
full of trouble; difficult
• Maggie's was a troublous life.—THE MILL ON THE FLOSS, GEORGE ELIOT

trousseau NOUN
a bride's collection of clothes and household items such as sheets and tablecloths
• Maggie had returned without a trousseau, without a husband.—THE MILL ON THE FLOSS, GEORGE ELIOT

trow (say troh) VERB
think; believe
• The night will be black as pitch, I trow.—LORNA DOONE, R. D. BLACKMORE

truck NOUN
1 an open trolley for moving heavy items; an open railway wagon
• A porter [had carried] off his baggage on a truck.—DOMBEY AND SON, CHARLES DICKENS
2 a wooden disc at the top of a ship's mast, with holes for ropes
• 'Nailed to [the ship's] main truck was a brazen lamp'—meaning a brass lamp.—MOBY DICK, HERMAN MELVILLE
3 goods; various items
• You always want more'n your share of the truck.—THE ADVENTURES OF HUCKLEBERRY FINN, MARK TWAIN

truckle VERB
to behave in a grovelling fashion towards someone
• And would you have me truckle to them?—SHIRLEY, CHARLOTTE BRONTË

truckle (also **truckle-bed**) NOUN
a low bed on small wheels or castors, also called 'truckles'
➤ **truckle bedstead** NOUN • Looking in, I saw ... a table, a bench, and a mattress on a truckle bedstead.—GREAT EXPECTATIONS, CHARLES DICKENS

true-hearted ADJECTIVE
loyal and honest
• a valiant and true-hearted comrade—WESTWARD HO!, CHARLES KINGSLEY

trump NOUN
1 a trumpet or horn, or a blast from one; used especially with reference to angels, and therefore death or judgement
• He could not speak again. The trump of the archangel would set his tongue free.—MARY BARTON, ELIZABETH GASKELL
2 an excellent person
• The man's a perfect trump.—TREASURE ISLAND, ROBERT LOUIS STEVENSON

trumpery NOUN
things that seem attractive but have no real value
• a wagon loaded with household trumpery—THE LEGEND OF SLEEPY HOLLOW, IRVING WASHINGTON

trumpery ADJECTIVE
attractive or interesting, but not important; worthless
• a very trumpery little incident—THE MOONSTONE, WILKIE COLLINS

truss NOUN
a bale of hay, corn, etc.
• Mrs Pipchin's chair is put onto the wagon *'in a convenient corner among certain trusses of hay'*.—DOMBEY AND SON, CHARLES DICKENS

trusser NOUN
a farm worker whose job was to tie up bales
• At length he obtained employment at his own occupation of hay-trusser, work of that sort being in demand at this autumn time.—THE MAYOR OF CASTERBRIDGE, THOMAS HARDY

trusty ADJECTIVE
trustworthy; reliable
• When the rajah put his jewels into the hands of Achmet he did it because he knew that he was a trusty man.—THE SIGN OF FOUR, ARTHUR CONAN DOYLE

tryst NOUN
a secret meeting, usually of lovers
• They laid her beside her husband in ... the churchyard where they had kept their love-trysts.—JOHN CHARRINGTON'S WEDDING, EDITH NESBIT

tucker NOUN
a piece of fabric worn around the neck or across the chest
• her lace tucker—DOMBEY AND SON, CHARLES DICKENS

tumbler NOUN
1 an acrobat, especially one performing somersaults
2 a type of pigeon with the ability to roll over whilst flying
3 a small rocking toy in the shape of a figure with a rounded base
4 a tumbril or cart

tumbril to typhus

tumbril NOUN
a cart, especially one of the type that carried condemned people to the guillotine during the French Revolution

turfy ADJECTIVE
grassy; covered with grass or a lawn
• Can you see many long weeds and nettles amongst the graves? or do they look turfy and flowery?—SHIRLEY, CHARLOTTE BRONTË

turkey-cock NOUN
a male turkey, often seen as aggressive or self-important
• She flushed up like a turkey-cock, and I thought fire would come out of her eyes.—MARY BARTON, ELIZABETH GASKELL

turn NOUN
1 a short walk or ride
• Miss Eliza Bennet, let me persuade you to … take a turn about the room.—PRIDE AND PREJUDICE, JANE AUSTEN
2 a shock
• What a turn you did give me!—THE ADVENTURES OF TOM SAWYER, MARK TWAIN
3 a natural tendency or inclination to do something
• Mrs Bennet had no turn for economy.—PRIDE AND PREJUDICE, JANE AUSTEN
4 a change in a situation
• A turn was thereby given to her thoughts; a new channel was opened for them.—SHIRLEY, CHARLOTTE BRONTË
5 a period of activity or piece of work
• I'm able and willing to do a turn o' work for him.—SILAS MARNER, GEORGE ELIOT

turnkey NOUN
a jailer
• The turnkey unlocked the door with one of a heavy bunch of keys that he carried at his girdle.—MOONFLEET, J. MEADE FALKNER

turnpike NOUN
a gate or small house where people had to pay a toll to use a road
• Enquiries were made about Lydia and Wickham 'at all the turnpikes, and at the inns in Barnet and Hatfield, but without any success'.—PRIDE AND PREJUDICE, JANE AUSTEN
• You should have kept along the turnpike road, friend, and not have strook across here.—THE MAYOR OF CASTERBRIDGE, THOMAS HARDY

tutor NOUN
a male private teacher, sometimes one who lived with a family and taught their children
• Liaisons between governesses and tutors should never be tolerated a moment in any well-regulated house.—JANE EYRE, CHARLOTTE BRONTË

tutor VERB
to teach or train someone
• 'Dombey and Son,' interrupted Paul, who had been tutored early in the phrase.—DOMBEY AND SON, CHARLES DICKENS

twain NUMBER
two
• The twain cantered along for some time without speech.—TESS OF THE D'URBERVILLES, THOMAS HARDY

twelvemonth NOUN
a year
• Mr Bingley and Jane remained at Netherfield only a twelvemonth.—PRIDE AND PREJUDICE, JANE AUSTEN

tyne (also **tine**) VERB
to lose something
• I'll wear you in my bosom, lest my jewel I should tyne.—JANE EYRE, CHARLOTTE BRONTË

typhus (also **typhus fever**) NOUN
an infectious disease transmitted by fleas, lice, rats, etc., causing many deaths during wars and famines
• [My father] caught the typhus fever while visiting among the poor.—JANE EYRE, CHARLOTTE BRONTË

ulster to unction

Uu

URBAN LIFE

In **1801** the population of London was **one million**, but by the end of the century it had exploded to **6.7 million** people. The streets were crowded and the first traffic lights were introduced in London in 1868. In the second half of the century, public toilets were built on the streets of London and led to the euphemism 'spend a penny' as they cost a penny to use. Across Britain, the smoke from factory chimneys and coal-burning fires caused thick fog, damaging public health.

ulster NOUN
an overcoat, originally one with a cape
• a slim youth in an ulster—THE ADVENTURES OF SHERLOCK HOLMES, ARTHUR CONAN DOYLE

unabashed ADJECTIVE
not embarrassed or ashamed
• Lydia was Lydia still; untamed, unabashed, wild, noisy, and fearless.—PRIDE AND PREJUDICE, JANE AUSTEN

unabated ADJECTIVE
no less strong or intense
• The subject still continued, and was discussed with unabated eagerness.—MANSFIELD PARK, JANE AUSTEN

unaffected ADJECTIVE
sincere; not artificial or pretended
• Elizabeth looked with unaffected astonishment.—PRIDE AND PREJUDICE, JANE AUSTEN
➤ **unaffectedly** ADVERB • Bingley is most unaffectedly modest.—PRIDE AND PREJUDICE, JANE AUSTEN

unamiable ADJECTIVE
unfriendly; not likeable
• For my part, unamiable as it sounds, I must say no.—SHIRLEY, CHARLOTTE BRONTË

unassailable ADJECTIVE
impossible to attack or defeat
• Laura is 'at the mercy of her worst enemy, of a man who is now absolutely unassailable'.—THE WOMAN IN WHITE, WILKIE COLLINS

unavailing ADJECTIVE
useless; unable to achieve anything
• Jane feels 'a sentiment of unavailing and impotent anger'.—JANE EYRE, CHARLOTTE BRONTË

unclose VERB
to open
• I heard the dining-room door unclose; a gentleman came out.—JANE EYRE, CHARLOTTE BRONTË

uncomely ADJECTIVE
unattractive
• Mrs Poole has a 'square, flat figure, and uncomely ... face'.—JANE EYRE, CHARLOTTE BRONTË

uncommon ADJECTIVE & ADVERB
extreme or extremely; to a remarkable degree
• They were overpowered afresh by his uncommon generosity.—BLEAK HOUSE, CHARLES DICKENS
• I'm uncommon fond of reading.—GREAT EXPECTATIONS, CHARLES DICKENS
➤ **uncommonly** ADVERB • You write uncommonly fast.—PRIDE AND PREJUDICE, JANE AUSTEN

unconscious ADJECTIVE
1 unaware
• The young man was quite unconscious of the action.—THE MAYOR OF CASTERBRIDGE, THOMAS HARDY
2 done without knowledge or realization
• I made this choice perhaps with some unconscious reservation.—THE STRANGE CASE OF DR JEKYLL AND MR HYDE, ROBERT LOUIS STEVENSON
➤ **unconsciously** ADVERB • I am sorry to have occasioned pain to any one. It has been most unconsciously done.—PRIDE AND PREJUDICE, JANE AUSTEN
➤ **unconsciousness** NOUN • He had not mentioned ... his unconsciousness of the child's entrance.—SILAS MARNER, GEORGE ELIOT

unction NOUN
1 the appearance of deep and sincere emotion, especially when this is not genuine
• These words he repeated with great unction and gravity.—DOMBEY AND SON, CHARLES DICKENS
2 oil or lotion, used as part of a religious ceremony or as a medicine
➢ **extreme unction**: a Roman Catholic sacrament of anointing a dying person with oil

undeceive to unreserve

undeceive VERB
to correct someone's wrong impression or belief
- *If I endeavour to undeceive people as to the rest of his conduct, who will believe me?*—PRIDE AND PREJUDICE, JANE AUSTEN

underbred ADJECTIVE
bad-mannered; badly brought up
- *The daughters of trades-people, however well educated, must necessarily be underbred.*—SHIRLEY, CHARLOTTE BRONTË

underlet VERB
to sublet; to rent out a room or house that you rent yourself
- *Pip plans to end the tenancy on his rooms as soon as possible, 'and in the meanwhile to underlet them'.*—GREAT EXPECTATIONS, CHARLES DICKENS

unequal ADJECTIVE
not able to deal or cope with something
- *[Tim] was quite unequal to any more conversation at the moment.*—NICHOLAS NICKLEBY, CHARLES DICKENS

unexampled ADJECTIVE
unparalleled; unprecedented; like no other
- *I can no longer help thanking you for your unexampled kindness to my poor sister.*—PRIDE AND PREJUDICE, JANE AUSTEN

unfit VERB
➢ **unfit someone for something**: to make someone unsuitable or unfit for something • *I must not stay here long. It would unfit me for the life I must begin again.*—THE MILL ON THE FLOSS, GEORGE ELIOT
➢ **unfitted** ADJECTIVE • *I found myself peculiarly unfitted for the situation offered to me.*—RIP VAN WINKLE, WASHINGTON IRVING

unfriended ADJECTIVE
without friends
- *Nicholas is worried about Smike wandering 'alone and unfriended'.*—NICHOLAS NICKLEBY, CHARLES DICKENS

unhallowed ADJECTIVE
unholy
- *I realized distinctly the perils of the law which we were incurring in our unhallowed work.*—DRACULA, BRAM STOKER

unhand VERB
to let go of someone
- *'Unhand me, sir, this instant,' cried Kate.*—NICHOLAS NICKLEBY, CHARLES DICKENS

unhappy ADJECTIVE
unfortunate
- *'I am,' said she, 'the cousin of the unhappy child who was murdered.'*—FRANKENSTEIN, MARY SHELLEY

unite VERB
1 to combine
- *Elizabeth tried to unite civility and truth in a few short sentences.*—PRIDE AND PREJUDICE, JANE AUSTEN
2 to marry
- *He loathed the idea that his daughter should be united to a Christian.*—FRANKENSTEIN, MARY SHELLEY

unman VERB
to make a man lose his courage, strength, or self-control
- *There was something in her face which quite unmanned him.*—NICHOLAS NICKLEBY, CHARLES DICKENS

unmingled ADJECTIVE
not mixed with anything else; pure
- *I passed a night of unmingled wretchedness.*—FRANKENSTEIN, MARY SHELLEY

unmixed ADJECTIVE
pure; not mixed with any other emotion
- *Nicholas … from a state of unmixed astonishment, gradually fell into one of irrepressible laughter.*—NICHOLAS NICKLEBY, CHARLES DICKENS

unmolested ADJECTIVE
not bothered or interrupted by anyone
- *I lived ungazed at and unmolested.*—FRANKENSTEIN, MARY SHELLEY
- *Let her sleep unmolested.*—JANE EYRE, CHARLOTTE BRONTË

unmurmuring ADJECTIVE
not complaining
- *Under this immediate personal trial Nancy was … firmly unmurmuring.*—SILAS MARNER, GEORGE ELIOT

unpretending ADJECTIVE
simple; unpretentious; humble
- *Miss Darcy is not 'a proud, reserved, disagreeable girl' but is 'amiable and unpretending'.*—PRIDE AND PREJUDICE, JANE AUSTEN

unpropitious ADJECTIVE
unfavourable; not likely to produce success
- *It seemed that the omen was an unpropitious one.*—FAR FROM THE MADDING CROWD, GEORGE ELIOT

unregarded ADJECTIVE
ignored; not considered
- *She had shed unregarded, unvalued tears.*—MARY BARTON, ELIZABETH GASKELL

unreserve NOUN
openness; lack of reserve
- *There was not a creature in the world to whom [Emma] spoke with such unreserve, as to [Mrs Weston].*—EMMA, JANE AUSTEN

unsuspicious *to* uttering

unsuspicious ADJECTIVE
not aware of something
• He declared himself to have been totally unsuspicious of her sister's attachment.—PRIDE AND PREJUDICE, JANE AUSTEN

unvitiated ADJECTIVE
pure; not corrupted by anything
• tenderly-nurtured unvitiated feeling—SILAS MARNER, GEORGE ELIOT

unwept ADJECTIVE
not cried over by anyone; unmourned
• On the bed 'unwatched, unwept, uncared for, was the body of this man'.—A CHRISTMAS CAROL, CHARLES DICKENS

Prefixes and suffixes

The prefix 'un-' can be added to a range of words. Recognizing prefixes and suffixes can help you to unravel the meaning of words.
• I could not **undeceive** her.—JANE EYRE, CHARLOTTE BRONTË
• To his friend's mind he was **faultless**.—SILAS MARNER, GEORGE ELIOT

Sometimes you may not realize immediately that something is a prefix, and you may need to read a section of text again in order to understand it.
• Here and there a ... **begrimed** face looked out from a gloomy doorway.—SILAS MARNER, GEORGE ELIOT

Sometimes a word does not have a prefix, although there would be one in modern English, as with the word 'cumber' in the following sentence. In modern English, the word is 'encumber'.
• I disgrace nobody and **cumber** nobody.—BLEAK HOUSE, CHARLES DICKENS

---

unwonted ADJECTIVE
unusual; untypical
• She asked this question, still without looking at me, but in an unwonted tone of sympathy.—GREAT EXPECTATIONS, CHARLES DICKENS

upas-tree NOUN
a tropical tree with poisonous sap, said to poison anything coming near it

uplong ADVERB
up; upright
• If any man in that neighborhood could stand uplong against Joe, I never saw the man.—GREAT EXPECTATIONS, CHARLES DICKENS

use VERB
to treat someone in a particular way, typically badly
• I think you and Mr Murdstone used me very cruelly.—DAVID COPPERFIELD, CHARLES DICKENS

usher NOUN
an assistant teacher
• He had been usher in a school, and was said now to be tutor in a private family.—SHIRLEY, CHARLOTTE BRONTË

usurious ADJECTIVE
charging an unreasonably high rate for lending money; extortionate
• Eliza ... consented to intrust [her money] to her mother, at a usurious rate of interest.—JANE EYRE, CHARLOTTE BRONTË

uttering NOUN
the act of putting money into circulation
• the uttering of forged one-pound notes—NIGHT WALKS, CHARLES DICKENS

Vv

VACCINATION

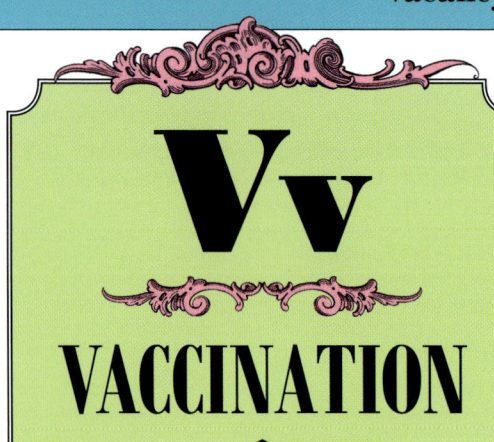

In 1796, **Dr Edward Jenner** carried out the first **vaccination** against smallpox, a deadly infectious disease. Jenner found that when people were treated with a mild dose of cowpox, a related, but less deadly disease, they were protected from smallpox. He called this procedure vaccination (from the Latin word for cow, *vacca*) and in **1853** laws were passed in Britain which made it compulsory for children to be vaccinated against smallpox.

vacancy NOUN
empty space
• Putting out his hand to feel around him, Mr Rochester 'met but vacancy'.—JANE EYRE, CHARLOTTE BRONTË
• The ladies had crowded round the table ... in so close a confederacy, that there was not a single vacancy near her.—PRIDE AND PREJUDICE, JANE AUSTEN

vagaries NOUN
unpredictable behaviour; changeability
• Your good friend there ... has so few vagaries herself ... that she cannot calculate on their effects.—EMMA, JANE AUSTEN

vainglorious ADJECTIVE
excessively proud of yourself; conceited
• Mr and Mrs Hubble ... were surpassingly conceited and vainglorious in being members of so distinguished a procession.—GREAT EXPECTATIONS, CHARLES DICKENS

valedictory ADJECTIVE
saying goodbye
• I should offer a few valedictory remarks.—DAVID COPPERFIELD, CHARLES DICKENS

van NOUN
a horse-drawn, covered vehicle, usually for transporting goods
• She could walk the remainder of the distance instead of travelling in the van by way of Casterbridge.—TESS OF THE D'URBERVILLES, THOMAS HARDY

vapours NOUN
➢ **the vapours**: a fit of fainting, sickness, etc., usually caused by shock or strong emotion
• Here, pass me the bottle or I shall get the vapours.—MOONFLEET, J. MEADE FALKNER

variance NOUN
➢ **at variance**: in conflict; different or opposing
• a feeling that is so utterly at variance with your own—DOMBEY AND SON, CHARLES DICKENS

varmint NOUN
a troublesome or mischievous person or animal; vermin
• Was ever such a sneaking varmint?—UNCLE TOM'S CABIN, HARRIET BEECHER STOWE

vassalage (say **vass-uh-lij**) NOUN
a situation of being inferior to, or dependent on, a more powerful person; people in this situation
• A man in my position ... is proud to offer some homage in acknowledgment of his vassalage.—DOMBEY AND SON, CHARLES DICKENS

vaunt VERB
to boast about something
• After all [Mr Elton's] own vaunted claims ... he had done nothing.—EMMA, JANE AUSTEN

vaunt NOUN
a boast
• It is no vaunt to affirm that if Nicholas had ten thousand pounds ... he would ... have bestowed its utmost farthing ... to secure her happiness.—NICHOLAS NICKLEBY, CHARLES DICKENS

vehement ADJECTIVE
forceful; very insistent
• My temper was sometimes violent, and my passions vehement.—FRANKENSTEIN, MARY SHELLEY
➢ **vehemence** NOUN • 'May she wake in torment!' he cried, with frightful vehemence.—WUTHERING HEIGHTS, EMILY BRONTË
➢ **vehemently** ADVERB • 'No, no, no,' she said vehemently.—THE WOMAN IN WHITE, WILKIE COLLINS

veneration NOUN
very great admiration and respect
• His veneration for the Doctor was unbounded.—DAVID COPPERFIELD, CHARLES DICKENS

venturesome to viewless

➢ **organ of veneration:** someone's capacity to feel veneration

venturesome (also **venturous**) ADJECTIVE
daring; willing to take risks
• *The journey was a fearfully heavy one ... It was most venturesome for a woman, at night, and alone.*—FAR FROM THE MADDING CROWD, THOMAS HARDY

verdure NOUN
green plants; greenness
• *Every day was adding to the verdure of the early trees.*—PRIDE AND PREJUDICE, JANE AUSTEN

veriest (say verr-ee-ist) ADJECTIVE
most complete; used for emphasizing a description
• *I knew no more than the veriest stranger could have known of what was really in her thoughts.*—THE MOONSTONE, WILKIE COLLINS

very ADJECTIVE & ADVERB
used for emphasis, to say that a description or action even includes a particular thing
• *[Mr Bumble] ascertained ... the exact condition of the furniture, down to the very horse-hair seats of the chairs.*—OLIVER TWIST, CHARLES DICKENS

vessel NOUN
a container
• *The dinner was served in two huge tin-plated vessels.*—JANE EYRE, CHARLOTTE BRONTË

vestibule NOUN
a hall or lobby next to an outside door
• *Charlotte Lucas came to spend the day with them. She was met in the vestibule by Lydia.*—PRIDE AND PREJUDICE, JANE AUSTEN

vestment NOUN
a garment
• *'You do not like these clothes?' he asked, pointing to the masculine vestments.*—VILLETTE, CHARLOTTE BRONTË

vesture NOUN
clothing
• *His drab vesture was buttoned up to his chin.*—MOBY DICK, HERMAN MELVILLE

vex VERB
to annoy or bother someone
• *I knew the pleasure of vexing and soothing him by turns.*—JANE EYRE, CHARLOTTE BRONTË

vexation NOUN
annoyance
• *I was half inclined to shed tears of vexation.*—GREAT EXPECTATIONS, CHARLES DICKENS
• *It was not in her nature ... to increase her vexations, by dwelling on them.*—PRIDE AND PREJUDICE, JANE AUSTEN

viands NOUN
food
• *Edward then set to with a good appetite at the viands which had been placed before him.*—THE CHILDREN OF THE NEW FOREST, CAPTAIN MARRYAT

vibrate VERB
1 to move rapidly backwards and forwards from one thing to another
• *His mind began vibrating between the wish to reveal himself to her and the policy of leaving well alone.*—THE MAYOR OF CASTERBRIDGE, THOMAS HARDY
2 (said about feelings) to respond to or match something
• *[Eppie's] feelings ... vibrated to every word Silas had uttered.*—SILAS MARNER, GEORGE ELIOT
3 to be heard
• *Milverton laughed, but fear vibrated in his voice.*—THE RETURN OF SHERLOCK HOLMES, ARTHUR CONAN DOYLE

vicinage NOUN
nearby surroundings; vicinity
• *The house looks deserted: 'the pattering rain on the forest leaves was the only sound audible in its vicinage'.*—JANE EYRE, CHARLOTTE BRONTË

vicious ADJECTIVE
immoral; full of vices
• *Was man ... at once so powerful, so virtuous and magnificent, yet so vicious and base?*—FRANKENSTEIN, MARY SHELLEY

victual NOUN (also **victuals, victualage**)
food (and sometimes drink or other supplies)
• *I'll come and clean up for you, and get you a bit o' victual.*—SILAS MARNER, GEORGE ELIOT

victual VERB
1 to store up food; to provide people, ships, or places with food
• *the soundest and best victualled ships*—WESTWARD HO!, CHARLES KINGSLEY
2 to eat
• *We found [the horses] ... victualling where the grass was good.*—LORNA DOONE, R. D. BLACKMORE
➢ **victualling** NOUN • *Her father had to do with the victualling of passenger-ships.*—GREAT EXPECTATIONS, CHARLES DICKENS

victualler NOUN
1 a person selling or providing food or drink, for example, a shopkeeper or the landlord of a pub
2 a ship providing food and other supplies for other ships

viewless ADJECTIVE
invisible
• *He said this as if he spoke to a vision, viewless to any eye but his own.*—JANE EYRE, CHARLOTTE BRONTË

vignette to vulgar

vignette (say vin-yet, vee-nyet) NOUN
a picture, especially a small one without definite borders
• *I used to … busy myself in sketching fancy vignettes.* —JANE EYRE, CHARLOTTE BRONTË

vinous (say vy-nuhss) ADJECTIVE
involving or related to wine
• Tom was *'flushed, either with his feelings, or the vinous part of the breakfast'*. —HARD TIMES, CHARLES DICKENS

violent ADJECTIVE
intense; forceful
• *[Scrooge] was taken with a violent fit of trembling.* —A CHRISTMAS CAROL, CHARLES DICKENS
• *Amongst the most violent against him was Mrs Bennet.* —PRIDE AND PREJUDICE, JANE AUSTEN
➤ **violently** ADVERB • *a man violently in love* —PRIDE AND PREJUDICE, JANE AUSTEN
➤ **violence** NOUN • *I was exhausted with the violence of my emotion and of my flight.* —THE WAR OF THE WORLDS, H. G. WELLS

Expressing emphasis

The words 'violent', 'violently' and 'violence' emphasize the forcefulness of something.

Other 19th century words used to add emphasis include 'excessively' and 'uncommonly'.
• *I … think our two youngest daughters* **uncommonly** *foolish.* —PRIDE AND PREJUDICE, JANE AUSTEN

Words used in order to lessen intensity include 'moderately' and 'tolerable'.
• *I tried to … keep the beating of my heart* **moderately** *quiet.* —GREAT EXPECTATIONS, CHARLES DICKENS
• *Elizabeth … was able to join the others the others with* **tolerable** *composure.* —PRIDE AND PREJUDICE, JANE AUSTEN

virtually ADVERB
in effect; in practice
• *Gabriel Oak is appointed as bailiff 'having virtually exercised that function for a long time already'.* —FAR FROM THE MADDING CROWD, THOMAS HARDY
USAGE In modern English, you might expect *virtually* to be used with strong words like 'impossible' or 'perfect', to mean 'almost'.

visage NOUN
a person's face
• *The Major's purple visage deepened in its hue.* —DOMBEY AND SON, CHARLES DICKENS

visit VERB
to afflict or affect someone
• *Godfrey Cass was fast becoming a bitter man, visited by cruel wishes.* —SILAS MARNER, GEORGE ELIOT
USAGE In modern English, you might only expect to be *visited* by a person, not by a feeling or event.

vital ADJECTIVE
deadly; fatal
• *the vital nature of the wound* —MEN OF IRON, HOWARD PYLE

vital NOUN
a basic part of something; one of your body's important internal organs
• *Jane would not be able to suppress her natural fire and keep it inside 'though the imprisoned flame consumed vital after vital'.* —JANE EYRE, CHARLOTTE BRONTË

vitiate VERB
to spoil something
• *His endless muttering monologue vitiated every effort I made to think out a line of action.* —THE WAR OF THE WORLDS, H. G. WELLS

vitriol NOUN
sulphuric acid
• *The brute had thrown vitriol on the poor fellow's ankles.* —MARY BARTON, ELIZABETH GASKELL

vittles NOUN
food; victuals
• *I … keep [the girls] on plain wholesome vittles.* —LITTLE WOMEN, LOUISA M. ALCOTT

votary NOUN
a devoted follower or seeker of something
• *St John thinks he has 'the heart of a politician, of a soldier, of a votary of glory'.* —JANE EYRE, CHARLOTTE BRONTË

V.R. ABBREVIATION
Victoria Regina, a title for Queen Victoria (who reigned 1837–1901)

vulgar ADJECTIVE
ordinary or common; not educated or refined
• *Not only the vulgar spectators … but even the ladies of distinction … saw the conflict with a thrilling interest.* —IVANHOE, WALTER SCOTT
➤ **vulgarity** NOUN • *The Miss Gunns … thought what a pity it was that these… people … should be brought up in utter ignorance and vulgarity.* —SILAS MARNER, GEORGE ELIOT

vulgar NOUN
➤ **the vulgar**: ordinary or uneducated people
• *My tale … would be looked upon as madness by the vulgar.* —FRANKENSTEIN, MARY SHELLEY

Ww

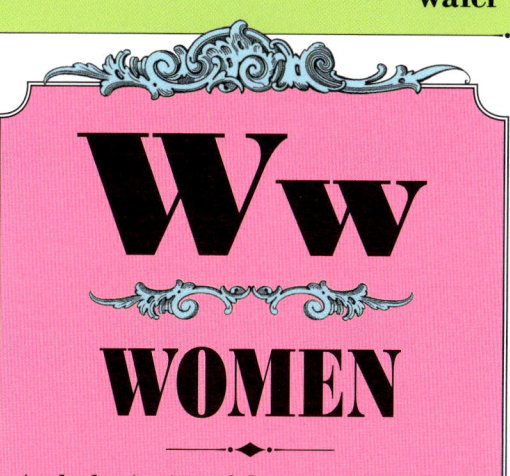

WOMEN

At the beginning of the century, middle-class women were seen as the 'angel in the house' providing homes, meals, and children. They were not expected to be educated, work, or vote, and they signed all their rights to their husband when they married. At the same time, many working-class women lived in poverty and laboured in factories. By the end of the century, women were protesting for their rights with Millicent Fawcett leading the **National Union of Women's Suffrage Societies** in **1897**.

wafer NOUN
a round piece of dried paste used as a seal on a document
• Here is an inkstand, here are pens and paper, here are wafers.—BLEAK HOUSE, CHARLES DICKENS

wafer VERB
to stick or fasten something with a wafer
• a few old prints from books ... wafered against the wall—BLEAK HOUSE, CHARLES DICKENS

waggish ADJECTIVE
joking in a mischievous way
• He followed up this remarkable declaration, by shaking his head in a waggish manner.—OLIVER TWIST, CHARLES DICKENS
➤ **wag** NOUN a joker • the merry wags in the taproom—THE MERRY ADVENTURES OF ROBIN HOOD, HOWARD PYLE
➤ **waggery** NOUN mischievous joking • He had ... a ... lurking waggery of expression that was irresistible.—RIP VAN WINKLE, WASHINGTON IRVING

waggoner (also **wagoner**) NOUN
a wagon driver
• 'The tailboard of the waggon is gone, Miss,' said the waggoner.—FAR FROM THE MADDING CROWD, THOMAS HARDY

wain NOUN
a wagon or cart
• Along one side of the field the whole wain went.—TESS OF THE D'URBERVILLES, THOMAS HARDY

wainscoting (also **wainscot**) NOUN
wooden panels on the lower part of a wall inside a room
• Here the walls and the dark wainscoting remained as good as ever—HEIDI, JOHANNA SPYRI
• It was a long and lofty room, with a high wainscot all round it.—MOONFLEET, J. MEADE FALKNER
➤ **wainscoted** (also **wainscotted**) ADJECTIVE
• the dark wainscoted parlour—SILAS MARNER, GEORGE ELIOT

wait VERB
➤ **wait on**: to pay a visit to someone • Well ... it will be abominably rude if you do not wait on him.—PRIDE AND PREJUDICE, JANE AUSTEN

waiting-woman NOUN
a female servant who looked after someone, usually a woman
• I do attend to her. I am her waiting-woman as well as her child.—SHIRLEY, CHARLOTTE BRONTË

Walker EXCLAMATION
used for showing surprise or disbelief
• 'Walk-ER!' exclaimed the boy.—A CHRISTMAS CAROL, CHARLES DICKENS

wall-eyed ADJECTIVE
1 blind, or with dim, gaping, or mis-matched eyes
• the wall-eyed pony—MOONFLEET, J. MEADE FALKNER
2 not understanding things properly
• muddle-headed [people] who, because they themselves were wall-eyed, supposed everybody else to have the same blank outlook—SILAS MARNER, GEORGE ELIOT
3 dark; dim
• [a] pale, wall-eyed, woebegone inn—BLEAK HOUSE, CHARLES DICKENS

wane VERB
1 to become duller, weaker, or smaller; to lessen
• The day waned into a gloomy evening.—BLEAK HOUSE, CHARLES DICKENS
• her waning hopes—MARY BARTON, ELIZABETH GASKELL
2 (of the moon) to become less full
➤ **on / upon the wane**: waning
• Smike's health has been 'long upon the wane'—getting worse for some time.—NICHOLAS NICKLEBY, CHARLES DICKENS

want NOUN
a lack; need
• I stopped for want of breath.—MOONFLEET, J. MEADE FALKNER

want *to* warrant

want VERB
1 to lack something
• Unlike the Squire, the ordinary farmers *'wanted ... self-possession and authoritativeness'*.—SILAS MARNER, GEORGE ELIOT
2 to be a particular amount of time until an event or hour
• *It wants twenty minutes, sir, to taking the medicine.* —WUTHERING HEIGHTS, EMILY BRONTË
• *It wanted but a few minutes of six.*—JANE EYRE, CHARLOTTE BRONTË

wanton ADJECTIVE
1 deliberately bad
• *Its origin—jealousy perhaps, or wanton cruelty—was yet to be unravelled.*—NORTHANGER ABBEY, JANE AUSTEN
2 lacking sexual modesty
• *It was a wanton thing which no woman with any self-respect should have done.*—FAR FROM THE MADDING CROWD, THOMAS HARDY
➤ **wantonly** ADVERB deliberately • *None surely would have been so wicked as to destroy me wantonly.* —FRANKENSTEIN, MARY SHELLEY

ward NOUN
1 a child being looked after by someone other than their parent
• *It is Mr Rochester's ward ... the little French girl.*—JANE EYRE, CHARLOTTE BRONTË
2 care or protection; guardianship
• *The little maiden shall be taken into ward under our own care.*—OTTO OF THE SILVER HAND, HOWARD PYLE
3 a guard or watch; guards
• *sentries keeping ward before the gate*—DOMBEY AND SON, CHARLES DICKENS
4 one of the rooms or areas in a prison, hospital, workhouse, etc.
• *Oliver ... was then hurried away to a large ward; where, on a rough, hard bed, he sobbed himself to sleep.*—OLIVER TWIST, CHARLES DICKENS
5 one of the ridges or grooves in a lock or key
• *the task of turning the rusty key in its still more rusty wards*—NICHOLAS NICKLEBY, CHARLES DICKENS
6 an area of a city or borough
• *The ladies 'would listen ... to Mrs Lamb's anecdotes of ... Portsoken Ward'.*—LITTLE BRITAIN, WASHINGTON IRVING
➤ **a ward in Chancery:** a child under the care of a law court • *Her father had died without a will, and so she must be made a ward of Chancery.*—MOONFLEET, J. MEADE FALKNER
➤ **watch and ward:** a look-out; care and protection • *Mrs Pipchin had kept watch and ward over little Paul and his sister for nearly twelve months.* —DOMBEY AND SON, CHARLES DICKENS

ward VERB
1 to guard or protect someone or something
• *This garment hung so loosely on the figure, that its ... breast was bare, as if disdaining to be warded or concealed.*—A CHRISTMAS CAROL, CHARLES DICKENS
2 to prevent something from causing harm
• *Robin warded two of the strokes, but at the third, his staff broke beneath the mighty blows.*—THE MERRY ADVENTURES OF ROBIN HOOD, HOWARD PYLE

ware (also **'ware**) EXCLAMATION & VERB
beware
• *'Ware!' cried Grace.*—JANE EYRE, CHARLOTTE BRONTË

ware NOUN
pottery; a pot
• *But hearing no breakage of ware ... I turned me about.*—LORNA DOONE, R. D. BLACKMORE

warehouse NOUN
a shop
• *Lydia ... does not know which are the best warehouses.*—PRIDE AND PREJUDICE, JANE AUSTEN

warming-pan NOUN
1 a wide, flat metal pan with a long handle, filled with hot coals and used for warming a bed
• *'Hear! hear!' cried Jo, clashing the lid of the warming-pan like a cymbal.*—LITTLE WOMEN, LOUISA M. ALCOTT
2 a person doing a job in order to keep it available for another person
• *We used to call him ... W. P. Adams, in consequence of his being Warming Pan for a young fellow who was in his minority.*—DOMBEY AND SON, CHARLES DICKENS

warmly ADVERB
fiercely or strongly; fervently
• *I again warmly repeated that it was a bad side of human nature.*—GREAT EXPECTATIONS, CHARLES DICKENS
USAGE In modern English, you might expect someone to speak *warmly* to a friend or loved one, meaning that they are affectionate rather than angry or insistent.

warrant NOUN
1 a guarantee
• *Your lordship's recommendation, or mine, would be sufficient warrant for him.*—BLACK BEAUTY, ANNA SEWELL
2 a reason or justification
• *I had no warrant to breathe a word on the subject.* —SHIRLEY, CHARLOTTE BRONTË

warrant VERB
to bet or guarantee something was true
• *'That shook them a bit, I'll warrant!' he continued.* —TESS OF THE D'URBERVILLES, THOMAS HARDY

wash-house to watering-place

wash-house NOUN
1 a small building or room for washing and doing laundry
2 a public place where people could go to have baths and do laundry
USAGE People would take puddings to the washhouse to be boiled or steamed.
• [They] bore [Tiny Tim] off into the wash-house, that he might hear the pudding singing in the copper.
—A CHRISTMAS CAROL, CHARLES DICKENS

washing-book NOUN
a book in which items sent to be washed were listed

washing-stand (also **wash-stand**) NOUN
a piece of furniture that held a basin, jug of water and other items for washing

washy ADJECTIVE
weak or worthless
• the chance of a gossip about ... their often very washy and paltry feelings—VILLETTE, CHARLOTTE BRONTË

Wast and wert

Wast and wert are past tense forms of the verb 'to be', used with the second-person singular pronoun thou. (See also the panel at thou.)
Thou wast and thou wert mean 'you were'.
• Thou **wast** a child.—MOONFLEET, J. MEADE FALKNER
• I felt as if thou **wert** all my own.—MARY BARTON, ELIZABETH GASKELL

waste VERB
1 to become weak or very thin; to make someone do this
• I do not recollect ... any change ... for the better; he wasted, and became slowly weaker.—GREAT EXPECTATIONS, CHARLES DICKENS
2 to destroy a place
• a storm that wasted all the region—THE PRINCE AND THE PAUPER, MARK TWAIN
3 to use something up
• The candle, wasted at last, went out.—JANE EYRE, CHARLOTTE BRONTË
4 (said about time) to pass
• The month of courtship had wasted.—JANE EYRE, CHARLOTTE BRONTË

waste NOUN
1 uncultivated land; wasteland
• the howling of the wind upon the barren waste
—A CHRISTMAS CAROL, CHARLES DICKENS

2 an instance of using up or losing something
• [a] great loss or waste of blood—DRACULA, BRAM STOKER

wasted ADJECTIVE
weak; dreadfully thin
• I saw her face, pale, wasted, but quite composed.
—JANE EYRE, CHARLOTTE BRONTË

watch-case NOUN
the hinged metal case or cover of a pocket watch

watch chain NOUN
a chain used for attaching a pocket watch to clothing
• I could see gleams of light on his studs and watch chain.—THE WAR OF THE WORLDS, H. G. WELLS

watch-guard NOUN
a chain or strap used for attaching a pocket watch to clothing
• He ... locked it ... with a small key attached to his watch-guard.—SHIRLEY, CHARLOTTE BRONTË
• [It] was a tiny coral lobster in the shape of a charm for her watch guard.—LITTLE MEN, LOUISA M. ALCOTT

watchman NOUN
a guard
• I went to the circus, and loafed around the back side till the watchman went by, and then dived in under the tent.— THE ADVENTURES OF HUCKLEBERRY FINN, MARK TWAIN

water NOUN
≫ **at / in low water:** in difficulties, especially financial ones • Inference,—that your brother was often at low water.—THE SIGN OF FOUR, ARTHUR CONAN DOYLE
≫ **of the first / finest:**
1 (said about gemstones) of the best quality
• a diamond of the first water—THE SIGN OF FOUR, ARTHUR CONAN DOYLE
2 very clearly the thing stated • This was manifestly a prig of the first water, and there was no use arguing with him.—DRACULA, BRAM STOKER

water-flag NOUN
an iris (type of flower) growing in water
• a group of reeds and water-flags—JANE EYRE, CHARLOTTE BRONTË

watering-place NOUN
a town with a natural spring thought to be good for health; a spa town
• During Miss Keeldar's stay at the fashionable watering-place of Cliffbridge, she ... had been introduced to Sir Philip Nunnely.—SHIRLEY, CHARLOTTE BRONTË

waterman to Welsh wig

waterman NOUN
someone who transported people in a boat; a boatman
• *They beckoned to some watermen, who … appeared in no hurry for a fare.*—MARY BARTON, ELIZABETH GASKELL

wattled ADJECTIVE
made using woven sticks, twigs, or branches
• *They have houses of wattled reeds.*—THE YOUNG KING, OSCAR WILDE

wax VERB
1 to become; to grow
• *high and light clouds which are sure to melt away as the day waxes warm*—JANE EYRE, CHARLOTTE BRONTË
• *'And he's a splendid fellow, I just know,' cried Jasper, waxing enthusiastic.*—FIVE LITTLE PEPPERS AND HOW THEY GREW, MARGARET SIDNEY
2 (of the moon) to become fuller
• *the waxing moon*—THE STAR, H. G. WELLS
USAGE In this meaning, *wax* is often used with *wane* (meaning 'become less full').
• *the waxing and waning of the moon*—THE MOONSTONE, WILKIE COLLINS

waxen ADJECTIVE
1 made of wax
• *a cone of waxen grapes and apples under a glass cover*—BEHIND THE SHADE, ARTHUR MORRISON
2 very pale
• *a gentleman with a waxen complexion*—THE MILL ON THE FLOSS, GEORGE ELIOT

wayfarer NOUN
a traveller on foot
• *Several wayfarers came along the lane, and of these my brother gathered such news as he could.*—THE WAR OF THE WORLDS, H. G. WELLS

way-worn ADJECTIVE
tired from travelling
• *Foot-sore, way-worn, half-starved looking men they were.*—MARY BARTON, ELIZABETH GASKELL

weasand (say **wee-zuhnd**) NOUN
the throat; the gullet
• *Food hath not passed my weasand for three livelong days.*—IVANHOE, WALTER SCOTT

weathercock NOUN
1 a pointer with a model of a cockerel on top, placed on a roof to show the direction of the wind
• *I have been looking at the weather-cock. I find it was a false alarm about the wind.*—BLEAK HOUSE, CHARLES DICKENS
2 a person whose feelings or moods change often
• *I'm afraid Laurie is … altogether too much of a weathercock, just now, for any one to depend on.*—LITTLE WOMEN, LOUISA M. ALCOTT

weazen (also **weazened, weasand, wizen**) ADJECTIVE
small or shrivelled; wizened
• *his grandfather—a weazen, old, crab-faced man*—DOMBEY AND SON, CHARLES DICKENS

weazen (also **weasand**) NOUN
your neck or throat
• *I know'd you … when you was so small … that I could have took your weazen betwixt this finger and thumb and chucked you away dead.*—GREAT EXPECTATIONS, CHARLES DICKENS

ween VERB
to think; to believe
• *Few of them would have helped the whale, I ween.*—MOBY DICK, HERMAN MELVILLE

welkin NOUN
the sky; heaven
• *I like that sky of steel … I like Thornfield … its grey facade, and lines of dark windows reflecting that metal welkin.*—JANE EYRE, CHARLOTTE BRONTË

well ADJECTIVE
1 good; fortunate
• *'It is well you are out of my reach,' he exclaimed.*—WUTHERING HEIGHTS, EMILY BRONTË
• *'It's my opinion he has not been frightened or ill-used while he was young.' 'That's well,' said the squire.*—BLACK BEAUTY, ANNA SEWELL
2 advisable; sensible
• *It is well to be accurate, and every minute is precious.*—DRACULA, BRAM STOKER

well ADVERB
1 sensibly; advisably
• *'They would do well,' returned Mrs Sparsit, 'to take example by you.'*—HARD TIMES, CHARLES DICKENS
2 carefully
• *Look well upon that gentleman, my learned friend there.*—A TALE OF TWO CITIES, CHARLES DICKENS
USAGE When it means 'advisable', *well* is often used with *as*.
• *It is as well to be ready for anything.*—A STUDY IN SCARLET, ARTHUR CONAN DOYLE
When it means 'advisably', *well* is usually used in the phrase *do well*, and is a way of giving advice.

well NOUN
a natural spring or water source
• *[He] filled a stoneware jar with water, for he knew by experience that the mountain wells were few and far between.*—A STUDY IN SCARLET, ARTHUR CONAN DOYLE

Welsh wig NOUN
a woollen cap
• *an old gentleman in a Welsh wig*—A CHRISTMAS CAROL, CHARLES DICKENS

wench to whereon

wench NOUN
a girl or young woman
• 'Why, what book is it the wench has got hold on?' he burst out ... 'Not quite the right book for a little girl.'
—THE MILL ON THE FLOSS, GEORGE ELIOT
• 'Come in, wench!' said her father.—MARY BARTON, ELIZABETH GASKELL

wend VERB
to go; to turn in a particular direction
• We entered the wood, and wended homeward.
—JANE EYRE, CHARLOTTE BRONTË

wert VERB (see the panel at wast)
were
• Thou wert loitering here after dark.—A DOG OF FLANDERS, OUIDA

westering ADJECTIVE
moving towards the west; setting
• the westering sun—VILLETTE, CHARLOTTE BRONTË

wet NOUN
a drink, typically alcoholic
• At the square-topped corner public houses business was just beginning, and rough-looking men were emerging, rubbing their sleeves across their beards after their morning wet.—THE SIGN OF FOUR, ARTHUR CONAN DOYLE

whalebone NOUN
a hard material from the jaw of a whale, used for stiffening clothing
• a vast bag, or rather a middle-sized balloon of black silk, held wide with whalebone—SHIRLEY, CHARLOTTE BRONTË

whaleman NOUN
1 a member of the crew of a whaling ship
• the whale as he actually appears to the eye of the whaleman—MOBY DICK, HERMAN MELVILLE
2 a whaling ship
• another homeward-bound whaleman ... manned almost wholly by Polynesians—MOBY DICK, HERMAN MELVILLE

whate'er (say wot-air) DETERMINER & PRONOUN
whatever
• God [is] our Father, and we mun bear patiently whate'er he sends.—MARY BARTON, ELIZABETH GASKELL

wheat-rick NOUN
a pile of wheat formed into a regular shape
• The wheat-rick was about shoulder-high from the ground.—TESS OF THE D'URBERVILLES, THOMAS HARDY

wheelwright NOUN
someone who made or repaired wooden wheels
• Anybody may know my trade—I'm a wheelwright.
—WESSEX TALES, THOMAS HARDY

whelm VERB
to completely cover or submerge
• an ocean, that ... had whelmed a whole world—MOBY DICK, HERMAN MELVILLE

whence ADVERB
from where; from which place
• He will not stay long: he will soon return whence he came.—JANE EYRE, CHARLOTTE BRONTË
• Who was I? What was I? Whence did I come?
—FRANKENSTEIN, MARY SHELLEY
USAGE 'From whence' means the same as whence.
• Lydia returned with Mrs Forster to Meryton, from whence they were to set out early the next morning.
—PRIDE AND PREJUDICE, JANE AUSTEN

whereat (say wair-at) ADVERB & CONJUNCTION
at which; in response to which
• [He] knocked ... on the table with a little hammer: whereat several gentlemen cried 'Hear!'—NICHOLAS NICKLEBY, CHARLES DICKENS
• [He] tried to open the door but found it locked, whereat the Steward laughed and rattled his keys.
—THE MERRY ADVENTURES OF ROBIN HOOD, HOWARD PYLE

wherefore ADVERB
for what reason; why
• My dear Frankenstein, wherefore are you desponding and sorrowful!—FRANKENSTEIN, MARY SHELLEY
• Wherefore such an order? Why guard the prison?—THE BLACK TULIP, ALEXANDRE DUMAS

wherefore CONJUNCTION
as a result of which
• This doctor had pronounced poor Lorna dead; wherefore Ruth refused most firmly to have aught to do with him.—LORNA DOONE, R. D. BLACKMORE

whereof ADVERB
of which
• his trim blue coat, whereof the buttons sparkled phosphorescently—DOMBEY AND SON, CHARLES DICKENS
• subjects whereof she knew little—SHIRLEY, CHARLOTTE BRONTË

whereon (also whereupon) ADVERB
on which
• He drew from his breast-pocket a poster whereon was printed the day, hour, and place of meeting.—TESS OF THE D'URBERVILLES, THOMAS HARDY

whereon to wild

whereon CONJUNCTION
at which time; immediately after which
• The man ... [told] him to 'shut up' ... whereon our man accused him of robbing him and wanting to murder him.—DRACULA, BRAM STOKER

wherewith ADVERB
with, which
• the mixture of pity and admiration wherewith he regarded her—LORNA DOONE, R. D. BLACKMORE

wherry NOUN
a light rowing boat or barge
• There is a boatman here with a wherry, Watson. We shall take it and cross the river.—THE SIGN OF FOUR, ARTHUR CONAN DOYLE

whether CONJUNCTION
used to introduce a question in which there are two alternatives
• 'Whether do you like me or Mr Sam Wynne best, Shirley?' inquired the boy.—SHIRLEY, CHARLOTTE BRONTË

whey-faced ADJECTIVE
pale; sickly-looking
• I'm bitterly disappointed with the whey-faced, whining wretch!—WUTHERING HEIGHTS, EMILY BRONTË

which DETERMINER
whichever
• At first ... turn my head which way I would, I seemed to see the gold.—SILAS MARNER, GEORGE ELIOT

while NOUN
➢ **between whiles:** from time to time, while something else is happening • The poor girl called to him, and shook him, and between whiles she wept.—THE BLUE FAIRY BOOK, ANDREW LANG

whilom (say **wy-luhm**) ADJECTIVE
former
• Vindex Brimblecombe, whilom servitor of Exeter College, Oxford—WESTWARD HO!, CHARLES KINGSLEY

whilom ADVERB
formerly; in the past
• the lion bold, which whilom so magnanimously the lamb did hold—THE LEGEND OF SLEEPY HOLLOW, WASHINGTON IRVING

whip VERB
➢ **whip up:** to use a whip to make a horse move
• [The driver] whipped up at once.—THE WAR OF THE WORLDS, H. G. WELLS
USAGE In modern English, you might expect a feeling or a crowd to be *whipped up*, rather than a horse.

whipcord NOUN
thin, strong, twisted cord used for making whips
• a loop of whipcord—THE ADVENTURES OF SHERLOCK HOLMES, ARTHUR CONAN DOYLE
• He was ... tough as whipcord. He never seemed to tire.—KING SOLOMON'S MINES, H. RIDER HAGGARD

whitewashed ADJECTIVE
painted with whitewash, a white substance containing lime (calcium hydroxide) and chalk
• A small room was visible, whitewashed and clean but very bare of furniture.—FRANKENSTEIN, MARY SHELLEY

whither ADVERB
where; to which place
• after his return from London, whither he was obliged to go the next day—PRIDE AND PREJUDICE, JANE AUSTEN
• Whither shall I drive them?—THE SECOND JUNGLE BOOK, RUDYARD KIPLING

whithersoever ADVERB
wherever; to whatever place
• Both her step-mother and her step-sister were always finding fault with her, whatsoever she did and whithersoever she went.—THE RED FAIRY BOOK, ANDREW LANG

wicket NOUN
1 (wicket-gate)
a small gate
• The vehicle had stopped at the wicket.—JANE EYRE, CHARLOTTE BRONTË
• They ... were turning out of the high road to pass through a wicket-gate into the meadows.—TESS OF THE D'URBERVILLES, THOMAS HARDY
2 an opening in a door or wall
• Elzevir knocked ... and ... a wicket in the heavy door was opened at once.—MOONFLEET, J. MEADE FALKNER

wife NOUN
a woman
• The old country wives, however ... are the best judges of these matters.—THE LEGEND OF SLEEPY HOLLOW, WASHINGTON IRVING
USAGE This meaning is mainly used in Scottish dialect, often with *auld* (meaning 'old').
• He saw an auld wife sitting beside the kitchen fire.—THE BLUE FAIRY BOOK, ANDREW LANG

wigged ADJECTIVE
wearing a wig
• a wigged gentleman, the prisoner's counsel—A TALE OF TWO CITIES, CHARLES DICKENS

wild ADJECTIVE
very enthusiastic or excited about something
• She was wild to be at home.—PRIDE AND PREJUDICE, JANE AUSTEN

wile NOUN
clever trickery; a clever trick
- *So wily, and we must follow with wile.*—DRACULA, BRAM STOKER
- *That might be an innocent girlish wile to lure on the true lover.*—VILLETTE, CHARLOTTE BRONTË

wimble NOUN
a tool for twisting threads, pieces of straw, etc. together so they can be used for tying up bales of hay or sheep's wool
- *gathering up the fleeces and twisting ropes of wool with a wimble for tying them round*—FAR FROM THE MADDING CROWD, THOMAS HARDY

wimble VERB
to twist threads, pieces of straw, etc. together so they can be used for tying up bales of hay or sheep's wool
- *Nance Mockridge ... worked in the yard wimbling hay-bonds.*—THE MAYOR OF CASTERBRIDGE, THOMAS HARDY

win VERB
to persuade someone to do something; to entice someone to something
- *She could not win him, however, to any conversation.*—PRIDE AND PREJUDICE, JANE AUSTEN

wind NOUN
breath; the ability to breathe normally
- *Mr Giles is carrying a pitchfork and has 'the shortest wind of the party'—he is more out of breath than anyone else.*—OLIVER TWIST, CHARLES DICKENS

USAGE The phrases *break a horse's wind* and *broken wind* refer to damage to a horse's lungs affecting its ability to breathe.
- *You ruined the last horse and broke his wind.*—BLACK BEAUTY, ANNA SEWELL

wind[1] VERB (past tense and past participle winded)
1 to detect a person's or animal's scent on the wind
- *[I knew] if once they winded us ... [the herd] would be off before we could get a shot.*—KING SOLOMON'S MINES, H. RIDER HAGGARD

2 to blow a trumpet or other instrument
- *Wamba winded the bugle.*—IVANHOE, WALTER SCOTT

wind[2] VERB (past tense and past participle wound)
➤ **wind up**: to end by saying or doing something; to conclude
- *'Unless, indeed,' I wound up, 'you really want NOT to go.'*—THE TURN OF THE SCREW, HENRY JAMES
- *He wound up his speech with a low chuckle.*—MARY BARTON, ELIZABETH GASKELL

winding sheet NOUN
a piece of cloth used to wrap a dead body; a shroud

windward (say wind-wuhd) ADJECTIVE
facing the wind
- *[The burning rick of straw] glowed on the windward side*—FAR FROM THE MADDING CROWD, THOMAS HARDY

windward NOUN
the side that the wind was blowing from
- *just to windward of us ... the cruelest rock on the coast*—CAPTAIN JANUARY, LAURA E. RICHARDS
- *[The fire] was now grown so hot that they could only approach it from the windward.*—TREASURE ISLAND, ROBERT LOUIS STEVENSON

wink VERB
1 to blink
- *staring at each other as if a bet were depending on the first man who winked*—SILAS MARNER, GEORGE ELIOT

2 to twinkle or flicker
- *The winking lights upon the bridges were already pale.*—GREAT EXPECTATIONS, CHARLES DICKENS

wink NOUN
➤ **not a wink**: not the smallest or slightest amount
- *The sea is 'not changed a wink since I first saw it'.*—MOBY DICK, HERMAN MELVILLE

wiper NOUN
a weapon
- *I have a wiper in the bag, an' I'll drop it on your 'ead if you don't hook it.*—THE SIGN OF FOUR, ARTHUR CONAN DOYLE

witch NOUN
a very beautiful woman or girl
- *Scrooge and the Spirit see 'a group of handsome girls ... artful witches'.*—A CHRISTMAS CAROL, CHARLES DICKENS

withal (say widh-awl) ADVERB
1 in addition
- *It was cold, bleak, biting weather: foggy withal.*—A CHRISTMAS CAROL, CHARLES DICKENS

2 nevertheless; even so
- *I sat upon the edge of the well telling myself that, at any rate, there was nothing to fear ... And withal I was absolutely afraid to go!*—THE TIME MACHINE, H. G. WELLS

withal PREPOSITION
with
- *And whence does an ostler like you get your shilling to pay withal?*—WESTWARD HO!, CHARLES KINGSLEY

withdraw NOUN
1 to leave a room or place and go somewhere else
- *Mr Bennet withdrew to the library.*—PRIDE AND PREJUDICE, JANE AUSTEN

2 to move something backwards
- *'I'd rather not,' she said, trying to withdraw her hand.*—LITTLE MEN, LOUISA M. ALCOTT

within to wordy

within PREPOSITION
➤ **within doors:** inside; indoors • *They were now a miserable trio, confined within doors by a series of rain and snow.*—MANSFIELD PARK, JANE AUSTEN

without ADVERB & PREPOSITION
outside
• *It is a strange-seeming place from without.*—MEN OF IRON, HOWARD PYLE
• *A sound is heard 'from without the castle walls'.*—OTTO OF THE SILVER HAND, HOWARD PYLE
USAGE When it has this meaning, *without* is often contrasted with *within* (meaning 'inside').
• *The lodge is made of wood, 'without and within'.*—RUPERT OF HENTZAU, ANTHONY HOPE

without CONJUNCTION
unless
• *And, without you start a third ship's company ... you'll have to [join] Cap'n Silver.*—TREASURE ISLAND, ROBERT LOUIS STEVENSON

withy NOUN
1 a flexible branch from a willow or similar tree
• *a withy basket*—TESS OF THE D'URBERVILLES, THOMAS HARDY
2 a willow tree
• *The stream is brimful now, and lies high in this little withy plantation.*—THE MILL ON THE FLOSS, GEORGE ELIOT

wittles NOUN
food (and sometimes drink or other supplies); victuals
• *You bring me, to-morrow morning early ... them wittles.*—GREAT EXPECTATIONS, CHARLES DICKENS

woe NOUN
1 sadness; grief
• *I was desolate and afraid, and full of woe and terror.*—DRACULA, BRAM STOKER
2 a sorrow; a source of trouble
• *'What is it?' cried Jo, forgetting her woes for a minute in her wonder.*—LITTLE WOMEN, LOUISA M. ALCOTT

wonder NOUN
surprise; a surprising thing
• *It was no matter of wonder to me to find Mrs Steerforth devoted to her son.*—DAVID COPPERFIELD, CHARLES DICKENS
➤ **for a wonder:** surprisingly • *The old man was sitting ... with his spectacles over his eyes, for a wonder, instead of on his forehead.*—DOMBEY AND SON, CHARLES DICKENS
➤ **in the name of wonder:** used for adding emphasis • *Where, in the name of wonder, should his sister ... have run from, or to?*—DAVID COPPERFIELD, CHARLES DICKENS

➤ **wonderful** surprising; astonishing • *It was strange; it was wonderful; yes, it was unaccountable.*—THE PRINCE AND THE PAUPER, MARK TWAIN

wonder VERB
1 to feel surprised or amazed
• *Can you wonder that such thoughts transported me with rage?*—FRANKENSTEIN, MARY SHELLEY
2 to express surprise or amazement
• *They were not welcomed home very cordially by their mother. Mrs Bennet wondered at their coming.*—PRIDE AND PREJUDICE, JANE AUSTEN

wonderment NOUN
amazement; wonder
• *Liddy's clear eyes rounded with wonderment.*—FAR FROM THE MADDING CROWD, THOMAS HARDY

wondrous ADJECTIVE
amazing; wonderful
• *mountains and streams and all the wondrous works with which Nature adorns her chosen dwelling-places*—FRANKENSTEIN, MARY SHELLEY

wondrous ADVERB
amazingly; wonderfully
• *A wondrous subtle thing is love.*—THE SIGN OF FOUR, ARTHUR CONAN DOYLE

wont (say wohnt) ADJECTIVE
accustomed; usually doing something
• *the half-sad, affectionate tone in which he had been wont to speak to her*—THE MILL ON THE FLOSS, GEORGE ELIOT
• *His heart beat more quickly than it was wont.*—MEN OF IRON, HOWARD PYLE
USAGE The adjective *wont* is often used in the phrase *be wont to*.
• *Mrs Bretton was never wont to make a fuss about any person or anything*—VILLETTE, CHARLOTTE BRONTË
➤ **wonted** ADJECTIVE customary; usual • *Our spirits rose to their wonted level again.*—DREAM DAYS, KENNETH GRAHAME

wont NOUN
someone's usual behaviour or habit
• *her yellow hair, which it was her wont to fasten up smartly with a comb behind*—SHIRLEY, CHARLOTTE BRONTË
• *Mr Jaggers stood, according to his wont, before the fire.*—GREAT EXPECTATIONS, CHARLES DICKENS

wool-stapler NOUN
a wool dealer; someone who bought wool from producers and sold it to manufacturers

wordy ADJECTIVE
using or involving many words
• *Not that Caroline made any wordy profession of love.*—SHIRLEY, CHARLOTTE BRONTË

work NOUN
an act or deed; something that happened
- 'It isn't Jem Rodney as has done this work, Master Marner,' said the landlord.—SILAS MARNER, GEORGE ELIOT

➤ **poor / terrible work:** a very bad thing
- And it 'ud be poor work for me to … make them as I'm fond of think me unfitting company for 'em.—SILAS MARNER, GEORGE ELIOT

work VERB
to form, decorate, or process something in a particular way
- [She practised] embroidering the fine cambric handkerchiefs which she could not afford to buy ready worked.—VILLETTE, CHARLOTTE BRONTË

workhouse (also poorhouse) NOUN
a place where people without jobs or homes were sent and given food and shelter in exchange for work
- If it hadn't been for you, they'd have taken me to the workhouse.—SILAS MARNER, GEORGE ELIOT

wormwood NOUN
a bitter plant; a feeling of bitterness
- 'Tis bitterer to me than wormwood the memory of what followed.—MOONFLEET, J. MEADE FALKNER

worrit (say wurr-it) NOUN
worry; trouble
- Susan says that Mrs Richard's son is 'the worrit of Mrs Richards's life!'—DOMBEY AND SON, CHARLES DICKENS

worrit (also worret) VERB
to worry; to bother or pester
- Florence is told she 'wasn't to go and worrit the wet nurse'.—DOMBEY AND SON, CHARLES DICKENS
- They aren't worreted wi' thinking what's the rights and wrongs o' things.—SILAS MARNER, GEORGE ELIOT

Local accents

Worrit and *worret* are dialect words related to 'worry'.

Characters may speak in dialect or with a local accent. When their speech is written to reflect this, it can be easier to understand it by saying it aloud. The context of the sentence (or the wider context) can also help you to understand the vocabulary.
- 'The owd maister was like other folk—naught mich out o' t' common way: stark mad o' shooting, and farming, and sich like.' The mistress was different.—JANE EYRE, CHARLOTTE BRONTË

worry VERB
1 to bite and shake another animal, an object, or a person; to attack other animals
- We … heard the baying of a hound … a scream of agony, [and] a horrible worrying sound.—THE ADVENTURES OF SHERLOCK HOLMES, ARTHUR CONAN DOYLE

2 to move something around with your fingers; to fiddle with something
- [The Martian] worried at the catch for a minute, perhaps, and then the door opened.—THE WAR OF THE WORLDS, H. G. WELLS

3 to attack or harass someone; to force someone to do something
- Dunstan felt sure he could worry Godfrey into anything.—SILAS MARNER, GEORGE ELIOT

worship NOUN
➤ **your worship:** used for addressing an important person • An old lady tells Mr Dombey that her house is 'a poor place for a great gentleman like your worship'.—DOMBEY AND SON, CHARLES DICKENS

USAGE In modern English, you would only expect *Your Worship* to be used to address a magistrate or mayor.

worshipful ADJECTIVE
1 honourable; deserving respect
- a gallant and courtly knight, of an ancient and worshipful family—WESTWARD HO!, CHARLES KINGSLEY

2 adoring; worshipping
- He would sometimes catch her large, worshipful eyes … looking at him.—TESS OF THE D'URBERVILLES, THOMAS HARDY

worshipful NOUN
➤ **your worshipful:** used for addressing an important person, especially a mayor • on the night of your worshipful's wedding—THE MAYOR OF CASTERBRIDGE, THOMAS HARDY

worthy NOUN
an important person
- 'Ah!' replied that worthy.—NICHOLAS NICKLEBY, CHARLES DICKENS

wot VERB
know or knows (from an old verb 'wit')
- God wot I need not be too severe about others.—JANE EYRE, CHARLOTTE BRONTË

would VERB
➤ **(I) would that:** I wish • Would that I had some brighter ending to communicate to my readers.—THE RETURN OF SHERLOCK HOLMES, ARTHUR CONAN DOYLE
- I would that I had a better head for remembering things.—THE MERRY ADVENTURES OF ROBIN HOOD, HOWARD PYLE

wrack to wry

USAGE Sometimes *that* is missed out.
- Would I were the Queen again ...—THE YELLOW FAIRY BOOK, ANDREW LANG

wrack NOUN
1 a type of brown seaweed
- The rocks are covered in 'slippery wrack'.—THE MYSTERIOUS ISLAND, JULES VERNE

2 things washed up on the shore
- the wrack of the sea-shore [that] came drifting in again at evening tide—A PLEA FOR RAGGED SCHOOLS, THOMAS GUTHRIE

3 a wrecked ship; a shipwreck
- Now ... it ain't a-goin' to be more'n two hours befo' this wrack breaks up and washes off down the river.—THE ADVENTURES OF HUCKLEBERRY FINN, MARK TWAIN

4 high, fast-moving clouds
- [The hours] passed like drift cloud—like the wrack scudding before a storm.—VILLETTE, CHARLOTTE BRONTË

wrapt ADJECTIVE
1 completely absorbed in something
- She sat in silence almost all the way, wrapt in her own meditations.—SENSE AND SENSIBILITY, JANE AUSTEN

2 a way of spelling 'wrapped'
- So he ... wrapt [the chain] round and round his neck.—THE ADVENTURES OF HUCKLEBERRY FINN, MARK TWAIN

wrathful (say roth-fuhl) ADJECTIVE
angry
- 'How dare you,' she said, with a wrathful glance.—THE RED FAIRY BOOK, ANDREW LANG

wreak VERB
to cause; to inflict
- He might remain in Switzerland and wreak his vengeance on my relatives.—FRANKENSTEIN, MARY SHELLEY

wreath (say reeth) NOUN
1 a spiral or curl of smoke, dust, mist, etc.
- Sherlock Holmes is described as 'sending up thick blue wreaths from his pipe'.—THE SIGN OF FOUR, ARTHUR CONAN DOYLE

2 snow that had formed a bank or pile; a snowdrift
- a light wreath of the new-fallen snow—THE SNOW-IMAGE, NATHANIEL HAWTHORNE

wreathe VERB
to cover or surround something
- The sun sank and the world was wreathed in shadows.—KING SOLOMON'S MINES, H. RIDER HAGGARD

wrest VERB
to get or take something from someone who does not want to give it
- He saw how she battled with herself ... but he wrested the answer from her.—DOMBEY AND SON, CHARLES DICKENS

wristband NOUN
part of a sleeve that goes around the wrist; a cuff
- [She] sat near her mother, stitching wristbands.—LITTLE WOMEN, LOUISA M. ALCOTT

writ NOUN
1 an order from a court
- I ... had a writ served upon me for 25 pounds.—THE ADVENTURES OF SHERLOCK HOLMES, ARTHUR CONAN DOYLE

2 someone's authority; the power to make people obey
- 'The king's writ runs but lamely in the Channel Isles.'—he does not have much authority there.—MOONFLEET, J. MEADE FALKNER

writ VERB
written; wrote
- [You've] not writ a line for the last two or three years.—WESSEX TALES, THOMAS HARDY
- I writ a letter.—DAVID COPPERFIELD, CHARLES DICKENS

wroth ADJECTIVE
angry
- But he was very wroth, and none can blame him for that.—THE RED FAIRY BOOK, ANDREW LANG

wrought (say rawt) VERB
1 worked
- His loom, as he wrought in it without ceasing, had in its turn wrought on him.—SILAS MARNER, GEORGE ELIOT

2 caused; created; brought about
- I saw little of the mischief wrought by the Martians.—THE WAR OF THE WORLDS, H. G. WELLS

3 formed, decorated, or processed in a particular way
- a royal crown wrought in silks and stones—THE PRINCESS AND CURDIE, GEORGE MACDONALD

wrought (also wrought up) ADJECTIVE
excited or upset
- Rachel was in high good spirits, just in that humour ... which you may sometimes have observed in young girls, when they are highly wrought up, at the end of an exciting day.—THE MOONSTONE, WILKIE COLLINS

wry ADJECTIVE
twisted, and showing disgust
- Miss Crocker tasted first, made a wry face, and drank some water hastily.—LITTLE WOMEN, LOUISA M. ALCOTT

Xx

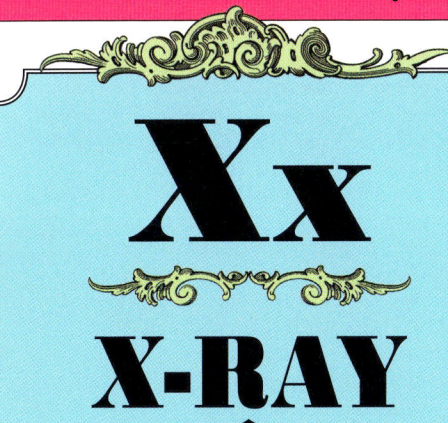

X-RAY

X-rays are a form of electromagnetic radiation accidentally discovered by the German scientist **Professor Wilhelm Röntgen** in **1895.** By experimenting with vacuum tubes he found that the X-rays he detected passed through flesh more easily than bone. He took an X-ray photograph of his wife's hand showing her bones and wedding ring. This discovery transformed medical science as medics could view the inside of the body without the need for risky operations.

xyloidin (also **xyloidine**) NOUN
a type of explosive substance
• *Some years ago ... a French chemist ... discovered this substance, which he called xyloidine.*—THE MOON-VOYAGE, JULES VERNE

Xantippe (say zan-tip-ee) NOUN
the wife of the ancient Greek philosopher Socrates. She was said to be bad-tempered.
USAGE This word was used, as it is now, to refer to a bad-tempered woman or nagging wife.
• The unhappily married Mr Barnet sees *'his handsome Xantippe'* driving away in the chaise.
—WESSEX TALES, THOMAS HARDY

Xerxes (say zerk-zeez) NOUN
an ancient Persian king
• *The shadows ... must have been long enough and broad enough to shade half Xerxes' army.*—MOBY DICK, HERMAN MELVILLE

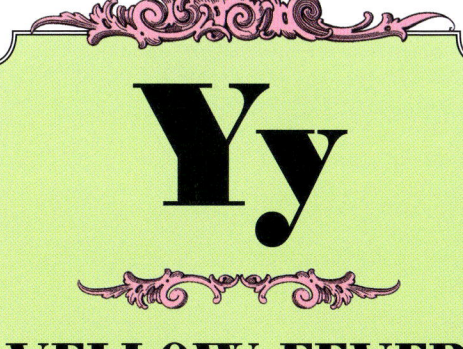

Yy

YELLOW FEVER

Disease and illness were rife in the 1800s. Yellow fever, which was common in tropical countries, was a viral disease spread by mosquito bites. Symptoms included yellowing of the skin and eyes. The 19th century saw several outbreaks of the disease in the United States of America. Cholera, smallpox, cowpox, typhus, and diphtheria were other dreaded diseases which ravaged Victorian society.

yawl NOUN
a small rowing boat carried on a larger ship, for taking people onto and off the ship
• *[The steamboat] sent out her yawl, and we went aboard.*—THE ADVENTURES OF HUCKLEBERRY FINN, MARK TWAIN

ye PRONOUN
1 you
• *Thank ye, Solomon, thank ye.*—SILAS MARNER, GEORGE ELIOT
2 yourself or yourselves
• *Sit ye down before the fire, my dear.*—A CHRISTMAS CAROL, CHARLES DICKENS
USAGE Ye was sometimes used when addressing or calling out to a group of people.
• *Come to me, O ye children!*—THE WATER BABIES, CHARLES KINGSLEY

yearn VERB
to feel compassion or affection
• *But his heart yearned towards the child.*—THE CHIMES, CHARLES DICKENS
USAGE In modern English, you might say that someone *yearns for* something, meaning that they want it very much.

yeomanry to yourn

yeomanry (say yoh-muhn-ri) NOUN
a force of volunteer soldiers who were small landowners
• They ought to make me a magistrate and a captain of yeomanry.—SHIRLEY, CHARLOTTE BRONTË

yesternight NOUN
last night
• It was him that roused [my old man] up yesternight.—THE SIGN OF FOUR, ARTHUR CONAN DOYLE

yet ADVERB
still
• 'I am in the presence of the Ghost of Christmas Yet to Come?' said Scrooge.—A CHRISTMAS CAROL, CHARLES DICKENS

yoke NOUN
1 a wooden frame or collar for attaching an animal to pull a vehicle, plough, etc.
2 something preventing someone from being free; oppression
• [Mrs Tulliver] had groaned a little in her youth under the yoke of her elder sisters.—THE MILL ON THE FLOSS, GEORGE ELIOT

yoke VERB
to attach an animal to a vehicle, plough, etc. using a yoke
• Six horses were yoked to [the waggon].—A STUDY IN SCARLET, ARTHUR CONAN DOYLE

yon ADVERB, DETERMINER & PRONOUN
that; that (one) over there
• Ask yon fireman, and he'll tell you more about it than I can.—MARY BARTON, ELIZABETH GASKELL
• Yon's our house, Mas'r Davy!—DAVID COPPERFIELD, CHARLES DICKENS

yonder ADVERB
over there
• Is that a boat yonder?—GREAT EXPECTATIONS, CHARLES DICKENS

yonder DETERMINER
that or those
• I wonder what thoughts are busy in your heart during all the hours you sit in yonder room.—JANE EYRE, CHARLOTTE BRONTË

yore
➢ **of yore**: past; in or of the past • There was an empty room … which, in days of yore, had been Walter's bedroom.—DOMBEY AND SON, CHARLES DICKENS

younker (say yung-kuhr) NOUN
a youngster
• Here … take this younker and make a tailor of him.—ALTON LOCKE, CHARLES KINGSLEY

yourn PRONOUN
yours
• These uncles of yourn ain't no uncles at all.—THE ADVENTURES OF HUCKLEBERRY FINN, MARK TWAIN

Zz

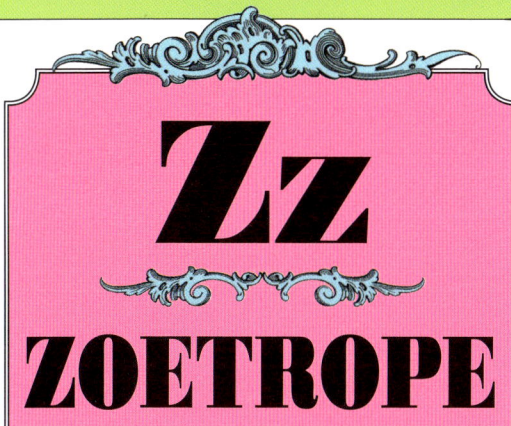

ZOETROPE

The zoetrope was patented by the American **William E. Lincoln** in **1867** when he was approximately eighteen years old. The **zoetrope** was a toy. It was made from a cylinder with a sequence of pictures on the inner surface. When viewed through vertical slits while the cylinder was rotated, it looked as though the image was moving in a continuous loop. The word comes from the Greek word *zōē* meaning 'life' and *tropos* meaning 'turning', and could be seen as an early form of animation.

zealot (say **zel-uht**) NOUN
a fanatic, especially a religious fanatic
• *[These deeds] would in some minds have stamped me as a dreamer and zealot.*—VILLETTE, CHARLOTTE BRONTË

zephyr (say **zef-uhr**) NOUN
a gentle breeze
• *There was not even a zephyr stirring.*—THE ADVENTURES OF TOM SAWYER, MARK TWAIN

zoophagous (say **zoo-off-uh-guhss, zoh-off-uh-guhss**) ADJECTIVE
eating animals
• *Renfield, who eats living insects, spiders and birds, is described as 'the zoophagous patient'.*—DRACULA, BRAM STOKER